Markets for Technology

Markets for Technology

The Economics of
Innovation and
Corporate Strategy

Ashish Arora, Andrea Fosfuri,
and Alfonso Gambardella

The MIT Press
Cambridge, Massachusetts
London, England

This book was set in Palatino by Graphic Composition, Inc., Athens, Georgia, using QuarkXPress 4.1.

Printed and bound in the United States of America.

Library of Congress Cataloging-in-Publication Data

Arora, Ashish.
    Markets for technology : the economics of innovation and corporate strategy / Ashish Arora, Andrea Fosfuri, Alfonso Gambardella.
        p. cm.
    Includes bibliographical references and index.
    ISBN 0-262-01190-5
    1. High technology industries—Management. 2. Technology—Marketing. 3. License agreements. 4. Technology transfer—Economic aspects. 5. Technological innovations—Economic aspects. 6. Globalization—Economic aspects. 7. Employees—Effect of technological innovations on. I. Fosfuri, Andrea. II. Gambardella, Alfonso. III. Title.

HD62.37 .A76 2002
338'.064—dc21

2001044324

This book is dedicated to Esther (AF), Sonal (AA), and Veevan (AG)

Contents

Preface and Acknowledgments   ix

1 Markets for Technology: Why Do We See Them, Why We Don't See More of Them, and Why We Should Care   1

I **Markets for Technology: Extent and Development**   15

2 Preliminary Evidence   17

3 The Division of Innovative Labor in High-Tech Industries   45

II **Limitations and Determinants**   91

4 Context Dependence, Sticky Information, and the Limits of the Market for Technology   93

5 Intellectual Property Rights and the Licensing of Know-How   115

6 Markets for Technology and the Size of the Market: Adam Smith and the Division of Innovative Labor Revisited   143

III **Functioning and Economic Implications**   169

7 Licensing the Market for Technology   171

8 Global Technology Suppliers and the International Division of Innovative Labor   197

IV Implications for Public Policy and Corporate Strategy   221

9   Implications for Corporate Strategy   223

10   The Institutional Context: Problems and Policy   253

11   Conclusions   281

     Notes   289
     References   309
     List of Figures and Tables   327
     Index   331

Preface and
Acknowledgments

This book is part of nearly a decade-old and ongoing research project focused on the process of technological change and its implications for industry structure, corporate strategy, and, ultimately, for economic growth. In the course of our earlier research, we have tried to understand the complex and variegated process of innovation and technical change, particularly during the 1980s and 1990s, decades that appear to differ from the post–World War II era of economic growth in many important respects.

Although economists and management theorists have made significant advances in understanding innovation, its determinants and its consequences, not enough attention has been paid to understanding innovation as an economic process, and the different ways of coordinating the actions of the various economic agents involved in such a process. In particular, it is not yet well understood how different economic actors, such as universities and firms, or large and small companies, or firms in developed and in developing countries jointly contribute to the process of creation, development, commercialization, and widespread use of new technologies. As a result, there is an insufficient appreciation of the implications, for public and business policy and for the rate and direction of technical change itself, when innovation involves trade in technology, or when firms specialize in developing technology as a part of a division of labor in innovation. This book tries to fill this gap.

In earlier research, we have individually and jointly addressed many of these issues. Our prior research has focused on topics such as technological alliances (particularly between large and small firms in high-tech industries), technological licensing, technological spillovers, the role of intellectual property rights in developing countries and their implications for industry structure, along with detailed studies of these and other issues in pharmaceuticals, biotechnology, and chemicals.

In many respects, this book is an important staging point in this intellectual journey and serves as an opportunity to consolidate and integrate and take stock. Some chapters draw from earlier studies. However,
the book is not a collection of previous articles. Even the chapters that
draw on earlier material have been refined and expanded in order to
adapt them to the logical sequence and the structure of the book. More
important, the core of the book stems from an entirely new effort to dig
into the topic of markets for technology, and to understand the implications for public and business policy, and for understanding the process
of technological change itself. This book is an attempt to systematize the
accumulated knowledge from our research and the insights of other
scholars working in the field as well as to provide some answers to these
questions. As is often the case, many of the answers are provisional and
often raise more questions that will form an agenda for our future research and, we sincerely hope, for others as well.

The book is eclectic in the methods it employs. We rely on historical
material, case studies, and other forms of qualitative discussion or evidence, as well as on systematic statistical analysis. Sometimes we develop formal propositions, which stem from more rigorous economic
models. However, we deliberately avoided presenting detailed technical proofs or material. We typically sketch the economic model to give a
flavor of it, and we focus on the proposition in order to highlight its implications. Our target readership is not solely the academic economist
for whom such formal proofs are essential. Instead, we hope to use this
book to reach economists and business scholars, as well as policy makers, industry analysts, and managers. Since the topic of technology markets is intimately linked to several legal and contractual issues, legal
scholars or professionals might also find this book useful. Accordingly,
the analysis and arguments of this book are grounded in rigorous economic analysis but nonetheless presented so as to be accessible to those
without advanced training in economic analysis. For technical details
we refer to the original papers, or we invite the reader to contact the
authors.

As is always the case, if we have succeeded, it is because we have been
able to draw on the wisdom of many scholars in this field. Several col-
leagues have contributed to our understanding of this topic, through
personal discussions, or in seminars, or with specific comments to parts
of this book. Many of their contributions are acknowledged in citations
to their work throughout the book. These citations do not always do justice to the intellectual debt owed to them. In particular, we are indebted

to Suma Athreye, Tim Bresnahan, Bruno Cassiman, Fabrizio Cesaroni, Wesley Cohen, Paul David, Giovanni Dosi, Walter García-Fontes, Ove Granstrand, Zvi Griliches, Bronwyn Hall, Mike Hobday, David Hounshell, Adam Jaffe, Steve Klepper, Ralph Landau, Franco Malerba, Jim Markusen, Myriam Mariani, Ben Martin, Robert Merges, Massimo Motta, David Mowery, Richard Nelson, Gigi Orsenigo, Fabio Pammolli, Keith Pavitt, Massimo Riccaboni, Thomas Roende, Nathan Rosenberg, Margareth Sharp, Ed Steinmueller, Salvatore Torrisi, and Eric von Hippel. While they deserve much of the credit for what is good in this book, they are not responsible for its many shortcomings, for which we alone are accountable.

We also gratefully acknowledge financial support from the following: The Italian Ministry of University and Research (Project's title: *The "technological" division of labor,* Protocol N.9913628915_002); the Italian Research Council (Consiglio Nazionale delle Ricerche, CNR, Project title: *Division of labor and the "market" for technology,* research grant N.99.00863.CT11); the European Commission, Directorate General (DG) XII (Project's title: *From Science to Products,* Contract N.SOE1-CT97–1059); the Spanish Ministry of Science and Technology (Grant SEC2000–0395); the Program *"Les Enjeux Economique de l'Innovation"* of the French Research Council (Centre Nationale de la Recherche Scientifique, CNRS); The Sloan Foundation (*The Indian Software Industry*); and the Center for Economic Policy Research at Stanford University (now the Stanford Institute of Economic Policy Research).

1

Markets for Technology: Why Do We See Them, Why We Don't See More of Them, and Why We Should Care

1.1 Objective

It is now a commonplace that we live in a knowledge economy. Like all cliches, this one is also wrong insofar as it suggests that earlier economies did not rely upon knowledge. If there is something different about the economic system that has characterized the majority of industrialized countries over the last two and a half centuries, it is arguably the increased importance of scientific and technological knowledge for economic activity. According to Simon Kuznets (1969), the distinguishing characteristic of modern economic growth has been the systematic application of science to economic ends. Understanding how scientific and technological knowledge is produced and applied to economic goals is the key to understanding the process of modern economic growth.

This book studies the nature and working of markets for technology, namely for intermediate technological inputs—and the implications for business and public policy. Although a wealth of scholarly research in economics exists on this subject, there is very little on how a market in knowledge would function, other than the appreciation that such markets would be characterized by a number of imperfections. Similarly, there is little guidance in the management literature on how managers should behave when markets for technology are present. This neglect is understandable. Although markets for technology have existed for a long time, with the advent of the corporate Research and Development (R&D) laboratory, firms began to develop their own technology. Drawing on the idea of imperfections in technology markets, Nelson (1959) provided the first rationalization for why and under what conditions firms would invest in R&D, an idea elegantly generalized by Arrow (1962a). But perhaps even more powerful has been the firm's-eye view of twentieth-century American economic growth offered by Chandler (1990). For Chandler, the systematic application of science takes place within the more organized confines of the firm, as the production of new knowledge is combined with its application through mutually complementary investments in research, manufacturing, and marketing.

This vision of knowledge creation integrated with knowledge use has become inadequate for understanding economic growth in the twenty-first century. Over the past ten to fifteen years, there has been a rapid growth in a variety of arrangements for the exchange of technologies or technological services, ranging from R&D joint ventures and partnerships, to licensing and cross-licensing agreements, to contracted R&D. Although we lack comprehensive empirical measures of the increase in such arrangements over time, all the available evidence suggests that the trade in technologies is more common than it was in the past. For instance, the industry cases collected in Mowery (1988) suggest that since the 1980s there has been an increase in the number of collaborative ventures among firms, especially of those involving R&D and technology. Grindley and Teece (1997) point to the increasing use of technology licensing by companies such as IBM, Hewlett-Packard, Texas Instruments, and AT&T during the 1990s. A number of firms and software products have emerged to help firms manage their patent portfolios. Firms specializing in the creation of new technology are now an important part of the industrial landscape in many technology-intensive industries. Finally, we have seen the development of electronic and online market places where technologies can be bought and sold.

Many practitioners and scholars have noted these trends (e.g., Rivette and Kline 1999; Teece 1998). However, what is still lacking is a thorough and systematic understanding of how markets for technology arise, how they work, their limits and implications for public policy and corporate strategy. This book is a step in that direction. First, we look at the role of industry structure, the nature of knowledge, and intellectual property rights and related institutions that facilitate the development of markets for technology. Second, we ask what the implications of such markets are for the boundaries of the firm, division of labor in the economy, industry structure, and economic growth. Third, we build on this discussion to draw implications for public policy and corporate strategy. We combine theoretical perspectives from economics and management and draw upon several rich data sources to exemplify and substantiate the theoretical points.

We do not wish to suggest that in-house R&D in corporations will be supplanted by externally conducted R&D. Rather, we want to understand the conditions under which technology can be traded, be it by established firms or by firms specializing in the production of technology. In addition to the diffusion of technology, such transactions could play an important role in fostering innovation. This is the case when the developers of the technology lack the resources necessary to commercialize the technology. Without the prospect of being able to capitalize on their innovations by trading them, many small technology-based firms would not invest in creating new and useful technologies.

1.2 Markets for Technology: Scope of the Analysis and a Typology

1.2.1 A Tentative Definition

Technologies come in very different forms, and it is difficult to provide a general definition that would satisfactorily encompass all interesting cases of technology trade that we, or the reader, could think up. For instance, technology can take the form of "intellectual property" or intangibles (e.g., a software program, or a design), be embodied in a product (e.g., a prototype, or an instrument, like a chip designed to perform certain operations), or take the form of technical services. We will not attempt to define *technology*. Rather, we treat technology as an imprecise term for useful knowledge rooted in engineering and scientific disciplines, but also drawing from practical experience from production.

Our task is further complicated by the fact that technological knowledge can exist in many forms, where the distinction between physical products and technology is not always easy to make. Some forms present no real difficulty. Transactions involving blueprints, designs, formulae, or flowcharts are clearly part of the market for technology. In general, when the right to produce something or the knowledge of how to do so are separated from the thing itself, there is a clear line between the market for the thing itself and the market for the technology used to create it.

But technology can also be embodied in physical artifacts. For instance, a new method for rapidly screening biological compounds may be embodied in a chip that performs the screening. In this case, by purchasing the good, one also purchases the technology. Increasingly, firms are embodying their technology in software programs. Once again, the purchase of the software brings with it the right to use the embodied knowledge—and hence, software is commonly licensed rather than sold outright.

Our general criterion is to look at whether the cost of developing the knowledge embodied in the artifact significantly exceeds the cost of creating the artifact. Another way to make our distinction is to say that in a market for technology, the suppliers have a great deal of autonomy in designing and developing the good, as compared to suppliers that produce according to detailed specifications by their clients. In this case, the value associated with the design and conceptualization of the product would considerably exceed the value to the buyer that is associated with the mere outsourcing of the manufacturing operations.

This criterion is the hardest to apply in the case where knowledge is embodied in a software program. For instance, knowledge about how to test and debug a microprocessor design may be most effective if embodied in a software program. Although in principle the two—the knowledge and the program—are separate, as a practical matter they may be very closely linked because the software makes the knowledge operational and accessible to a much larger group of users. Having the required knowledge of microprocessor design is clearly a prerequisite for developing the software in question but is by no means sufficient, and considerable ingenuity and thought may go into the development of the software itself. In other words, we cannot hope to eliminate all the "gray" areas. Nor is it necessary. All that is needed is that there be enough of a "core" of transactions where the principal focus of the trade is knowledge rather than a physical artifact.

We also use the term *market* in a broad sense. Strictly speaking, market transactions are arms-length, anonymous, and typically involve an exchange of a good for money. Many, if not most, transactions for technology would fail one or the other of these criteria. Often these transactions involve detailed contracts and may be embedded in a technological alliance of some sort. Although the specific form of the transaction may affect the outcome in subtle ways, we shall ignore many of these subtleties in an effort to focus on the issues common to these transactions, such as the role of specialized technology suppliers, the role of intellectual property rights, and the nature of demand.

A final clarification is that we shall ignore some relevant forms of technology exchange. The trend toward acquisition of small, technology-based companies has become an important phenomenon in recent years. Insofar as they are driven by the need to acquire external technology, outright acquisitions should be included in the market for technology. However, acquisitions encompass not only existing technology, but also the capability and competence to develop new technologies. The issues surrounding the acquisition of technological capability are different from those pertaining to the acquisition of technology. Therefore, we exclude corporate mergers and acquisitions from our analysis. We also disregard another channel through which technological knowledge moves across firm boundaries—the movement of people. Neither omission is indicative of the importance of the phenomenon. Yet, ambitious as this book is, to include inter-firm movement of engineers and researchers would be unworkable.[1]

1.2.2   Markets for Technology and for Innovation

One can distinguish between markets for existing technologies and markets for technologies still being developed. Put differently, our definition of markets for technology covers both "current" and "futures" markets. Both share a number of common features, but there are also some interesting differences that we shall discuss in various chapters.

The U.S. Department of Justice, in its *Antitrust Guidelines for the Licensing of Intellectual Property* (U.S. Deptartment of Justice 1995) makes a similar distinction. The guidelines distinguish between markets for "goods," markets for "technology," and markets for "innovations." Markets for technology are markets for "intellectual property that is licensed and its close substitutes—that is, the technologies or goods that are close enough substitutes significantly to constrain the exercise of market power with respect to the intellectual property that is licensed." Markets for innovation include arrangements in which the parties involved agree to conduct activities, jointly or independently, leading to future developments of technologies that will be exchanged (or jointly owned) among them. This is typically the market for contract R&D and technological joint ventures and collaborations (U.S. Deptartment of Justice 1995, 6).

Roughly speaking, the distinction between the market for technology and the market for innovation as defined by the United States Department of Justice, corresponds to the distinction between transactions for the use and diffusion of technology on one hand, and transactions for the creation of new technology on the other. In addition to contract research, technology licensing, and R&D joint ventures of various kinds, transactions for the creation of new technologies also include the sale or licensing of research tools and transactions for research tools, as well as other types of technical services. Therefore, for this book, the market for technology includes transactions involving full technology packages (patents and other intellectual property and know-how), and patent licensing. Also included are transactions involving knowledge that is not patented and perhaps not even patentable (e.g., software, or many nonpatented designs) but excluding standard software site licenses.

1.2.3   The Division of Innovative Labor

Transactions in the market for technology can be classified in another way, depending on whether they involve "horizontal" transactions among established producers or "vertical" transactions between specialized firms that do not compete. Horizontal transactions (e.g., licensing and technology joint ventures), especially between firms in an industry and particularly at the international level, have been the focus of much of the literature on this subject (e.g., Teece 1977; Contractor 1981; Caves, Crookell, and Killing 1983; Mowery 1988; Anand and Khanna 2000).[2] However, vertical markets, where the technology is supplied to the downstream firms or industries by an upstream sector of specialized technology producers with no stake in the downstream operations, have become increasingly important in several high-tech industries. Further, the development of these vertical markets constitutes a division of labor in the innovation process itself and thus is closely linked to a much older and more powerful set of economic ideas.

As Smith (1776) and Stigler (1951) pointed out, an input produced under increasing returns is supplied more efficiently by a specialized upstream supplier that serves many firms, rather than by the individual downstream companies. Thus, division of labor is more extensive in larger markets. Young (1928) added a dynamic dimension to this analysis. As the more efficient production of the input lowers its unit cost, users are induced to invest, and the demand for the input increases. In turn, this increase in market size further expands the division of labor.

But while extensive specialization and division of labor mark many economic activities, this has not usually been the case in the production of technology. As noted earlier, R&D and technology have been integrated in large firms for many years. As we shall see in chapter 4, economists like Nelson and Winter (1982), and other scholars who built on their work, provided an economic justification for this pattern. The production of technology is a cumulative process based on tacit knowledge and expertise, requiring extensive interactions among the groups and individuals involved. These interactions can be realized more effectively when the individuals or groups belong to the same organization. In essence, there are transaction costs, both static and dynamic, in the exchange of technological knowledge across organizations, which may offset the advantages of a division of labor.

As discussed more fully in later chapters, especially chapters 3 and 6, there are two potential productivity benefits from a division of innovative labor. The first is specialization according to comparative advantage. If firms specializing in research are more efficient at developing new knowledge, while others, possibly those experienced in production and marketing, are more efficient at exploiting the new knowledge, then a division of innovative labor promotes innovation and productivity growth. A second potential benefit arises due to the increasing returns associated with new knowledge (David 2000; Romer 1990). This point can be clarified by looking briefly at what is happening in markets where an active division of innovative labor is taking place. A recent trend in biotechnology, software, and semiconductor sectors is the growth of firms specializing in the production of research methods and "tools" that can be used for several applications. For instance, many biotech companies have developed general-purpose technologies for drug discovery. These include rapid screening of chemical compounds, combinatorial chemistry techniques, and automated tools to assess the relationships between genes and diseases. Specialized tool developers can spread the fixed cost of development over many users. In contrast, a tool developed by a downstream user is applied far more narrowly. From a social point of view, each user developing its own tools means that the fixed costs of development are incurred several times over.

Our distinction between the division of labor and the division of "innovative" labor is meant only to emphasize that the division of labor we focus upon concerns technologies rather than specific products. The properties and implications of a classical division of labor apply to the division of innovative labor as well. However, insofar as the division of innovative labor deals with knowledge and technologies rather than material goods, there are additional factors that affect the form and extent of the division of labor.

One can summarize the foregoing discussion in the form of a simple typology shown in table 1.1. The table also provides a canonical example, taken from a commercial database, of each cell.

Table 1.1
A Simple Typology of Markets for Technology

	Existing Technology	Future Technology or Component for Future
Horizontal market/ Transactions with actual or potential rivals	Union Carbide licensing Uniopol polyethylene technology to Huntsman Chemicals	Sun licensing Java to IBM; R&D joint ventures between rivals
Vertical market/ licensing to nonrivals	Licensing of IP Core in semiconductors	R&D joint ventures; Affymax licensing combinatoric technology to pharmaceutical firm

1.2.4 Markets for Technology: Why We Should Care

Markets for technology promote the diffusion and efficient use of existing technology and can enhance the rate of technological advance by providing additional incentives to invest in research and development. In particular, they can encourage firms to specialize in the production of technology.

Companies, particularly large companies, often develop technologies that they do not commercialize. In many cases, there could be other companies that could profitably use these technologies. Often there are strategic reasons for not licensing unused technologies, including the fear of creating new competitors or of cannibalizing existing markets. Often the reason is different. Technology contracts are thought to be inefficient, and the returns from licensing inadequate to offset other costs. As a result, firms have tended to ignore the option of licensing their technologies.

Technology licenses, and especially international licenses, do exist. However, there is anecdotal evidence that the licensing market is less developed than socially desirable. For instance, a recent study by British Technology Group (BTG), a consulting firm, found that large companies in the United States, Western Europe, and Japan ignore a substantial fraction of their patented technologies, which could be profitably sold or licensed (British Technology Group 1998). Moreover, the study found that companies fail to license not because licensing is unattractive, but simply because they do not take this possibility into account. Similarly, the European Union estimated that 20 billion U.S. dollars are spent every year in Europe to develop new products or ideas that have already been developed elsewhere.[3] Well-functioning markets for technology can improve efficiency by reducing duplicative R&D and by matching technology producers and users.

One objective of this book is therefore to understand the factors that induce established companies to license their technologies and become active suppliers in the market. In particular, we examine how industry structure and competition affect these incentives. Moreover, there are important managerial implications that flow from dealing with technologies as "products." As Grindley and Teece (1997) have noted, this may require different modes of managing the firms; in particular, it requires a different approach to the management of intellectual capital compared with the use of technology merely as an input for the company's final products. Even competitive strategy may change substantially when there are well-functioning markets for technology. For example, in industries like chemicals, extensive technology licensing among established producers has contributed to increased competition in many product markets (Arora and Gambardella 1998).

Technology markets are also a precondition for the existence of specialized technology suppliers operating in vertical markets. Specialization and division of labor is a powerful determinant of industry and economic growth. But specialized suppliers can also act as a mechanism for knowledge transfer that resembles technological spillover across firms, a subject that has attracted a great deal of attention from economists. While spillovers may reduce the private incentives to do R&D, they increase the social returns to R&D and technological investments, and therefore are another source of technological diffusion and growth. There is a large empirical literature that attempts to measure the extent and impact of such spillovers on economic measures of performance such as productivity (Griliches 1979, 1984; Jaffe 1986; Coe and Helpman 1995; Cohen and Levinthal 1989).

However, some so-called spillovers may in fact be market-mediated transfers of knowledge. One thesis of this book is that the intermediation of an upstream sector of technology suppliers can be a powerful mechanism through which spillovers can take place. This recognition that spillovers are not simply "in the air" suggests that they do not arise merely because of geographical agglomeration but require well-defined institutions to work. Moreover, benefiting from spillovers may well require the development of cooperative links or other types of relationships with upstream technology suppliers. Nathan Rosenberg's work provides a compelling historical account of this process. For instance,

Rosenberg (1963) describes how specialized machine tool suppliers absorbed and improved the metal-working technology first developed in armament manufacture, and made this improved technology available to other sectors that followed, including sewing machines and bicycles.

In sum, if markets for technology were more extensive and more widespread, existing technologies would stand a better chance of being used, and being used more extensively. New technologies would be more likely to be developed, because even if the technology's inventor did not commercialize the technology itself, the inventor could still profit by licensing the technology to others better able to commercialize it. Not only would there be an increase in the rate of inventive activity, but there would also be profound influences on conditions of entry for new firms and new types of firms, on the competitive position of existing firms, and on the structure of the industry itself.

1.3   Structure of the Book

This book is divided into four parts. Part I provides evidence of the existence of markets for technology. Chapter 2 presents evidence from the available literature, systematic data on worldwide technology licensing deals and related technology transactions in recent years. Using the available data on the values of these transactions, we estimate the total value of worldwide technology transfer deals by the granting and receiving of two-digit SIC sectors. This enables us to quantify the extent of the worldwide market for technology, and to gain insight into market mediated inter-sectoral technology flows.

Chapter 3 provides additional qualitative evidence about markets for technology from four high-tech industries: chemicals, software, biotechnology, and semiconductors. We document the development of markets for technology in these sectors, with a special focus on the division of innovative labor in these industries. These cases illustrate many of the issues discussed in later chapters of the book.

Part II focuses on the limitations and determinants of markets for technology. Chapter 4 deals with the "cognitive" limitations to markets for technology. These limits arise from context dependence, the idea that knowledge created in one context is not readily transferred and used in another context (Arora and Gambardella 1994a). This raises the costs of technology transfer, especially in the context of a division of innovative labor, because context dependence makes it difficult to partition the innovation process into independent activities to be assigned to independent actors.

Chapter 4 begins by illustrating the problems involved in partitioning innovation activities, and continues to review the available literature. It first discusses the literature that follows Nelson and Winter (1982) and Teece (1988), who argue that innovation is largely the outcome of organizational routines, and hence is more effectively performed within organizations. Building on this literature and particularly on the work by Eric Von Hippel (1990, 1994) and Kogut and Zander (1992), we argue that industries and technologies differ in the extent to which task-partitioning is possible. We discuss these conditions and the related differences across industries and technologies. We also argue that changes in the technology of technical change itself, and specifically, the growing use of computers, and information technology in research are enhancing the market for technology and division of innovative labor.

Context-dependent knowledge is less likely to be articulated and codified. Put differently, much of what is useful about technology may be tacit, neither codified nor embodied in machinery or equipment. Not only is tacit knowledge costly to transfer for reasons discussed in Chapter 4, its transfer also raises potential contracting problems. Indeed, the existence of tacit knowledge is a commonly advanced as a reason why technology trade may be inefficient. Chapter 5 develops a formal model showing that when tacit know-how is bundled with complementary codified technology inputs, and the latter is protected by patents or other means, simple contracts can accomplish the transfer of tacit knowledge.

Chapter 5 addresses the suggestion in the literature that part of the difficulty in creating markets for technology is that one cannot exchange tacit knowledge through arm's-length contracts. The chapter shows that the problem of contracting for know-how can be overcome by bundling know-how with complementary codified inputs and leveraging the superior enforceability of contracts over the latter. The chapter also provides empirical support using data on 144 technology import agreements by Indian firms during 1950–1975.

Chapter 6 analyzes the tradeoff between increasing returns to knowledge production and the superior ability of users to understand their own needs. Whereas the latter favors each user developing its own technology, the former favors specialized technology suppliers. This tradeoff determines whether an upstream sector of technology specialists will arise. This chapter examines how two different dimensions of demand—its breadth (the number of users) and depth (the average size of each user)—affect the terms of this tradeoff and hence, have very different effects on the division of innovative labor. We draw on the experience of specific industries like biotechnology and software to provide evidence supporting the theoretical reasoning developed in the chapter.

Part III discusses the functioning of markets for technology. Chapter 7 examines the incentives of established producers to license their own technologies. Here we focus on the interaction between the downstream "goods" market and the market for technology. The key insight is that competition in the goods market can induce licensing of in-house technology by established producers. The logic of the argument is straightforward: Incumbent producers have a disincentive to license because licensing increases competition in the downstream goods market and dissipates rents. However, licensing also creates revenue. Although the existing literature often implicitly assumes that the revenue effect is smaller than the rent dissipation effect, this is not always true. We rigorously explore how market share, the extent of product differentiation, and the efficiency of licensing contracts affect the balance between the two. We also introduce a third effect—the role of competition in the market for technology itself. We show how the presence of other technology holders, particularly firms that only supply technology, can create additional incentives for licensing by established incumbents. The chapter also explores the empirical validity of these ideas using data on chemical process technology licenses.

Chapter 8 focuses on the role of an upstream industry of technology suppliers as a vehicle for transmitting investment opportunities across downstream companies and industries. This chapter highlights how technology is transferred internationally as the outcome of a functioning market for technology. The chapter focuses on the story of the specialized engineering firms (SEFs) in the chemical processing industry (discussed in chapter 3). Beginning in the 1930s and continuing into the 1960s, the rapid growth of the chemical industry in the developed countries stimulated the growth of firms that specialized in the design and engineering of chemical plants—the SEFs. Since the 1970s, as a modern chemical industry emerged in the less developed countries (LDCs) the presence of an upstream sector of technology suppliers in the first world proved very valuable. SEFs had already accumulated expertise in plant design and technology, which could be supplied to the chemical firms in LDCs.

We exploit a rich database on investments in chemical processing industries worldwide from 1980–1990. The empirical analysis shows that the greater the number of technology suppliers (SEFs) that operate in the first world, the greater the investments in chemical plants in LDCs. Moreover, the effect of SEFs is greater for LDC firms rather than multinationals. A major contribution of the analysis developed in this chapter is that it identifies an important and understudied mechanism through which technology is made available and through which spillovers take place—notably, the intermediation of an upstream sector of technology specialists.

Part IV examines the implications for corporate strategy and policy. Chapter 9, which focuses on implications for corporate strategy, also links the discussion in the earlier parts of the book to the "resource-based" view of the firm and clarifies how the development of a market for technology affects corporate boundaries and corporate strategy. It documents the growing recognition by established firms of the importance of technology licensing in relation to their overall business. As the sale of technologies becomes a business of its own, some of these companies are organizing internal divisions focusing on licensing and seeking better ways to manage their intellectual capital and patent portfolios. Second, the chapter argues that for many technology-based smaller firms, licensing may be a better strategy than bearing the costs and risks of downstream manufacturing and commercialization. Third, it points out that markets for technology increase the "penalty" of company strategies based on the notorious "not invented here" syndrome. Finally, markets for technology have natural implications for industry structure. Such markets lower entry barriers and reduce concentration.

Chapter 10 addresses institutional changes and policy implications. This chapter argues that the growth of markets for technology is enhanced by the growth of complementary institutions. It discusses some of these institutions, and the ways in which they can reduce the transaction costs involved in trading technology. In addition to standards, and standard-setting bodies, a key consideration in this respect is intellectual property rights. As discussed in chapter 5, much of the literature on intellectual property rights has focused on the extent to which they provide incentives for firms to invest in R&D. However, as property rights, they can be traded, implying that they can facilitate the efficient utilization of innovations. Such trades could also play an important role in inducing innovation, when the developers of the technology are not the firms best able to commercialize the technology. Without the prospect of being able to capitalize on their innovations by trading the property rights protecting the innovation, many small technology-based firms would not invest in creating new and useful technologies.

In other words, intellectual property rights are the means for defining the object of the transaction and the property rights in the markets for technology. That said, intellectual property differs from tangible property in many important ways. Some scholars have argued that these differences make intellectual property rights more prone to "fragmentation." In this chapter we discuss this theory and some possible policy responses. Finally, the chapter notes that one consequence of markets for technology is the possible encouragement of a greater "privatization" of knowledge. This may weaken norms of conduct commonly associated with academic research and undercut the important role of academic research based on open disclosure and information sharing in the generation and the diffusion of knowledge. Chapter 11 concludes the book, summarizing its main issues and discussing further developments in this line of research.

I

**Markets for Technology:
Extent and Development**

2   Preliminary Evidence

2.1   Introduction

Can and do markets exist for technology not embodied in capital or products? In this chapter, we marshal the available evidence on the topic.

We start with an illustrative case study from the chemical sector.[1] The purpose of this case is to introduce the reader to the subject of this book by providing a concrete example of what markets for technology are, how they function, along with their intricacies and implications. Our objective is to illustrate a phenomenon that is difficult to define in general terms. The chapter continues with a discussion of evidence from the literature. Finally, we use material from an extensive database on technology transactions to present an aggregate picture of the size and scope of markets for technology in the 1990s.

2.2   The Market for Metallocene Technology: An Illustrative Case Study

Polyethylene is an important chemical product. Along with polypropylene, polyethylene is the basic material used to produce a variety of plastics, packaging films, electrical wire, and fibers. Advances in catalyst and process technology are the main sources of technical advances for polyethylene producers. Metallocenes, or "single site catalysts," are a new type of catalyst system for polymers that provide much greater control over molecular size and architecture than previously possible. Hence, the physical properties of the plastic can be more finely tailored.

Conventional polymers are produced via Ziegler-Natta catalysts, which have multiple active sites. Multiple active sites create polymers with varying molecular structures, resulting in the variable distribution

Table 2.1
Market for Polyethylene Technology
(a) Leading Firms in Major Polyolefin Segment

Polymer	Major Use	United States	Europe	Japan
LLDPE	Film	Dow, Exxon, Phillips, Mobil	BASF, Borealis, BP	Mitsui, Sumitomo, Ube
HDPE	Film	Dow	Fina	Asahi
PP	Fibers, Nonwoven	Exxon, Fina	Targor, Montell	Mitsui

Source: Hernandez-Tozo 2000 (adapted from *Chemical News*).

(b) Key Technology Providers for Polyethylene (PE)

	Gas Phase PE Process	Catalyst
Dow-BP	Innovene (BP)	Insite (Dow)
Exxon-UC (Univation)	Unipol (UC), SCM-T (Exxon)	Exxpol (Exxon)

of the co-monomer between polymer chains. Metallocenes, a family of metal complexes, have only one active site. A single site tends to polymerize in a more uniform fashion, so that every molecule is similar, producing a polymer with exceptionally predictable physical, optical and mechanical properties. Key applications for metallocene-based polyethylene include pharmaceutical and medical packaging, capacitor films, flexible food packaging, optical parts and lenses, and toner binder resins.[2]

In recent years, the polyolefin (polyethylene and polypropylene) industry has consolidated greatly. Table 2.1a shows some of the leaders in different market segments. Many of these firms are actively investing in the development of new technologies and have entered into a variety of alliances and agreements, as shown in table 2.1b. Dow and Exxon are the leaders in metallocene technology, followed by Phillips and Hoechst, which also have patents in this area. Union Carbide (recently acquired by Dow) and BP chemicals are among the leaders in polyethylene process technology. The major suppliers of process technology in polypropylene are Montel, a joint venture of Shell and Montedison, and Union Carbide, followed by BP, BASF, Hoechst, Mitsui, and Sumitomo.[3] The most important agreements in polyethylene concern firms with catalyst technology pairing up with firms with process technology, as shown in table 2.1b.

Demand for global polyethylene in the year 2000 is estimated to be about 51 million tons, of which metallocenes represent about one million tons, or 2 percent. However, by 2010, the total demand for polyethylene is estimated to be around 83 million tons, and metallocenes are expected to account for about 17 millions tons, or about 20 percent. Moreover, a number of metallocene-related patent suits have recently been settled, and industry executives believe that this has cleared the way for a more extensive deployment of the technology. Industry sources estimated the size of the market in 1997 at around $3.5 billion.

The technology is still new and diffusing. Metallocene technology has been commercialized in polyethylene, but it is still in its early stages in polypropylene. Integrating the catalyst technology with an established process technology has been a major technical challenge in the development of the technology. The total investment in developing metallocene technology is estimated to be $3 billion (Moore and Scott 2000).

2.2.1 Market for Metallocene-Based Polyethylene Technology

Dow Chemicals and Exxon, the leaders in metallocene technology for polyethylene, are also leading producers of polyethylene.[4] Both are also leading technology suppliers, licensing their technology on a worldwide basis in cooperation with other prominent firms (BP Chemicals and Union Carbide, respectively) who possess important complementary technologies, notably gas phase process technology for polyethylene.

The major licensors of metallocene technology have taken different paths to arrive at the decision to license. Both Union Carbide and Dow have been major producers of polyethylene for many years, each using a proprietary technology. Union Carbide (UCC) started licensing its gas phase process, the Unipol process, in 1975. Over time, licensing became a very important source of revenue for the firm.[5] BP had entered the polyethylene business by licensing the Ziegler-Natta catalyst technology from Ziegler himself in the 1960s, and built its first polyethylene plant in 1969.[6] BP Chemicals began producing metallocenes at a later date, and found that Exxon and Dow already had the lead. Dow had developed a metallocene catalyst technology, the Insite system, that was judged by BP to be better in some respects than Exxon's, but had relatively little experience in the market for technology. Hence, BP offered its gas phase technology as well as its licensing expertise. Accordingly, Dow negotiated a joint development with BP shortly before the creation of Univation by Exxon and UCC. Although the joint venture is reported to have met its technological goals, its commercial activities were hamstrung by the acquisition of UCC by Dow in late 1999. The acquisition effectively made Dow a partner with Exxon through Exxon's joint venture with UCC.[7] The first licensee of the joint venture, Chevron, has publicly announced that it would begin production using the licensed Dow-BP technology in 2001.

Exxon began polyethylene production by licensing Union Carbide's gas phase technology (Unipol) in the 1980s. This licensing contract required Exxon to share any process improvements with the licensor. Increasing competition in the polyethylene market implied great pressures for product differentiation, which lead Exxon to develop a new catalyst system. However, when Exxon used its new metallocene catalyst system in a modified Unipol process in its French plant, it prompted a lawsuit by UCC. The lawsuit was settled with the formation of a joint venture, Univation Technologies, in 1997, to jointly license polyethylene process technology. Exxon provided its Super Condensing Mode process technology (SCMT) and the Exxpol metallocene catalyst technology and UCC provided its Unipol single reactor gas phase technology and expertise in the technology licensing business.

Univation is a technology licensing business providing both patents and know-how, including detailed engineer flow sheets, with six specialized engineering firms (SEFs) as approved contractors for the actual construction of the plant. Although in principle the technology can be used in existing plants, in practice it is primarily sought for use in new plants. By early 2000, Univation had sold six technology licenses.

2.2.2   The Market for Technology in Chemicals More Generally

There is an active market for technology in chemical processes. There are some standard templates for licensing contracts, such as the one offered by the Institute of Chemical Engineers in the United Kingdom, which are broadly followed in the polyethylene market. However, actual contracts tend to be more complex and particularized to accommodate variations in commercial conditions. The typical licensing arrangement consists of an up-front payment plus a royalty. From 15 to 30 percent of the total value is typically paid in a lump sum, but terms vary from contract to contract. The licensing contract may include improvements in the technology that are made during a specified period of time, or it may not include improvements at all. The usual license contract specifies the site at which the technology is to be used and production capacity. However, sales of the output can be made worldwide, with no restriction in terms of markets.

The level of service a firm provides to its licensees is one of the most important ways a firm can differentiate itself from its competitors in the technology market. Some firms offer technical support and other know-how critical for the effective operation of the licensed technology. In chapter 5, we shall analyze how simple licensing contracts common in the industry can efficiently provide such know-how, and the crucial role of patents.

Licensing revenues are still small in relation to the large revenues from chemical production at firms like UCC, BP, Dow, and Exxon. This is hardly surprising, given the extremely large volume of chemicals that these companies produce. Even so, the profit margins in licensing are much higher than in polyethylene production. Indeed, it is likely that profit margins in licensing are higher than margins for most chemical products. Growth in licensing has meant that licensing revenues comprise a substantial portion of R&D spending. Estimates from interviews with industry participants suggest that licensing costs are well over two-thirds of the R&D spending in polyethylene in BP Chemicals. Rough estimates suggest that licensing revenues are approximately 10–20 percent of the R&D budget for polyethylene and related polymers at Exxon Chemicals, and about 33 percent in Phillips Chemicals. Even though licensing revenues are only a small fraction of the revenues of total revenues for Exxon Chemicals, it has aggressively defended its metallocene patents. Exxon has chosen to do so primarily with an eye to its licensing business—not merely to preserve its own polyolefin business.

For both BP and Exxon, the decision to license technology was a response to the changing nature of product market competition. Exxon Chemicals had not been a major technology licensor before the metallocene licensing thrust; managers we interviewed noted that Exxon could not exploit the technology on a large enough scale by itself. Therefore, licensing was a means of getting returns on R&D.

BP had developed its own polyethylene process technology in the 1960s. However, it found there were other sources of technology, notably Union Carbide in gas phase, and more than a dozen other suppliers of other types of process technology. Among the many producers of polyethylene, BP had less than 2 percent of the market share. Even so, BP initially restricted technology licensing to outside Western Europe, where it had a larger market share. BP later moved to a global policy in response to UCCs aggressive licensing activity. BP decided to license its polyethylene technology (Innovene) globally in 1982, and over time achieved a 25 percent market share, with the market leader, UCC, holding a 50 percent market share. BP's polyethylene licensing operation grew from a small operation inside the Engineering Division of BP Chemicals to an independent profit center. However, in acetic acid, where BP has strong proprietary technology licenses are granted in select cases only.

Clearly, the changing competitive conditions are driving the changed attitudes toward licensing. Dow itself changed its attitudes to licensing in the early 1990s, stimulated by a need to derive more value from its investments in R&D.[8] While Dow had earlier been very reluctant to part with its technology, rising R&D costs and falling profit margins, as well as Union Carbide's success with licensing technology, were important factors in Dow's decisions to change its licensing strategy. Indeed, during Dow's acquisition of UCC, the latter's expertise in technology licensing was explicitly noted as an important asset by Dow's CEO in his communications with investors and analysts.

However, not all technologies are licensed. For instance, licensing is not seen as a sensible strategy for fine chemicals. In butyl rubber, for example, the market size is small and Exxon Chemicals does not license its technology. Similarly, even though Union Carbide has pioneered the use of licensing as a business model, they do not license technology in wire and cable applications, because they have a strong position in this market niche. As one of the managers we interviewed told us, "if you license out, the specialty will turn into a commodity rapidly."[9]

Globalization implies that under some conditions, firms license as a way of exploiting their technology in markets in which they do not wish to produce. Competition reduces profit margins while increasing the size of the market. Under some conditions, analyzed more fully in chapter 7, this makes it profitable even for large producers to license proprietary technology. Even though licensing in the chemical industry has increased in response to globalization and increased competition, technology licensing in this industry is not new (Arora 1997). More than thirty years ago ICI, Mitsui, and Amoco were among chemical producers that offered technology for license, along with firms specializing in process design and engineering.[10]

2.3   Markets for Technology: Evidence from the Literature

2.3.1   Markets for Technology in the Nineteenth and Early Twentieth Centuries

The market for metallocene technology is a recent and more fully elaborated instance of a much older phenomenon. A sequence of papers by Lamoreaux and Sokoloff (1996, 1997, 1998) provide a detailed account of U.S. markets for technology in the nineteenth and early twentieth centuries. Their 1996 paper addresses this issue from several perspectives. First, they show that between 1840 and 1911, the annual number of patents per resident varied across regions of the United States. For example, during 1850–1859, the number of patents per resident in these regions were, New England: 175.6; Middle Atlantic: 129.4; East North Central: 57.3; West North Central: 22.9; South: 15.5; West: 24.8. The U.S. average was 91.5 patents per resident. This discrepancy became less pronounced over time. During 1910–1911, the number of patents per resident in these regions became 534.3; 488.6; 442.3; 272.0; 114.4; and 458.4, respectively, with a U.S. average of 334.2. The convergence notwithstanding, Lamoreaux and Sokoloff argue that in this period, inventive activity was more concentrated geographically than production. Therefore the location of the inventive activity cannot be explained solely by the location of manufacturing. (See also Audretsch and Feldman 1996.)

Further evidence is provided by Lamoreaux and Sokoloff's examination of a sample of more than 6,600 U.S. patents issued in 1870–1871, 1890–1891, and 1910–1911. From the *Annual Report of the Commissioner of Patents*, the patent records in the sample provide information on full or partial assignments of patent rights, allowing the researchers to assess the extent to which patentees transferred their patent rights to other parties when the patent was issued.[11] Lamoreaux and Sokoloff found that the percentage of patents assigned to third parties was higher in regions that also featured a higher number of patents issued per resident. For instance, in 1910–1911, the percentage of patents assigned to third parties was 50 percent and 36.1 percent in New England and Middle Atlantic as compared to 32.3 percent in East North Central; 17.5 percent in West North Central; 22.7 percent in the South, and 21.4 percent in the West. (The U.S. average was 30.5 percent.) Moreover, the percentage of patents assigned to companies increased considerably in all regions over time. In New England, for example, the percentage of patents assigned at issue to companies, as compared to all patents assigned increased from 33.3 percent in 1870–1871 to 75 percent in 1910–1911.

The higher intensity of assignment in regions that feature a higher concentration of innovative activity suggests a relationship between a market for inventive services and the extent of inventive activity. This relationship is further mediated by the growth in services that facilitate the trade of technology. Lamoreaux and Sokoloff noted, for example, that over time many lawyers became increasingly active in finding buyers for patents and related technologies, and in connecting demand and supply—especially in areas where the inventive activity was pronounced. Many were patent advisors, specializing in patent litigation or in the preparation of patent filing and documentation for the Patent Office. But they gradually became involved in creating networks between buyers and sellers of patents, and in so doing they played an important role in "organizing" the market for technology. By the same token, the increasing share of patents assigned to companies suggests that the market grew over time to become one in which full-fledged companies, with sizable assets for development and commercialization, were the primary buyers.

Lamoreaux and Sokoloff also make the more general point that the Patent System was the critical institution for the rise of markets for technology. In the first place, patents provided a clear and recognized right to inventions, so that inventors were assured of their ability to benefit from their invention without having to commercially exploit the innovation themselves. Second, the Patent System diffused information about innovations, enhancing opportunities for technology trade. Information was not only diffused directly, but also through journals such as *Scientific American,* which started publishing information on new patents and the technology development they represented.

One possible objection to interpreting Lamoreaux and Sokoloff's results as a market for technology is that these patent assignments may reflect employment contracts or other types of market transactions rather than a market for technology.[12] For instance, the patentee may be an employee of the firm, or otherwise related to the owner of the firm. To address this concern, Lamoreaux and Sokoloff examined the career profiles of all patentees with last names starting with the letter *B* in the initial sample of 6,600 patents, focusing on their patenting behavior in 1870–1871, 1890–1891, and 1910–1911. This information was combined with available information about patentees (Sokoloff and Khan 1990). They found that there was a substantial decline in the number of occasional inventors. The number of patentees with 1 or 2 "career patents" (i.e., with one or two patents over the entire period) fell from 70 percent of total patents to 40 percent from the early to the late nineteenth century. By contrast, the share of patentees with ten or more career patents increased from 5 percent to 20 percent.

Three additional results of this analysis are particularly relevant for our purposes. First, the patentees with a higher number of career patents resided in geographic areas with higher patenting and assignment rates and better-developed institutions for technology trade. Second, the percentage of assignments for a given patentee increases progressively with the number of career patents. Thus, for example, the patentees with eleven to nineteen and twenty or more career patents assigned respectively 47.4 percent and 66.8 percent of their patents to third parties, compared with 20.1 percent and 24 percent of those with one or two to five career patents. Third, about 36 percent and 41 percent of the patentees with eleven to nineteen and twenty or more career patents assigned their patents to four or more different assignees. Though far from conclusive, the combination of a high number of career patents, high percentage of assignments, and their location in higher patenting areas suggest that certain areas increasingly hosted several specialized inventors, who were generally more productive and typically sold their patents to others.[13]

Their subsequent papers provide further evidence of a functioning market for technology in the nineteenth century. Lamoreaux and Sokoloff (1997) analyze the relationship between the location of manufacturing and the location of inventive activity in the U.S. glass industry in the late nineteenth and early twentieth centuries. Given that technology producers "learn by doing," and given the importance of proximity in facilitating information flows, one might expect technology development activities to be located close to production.

Instead, Lamoreaux and Sokoloff find no systematic relationship. Some U.S. regions showed a high percentage of U.S. output or labor force in the glass industry, but a far lower percentage of glass patents, while the opposite was true for other regions. Other regions showed fairly similar percentages of production and invention. Moreover, very little consistency is observed over time. For instance, the U.S. share of glass production in Southern New England fell from 14 percent in 1870 to 0.7 percent in 1918, while the percentage of U.S. glass patents in the region fell only from 15 percent to 7.3 percent. By contrast, West Virginia was responsible for 9.1 percent of all U.S. glass patents and only 1 percent of production in 1870, compared with 5.1 percent and 15 percent respectively in 1918. Unlike these regions, Indiana showed a consistent pattern over time, with 4.1 percent of the U.S. glass production in 1870 and practically no patents, compared to 11.1 percent of the U.S. production and 3.7 percent of glass patents in 1918. These statistical patterns are consistent with qualitative evidence, which shows that in some cases new technologies were developed next to production sites, whereas in others technologies were developed by independent engineers and technologists located elsewhere.

If the location of production does not explain the location of innovative activity, the natural question is—what explains the observed patterns of location of the inventors? Lamoreaux and Sokoloff show that for the glass industry, inventive activity was concentrated where the environment was conducive both to the innovation process and to technology trade, particularly due to institutions that facilitated the diffusion of technological information and the related technological exchange. Moreover, they find that a higher proportion of the patents assigned at issue occurred in regions where the share of total U.S. glass patents exceeded that of the total U.S. glass production or labor force, and that patentees who assigned their patents at issue produced on average more patents over their careers than those who did not.

Lamoreaux and Sokoloff (1998) examine the same issue from a slightly different perspective.[14] They start by suggesting that the difficulties in contracting for technological information have been overemphasized by the literature. Based on their analyses of their previous two papers, they argue that an organized market for technology existed prior to the growth of in-house R&D laboratories by the larger companies. One important step in the growth of in-house R&D was the effort to convince inventors of the advantages of stable employment relationships in exchange for contracts that relinquished the rights to the inventions to their employers. Using historical examples, Lamoreaux and Sokoloff argue that one of the major obstacles was the reluctance of inventors to relinquish their patent rights. However, many successful inventors, faced serious difficulties in finding the financial sources to develop their own new technologies and prototypes. This convinced many of them to accept employment relationships that ensured greater financial security. The problem was intensified because, in the twentieth century, many innovations became more complex and costlier to develop. Asymmetric information and related problems between inventors and prospective financiers intensified. According to Lamoreaux and Sokoloff, financial constraints, rather than inefficiencies in contracting for technological information, were the main force in entrepreneurial inventors' acceptance of employment in corporate R&D laboratories instead of the more uncertain (but often higher) returns as an independent inventor.

This conclusion is intriguing, for it suggests that an important limitation on the rise of markets for technology may be the inability of financial markets to fund risky inventive activity, and not inherent features of the nature of knowledge and technologies. This conclusion is consistent with the broad observation that in areas where there are more effective institutions for financing risky innovation projects (e.g., Silicon Valley, Israel), one observes a proliferation of technological spin-offs and start-ups. Of course, the development in financial institutions, especially for financing technology based start-ups, over the last century may qualify this conclusion. The willingness of venture capital firms from the United States to set up offices and subsidiaries in countries such as India and Ireland to fund technology based startups in those countries suggests that financial constraints may be less of a problem today.

2.3.2   Knowledge Spillovers, or Markets for Technology?

The notion of markets for technology is related to another prevalent concept in economic literature—knowledge or technological spillovers. The idea is that R&D investments by a firm spill over to other firms, thereby increasing the productivity of R&D in other firms, or directly improving efficiency and productivity in other firms. Such spillovers are real externalities and imply public subsidy for R&D.

The existence of technological spillovers has been widely documented (see Griliches 1979; Jaffe 1986). Moreover, it has been suggested that technological spillovers are more pronounced when the agents are geographically close. For instance, patents are more likely to cite other patents or scientific literature produced by people located in the same geographical area of the patentee; companies located in areas where there are scientifically or technologically active universities or firms exhibit higher innovation productivity or higher performance than predicted by their own investments in R&D or technology (Jaffe 1986; Jaffe, Trajtenberg, and Henderson 1993; Audrestch and Feldman 1996). Similarly, geographic clusters enhance complementarities and other relationships that generate technological externalities (Saxenian 1994; Swann, Prevezer, and Stout 1998). Technological spillovers can also span wider geographical boundaries. Coe and Helpman (1995) have documented the existence of international spillovers. (See also Eaton and Kortum 1996, and Keller 1998.)

One limitation of these studies is that they do not explain the mechanisms that give rise to the spillovers. In this respect, they all seem to abide by Alfred Marshall's oft-used phrase, "the secrets . . . are in the air" (Marshall 1990). But, as suggested by the findings reported in Lamoreaux and Sokoloff, and as we document in later chapters, some of the observed correlation between productivity in individual firms or countries with R&D investments by others may not reflect real externalities. Instead, they may reflect knowledge transfers through markets. Put differently, they may reflect at best pecuniary externalities rather than real ones.

Zucker, Darby, and Armstrong (1998) provide some suggestive evidence consistent with this idea. They analyze the performance of 110 California-based biotechnology firms, and relate their performance to the relationships of the firms with California-based "star" scientists. Star scientists are defined as those responsible for a substantial number of genetic sequence discoveries, based on their authorship of articles reporting these discoveries (up to 1990). Zucker, Darby, and Armstrong found fifty-five California star scientists defined in this way. They distinguished between "affiliated," "linked," and "untied" articles by each of the firms in their sample. Affiliated articles are those in which a star scientist gives the name of the firm as the affiliation; linked articles are those co-authored by non-star authors affiliated with the firm and at least one star scientist not affiliated with the firm; untied articles are those by star scientists not linked or affiliated with the firm. To measure performance, Zucker, Darby, and Armstrong used the 1989–1994 growth in the firm's employment, the number of products in the market and the number of products in development in 1991.

Simple statistics already show the importance of ties to a star. Firms with affiliated or linked scientists showed an average growth in employment of 366 workers from 1989 to 1994, compared to eighty-two workers for firms without such ties. Firms affiliated or linked with star scientists also averaged 8.8 to 10.7 products in development and in the market, compared to between 1.2 and 3.5 for those firms with no such affiliation or linkage. These basic statistics are confirmed by multiple regressions. Using firm age and other controls, Zucker, Darby, and Armstrong report that unlike untied articles, linked and affiliated articles are associated with better firm performance. In fact, in some cases they find that untied articles are associated with below-average firm performance.

Zucker, Darby, and Armstrong conclude that it is important to distinguish whether a firm is tied or not to the sources of these spillovers. The negative sign of untied articles is particularly interesting. It suggests not only that the spillovers accrue to those who actively pursue formal ties with the sources of the spillovers, but also that those who do not do so bear only the costs of being in economically and technologically active areas without reaping the benefits. Examples of such costs include congestion effects, and higher cost of local resources like land and labor.

The work by Zucker, Darby, and Armstrong does not clarify the specific causal relationship that drives their empirical results. It may be that the proliferation of linked articles does not improve performance in biotech firms, but rather well-performing biotech firms attract star scientists to work with them. While both effects are probably relevant here, it is nonetheless revealing that there is mutual attraction between high performance firms and leading scientists in a region, suggesting those who belong to the "club" may derive greater benefit in such geographical clusters compared to those who stay at the margins of this system of relationships.

2.4   The Size and Scope of Markets for Technology

2.4.1   Technology Trade in the 1990s

How large and important are markets for technology today? The available information is fragmented. To date, no systematic assessment of this phenomenon exists. Some evidence is provided by a recent study by a British consulting company (British Technology Group 1998), based on interviews with 133 companies and twenty universities in Europe (49 companies and 11 universities), North America (51 companies and 9 universities), and Japan (33 companies). These are all R&D-intensive companies or research universities. Though the sample is small and not representative of all firms performing R&D, and BTG presumably has a vested interest in showing the existence of underutilized technologies, the findings of the report are nonetheless suggestive.

The BTG report shows that companies have a sizable pool of unutilized patents. Only 15 percent of the survey respondents said that they had no unutilized patents in their portfolio, while 24 percent said that they had more than 100 unutilized patents, and 12 percent had more than 1,000. Unutilized patents were especially common among the Japanese companies (30% had more than 2,000).

Interestingly enough, 78 percent of the respondents were unable or unwilling to estimate the value of technology they possess. It therefore appears that companies or universities have seen little benefit in estimating the commercial value of the technological assets that they possess.[15] Not surprisingly, the same companies tend not to estimate the value of their unused patents. Only 25 percent of university respondents, and a mere 8 percent of industry respondents said that they made efforts to measure the value of their "orphan" patents.

The orthodox economic model of rational behavior would interpret these results as evidence that a large fraction of patents, perhaps the bulk of them, are of very low value. Indeed, this is the finding as reported by Pakes (1986) and Schankerman and Pakes (1986), based on patent renewal data. However, a substantial fraction of the respondents—40 percent of the universities and 32 percent of the companies—said they thought their unused patents were very or quite important. Although economists are inclined to place much greater weight on what economic agents do rather than what they say, in at least some cases the neglect of patents does not necessarily reflect the true economic value of the patent, but rather established management practice and norms. These norms may have been appropriate in an era when courts were far more likely to find patents invalid than they are now. In other words, corporate practice may not have fully caught up to the changing economic conditions, where patents appear to have much greater value than before.[16] This points to the potential for the growth of markets for technology, and suggests that the sluggishness of this market can be partly attributed to the fact that it is unstructured and poorly organized. Consistent with this hypothesis, 44 percent of the respondents (including 39 percent of the companies) found the possibility of licensing out their unused patents very or quite attractive.

As far as licensing behavior is concerned, the survey showed that while only 6 percent of the universities license technology from others, 77 percent of the companies do so. At the same time, 90 percent of the universities and 62 percent of the companies responding to the survey had licensed technologies to others. Licensing appears to be more frequent in Japan (82% of the respondents had licensed from others and 67 percent had licensed to others) and North America (80% and 72%, respectively) than in Europe (71% and 53%). When compared to internal R&D, however, licensing is a fairly modest activity in terms of budgets involved. The survey estimated that expenditures for licensing technology from others amount to 12 percent, 5 percent, and 10 percent of the total R&D budgets of the North American, European, and Japanese respondents, respectively. Licensing to others in the three regions accounted for 4 percent, 1 percent, and 4 percent, respectively.

2.4.2   Inter-Industry Technology Flows

Insofar as these percentages of licensing expenditures are representative, they provide a rough estimate of the order of magnitude of the size of the markets for technology in the three regions. The Organization for Economic Development and Cooperation (OECD 1998) estimates indicate that in 1996 Gross Domestic Expenditures on R&D (GERD) amounted to $207 billion in North America, $132 billion in the European Union, and $83 billion in Japan. Using the shares of expenditures for licensing-in, these numbers suggest that the size of the market for technology in North America is approximately $25 billion; while in Europe and Japan it is approximately $6.6 and $8.3 billion, respectively. This would imply a world market for technology of over $40 billion. To put these figures in perspective, $25 billion is about the size of the 1996 GERD of France, and it is higher than the size of the 1996 GERD of the United Kingdom. In comparison, $6.6 and $8.3 billion are respectively slightly smaller and slightly higher than the 1996 GERD of the Netherlands. The licensing market thus appears to be especially underdeveloped in Europe. As noted in Chapter 1, the European Union estimated that $20 billion are spent in Europe every year to develop new products or ideas that have already been developed elsewhere. If so, the European market for technology has a potential for increasing from its present size of between $6 and $7 billion to perhaps four times that.

These are obviously very rough estimates of the size of technology markets. Nonetheless, they are comparable to two other independent estimates of the volume of technology transactions. Using data from the Internal Revenue Service (IRS) and the Bureau of Economic Analysis (BEA), a recent paper by Degnan (1998) estimates that U.S. firms, individuals, and government and nonprofit organizations received about $73 billion as licensing and royalty payments from unaffiliated entities in 1996, with corporations accounting for over $66 billion. Individual inventors received nearly $6 billion in such income. Further, slightly over $8 billion came from foreign firms. One should note, however, that the figure of $73 billion includes payments for technology, software licensing, trademark and service mark licensing, copyrights for books, movies, and songs, and franchising fees. Thus, the true value of technology-based royalties is likely to be smaller.

We lack definitive information on the relative proportion of royalties on technology compared to royalty on trademarks or brands. However, BEA figures on the receipts of licensing and royalty income from foreign unaffiliated entities show that of the $8.3 billion in total receipts, slightly less than $4 billion is for "industrial processes and products."[17] Other major items include $2.1 billion for computer software and $1 billion for trademarks. In other words, about half of the foreign receipts from unaffiliated companies might be considered payments for the sale or licensing of technology. If one believes that similar proportions hold for domestic royalty receipts, this would put the market for technology in the United States at about $36.5 billion. Even this figure may involve some double counting. IRS figures indicate that U.S. firms collected only $57 billion in technology receipts, implying that the U.S. market for technology is slightly under $32 billion. The U.S. accounts for about 45 percent of world non-defense R&D. However, there are strong a priori reasons to believe that the U.S. share of the market for technology is larger than its share in global R&D spending. Assuming that the U.S. accounts for 60 percent of the world market for technology, that market would amount to a little over $53 billion.

The estimates based on the BTG and Degnan studies are measures of the annual flow of revenues from the stock of technology that has been traded. One could also measure the market for technology as the value of the annual flow of technology transactions. This amounts to measuring the present value of all future revenues from the technology traded in a particular year, or roughly speaking, the value of all technology deals in a year. To this end we collected data from a commercial database compiled by the Securities Data Company (SDC 1998). The SDC database covers about 52,000 joint ventures, alliances, licenses, R&D funding, R&D collaborations, and other similar deals worldwide. The SDC sources are the Security Exchange Commission filings in the United States, their international counterparts, trade publications, newswires, and other news sources. The database reports the name of the companies involved, their ultimate parent companies, the main SIC code of the partner companies and their parents, the SIC code of the alliance, the date when the deal was announced, and a description of the deal.

We collected information on all transactions involving technology transfer. These transactions involved licensing and joint R&D. We read through the description of every transaction to ensure that each deal related to a technology transaction, be it the licensing of new products, process technologies, new designs, or collaboration in the development of the technology. A number of the technology licensing agreements also involved other types of relationships, such as a marketing agreement or joint production. We included those agreements in our sample of technology transactions, as they did involve some technology trade, though associated with other types of relationships as well. Finally, we aggregated all deals to the ultimate parent company.

Table 2.2 reports some of the leading dealmakers and the type of deal in a number of technology-intensive industries, based on information from the SDC database. As the table shows, many of the leading information technology and life sciences firms are also among the leading dealmakers. The table also shows that the larger firms are active both as buyers and sellers of technology, and also participate actively in R&D collaborations. In addition to large established players, the table lists some smaller firms that are active licensors of technology, such as Qualcomm in telecommunication equipment. One can also see the large number of licensing and R&D deals in business services (mostly software), electronics (mostly computers and semiconductors), and chemicals (mostly pharmaceuticals). The table suggests that technology transactions tend to be most prevalent in sectors where technological change is advancing most rapidly.

For some of these deals, the SDC database reported the estimated value of the transaction. The value typically is comprised of licensing and royalty payments, equity purchase in the technology provider, and R&D funding to the technology provider. We computed the average value of these deals by two-digit SIC sectors using the available information. To avoid overestimation of the transaction in technology, we computed these averages using only available information about the value of the deal when the latter was involved only licensing or R&D collaboration and licensing, with no other forms of collaboration in marketing or manufacturing. We computed the averages only for the two-digit sectors for which four or more observations were available for licensing and royalty payments, equity purchase in the firm providing the technology, and R&D funding.[18] To obtain more conservative estimates, we averaged licensing and royalty payments, and equity purchase and R&D funding. For the remaining sectors, we conservatively estimated the average value of each deal at $5 million. To estimate the total value of the technology transactions by sector, we multiplied the sector average by the number of technology deals in each sector.

Tables 2.3a and 2.3b show the total number and value of such transactions by industry sector between 1985 and 1997. The value of a transac-

Table 2.2
Leading Deal Makers in the Market for Technology and Type of Deals, by Industry, 1985–1997

Sector and SIC	Firm	Total Deals	Licenses Given	Licenses Taken	Cross Licenses	R&D Agreements	Cross-Border Deals
Eng. and Mgmt. Service							
SIC 87	AT&T	13	0	0	1	13	5
	Baxter International	9	1	4	3	7	3
	Bristol-Myers Squibb	10	0	4	1	10	5
	IBM	17	1	0	3	15	10
	Monsanto	10	2	4	1	9	6
	Motorola	8	0	1	1	7	6
	Roche	21	2	5	11	21	17
	Sandoz	10	0	1	1	10	10
Business Services							
SIC 73	AT&T	97	11	22	21	79	16
	Digital Equipment	83	8	20	21	64	15
	Fujitsu	62	6	11	34	54	58
	Hewlett-Packard	132	13	24	28	104	27
	IBM	277	34	48	69	222	78
	Microsoft	204	44	45	55	140	39
	Apple Computer	86	25	18	15	58	20
	Novell	100	17	17	22	73	13
	Oracle	88	10	9	35	73	18
	Sun Microsystems	105	24	16	16	73	17

Communications						
SIC 48						
AT&T	18	4	3	5	13	5
Bell South	8	1	0	1	8	2
Cable & Wireless	8	2	0	1	7	6
IBM	9	0	2	5	6	2
Japan	7	0	0	4	7	6
Kokusai Denshin Denwa	7	2	0	2	7	7
Motorola	14	3	1	2	8	6
Pacific Telesis Group	7	3	0	1	7	5
Qualcomm	17	15	0	1	3	8
Sprint	9	0	1	3	8	6
Instruments						
SIC 38						
Baxter International	9	3	4	1	4	1
Daimler-Benz	10	2	0	4	9	10
Eastern Kodak	13	1	3	1	10	5
General Motors	11	4	2	3	11	6
Hewlett-Packard	11	2	1	5	9	4
Honeywell	14	4	0	4	7	8
Johnson & Johnson	10	0	7	2	10	4
Eli Lilly	10	3	4	3	6	1
Philips Electronics	13	2	2	1	7	10
Siemens	14	1	3	4	9	11

Table 2.2 (continued)

Sector and SIC	Firm	Total Deals	Licenses Given	Licenses Taken	Cross Licenses	R&D Agreements	Cross-Border Deals
Transport							
SIC 37	Boeing	15	1	1	3	14	5
	Daimler-Benz	27	0	0	10	27	22
	Fiat	14	1	0	2	13	13
	Ford Motor	26	1	1	7	26	14
	France	20	0	0	7	20	18
	General Electric	13	0	0	3	13	10
	General Motors	25	2	1	3	25	9
	Siemens	14	1	0	1	14	12
	United Technologies	22	3	1	6	19	12
Electronic equipment							
SIC 36	AT&T	83	11	11	36	63	32
	Intel	70	19	8	20	52	21
	IBM	104	18	9	38	87	37
	Motorola	113	23	15	33	84	51
	NEC	66	0	21	27	51	60
	Philips Electronics	72	7	8	35	56	72
	Samsung	62	4	39	15	22	62
	Siemens	56	7	7	26	46	57
	Texas Instruments	88	18	14	39	42	49
	Toshiba	75	5	23	30	56	69

Industrial machinery	AT&T	24	5	5	7	17	9
SIC 35	Digital Equipment	26	6	0	6	22	4
	Fujitsu	32	5	8	10	19	27
	Hewlett-Packard	37	7	4	15	28	14
	Hitachi	27	2	8	9	19	22
	IBM	75	5	10	22	63	32
	Matsushita Electric Industrial	21	0	12	2	10	19
	NEC	29	2	9	8	23	28
	Apple Computer	27	7	6	6	17	16
	Toshiba	28	0	8	12	18	28
Chemicals	American Home Products	56	21	19	7	31	20
SIC 28	Dow Chemical	67	13	20	11	40	32
	Hoechst	72	7	34	14	42	69
	Johnson & Johnson	42	3	22	8	25	11
	Eli Lilly	58	5	25	12	38	14
	Merck	47	7	16	10	33	19
	Monsanto	55	14	14	16	38	35
	Rhone-Poulenc	48	10	15	11	31	43
	Roche Holding	94	29	32	21	53	92
	SmithKline Beecham	65	10	38	9	41	60

Source: SDC 1998.

Table 2.3
The Size and Sectoral Composition of the Market for Technology
(a) The Market for Technology: Number of Technology Transactions, 1985–1997, by Sector

YEAR	1985–1989	1990	1991	1992	1993	1994	1995	1996	1997	Total Number
SIC 28	439	310	461	395	486	596	351	208	222	3496
SIC 35	129	115	210	188	195	192	164	63	69	1360
SIC 36	234	190	310	316	366	415	326	135	151	2479
SIC 73	143	207	360	334	363	610	770	405	424	3689
SIC 87	11	9	45	253	156	73	34	22	17	707
All Others	174	209	468	523	560	540	545	289	293	3858
TOTAL	1130	1040	1854	2009	2126	2426	2190	1122	1176	15073

(b) The Market for Technology: Value of Technology Transactions, 1985–1997, by Sector (millions of 1995 dollars, all countries)

YEAR	1985–1989	1990	1991	1992	1993	1994	1995	1996	1997	Total Value
SIC 28	5809	4102	6101	5227	6431	7387	4645	2753	2938	45893
SIC 35	6280	5599	10224	9153	9493	9347	7984	3067	3359	64506
SIC 36	10971	8908	14534	14816	17160	19457	15234	6329	7080	114539
SIC 73	1740	2518	4380	4063	4416	7421	9368	4927	5158	43991
SIC 87	171	140	701	3939	2429	1137	529	343	265	9654
SIC All	2781	2901	5471	6373	6549	6354	6658	3342	3156	43585
Others										
TOTAL	27753	24169	41410	43571	46479	51634	44469	20761	21956	322172

Source: Our computations based on SDC data files. Values are estimated by weighting the number of transactions in technologies reported by SDC 1998 by the average value of the technology transactions for the sector computed from available information in the SDC database. See the text for details.

Note: SIC28 = Chemicals; SIC35 = Industrial Machinery & Equipment; SIC36 = Electronic & Other Electric Equipment; SIC38 = Instruments & Related Products, SIC49 = Electric, Gas, and Sanitary Services; SIC50 = Wholesale Trade – Durable Goods; SIC73 = Business Services; SIC 87 = Engineering and Management Services.

tion is calculated here as the sum of licensing and royalty payments and equity investments and R&D funding provided in return for licensing rights. These tables show that there have been over 15,000 transactions in technology with a total value of over $320 billion, implying an average of nearly 1,150 transactions worth $25 billion per year. Since it is likely that we are undercounting transactions both early in the sample period (when SDC data collection was likely to be not as systematic) and late in the sample period, this figure is probably a lower bound. As well, the SDC data may have gaps in the coverage of deals not involving U.S. firms. It is also possible that the figure is lower than the other two estimates because the average value is taken over more than a decade. The available evidence suggests that technology transactions were more frequent in the mid– to late–1990s than the early 1980s. Indeed, if we confine ourselves to the sample of transactions from the 1990s, the average value increases to about $36 billion. Although all estimates based on all three sources—BTG, Degnan (1998), and SDC—are subject to numerous caveats and qualifications, it is remarkable that they are fairly close to each other. Thus, though our measures are quite crude, they suggest that volume of transactions for technology are of the order of $35–$50 billion per year.

Table 2.3 confirms that markets for technology are most developed in Electronics and Electronic Components, Business Services, and Chemicals.[19] Although our Electronics sector did not include computers (which we classified as Industrial Machinery), it did include all sorts of electronic components, as well as semiconductors and other electronic devices. As we shall see in the next chapter, qualitative accounts of the dynamics of the semiconductor business also suggest that these are very active fields in terms of technology transfers through various arrangements among independent companies. Business Services include software, which is likely to account for a large share of the value of technology deals covered by this sector. Software is another industry in which such deals have developed significantly in recent years. Finally, the chemical industry is one in which transactions in technology have been common for many years, from the licensing of chemical process technologies, to the licensing of chemical compounds and especially pharmaceuticals, to the large number of technology transactions that characterize the modern biotechnology industry.

Table 2.3b also shows that the value of technology transactions has increased significantly during the early 1990s. In part, this may reflect the increase in the number of sources employed by SDC to collect the information. However, the values for some sectors drop in 1992 or 1993, which roughly corresponds to the recession of the early 1990s. Moreover, there are differences in the growth of markets for technology in the different sectors. For instance, compared to the other sectors, a significant growth occurred in our three top sectors, and in Engineering Services in 1994. This growth parallels the significant development of these technologies just before the mid–1990s. Thus, while it is likely that the increase is overestimated because of the addition of new sources (or better technologies to acquire the information, including computerized sources), a real expansion of markets for technology has also occurred.[20]

Table 2.4 focuses on inter-industry technology flows. To construct this table, we analyzed all the available technology transactions in the SDC database that took place between 1988 and March 1998. Because our focus is now on the cross-section among sectors, this broader sample reduced the problem of the underestimation of the technology transactions in earlier or later years. We assigned a technology deal to a granting sector by attributing it to the two-digit SIC sector of the company that granted the technology (not the ultimate parent). Similarly, we assigned it to a receiving sector according to the two-digit SIC of the company receiving the technology.[21] As with table 2.3b, we computed the values by weighting the number of transactions in each sector pair by the average value of the technology transactions in the receiving sector.[22] Table 2.4 also reports two Herfindahl indices for each sector. The Herfindahl is a measure of the industry diversification of technology supplies to that sector. Along the columns, we have the analogous measure of the spread of industries from which the given sector obtains technologies.

Note that Business Services (SIC 73) and Electronics (SIC 36) show a low Herfindahl for technology supply, and a fairly high one for technology demand. These sectors receive mostly their own technologies, while they supply technologies to a number of sectors.[23] The latter result is suggestive of the "general-purpose" nature of the software and electronics technologies. In contrast, the chemical sector shows the highest concentration of technology supply, with companies offering about 40 percent of their technologies to other companies within the chemical sector. Clearly, within the chemical sector there are many segments that would probably show different degrees of "generality," but by and large, it appears to be the one in which much of the technology produced is used within the sector itself.

Table 2.4
Values of Inter-Industry Technology Licenses, 1988–1997 (millions of U.S. dollars)

	SIC	Receiving Sector												Row Total	Herf Grant.
		28	73	36	35	87	38	82	50	37	48	80	REST		
Granting Sector	28	22344	259	388	410	3710	1790	237	388	194	22	474	4615	34832	0.444
	73	949	16214	6551	7825	563	919	119	1690	534	1571	296	5069	42299	0.224
	36	1108	4985	30907	9638	609	2437	166	2105	1329	1495	55	5483	60318	0.308
	35	343	2475	3941	6644	152	704	19	571	381	247	0	1637	17115	0.238
	87	9785	419	1090	615	4333	1062	280	224	224	84	335	2628	21080	0.280
	38	2121	513	1352	1025	350	4334	70	373	140	70	93	1305	11745	0.206
	82	2083	128	112	48	833	288	144	48	0	0	80	305	4071	0.318
	50	110	150	120	170	20	160	10	270	20	30	10	150	1220	0.135
	37	63	27	135	108	27	54	9	36	414	0	0	171	1044	0.220
	48	95	1040	1607	662	284	189	0	378	95	3780	0	1323	9450	0.229
	80	2802	65	0	65	652	587	65	0	0	130	587	391	5344	0.320
	Rest	895	220	280	370	240	180	5	125	90	65	30	1945	4445	0.251
	Col. Tot.	42697	26495	46482	27580	11773	12705	1124	6207	3420	7495	1962	25022	212962	
	Herf Rec.	0.337	0.421	0.472	0.264	0.250	0.192	0.164	0.212	0.213	0.340	0.205	0.150		

Notes: Values are estimated as indicated in table 2.3. See the text for details. Herfindahl indices for "spread" of granting and receiving sectors are also reported (Herf Grant).

SIC codes: 28 = Chemicals and allied products; 73 = Business services; 36 = Electronic & other electronic components, except computer equipment; 35 = Industrial & commercial machinery and computer equipment; 87 = Engineering, Accounting, Research, Management & Related Services; 38 = Measuring, Analyzing, and Controlling Instruments; Photographic, Medical and Optic Goods; Watches and Clocks; 82 = Educational Services; 50 = Wholesale Trade – Durable Goods; 37 = Transportation Equipment; 48 = Communications; 80 = Health Services.

2.5   Synthesis of the Available Evidence

Markets for technology are not new. The work by Lamoreaux and Sokoloff shows that there was an active market for patents, and possibly an active market for technology as well, before the early twentieth-century institutionalization of R&D large corporations.

The evidence provided by Zucker, Darby, and Armstrong (1998) in the California biotechnology industry is intriguing as it suggests that a good deal of what are typically seen as unintended technological spillovers stem from intentional linkages and economic relationships. The BTG study indicates that there is a great potential for the growth of markets for technology. Many companies simply ignore a large number of patented technologies that they have developed internally. Moreover, they often fail to license their inventions not for strategic reasons, but simply because they do not take this possibility into consideration. In short, markets for technology require organization and the development of proper supporting institutions.

Other evidence, both aggregate evidence based on IRS records and information on individual technology transactions, is consistent with an estimate derived from the BTG report of the size of the market for technology. These estimates indicate a worldwide market for technologies in the range of $35–$50 billion per year. Though each type of estimate is subject to a variety of caveats, the consistency between these three types of estimates is reassuring.

Markets for technology also appear to have grown in the 1990s. This is especially true for some leading high-tech industries: software, electronics, and certain branches of the chemical sector. Moreover, if one examines how technology flows across sectors, one notes the role of some key general-purpose technology industries, in particular software and electronics, which supply a wide spectrum of other industries. There also seems to be a fairly generalized pattern of inter-industry technology flows. While the largest share of technology transactions is within each two-digit SIC industry, practically all two-digit SIC industries supply and receive technologies to and from many other sectors.

These conclusions are not meant to suggest that markets for technology are spreading and that we shall soon observe that most technologies will be traded in the market. In-house technology development is still very important, and the size of in-house technological activities is most likely larger than that of external technology flows. In the following chapters, we see that there are many constraints to the rise of markets for technology. Some of these can be relaxed, while others are likely to prove more formidable. What is important for our purposes, however, is to note that markets for technology are not inconsequential. Even more important, they seem to grow or at least possess a significant potential for expanding if certain conditions—in particular, an effective organization of such markets—are created.

3 The Division of Innovative Labor in High-Tech Industries

3.1 Introduction

Quantitative measurements of the volume of technology-related transactions, described in the previous chapter, indicate that, taken together, markets for technology are of substantial size. These measures are subject to a variety of caveats and qualifications. Given the availability of data, this is the best one can do at this stage—there are as yet no measures without caveats attached. However, it is possible to obtain further insight by qualitative analysis.

This chapter explores the market for technology in four high-tech industries: chemical processing, software, biotechnology, and semiconductors. The knowledge bases in these industries have evolved in ways conducive to trade in technology, and markets for technology have developed at a significant rate in these industries in recent years. In chemical processing, specialized suppliers and a market for process technology have existed at least since the end of World War II. The fifty-year history of the division of labor in this sector provides a good basis for studying the major features of markets for technology and their evolution over time. In the other three industries, markets for technology have grown primarily during the past two decades, with a possible acceleration in the 1990s.

The various sections of this chapter are not meant to provide an extensive and detailed account of the evolution of these industries.[1] Several other studies have recounted these stories in far greater depth than we do here, and we refer to them at the appropriate points in the discussion. Our aim is to bring out some key aspects of the nature and functioning of markets for technology. In particular, we focus on the division of innovative labor and the factors that condition it.

3.2   Specialized Engineering Firms and the Market for Technology in the Chemical Processing Industry

3.2.1   Chemical Engineering: A Paradigm for Chemical Processing Technologies

We start with the chemical processing industry, where a market for chemical process technology began to emerge in the early 1950s. The factors that lead to the growth of this market are described in Arora (1997). They include the convergence of oil refining and chemical processing. Oil companies brought with them more open attitudes toward licensing. In addition, World War II and a more active U.S. antitrust policy in the 1940s tended to shake up and dismantle cozy oligopolies. We shall focus on the role played by the division of innovative labor between chemical producers and engineering companies specializing in the design and engineering of the chemical process. Not only did this division of labor give rise to specialized suppliers of chemical process technologies, it also encouraged some established chemical firms to be more open to licensing their technology.

This division of labor is rooted in the development of chemical engineering as a discipline back in the 1920s. Chemical engineering addressed both the science and economics of the chemical process. The objective of chemical engineers was to design and optimize plants to reduce manufacturing cost, and improve product quality.[2] The concept of "unit operations" played a key role in the development of chemical engineering in the twentieth century. The idea was that all diverse chemical processes could be conceived of as a combination of a small number of well-defined operations, such as distillation, evaporation, drying, filtration, absorption, and extraction. Unit operations was thus a first attempt at producing a unified framework for thinking about the design of diverse and differentiated processes in oil refining and chemical production (Rosenberg 1998).

By separating the task of process design from the details of the particular product being produced, chemical engineering enabled process designers to think about chemical processes in general rather than about the specific chemical process for a particular chemical such as ethylene or ammonia. Thus, process engineers could work without having to become experts in the chemical for which they were designing the production process. By providing a unified framework, chemical engineering allowed for the experience gained in one chemical process to be applied to others, further enhancing the benefits of specialization. As a result, chemical engineering made possible the rise of specialized firms that focused on engineering and process design services for chemical plants—the specialized engineering firms (SEFs).

With a few notable exceptions, most SEFs did not develop radically new processes. The large oil and chemical companies typically produced most major process innovations (Mansfield et al. 1977). However, the SEFs did undertake incremental innovations, effectively moving new processes down the learning curve. Equally important was that, as independent vendors of process technology, SEFs facilitated entry in the postwar decades. Initially, the entrants were firms from the developed countries themselves. More recently, SEFs have helped firms from developing countries enter the market as well (see also chapter 8). By acting as independent licensors, SEFs also stimulated chemical firms themselves to license their technology. In essence, SEFs helped create a market for technology, making process technology into a "commodity" that could be bought and sold (Arora and Gambardella 1998).

The development of an independent engineering design sector is an example par excellence of the economies of specialization at the level of the industry. A large market for basic petrochemicals, such as the one that was rapidly growing in the 1950s, combined with the relative independence of process design from products, implied that SEFs could design many more plants for a variety of closely related processes than any single chemical company could. The accumulated knowledge of SEFs formed the basis of their comparative advantage in process design. In turn, the cost reduction from better and cheaper process lowered prices, and hence stimulated the substitution of chemical products for natural fibers, resins, and metals, which resulted in further market growth.

3.2.2 Origins and Comparative Advantages of SEFs

The first SEFs were formed early in the twentieth century. Typically their clients were large oil companies that concentrated their energies upon "searching for crude oil and establishing retail market facilities" (Landau and Brown 1965, 7). In the years before World War II, the chemical companies did not rely much upon SEFs for the design and engineering of entire production processes, although SEFs were prominent in improvements in ammonia and sulfuric acid plants (Arora and Rosenberg 1998). SEFs were mostly employed as suppliers of specialized equipment and the like. In part, this was due to the long-standing traditions of secrecy that characterized chemical companies. Further, most chemical operations tended to be batch, with relatively low volumes, emphasizing "art" and embodying a great deal of company-specific know-how. Unlike chemical processes, oil refining involved relatively little product innovation (with some important exceptions such as the development of high-octane diesel during World War II), so the focus tended to be on process innovation.

The situation changed markedly after World War II. The growing importance of petrochemicals and the increase in the scale of production raised the payoff to improvements in plant design in the chemical industry. In addition, the growth in the size and complexity of plants, as well as the concomitant development of chemical engineering laid the foundations for division of labor and vertical specialization in the chemical processing sector. By the 1960s, SEFs had come to occupy an important place in the industry. In a pioneering study, Freeman noted that for the period 1960–1966, "nearly three quarters of the major new plants were 'engineered', procured and constructed by specialist plant contractors" (Freeman 1968, 30). Moreover, Freeman found that SEFs were an important source of process technologies. Between 1960 and 1966, they accounted as a group for about 30 percent of all licenses of chemical processes.

Freeman's findings are confirmed by more recent data. Table 3.1 uses information from a comprehensive database of investments in the chemical sector, Chemintell (1991).[3] It shows that for the period between 1980 and 1990, SEFs engineered three-fourths of the total number of plants in the world. Although the share of SEFs varies across sectors, in almost all sectors the share is above 50 percent. The extent of division of labor and vertical specialization is apparent in that, in most sectors, the percentage of plants engineered in-house is below 10 percent.

As table 3.1 shows, the division of labor in licensing is less marked than in engineering. Both the share of in-house technologies and that of technologies coming from sources other than SEFs are higher than the corresponding shares for engineering. The lower shares of SEFs in technology licensing reflect the difficulties of financing research into radically new processes, as well as the specialized, product-specific knowledge that such research may need. Nonetheless, SEFs still account for about 35 percent of the licenses in which the source of technology was reported. At the same time, the active licensing by both SEFs and established chemical companies suggests that in this industry the market for technology involves both a vertical division of labor between SEFs

Table 3.1
The Market for Engineering Services and Licenses in Chemicals, 1980–1990, by Sector

Sectors	Percentage of Plants Engineered			Percentage of Licenses		
	In-house	by SEF	by other firms (*)	Own technology	by SEF	by other firms (*)
Air Separation	32.4	34.1	33.5	27.2	33.7	39.0
Fertilizers	4.8	79.6	15.6	4.8	61.5	33.7
Food Processing	5.0	74.8	20.3	20.4	38.8	40.8
Gas Handling	5.0	78.0	17.1	4.9	62.3	32.8
Inorganic Chemicals	14.1	66.9	18.9	24.4	29.2	46.4
Industrial Gases	21.9	60.3	17.8	12.9	36.1	51.1
Minerals & Metals	7.8	71.3	20.9	23.9	24.4	51.7
Miscellaneous	6.6	78.9	14.4	16.8	34.6	48.5
Organic Chemicals	24.3	53.8	21.9	44.2	19.4	36.4
Oil Refining	6.4	83.7	10.0	9.3	48.6	42.1
Petrochemicals	13.3	75.9	10.8	18.5	32.4	49.1
Pharmaceuticals	19.4	63.0	17.6	54.8	3.2	41.9
Plastics & Rubber	23.8	63.1	13.2	41.2	6.1	52.8
Pulp & Paper	4.0	79.0	17.0	3.8	46.2	50.0
Misc. Specialties	31.0	52.1	16.9	61.5	2.9	35.6
Textile & Fibers	7.4	72.2	20.3	17.9	52.9	29.2
Total	12.7%	71.6%	15.6%	21.5%	34.6%	43.9%

Source: Chemintell 1991.
*Typically chemical companies or other downstream manufacturers.

and chemical manufacturers, and horizontal technology trades among the chemical companies themselves.

The SEFs began as an American phenomenon. In his study, Freeman (1968) estimated that between 1960 and 1966 the U.S. firms accounted for more than 50 percent of the total value of engineering contracts worldwide. Table 3.2 shows that during 1980–1990, U.S. SEFs accounted for 26% of the total number of engineering services in the world market, with the German, British, Italian, French, and Japanese companies being important competitors.[4] Moreover, if one compares the shares of U.S. SEFs outside of the three main regions with the total world shares in table 3.2, the U.S. SEFs have comparatively larger shares in the latter case. This suggests that they are relatively more effective as competitors in first world countries than in the third world. Table 3.2 also shows that while the U.S. SEFs have a sizable share of the market in Europe, the

Table 3.2
Market Shares of SEFs: Engineering services, 1980–1990 (shares of total number of plants by region)

	United States	Western Europe	Japan	Rest of the World	Share of Total World Market
United States	58.8	19.8	3.7	18.9	26.0
West Germany	1.9	18.5	4.6	12.7	11.7
United Kingdom	6.9	12.2	2.0	7.3	8.1
Italy	0.3	8.2	0.0	5.8	5.1
France	0.2	2.3	0.3	4.6	3.2
Japan	0.2	0.2	34.0	5.1	4.0

Source: Chemintell 1991.

Table 3.3
Market Shares of SEFs: Licenses, 1980–1990 (shares of total number of plants by region)

	Regions				
Nationality of SEFS	United States	Western Europe	Japan	Rest of the World	Share of Total World Market
United States	18.0	10.3	6.5	16.9	15.1
West Germany	3.1	11.3	1.0	10.2	8.8
United Kingdom	1.2	3.0	2.7	2.4	2.4
Italy	0.1	1.4	0.0	2.2	1.6
France	0.1	0.6	0.0	0.9	0.7
Japan	0.1	0.1	1.5	1.1	0.7

Source: Chemintell 1991.

European firms have only a small market share in the United States. This is a legacy of the period following World War II, when American companies, including many SEFs, moved to Europe with new technologies and process know-how. Many American SEFs were able to establish local subsidiaries, and some of these subsidiaries, such as Foster-Wheeler, even succeeded in becoming full-fledged "national" companies.

Japanese SEFs account for the bulk of the engineering services in Japan, where even the U.S. SEFs have only a modest presence. As discussed in Hikino et al. (1998), while Japan allowed an inflow of Western (especially American) technologies in the period following World War II, it protected its markets for products and other services. Thus, although American firms license technology to Japanese firms in Japan, their entry in the market for engineering services was restricted. As a result, U.S. SEFs have only a modest presence in Japan compared with Europe.

Table 3.3 reports the shares of SEFs from leading countries in licensing. The U.S. share is about 15 percent. Comparing table 3.3 with table 3.2, U.S. SEFs have a larger share of the market in licensing than engineering, when contrasted with its competitors, (Germany is the only exception). The comparative advantage of U.S. SEFs in licensing is even more apparent if one compares their shares in Europe and Japan with the corresponding shares of their competitors. In Europe, for instance, the share of U.S. SEFs in engineering is only about 1.6 times that of British SEFs, while it is 3.4 times that of British SEFs in licensing.

3.2.3 SEFs and Technology Diffusion

As table 3.1 above shows, SEFs are the dominant source of the general design services for a new plant and an important source of technology as well. In addition, many SEFs also specialize in construction services, and can provide "turnkey" plants to their clients. In other words, chemical process technology has diffused through SEFs, as licenses or embodied in engineering services (or both)—first to Europe, then worldwide to Asia, Eastern Europe, Latin America, and the Middle East.

The implications for industrial structure have been profound. Spitz (1988, 313) notes that, in the 1950s and in the 1960s, for most major products there were between five and fifteen main producers. In contrast, in the pre–World War II era it was unusual to have more than three manufacturers of any major product (see also Backman 1964, 47–50). The growth in the number of producers came about even though the minimum efficient scale of plants was increasing, albeit in a growing market. The fraction of entry that can be attributed to the SEFs cannot be estimated precisely, and the changed licensing policies of chemical firms, partly motivated by antitrust concerns, also lowered entry barriers.

Other studies provide evidence consistent with the hypothesis that SEFs were major suppliers of technology and know-how to new entrants. In a study of thirty-nine commodity chemicals in the United States in a period from the mid–1950s to the mid–1970s, Lieberman (1989) found that after controlling for demand conditions, experience accumulated by incumbents did not deter new entry. Given the importance of learning by doing, this suggests that entrants had access to other sources of know-how, most likely SEFs. This interpretation is further supported by Lieberman's finding that entry into concentrated markets, which were also marked by low rates of patenting by non-producers (both foreign firms and SEFs), usually required that the entrant develop its own technology. In contrast, less concentrated markets were associated with high rates of patenting by non-producers and high rates of licensing to entrants. In a related study (based on a subset of 24 chemicals), Lieberman (1987) found that high rates of patenting by non-producers were also associated with faster rates of decline in prices. Once again, this evidence is consistent with an interpretation where patenting by non-producers (especially SEFs) led to entry by new firms through licenses.

As SEFs became important sources of plant design, their importance as sources of process innovation also increased (Mansfield et al. 1977). SEFs have been particularly innovative in two areas: catalytic processes, and engineering design improvements.[5] SEFs have relied on licensing to appropriate rents from their innovations. Not only did the licensing activity of SEFs affect market structure by inducing entry, but it also had notable effects on how the chemical firms themselves have used their technologies. In a marked departure from their pre–World War II strategy of closely holding onto technology, after the war several chemical and oil companies began to use licensing as an important means of profiting from innovation. As Spitz (1988, 318) put it:

[S]ome brand new technologies, developed by operating (chemical) companies, were made available for license to any and all comers. A good example is the Hercules-Distillers phenol/acetone process, which was commercialized in 1953 and forever changed the way that phenol would be produced.

In addition, SEFs often acted as licensing agents for chemical firms. Chemical producers often lack licensing experience and are unwilling to provide the various engineering and design services that licensees need in addition to the technology, and subsequently use SEFs as licensing agents. In this arrangement, a chemical firm authorizes an SEF to license its technology to others. The SEF offers a complete technology package, consisting of the core technology licensed from a chemical producer, along with know-how and installation and engineering services.[6]

The available evidence suggests that technology licensing in the chemical processing industry is widespread. As shown in table 3.1, during the 1980s, only one-fifth of the technology used in new chemical investments worldwide was developed in-house by the investors. The rest was licensed in from unaffiliated sources. At the same time, as noted earlier, the share of licenses sold by non-SEFs is significant (an average of 43.9 percent of the total number of plants in which the source of technology is reported), especially if compared to the corresponding share of engineering services provided by non-SEFs (15.6 percent). Some chemical companies that have been major licensors of their patented technologies include ICI in ammonia; Union Carbide in polyethylene, polypropylene, and air separation technologies; Montecatini (including affiliates such as Himont) in polypropylene; and Mitsui, also in polypropylene. Oil companies, especially Shell, Mobil, BP, and Amoco, have been active in licensing their technologies as well. More generally, our Chemintell database indicates that practically all the leading chemical, petrochemical and oil companies of the world, whatever their nationality (United States, Britain, Germany, etc.) have issued dozens of licenses to unaffiliated parties. Arora and Fosfuri (2000) estimate that world leading chemical firms were able to recoup about 10 percent of their R&D expenditures through licensing revenues during the 1980s.

3.3   The Role of Software in the Growth of Markets for Technology

3.3.1   The Dual Nature of Software: Product or Embodied Technologies?

One issue we have to confront at the outset of our discussion is that in relation to markets for technology, the peculiar nature of software is a potential source of confusion.[7] Software shares a key characteristic of technology, namely that production is characterized by a high fixed cost of producing the first unit and a low marginal cost of reproducing it. Moreover, software is typically licensed rather than sold, resembling the manner in which technology is transferred. In some cases, however, the resemblance is only superficial and licensing reflects merely the extremely low marginal cost of reproduction compared to the fixed costs of development. In other cases, software represents technology embodied in code. It can therefore be seen as one form (and an increasingly important one) in which knowledge is held and transferred.

While software does embody knowledge or technologies in various forms, it is hard to make a distinction between software as embodied knowledge and software as a product (sold to other companies or the final users) or component (sold to other companies and embedded in larger and more complex systems). In many cases, the low reproduction cost of software can be thought of merely as a peculiar feature of its nature as a commodity, rather than a manifestation of the fact that it is technology or knowledge transferred in a particular form. The sale of ready-to-use software designed to be incorporated in more complex products is akin to the provision of manufactured components by a given supplier to downstream companies that embody them in more systemic goods. Likewise, the sale of software products to final users (video games) often appears to be quite similar to the sale of goods on the market. In sum, the distinction is blurred between software as a technology (or embodied knowledge) and software as an industrial component or good.

3.3.2 Software as a Knowledge Tool

There are two issues regarding the present dynamics of the software industry that we want to discuss here because of their relevance for markets for technology. The first is the growing use of software as a tool for embodying knowledge and expertise in several areas and sectors—for example, expert systems, design tools embodying design knowledge, and the like. The second one is the disintegration of the production of software modules and components, which is giving rise to a substantial pool of available self-contained modules performing well-defined functions to be "plugged" into more complex systems.

The two issues are related. In particular, the disintegration of software production into separate compatible modules represents the incorporation of independent "pieces" of knowledge into such modules. The development of readily available software components is a response to rising software costs and the growing complexity of software systems. Software reuse is akin to the reuse of knowledge developed earlier, avoiding the cost of having to rediscover it for oneself. But the need to reuse knowledge also encourages the search for effective ways to disentangle it from the more complex context in which it was initially embedded and developed.

For example, the semiconductor industry is giving rise to a significant development of software tools that embody knowledge and expertise about chip design. As we see in section 3.5, the industry is witnessing a trend toward increasing complexity of chips. This, in turn, has led to the growth of firms that develop and supply electronic design automation (EDA) software tools. These software tools are critical for managing the design of the complex systems embedded in chips. Typically, EDA tools are based on systems of equations that represent the various functions and subfunctions to be performed by the chips, and the way they connect to each other. By operating and simulating the system through these equations, designers can build the functions, link them, and test the working of the devices or parts thereof. Clearly, the development of such tools requires a great deal of knowledge about the way the chips function, which is "codified" into such systems of equations.

Some users develop their own EDA software.[8] However, for most applications, they rely on software tools supplied by firms such as Cadence Design Systems, Mentor Graphics, and Synopsis (Linden and Somaya 2000). The development of EDA tools is facilitating the rise of independent providers of software modules for specific functions common to a large variety of integrated circuits for semiconductors. Linden and Somaya (2000) note that EDA companies provide libraries of pretested software design elements, called "cells," along with their tools. Moreover, they note that the most recent strategy of companies like Mentor or Synopsis is to buy and resell modules produced by specialized parties, while shifting their focus to support services for their customers' engineers. Similarly, Cadence is specializing in the integration of third party and customer modules within complete chip designs. The knowledge content of the activities performed by these companies is apparent from the fact that EDA firms typically help design engineers to develop design methodologies and practices. Mentor Graphics and Synopsis have even written a comprehensive manual on design reuse, widely employed by the industry, which is a quintessential example of the codification of knowledge into standard practice (Linden and Somaya, 2000). Software tools that embody expert knowledge have diffused far beyond the semiconductor industry.[9] As we see in the next section, biotechnology is another sector that, like semiconductors, is emerging as a growing market for software systems, databases, and related knowledge tools.

Interestingly enough, software tools are also being developed to manage intellectual property, and specifically, to help firms manage their patents and patenting activity.[10] For example, a start-up firm called SmartPatents has developed a knowledge information system that enables users to access more than 2.2 million U.S. patents filed since 1971. SmartPatents' customers today include Hewlett-Packard, Lucent Technologies, and Dow Chemicals.

Another start-up, Invention Machine, has developed software that uses a database of more than five million patents to search for solutions to technical and scientific problems faced by engineers and scientists. For instance, an engineer looking for a way to cool an engine can select the goal "change temperature" from a pull-down menu. The program will present a list of all the ways temperature can be changed, along with formulae, limitations, necessary materials, references, real-world examples, and animated diagrams. While the software technology of this tool is a fairly traditional one—creation of a database and software which queries it effectively—the tool's value lies in its ability to help avoid costly duplication of research. In this respect, Invention Machine's software is an interesting way of leveraging existing knowledge from patents, and it shows how software can greatly enhance the power of codification.

These examples also illustrate Lamoreaux and Sokoloff's point that the growth of technology trade in the United States in the nineteenth century was accompanied and sustained by the growth of patent attorneys, patent agents, and other services that helped bring buyers and sellers together. Patent databases and smart tools for searching these databases and using the knowledge contained in them are another means for reducing search costs in the market for technology.

3.3.3 The Market for Compatible Components

The production of software itself is undergoing a change, with an increase in the use of predeveloped modules and components for functions that are common to a large variety of software programs (Mowery 1996). Production and exchange of specific software modules, largely developed by specialized producers, has been a long-standing feature of this industry, although thus far, not very significant in quantitative terms. In the 1990s, however, this process appears to have accelerated, especially because of the development of software architectures that provide opportunities for plugging in standard components that can be developed independently, provided that they are compatible with the architecture. This, in turn, has given rise to the production of independent modules by a wide array of specialist producers, often individual programmers, who can focus on these parts without having to invest in the more complex systems.

Reusable software requires standards and general architectures. One well-known example is a component management technology standard, called CORBA, controlled by a U.S.-based nonprofit consortium, Component Management Group (CMG), which lists 20,000 members (individuals and companies) in the United States, Canada, Italy, Japan, and India. CORBA is an architecture that provides standard interfaces for building components that are interoperable with any other CORBA compliant component. CORBA is said to allow applications to communicate with one another, regardless of where they are located, in which software language they have been written, or on what operating system they reside. The consortium also develops menus of orders and rules which, along with the technical features of the architecture, can give rise to a diffused worldwide repository of components, and will encourage the development of object-oriented based component methodologies. The development of technologies like CORBA is necessary, though not sufficient, for integrating components or modules developed by a number of individual developers or firms acting independently of each other, and possibly, without being aware of each other. In some cases, these components may be produced using a market or market-like mechanism. Evidence of this trend is provided by the creation and organization of markets for components which are encouraging the growth of "component by design" activities. For example, Flashline Inc., an Ohio-based company, has set up a worldwide Web-based market for software components, whereby companies or individuals can post their components and buyers can search for special modules performing the functions that they may need. (See <www.flashline.com>.) The obvious implication of the rise of these "brokerage" companies is that they reduce the transaction costs of the market for technology, thereby reinforcing the opportunities for specialization and division of labor.

The impact of standard architecture on innovation has been emphasized by Langlois (1992) and Langlois and Robertson (1992), who have pointed out how "open" architecture, into which individual producers can easily plug their own components, provides opportunities for widespread experimentation. Increased experimentation enhances the rate of innovation at the level of the industry. Langlois and Robertson note how the choice of an open slot architecture in the first Apple PC was critical for the rise of specialist suppliers, who provided many innovative individual PC components. Well-defined architecture in software, and the diffusion of common rules, standards, and practices, can similarly enhance innovation in software.

3.3.4   Some Evidence of Technology Trade in Software

Companies specializing in the production of software modules and components are on the rise. These include tiny start-ups, firms in developing countries like India that are increasingly specializing in this business, or even individuals posting their software components or modules on the Internet. Many of these companies have limited investments in downstream commercialization capabilities, and choose to license their components to larger software producers.

Table 3.4
Types of Technology Transactions in Software, Some Representative Examples

---

Transfer of Market Rights

Open Market Inc. licensed Raptor Systems Inc. marketing and distribution rights to its Axcess software which controls access to content on the World Wide Web. (1997)

Promatek Industries and Control Systems granted worldwide exclusive marketing rights for certain software products to Hewlett-Packard Co. (1997)

Iomega Corp licensed Matsushita Communication Industrial Co. Ltd., a unit of Matsushita Electric Industrial Co. Ltd., the (non-exclusive) right to manufacture and market Iomega's Zip drive technology. (1996)

Data dimensions granted Tecnologica Telecommunicaciones E Informatica S.A. a license to market its Ardes 2K Millenium software in the year 2000 in Technologica's consulting work in Argentina and Uruguay. (1997)

Informix Software, a unit of Informix Corp , and Fulcrum Technologies entered into a strategic alliance; whereby both companies agreed to a cross-licensing, cross-distribution agreement of Fulcrum DataBlade module and Informix knowledge-retrieval software. The companies planned to market the integrated technology in Europe. (1997)

Software Components

Centigram Communications Corp. granted a license to Parlance Corp. for Centigram's Truvoice text-to-speech software to provide voice recognition software. Under the terms of the agreement, the software was to be in Parlance's Nameconnector service to combine speech recognition with computer and telephony technology. (1997)

Macrovision Corp. and Zoran Corp. entered into a strategic alliance; whereby Zoran licensed Macrovision's digital video disc (DVD) copy protection technology to incorporate into its NTSC/Pal encoder intellectual property core to ensure against unauthorized duplication. (1997)

Motorola Inc. entered into a licensing agreement with LSI Logic Corp. to embed its V.34 software modems into LSI's custom semiconductors. (1997)

One example of this strategy is Inktomi, a California-based Internet company, which has developed a new search engine capable of handling the problem of the soaring number of Web users worldwide by minimizing "redundant" net traffic. Inktomi's software engineers realized that a critical tie-up of the bandwidth of the network stemmed from individuals requesting the Web to provide the same information and material from the same location several times. The engine works by effectively storing frequently requested information from the same location so as to free up the network and reduce telecommunications costs. Inktomi's technology is said to have been critical in order to handle the huge growth in Internet traffic in recent years (Financial Times 1999). At the same time, Inktomi chose to license its technology to other companies rather than becoming another supplier in this business. Inktomi targeted search site, traffic server, and telecommunications companies, and has licensed its technology to firms like America Online, GeoCities,

Tools and Technologies
Oxford Molecular Group granted a license to Hoffmann-La Roche to use its RS3 Discovery software, which transforms standard relational database systems into a high-performance, chemical-structure search engine. Oxford also granted a similar license to Abbott Laboratories. (1996)

International Software group licensed Computer Associates International (CAI) its Navigator software which provides visual paradigm for programmers to build intranet solutions that can access and update transactions from any location through any internet browser. (1997)

Tandem Computers Inc. and Computer Associates International Inc. entered into an agreement to cross-license and develop a fault-tolerant version of computer Associates' Unicenter Enterprise management software. Under the terms of the agreement, Tandem was to standardize the Unicenter software for a number of server platforms, including UNIX, Windows NT, and Tandem Himalaya. (1996)

Licensing the Right to Use Software Products
Neomedia Technology Inc. licensed Maxwell Technologies the right to use its WIS2000 technology. Maxwell is to pay a licensing fee and royalties for any conversions it performs based on Neomeida's WISP2000 tools. (1997)

Ross Systems Inc. entered into a licensing agreement with Dragoco Gerberding und Co. AG. Ross provided client server software and services to Dragoco's subsidiaries. The software was scheduled to be fully implemented in all of Dragco's subsidiaries within 18–24 months. (1997)

Modacad Inc. granted Fleetwood Enterprises Inc. a license to use its CAD design software. Under the terms of the agreement, the software enabled Fleetwood to create sophisticated interior designs through a photo-realistic computer simulation before actual construction would begin (1997)

Source: SDC 1998.

HotBot, NBC's Snap!, Yahoo!, the Disney Internet Guide, PSI Net, Bell Canada, NTT in Japan, and Telenor Nextel in Scandinavia. This strategy was based explicitly on the recognition that the main strength of the company was its focus on the technology without diverting resources to move into an already crowded and competitive arena.

To provide a more general overview of the nature and type of technology transactions in software, we also examined each of the 1665 technology deals in software (SIC 7371–7376) during the 1990s in our SDC database. Since transactions in software occur in other industries as well, we also included all deals where the description of the deal mentioned software. Using this data, we found that technology deals in software during the 1990s can be classified into four main groups. Table 3.4 summarizes our findings by reporting some representative examples of technology deals in each group.

First, a number of these transactions take the form of transfer of *market rights* by a company developing a given piece of software to other companies marketing or distributing it. These arrangements involve a variety of technologies including multimedia, graphics, video games, and network management. In some cases, software companies allowing other firms to distribute the software in other countries or to specific users with which the partner has some special relation.[11] In other cases, the transfers of market rights were co-marketing agreements between two or more software suppliers, which pooled resources to undertake commercial operations.

The second group of transactions can be labeled as transactions in *software components*. The typical case here is ready-to-use software licensed to another company which incorporates it in larger software systems or other technologies. This clearly embraces the case of the software component modules discussed earlier, as well as the supply of software components for use in other technological systems. The sectors or areas where these types of transactions were most frequent included software to be embedded in larger software systems, semiconductor devices, computers, communication technologies, and Local Area Networks (LANs).

The third group of transactions can be classified as transfers—exchange or integration of *technologies* or supply of *software tools* such as EDA tools; tools for drug research, testing, and screening; or other R&D and testing tools. In some cases, this involves integration of the two partners' software technologies or of the software technology of one partner into the technological system of the other, with further development of the technology. Design and R&D tools are the objects of the other major type of transactions in this group. Apart from EDA and other design tools for semiconductors, many of the cases that we examined involved software for drug and chemical research and testing (see also section 3.4).

The fourth type of software transaction are primarily licenses for the transfer of the rights to use a given *software product*. This is the typical way in which software is sold in the final market. The most frequent cases in this area are licenses for the supply of databases and management information systems to banks and financial institutions, companies, and other organizations.

3.3.5   Software Patents and the Market for Technology

The extent to which software can be patented has important implications for the nature and functioning of markets for technology in this as well as other industries that employ software as a tool embodying design or other knowledge. We shall discuss the role of patents in markets for technology in other chapters of this book (see, e.g., chapters 5 and 10). However, we briefly address the issue here as well because of the controversy surrounding software patents.

In 1972 the U.S. Supreme Court ruled unanimously that software could not be patented. Software was equated to a set of mathematical algorithms, which did not fall into the patentable objects covered by the U.S. Patent Act. That decision forced software producers to rely on trademarks (which do not prevent duplication), and copyrights (which cover the product but not the idea on which that product is based). Some later decisions by the Court opened the issue anew. In particular, several decisions since the early 1980s implied that various devices that contained important software components could be patented, extending patentability to cases in which all hardware components were well known and the only novelty was the software, or in which the devices were almost entirely composed of software. Indeed, in specific cases, such as the patented LZW compression method (also called the GIF patent) for graphics files held by Unisys, the patented methods do deal with software objects. This prompted the software makers to develop ways to patent software by embedding it into more traditionally patentable devices (Schaaftsma 1998).

The process toward software patenting has progressed further in recent years, as the U.S. Patent Office has begun granting a large number of software patents. Moreover, the U.S. Patent Office has increasingly allowed for business processes to be patented. In this respect, a critical 1998 decision by the Supreme Court was the ruling that a software process which makes calculations about potential financial investments was patentable (*State Street Bank & Trust Co. v. Signature Financial Group Inc.*, July 1998—see Ellis and Chatterjee 1998). Similarly, a great deal of controversy has been raised recently by several decisions of the U.S. Patent Office to grant patents for business processes provided through the Web. For example, a company called E-Data has already initiated legal action, stating that its patents on music-store kiosk technology entitle it to licensing revenues from almost all forms of Internet commerce. An even more controversial case is the patent assigned to Priceline.com in 1998: This Web-based company was granted protection for its website auctioning products with customers. In Priceline's "reverse" auction model, consumers name the price they are willing to pay for items including plane tickets and car rentals, and Priceline solicits the best offer from a group of vendors with excess inventory. Many believe that the patented method was not significantly novel. However, the primary source of controversy appears to be the belief that such patents are contradictory to norms cherished by many in the software development community.

The increasing patentability of software has a variety of implications. For one, it removes the asymmetry between technologies embodied in hardware and those embodied in software. Since copying software is much easier than copying machinery, such protection against copying is desirable. Proponents of software patenting argue, with considerable justification, that there is no reason why such software innovations ought not to be patentable whereas a similar innovation implemented in hardware would be protected.

The problem is the history of software development. Many software developers see themselves as a part of a broad community with open and free exchange of ideas, code, and programs, similar in many respects to academic communities. Many within the community have responded with alarm and outrage to what they see as the "privatization" of what were previously the "commons." In the short run, the problem is exacerbated by the inability of the U.S. patent office to adequately search for prior art—articles, patents, and other published material that establishes the state of the art in the field. This inability of the patent office arises because it tends to rely primarily on earlier patents to discover prior art, and much of the progress in software has not been patented. The result has been a few well-known cases of extraordinarily broad patents that the patent office was compelled to reexamine and invalidate in response to protests from the software development community. In the long run, software patents could give rise to problems similar to those envisioned by Dasgupta and David (1994) of the contamination of academic values once university research outputs become potentially patentable. (See also chapter 10.) From talking to academic and nonacademic computer scientists in person, as well as through internet newsgroups, our sense is that the debate has been defined in terms of incentives to invest versus the inefficiencies of imposing property rights that conflict strongly with the norms and culture of a community. The recent success of open source software implies that, court decisions notwithstanding, software patents are likely to be contentious for some time.

Lost in the debate are potential benefits for the efficient use of software. For example, Lemley and O'Brien (1997) argue that one possible effect of the shift from copyrights to patents as a means for protecting computer software, is to encourage software reuse. Copyright allows competitors to appropriate the value of new software without having to pay a fee, but it prevents them from copying the code. It therefore encourages competitors to make use of others' innovations while continuing to write their own code. However, this process is inefficient because the competitors must rewrite code that could be copied directly from the inventing firm. Patents instead force competitors to obtain a license for using the invention. While this implies a royalty fee, it also allows for the direct, unadulterated use of the patented idea and its code. It can then foster a more efficient organization of the industry, with greater trade and reuse of code, by promoting a market for software technology.

The U.S. patent system however substantially reduces the possibility of software reuse on a significant scale. The current U.S. system does not require publication of the patent application until the patent is granted. In sectors such as software where technology is advancing rapidly, the long delays between patent application and patent grant implies that a patent search conducted at the start of a product development program may not uncover many relevant patents until product development is far advanced. The problem is compounded in many cases because the number of relevant patents may be very large. The result is that many software developers simply do not bother to undertake a patent search, negating the putative benefit of patents in preventing the rediscovery of the wheel.[12]

3.4   The Division of Innovative Labor in Life Sciences

3.4.1   *The Rise of the Biotechnology Industry: 1970–1980*

The origins and the evolution of the biotechnology industry are well known, and they have been studied in detail.[13] The industry emerged in the early 1970s following two major scientific breakthroughs: Cohen and Boyer's famous discovery of the recombinant DNA process by which strands of DNA of different organisms could be combined to obtain new genetically modified organisms; and the development of monoclonal antibodies, a technique for cloning and fusing cells with great potential for therapeutic, diagnostic, and other purposes. Starting with Genentech's $35 million public offering in 1976, several small R&D-intensive biotech companies, the Dedicated Biotechnology Firms (DBFs) as they are sometimes called, entered the industry. These firms were mostly U.S.-based and focused on discovering new therapies for ailments such as diabetes, heart attacks, and cancer, as well as creating new diagnostic kits. In addition to pharmaceuticals, where the bulk of the attention was focused, a few DBFs targeted other branches of the chemical industry such as agricultural chemicals and the environment. The research outputs and the competencies of the DBFs turned out to be important resources for the larger, established chemical and pharmaceutical firms. The larger firms developed several linkages through alliances, R&D joint ventures, and acquisitions. Some of the early biotech companies, like Genentech or Amgen, aimed to become full-fledged pharmaceutical companies, selling their products to final markets, and partly succeeded in this strategy. However, it soon became clear that the high costs and high failure rates of product development and commercialization in pharmaceuticals were a serious barrier to the vast majority of the other biotech start-ups. The industry developed into one in which a large number of small DBFs, which specialized in the earlier research stages, become linked to the larger companies that were endowed with the necessary complementary resources in research, product development, and commercialization. The universities were an additional source of technologies and competencies for the industry. As a result, innovations in biotechnology became the output of complex networks of relationships among the universities, the DBFs (which were frequently university spin-offs or linked to university research), and the larger companies (see Pisano, Shan, and Teece 1988; Orsenigo 1989; Arora and Gambardella 1990; Gambardella 1995). In sum, we see a market for technology with a well-defined division of innovative labor, involving DBFs as technology suppliers and established pharmaceutical and chemical firms as buyers (Arora and Gambardella 1994).

The role and behavior of the larger companies have been confirmed by Galambos and Sturchio's (1998) recent study on the transition of the pharmaceutical industry to biotechnology. They argue that during the 1980s, the established drug and chemical manufacturers were, on the one hand, cautious about moving rapidly into the new technology, while on the other, they followed its evolution attentively. They did so by developing alliances, funding R&D, doing joint research, and occasionally acquiring some DBFs outright. Clearly, larger companies also invested in-house R&D resources in biotechnology. But even the companies that invested considerable internal resources in biotech were very active, if not the most active, in creating linkages with DBFs and universities (Arora and Gambardella 1994b).

Along with the U.S. firms, the European and Japanese large chemical and pharmaceutical companies also took advantage of the new technological opportunities by creating alliances, funding operations, and acquisitions of U.S.-based DBFs, or through collaborations with U.S. universities. Moreover, large firms typically established relationships with many DBFs and universities at once in several areas, thereby creating wide networks of linkages. This marked a significant departure from the earlier days of the pharmaceutical industry, in which the large companies integrated all the activities for drug R&D and marketing, possibly developing only occasional collaborations with universities or specific university professors who consulted with them.

3.4.2   The Growing Biotech Industry in the 1990s

To understand the developments of the biotech industry in the 1990s, one must understand two important aspects of the technology involved. First, as suggested by Cockburn et al. (1999), since its very origin biotechnology followed two distinct research trajectories. On the one hand, by elucidating the structure of proteins and their functions, the new technology enabled the development and production of large and complex molecules that mimicked the functions of proteins, and could therefore perform complex therapeutic activities. On the other hand, knowledge of the structure and functions of human proteins, along with other advances in genetics and molecular biology, enabled researchers to develop tools to select traditional small molecule drugs. While in the 1980s, the biotech opportunities for human therapeutics and other products were largely seen as associated with the first trajectory, the 1990s witnessed the increasing development of biotechnology as a research tool.

A second and related aspect is that advances in the life sciences and their technologies continued at a significant pace during the 1990s, with new breakthroughs and therapies. Thus, not only were the structure of many new genes and proteins uncovered and their actions and functions clarified, but also new techniques like Polymerase Chain Reaction (PCR) were developed, new types of diseases and pathologies were targeted, and major advances took place in cloning and in gene therapy (therapy based on modification of malfunctioning genes). In short, the biotechnology industry of the 1990s showed signs of continuing technological growth.

These developments have been paralleled by a continuing role of the DBFs. The 1999 Ernst & Young biotech report (Ernst and Young 1999) counts 327 publicly traded U.S. DBFs in 1998, up by thirty companies or so from a few years earlier (see Ernst and Young 1997), along with at least three times as many privately held DBFs. Many DBFs were founded in continental Europe as well, especially after 1995. (See Ernst and Young 1999.) Moreover, Zucker and Darby (1996) show that out of twenty-one new biological entities approved by the FDA in the U.S. by 1994, nineteen were discovered by DBFs. Similarly, DBFs were responsible for the vast majority of the three hundred biotech-based drugs in Phase III of clinical trials in 1998, for their substantial increase with respect to the previous years (120, 150, and 160 in 1995–1997), and for the vast majority of the forty-one biotech drugs approved in the United States between 1995 and 1998.

Alliances and networks between DBFs, large firms and universities also continued in the 1990s. Powell, Koput, and Smith-Doerr (1996) studied the behavior and performance of a sample of 225 independent DBFs operating in human therapeutics during 1990–1994. Their statistical analysis shows that the companies with a larger number of such R&D ties are also larger and grow faster. Moreover, these companies tend to become central in their networks over time, which spurs new alliances and growth. Powell, Koput, and Smith-Doerr conclude by emphasizing the importance of network learning and the role of alliances in creating opportunities for monitoring and acquiring external knowledge and capabilities.

Orsenigo et al. (1998) tracked the agreements and R&D collaborations of 174 independent companies operating in human therapeutics during 1978–1993.[14] They distinguish between different "generations" of companies, and particularly the incumbent firms, and the DBFs of the first (DBF-I), second (DBF-II), and third (DBF-III) generation. The latter were founded respectively in 1973–1980, in 1981–1986, and after 1986. They note that each new generation of DBFs was more narrowly specialized than the earlier generation. Specifically, they argue that since the early 1970s, the life sciences have evolved by deepening more specific research hypotheses arising from fundamental scientific theories and domains. The entry of the DBFs conformed to this hierarchical structure of scientific developments; that is, the new generation DBFs tended to focus on more specific domains within each research paradigm. This points to the "vertical" complementarity among companies of different generations. Consistent with this hypothesis, Orsenigo et al. (1998) find that intergenerational agreements are more common than intragenerational agreements.

The continuing importance of technological alliances in biotechnology is also highlighted by Ernst and Young (1999). The Ernst and Young report indicates that a growing number of alliances took place in 1997–1998, particularly in the technologically more dynamic applications of biotechnology—pharmaceuticals and agricultural biotechnology. Moreover, the same source reports that 1998 was a record year in terms of number of deals, and especially of those valued $100 million or more. As table 3.5 shows, technological alliances in the late 1990s focused on both biotechnology product R&D, and biotech research tools or "platforms." Mergers and acquisitions in both products and platforms also took place in this period.

However, as table 3.6 shows, the late 1990s witnessed a substantial reduction in equity financing for biotech companies in the U.S. market. Total equity financing for biotechnology firms in the US dropped from $8 billion in 1997 to between $5 and $5.5 billion in 1998 and 1999. Although seeming to conflict with other indicators of growth, this fall represents the greater selectivity in the supply of financing to DBFs, as well as the tremendous attraction of Internet and related opportunities. Financial markets in continental Europe still offer high evaluations for the "local" biotech concerns. This is because, unlike the United States, there are fewer biotech firms in Europe. Because of the greater difficulties involved in forming high-tech start-ups there, these companies are probably preselected. The reduced funding from financial investors is also partially compensated by an increase funding from the larger companies through deals, licensing agreements, and R&D collaborations. Because of their experience with the industry and technology, established pharmaceutical companies can better evaluate the DBFs than financial investors relying upon signals from more informed agents for assessing the potential of the DBF and its technology. Indeed, we observe that DBFs allied with pharmaceutical firms are more likely to attract funding from other investors as well.

In short, what seems to be happening in the biotech industry today, particularly in the leading biotech market, the United States, is a consolidation of the sector toward a structure in which an upstream industry of specialized technology suppliers has become a stable source of new products and technologies. While some of the largest biotech companies have become suppliers in the final markets as well, the vast majority of them are consciously becoming suppliers to the downstream producers,

Table 3.5
Selected 1998 Alliances in Biotechnology Products and Platforms

Companies	Object of Alliance	Alliance Value
Products		
Guilford; Amgen	Amgen gets worldwide rights to a class of small molecules to treat neuro-degenerative disorders	$50+25M to Guilford plus $390M if further results are achieved
Ligand; Eli Lilly	Metabolic and cardiovascular diseases associated with insulin resistance and obesity	$204M to Ligand
Biogen; Merck	To develop Biogen's anti-VLA-4 small molecule for asthma and other inflammatory diseases	$145M to Biogen
Alteon; Genentech	Alteon's Pimagedine inhibitor of advanced glycosylation end products (AGEs)	$63M of assured cash to Alteon, plus more than $100M in other payments
GenVec; Parke-Davis	Agreed to develop and market GenVec's BioByPass adenoviral via local injection. (Gene therapy)	$100M to GenVec
Transgene; Schering-Plough	Adenoviral delivery of Schering-Plough genes. (Gene therapy)	$88M to Transgene
Transgene; Human Genome Science	Gene therapy	10% stakes of HGS in Transgene
Vascular Genetics; Human Genome Science	Gene therapy	19.9% stakes in Vascular Genetics
Centocor; Roche	Centocor acquired US and Canadian rights to Roche's Retavase reteplase tPA	$335M to Roche

Platforms

Millennium Pharmac.; Bayer	Millennium provides Bayer with 225 gene and protein-based targets for small molecule compounds applicable to a wide array of different diseases	$465M to Millennium
Incyte Pharmac.; Smithkline Beecham	Joint-venture to apply the companies' genomics and bioinformatics technologies to discovery and development of molecular diagnostics	Undisclosed
Genset; Genetics Institute	Development of proteins by combining proteins from Genset's SignalTag library with GI's DiscoverEase protein development platform	Undisclosed
Perkin-Elmer; J. Craig Venter; The Institute for Genomic Research	Created Celera Genomics to complete sequencing of human genome in three years	Undisclosed
Oncogene Science; Roche; Cold Spring Harbor Lab	Created Helicon Therapeutics to perform research on the genetics of the central nervous system	Undisclosed
Millennium Pharmac.; Monsanto	Wide genomics collaboration involving Monsanto's agricultural, pharmaceutical and nutrition products	$218M to Millennium
Incyte Pharmac.; Monsanto	Expanded 1996 plant genomics deal to include all Monsanto's life science businesses	Undisclosed
Gene Logic; Hoechst Schering AgrEvo	Discovery of genes to develop crop protection and improvement products	$45M to Gene Logic
Axys Pharmac.; Xyris Corp.	Axys gave Xyris worldwide exclusive license to apply Axys tools for drug discovery to the development of new agricultural products	Undisclosed

Source: Ernst & Young 1999.

Table 3.6
Biotech Equity Financing in the United States, 1997–1999 (millions of U.S. dollars)

Form of Financing	1997	1998	1999
Initial Public Offering	1745	707	731
Follow-ons	3406	1099	1204
Other	2169	2220	2181
Venture	708	863	1268
TOTAL	8028	4889	5414

Source: Ernst and Young 1999.

as we shall also see in the next section. Moreover, as noted earlier, alliances are still a major factor in the industry, and these are the forms through which exchange takes place in this market for technology. However, new generation DBFs continue to enter into new niches of the industry, usually to respond to new technical opportunities.

3.4.3 "General-Purpose" Tools in Biotechnology: The Convergence Between Life Sciences and Information Technologies

One of the most striking technological advances of biotechnology in the 1990s has been the development of drug discovery and research tools. This has been spurred by several developments: computer-based tools and software; the Human Genome Project; and the concomitant growth of knowledge about human genes, the structure of proteins and the relationships between genes, proteins, and diseases. Moreover, "genomics" and related fields are creating new opportunities for using molecular biology and genetics as tools for developing new drugs. These opportunities are related to the ability of the researchers to manipulate and process the massive amounts of information gradually disclosed by the Human Genome Project and its private competitors.[15]

The increased use of information technology and software in biotechnology reflects their general-purpose nature, and the changing nature of biotechnology research. First, biotechnology uses chemistry to understand proteins and structures of proteins that conform to fundamental physical laws such as the minimization of potential energy, and researchers require fast computers and efficient algorithms to find and visualize these structures. Second, while biochemical and drug researchers typically worked in small groups and shared information mostly among themselves, the massive amount of information that is becoming available can only be accessed and managed by creating powerful tools for sharing information both within a company and between companies and other institutions. Third, the development of robotic techniques to conduct laboratory experiments, which has significantly augmented the productivity of laboratory experiments in the pharmaceutical industry, requires suitable software to analyze and report the data. Finally, the use of combinatorial chemistry for producing libraries of chemical compounds rests on the development of complex software programs and substantial increases in computational power.

Table 3.7 presents a list of selected DBFs and their fields of activities in these areas. This list is not meant to be exhaustive, but simply to provide a picture of the kind of tools that have been developed in recent years. Several companies have invested in the development of software tools and programs for drug research. Thus, for instance, two U.S. DBFs, Pangea System and NetGenics, are independently developing two software systems for genetic and biochemical data synthesis and analysis. Both systems are "generic" and modular enough to be combined with other tools and operating systems to perform a wide array of data analyses. Similarly, Oxford Molecular Group (OMG), a British bioinformatics concern, is specializing in software development and services for large pharmaceutical firms, and it is currently undertaking a project for unifying and centralizing Glaxo Wellcome's scattered data and information in one enterprise system.

Integration of tools is another strategy in this area. For example, in 1997, PE Applied Biosystems, a California-based subsidiary of Perkin-Elmer, acquired a privately held company, Molecular Informatics, primarily for its BioMerge product. BioMerge is an object-oriented relational database in which users can store and manage results of DNA and protein sequence analysis, typically supplied by PE Applied Biosystem's sequencing instruments. In a sense, these companies are both biotech and information technology companies. For example, NetGenetics employs more than twenty programmers and about as many researchers in the life sciences. While these companies have specialized mainly in the development of software tools for analyzing and processing information, other DBFs have integrated further down by producing services or even research leading to drug discovery. Thus, some companies have invested in combinatorial chemistry techniques to develop libraries of new compounds to be sold to pharmaceutical companies. Others, like DeCode Genetics, Millennium Pharmaceuticals, and Incyte

Table 3.7
Selected DBFs Developing Research Tools

Company, Nationality	Product/Activity	Field of Activity
Pangea Systems, U.S.	Gene World: software system for organizing and processing genetic and biochem data	Software systems and services
NetGenics, U.S.	Synergy: software system for organizing and processing genetic and biochem data	Software systems and services
Oxford Molecular Group, U.K.	Software systems and services for central management of drug discovery data	Software systems and services
Pharsight, U.S.	Software to simulate and optimize design of clinical trials	Software systems and services
PE Applied Biosystems, U.S.*	Integration of relational database BioMerge for storage and management of results of DNA and protein sequence analysis with PE sequencing instruments	Software and integration with DNA and protein sequence instrumentation
Pharmacopeia, U.S.	Library of 3.8 million compounds using combinatorial chemistry techniques	Combinatorial chemistry
Incyte Pharmaceuticals, U.S.	Genetic database and tools for drug design	Genomics databases and analysis
Millennium Pharmaceuticals, U.S	Genetic database and tools for drug design	Genomics databases and analysis
Human Genome Science, U.S.	Genetic database and tools for drug design	Genomics databases and analysis
Genomica, U.S.	Genetic database and tools for drug design—claims that its database performs more elaborated functions than competitors	Genomics databases and analysis

DeCode Genetics, Iceland	Genetic database of Iceland population and tools for drug design—claims that Icelandic homogeneous population eases targeting of genes for diseases	Genomics databases and analysis
Cytokinetics, U.S.	Genetic database and tools for drug design—developed a method for testing disease prone genes in vivo rather than in vitro	Genomics databases and analysis
Oxford GlycoSciences, U.K.	Genetic database and tools for drug design—developed database and tools for proteins functions beside genes	Genomics databases and analysis
Affymetrix, U.S.	GeneChip to analyze and test gene samples	Testing chips
Nanogen, U.S.	Apex Chip to analyze and test gene samples	Testing chips
Synteni, U.S.**	Chip to analyze and test gene samples	Testing chips
Hyseq, U.S.	Gene discovery platform, a gene chip associated with other tools (e.g., robotic testing)	Testing chips
Caliper Technology, U.S.	"Laboratory-on-a-chip" to rapidly test various substances beside genes (proteins, carbohydrates, cells)	Testing chips
Aclara BioSciences, U.S.	"Laboratory-on-a-chip" to rapidly test various substances	Testing chips
Orchid Biocomputer, U.S.	"Laboratory-on-a-chip" to rapidly test various substances	Testing chips
Lumisense, U.S.	"Laboratory-on-a-chip" to rapidly test various substances	Testing chips

Source: Red Herring Magazine, various issues, available at <www.redherring.com>.
*Subsidiary of Perkin-Emler.
**Acquired by Incyte.

Pharmaceuticals, have gone even further by developing detailed genetic databases about various diseases.

With the completion of the Human Genome Project, much genetic information is becoming a widely diffused "commodity." Thus, it is probably no longer sufficient to supply a database of genetic sequences and related information. Thus firms such as Genomica are trying to add value to their genetic database by developing software technologies that increase the value of the database. Genomica claims that, unlike the "simple" databases of its competitors, its software can track every aspect of the gene discovery process, including human genetics, genotyping, molecular cloning, and functional analysis of a gene sequence. Finally, there are companies that develop software to simulate other steps of the drug discovery process, including software that optimizes the design of the clinical trials in order to maximize the prospects for FDA approval.

In addition to managing and analyzing vast amounts of information, information technology is finding other applications in biotechnology. Semiconductor technology applications are probably the most important example. In 1996, the Santa Clara–based biotech company Affymetrix introduced its first Gene Chip. The function of the chip is to detect the presence of gene mutations from a blood sample through a series of steps including chemical reactions on simulated strands of DNA and a final analysis of data reported on a PC. The first application of the gene chip was customized to help researchers understand HIV mutations. But the chip can be reconfigured to assess other infectious diseases as well as genetic conditions like cystic fibrosis, diabetes, and coronary artery disease. Affymetrix is developing alliances with pharmaceutical and genomics companies to develop other versions of the chip. It has announced its collaboration with another biotech company, OncorMed, on a chip that will screen a gene called P53 for more than four hundred known mutations closely associated with many types of cancer. Another biotech company, Nanogen, has developed a similar product. Using a different technology, the Nanogen Apex Chip can screen for five different diseases at once. One notable feature of Apex is that it is essentially an Application-Specific Integrated Circuit (ASIC), of the kind commonly used in electronic products. As a result, Apex can be most easily reconfigured to test for new diseases simply by changing its software.

Some biotech companies are taking an even more profound approach to the problem. The idea is to develop what is called a "laboratory on a chip," analogous to the "system on a chip" idea in semiconductors. For example, a Palo Alto start-up, Caliper Technology, claims that unlike the other gene chips which perform somewhat fixed functions, its chip can conduct a much wider range of tests on varying substances like proteins, carbohydrates, and cells. Another "laboratory on a chip" product is currently being developed by another California-based DBF, Lumisense. Lumisense is developing a method for placing 250,000 small chemical wells on a 0.1 millimeter-square of fiber-optic wire. This would tremendously increase the productivity of current laboratory testing typically conducted using a small tray containing ninety six test tubes to perform only ninety-six tests on a single plate. The complementarities with other technologies being developed in this field, and by other DBFs, are also apparent. For example, savings in the reagent costs and other factors would significantly reduce the costs of testing a library of millions of compounds created by combinatorial chemistry companies.

Whether these technologies will ultimately fulfill their promises is yet to be seen, but this is not truly the point at stake. The point is that many DBFs have now realized that their market is not the large, but also very competitive, risky, and difficult-to-tap market of the final consumers of drugs or agrochemical products. Rather, they are better off focusing on another large and growing market which they can tap more effectively given their resources and competencies—the market for R&D drug discovery.

Moreover, while there is a continuing controversy as to whether the larger companies will absorb the biotech firms, there is increasing recognition that they may in fact take advantage of the opportunities that a market for technology can create:

Licensing agreements also are the preferred way that major pharmaceutical companies work with smaller biotech companies. "If a big company likes the products in a startup's pipeline, . . . they'll simply license them instead of absorbing the whole entity" (*Red Herring Magazine* 1998a).

The biggest question for biotech as it moves through this entrepreneurial stage is how it will consolidate and shake out. Some industry watchers . . . predict that the massive drug companies will soak up the smaller ones in an effort to become end-to-end drug, therapy, and service providers. Others say the drug conglomerates will remain content to license intellectual capital from the startups. "We'll see horizontal integration with like-sized companies merging, but the big companies won't gobble up the guppies," says Hunt Williams, CEO of the Community of Science, a for-profit database consortium for research universities. "They'll do licensing deals to get the commercialization rights, but they want the small companies to stay small and keep the food chain alive" (*Red Herring Magazine* 1998b).

3.5 Intellectual Property, Fabless Companies, and the Market for Technology in Semiconductors

3.5.1 Fabless Fabs and the Division of Innovative Labor in the U.S. Semiconductor Industry

The story of the semiconductor industry is also well known.[16] Since the post-World War II invention of the transistor and the integrated circuit, the industry has undergone a bewildering process of miniaturization. The number of transistors placed on a silicon chip has increased exponentially, while chip size and the price/performance ratio have fallen dramatically. Applications of semiconductor devices have diffused to a growing number of industries ranging from telecommunications to computers, military systems, automobile, consumer electronics, home appliances, and computer networks. The industry has also developed impressive manufacturing technologies for the fabrication of these very small devices. As noted in our discussion of biotechnology, some of these manufacturing technologies have found applications in other industries as well.

The production of semiconductors has increased from $19 billion in 1980 to $137 billion in 1997 (in 1997 dollars) and alongside, R&D and manufacturing costs have also soared. The capital cost of a fabrication facility for semiconductor devices of approximately three microns linewidth was about $20 million in the early 1970s. Today it is over $1 billion for devices of 0.35 microns linewidth (Macher, Mowery, and Hodges 1999, 245, 268.) Apart from traditional products like memory products such as DRAM (which have become a commodity), semiconductor devices include highly complex technological, and design-intensive products like Application Specific Integrated Circuits (ASICs), and various types of microprocessors, microcontrollers, and digital signal processors (DSPs). Several new trends have characterized the industry during the 1990s. While integrated companies still play an important role, over the past few years there has been a growth of several specialized producers, and particularly of the so-called fabless semiconductor companies. These companies rely on other companies specialized in manufacturing semiconductor devices—the "foundries"—for the production of their designs. Further, the growing complexity of semiconductor devices—particularly the development of "superchips" which incorporate functions previously performed by separate chips within an extremely complex system—has given rise to new "chipless" firms specialized in the production of design modules. The industry has also witnessed a marked increase in semiconductor patents, and an expansion of licensing and cross-licensing agreements among semiconductor firms. U.S. firms are leading these new trends, and it is in the United States that this new evolution of the industry is most visible. For instance, it is estimated that in 1998 out of a total of 500 fabless semiconductor firms, about 300 are located in North America (Macher, Mowery, and Hodges 1999, 268).

The fabless companies specialize in the design of chips or components of chips that perform specific functions. These are typically integrated within larger chips or systems that interconnect several of these functions. The trend in the industry has been to embed in one chip functions—such as graphics, networking, and communications capabilities that were earlier performed by stand-alone chips linked together. The fabless companies provide only the design of the components or sub-components; they have no manufacturing operations of their own. There are often several layers of specialization among the design firms, with smaller design companies producing modules that are licensed to other design firms until the whole chip system is created by a final assembler, who typically contracts with a foundry or a large semiconductor company for the manufacturing of the product. The term *chipless companies* has been employed more recently to emphasize the further specialization of firms that focus on design modules, without producing even a physical prototype of the chip.

The role of these firms is growing. The total revenue of the fabless industry in 1997 was estimated to be $7.8 billion, and it is expected to rise to $11.7 billion in 2000 and to 40 percent of the world's chip production by 2010 (Macher, Mowery and Hodges 1999, 269). Trade in semiconductor design modules is also increasing rapidly. Using Dataquest estimates, Linden and Somaya (2000) note that the total licensing revenue from semiconductor design modules grew from $16 to $140 million U.S. from 1995 to 1998, and it is expected to reach almost $300 million by 2001.[17]

The fabless and chipless firms are a response to the growing complexity of chip design. As chipmakers attempted to embed more functions into a single chip, it became clear that the design of the chip could no longer be conceived as an integrated and unified process. This complexity could only be faced by partitioning the problem into more elementary problems that could be addressed independently. Moreover, the growth of the market for customized applications implied that each chip had to have different properties or characteristics. Reusability of functions became critical for creating economies in the design and production stages.

As we also discuss in the next chapter, one way designers coped with this complexity was to create modular designs, with specific functions to be performed by self-contained chip-modules. Each module was conceived as an "isolated" component identified by the function it performed rather than by the way it was designed and built. These functions could be combined to create systems that performed more complex functions. Standardized interfaces among the modular components ensured that the modules could be combined, and that the designer of each module or function could focus on the design and the properties of his or her component without being excessively constrained by the properties and the architecture of the whole system.[18] These days component designs are called "intellectual property," indicating that they are proprietary designs. As in any division of labor, the growth of the size of the market was crucial. Thus, in the United States, the increase in demand for design-intensive semiconductors in the 1990s (such as ASICs and DSPs), was a major factor behind the increasing specialization of the design companies, foundries, and larger semiconductor firms (Macher, Mowery, and Hodges 1999).

Today, semiconductor design companies like ARC Cores, ARM and MIPS Technologies are supplying the chip processor market with new solutions. The case of ARC Cores is worth noting. This is a U.K.-based company which evolved from a business unit of Argonaut Software (a developer of games and technologies) into an independent concern in 1998. However, well before then, it began acting as an independent unit licensing its designs. ARC Cores develops third generation user-customizable processors. A notable feature of its design is that customers can easily build their own process configurations by employing easy-to-use tools. Moreover, the company has chosen a business model whereby it licenses its intellectual property rather than attempting any downstream integration into manufacturing. In 1999, ARC Cores is said to have obtained about thirty licenses, and it is expected to reach 250 licenses by 2000 (*Red Herring Magazine* 1999).

Another successful company with a similar strategy is Artisan Components, a U.S. concern that licenses RAM, ROM, standard cells, data-path elements, and I/O cells to companies like SGS-Thomson, Fujitsu Microelectronics, Oki Electric, and NEC Electronics for use in cellular phones, PCs, and automotive electronics. The semiconductor intellectual property market covers a wide and increasing range of functional areas. Among these, two important areas are communications and graphics. The former is spurred by the growth of the Internet business and by the opportunities for integrating multimedia communications with broadband frequencies like TV frequencies, cables, and wireless communication.

Also an important market for semiconductor intellectual property are those companies that design paths and elements for interconnecting the various functions on the chip, or for improving and speeding up these interconnections. One company with a leading technology in this field is Rambus. Its technology is a chip-to-chip interface device to speed communication between memory chips and microprocessors. While Rambus does some component manufacturing itself, it sees its revenues as coming largely from licensing the technology. Rambus has signed agreements with several leading manufacturers, of which the agreement with Intel is easily the most significant. Similarly, Virtual Socket Interface (VSI) developed a technology for linking subsystems on complex chips which allows mathematical simulations of chip behavior. Using VSI's technology, design companies can bypass the creation of physical prototypes in silicon by using simulations to assess the performance of the design. PDF Solutions, founded in 1992, has developed software that can simulate chip production and design activities. PDF provides this technology through licenses and consultancy services.

3.5.2 The Rise of Semiconductor Patents in the United States and the Growth of Licensing and Cross-Licensing in the Industry

Another important trend in the semiconductor industry during the 1980s and the 1990s has been the growth in the number of semiconductor patents. Hall and Ham (1999) studied this phenomenon using a sample of 97 U.S. semiconductor companies during 1980–1994. Their techniques included both field interviews and a statistical analysis of these firms' propensity to patent their technology.

They show that U.S. semiconductor patents per million dollars in R&D expenditures doubled between 1982 and 1992, from 0.3 to 0.6. The ratio of patents per million dollars in R&D has remained constant for the manufacturing industry as a whole, though it has declined for pharmaceuticals, suggesting that the rise in semiconductor patenting is due to an increase in the propensity to patent of the U.S. semiconductor firms. Moreover, they show that both the established firms and the new entrants exhibit higher rates of patenting compared to the early 1980s. Hall and Ham argue that established semiconductor firms have increased their patenting for different reasons than those for the smaller firms. Established firms increasingly use patents as bargaining chips in cross-licensing negotiations with rivals, an argument put forth by other studies as well (Grindley and Teece 1997, Cohen, Nelson, and Walsh 2000). In turn, several events have contributed to this behavior. First, since the 1980s, there has been an increase in the strength of intellectual property rights in the United States (e.g., Kortum and Lerner 1999). Second, in the mid–1980s, some companies, particularly Texas Instruments, began suing other companies for patent infringements. The rulings were largely to be in favor of the patent holder. Since then, patent infringement cases have soared, and several semiconductor producers have found themselves in a position whereby any development of new technologies was likely to infringe some existing patent. The fear of long and costly patent litigation caused many companies to license and cross-license patents so they could be free to develop their own technology. Whereas initially the cross-licensing arrangements were essentially barter trades, in that technology was exchanged for technology, recent arrangements appear to involve significant monetary transfers as well, from companies with weak patent portfolios to those that hold critical patents or those with more substantial portfolios. If true, this suggests that even established producers are participating as sellers, not just buyers, in the market for technology.

Thus, for instance, Texas Instruments' royalty income from technology licenses has grown from about $200 million in 1987 to more than $600 million in 1995. Similarly, licensing incomes have become an important component of the profits for firms like AT&T, IBM, Intel, and Hewlett-Packard (see Grindley and Teece 1997). Table 3.8 reports the firms from our SDC (1998) database (described earlier) with the highest number of licenses granted, the highest number of cross-licensing deals, and the highest number of licenses received in semiconductors (SIC 3674). Note that the top-granting firms are practically all U.S. firms. In contrast, five out of the eight top licensees in table 3.8 are Japanese or East Asians (Samsung, Toshiba, NEC, Oki, Lucky-Goldstar). Moreover, the overall picture provided by the Table shows that the market for semiconductor technology is largely a U.S. or U.S.-East Asian market. European firms, and particularly the continental European firms (e.g.,

Philips, Siemens, SGS-Thomson, Bull, Thomson-CSF), play a more limited role.

As far as the smaller semiconductor companies are concerned, interviews conducted by Hall and Ham (1999) with two leading semiconductor design firms suggest that their main motive is to establish rights in well-defined product niches. Since the nature of their products is largely intangible, patents are a critical means to identify and secure rights on them, and to expand market shares vis-à-vis their rivals. Moreover, patents are a means to make intangible products, and their quality, visible, which also helps secure resources from the financial market. Once again, what is relevant for our purposes is that the increasing concern about patenting semiconductor designs, especially for these smaller firms, is linked to the goal of selling the intellectual property itself, and not the specific products that would embody that intellectual property.

In sum, trends in the U.S. semiconductor industry during the past decade or so show that in this industry markets for technology are expanding. Many leading semiconductor producers are adopting strategies to license their technologies much the same way that products are sold in the marketplace. Fabless design firms are thriving, and this is giving rise to vertical specialization and an increased exchange of new and innovative designs disembodied from the larger systems in which they have to operate.

3.5.3 Technological Intermediaries, Industry Consolidation, and the U.S. Competitive Advantages Stemming from the Division of Innovative Labor

Another consequence of the growth of a market for technology is the rise of firms or other institutions specializing in technological intermediation between design companies and downstream producers. As noted earlier in this and the previous chapter, these intermediaries are both a natural outcome of the growth of markets for technology and a critical factor in expanding them. Moreover, today many of these intermediaries have taken the form of Internet companies which provide their services largely (and sometimes exclusively) through the Web.

Table 3.9 presents a selected list of these intermediaries and their main activities. HTE Research is an intermediary specialized in semiconductors. It offers detailed information about eighty intellectual property and technology licensing companies in this business, along

Table 3.8
Main Licensors, Cross-Licensors, and Licensees in Semiconductors, Worldwide, circa
1988–1997

Licensors

Licensor	Number of Licenses Granted	To companies from			
		United States	Japan	Western Europe	Other (*)
Sun Microsystems Inc.	15	5	6	3	1
Intel Corp.	13	5	3	4	1
MIPS Computer Systems Inc.	13	2	5	4	2
Texas Instruments Inc.	12	5	6	0	1
IBM Corp.	12	6	1	4	1
Motorola Inc.	9	5	1	0	3
Rambus Inc.	9	3	4	0	2
Advanced RISC Machines	6	4	1	0	1
Ramtron Holdings Ltd.	6	3	1	2	0

Cross-Licensors

Cross-Licensor	Number of Cross-Licenses	With companies from			
		United States	Japan	Western Europe	Other (*)
Texas Instruments Inc.	26	7	15	1	3
Intel Corp.	7	5	1	1	0
Hitachi Ltd.	7	7	0	0	0
Samsung Group	7	5	1	0	1
Philips NV	7	4	3	0	0
Advanced RISC Machines	6	4	1	1	0
Standard Microsystems Corp.	6	0	3	2	1

Licensees

		From Companies from			
Licensee	Number of licenses Received	United States	Japan	Western Europe	Other *
Samsung Group	28	24	1	3	0
Toshiba Corp.	17	17	0	0	0
NEC Corp.	11	9	2	0	0
Texas Instruments Inc.	12	7	4	1	0
OKI Electric Industry. Co. Ltd.	11	10	1	0	0
Lucky-Goldstar Group	10	8	1	1	0
LSI Logic Corp.	9	7	1	1	0
VLSI Technology	8	7	1	0	0

Source: SDC 1998.
*Other includes mainly South Korean firms.

with detailed descriptions of the technologies to be licensed, as well as the profiles of about four hundred other semiconductor design houses. Companies like these often also supply complementary services like assistance in developing contracts or consulting services on technical or managerial issues, and even undertake some product design and engineering activities themselves. The other companies listed in table 3.9 offer scouting services in a wide range of technologies. Venture Capital Online was founded on the premise that the venture capital sector itself needs to be systematically informed about new opportunities. This company provides intermediation services between venture capital firms and new start-ups. The European Union (EU) has set up its own online service CORDIS. CORDIS provides information on technologies coming from E.U.-funded R&D programs, as well as a bulletin board of technologies available for licenses, or for collaborative R&D, manufacturing and marketing agreements.

The presence of these technological intermediaries suggests that this industry is gradually developing all the relevant features of a full-fledged market for technology. Further evidence of the increasing stability of this market is provided by the difficulties that some design firms have encountered when they have tried to integrate downstream in manufacturing. The different fortunes of two producers of broadband communications chips, MicroUnity and Broadcom, which both focused on the development of the next generation TV-based digital media

Table 3.9
Selected Technology Intermediaries and Their Services

Company	Description and Services	Web Site or Other Sources
HTE Research, U.S.	Specializes in semiconductor business. Provides information about intellectual properties (IP), design companies, market opportunities. Consultancy services in management of IP and licensing in semiconductors. Finds partners.	\<www.hte-sibs.com\>
First Principals Inc., U.S.	Technology assessment, sourcing, and transfer services (patent licensing). Information services about capital sources and industry/market analysis. Consultancy services in IP management decisions. Wide range of technologies covered.	\<www.firstprincipals.com\>
Refac, U.S.	Consultancy on licensing strategies, IP management, product design and engineering. Various technologies.	\<www.refac.com\>
Object Technology Licensing Corp., U.S.	Owns worldwide patent rights to inventions in object oriented technologies (e.g., network applications, development tools, multimedia). Finds potential users.	\<www.otlc.com\>
TechSearch International, U.S.	Provides intermediation and related services for technology licensing, especially in electronics and semiconductors.	\<www.techsearchinc.com\>
TechExchange Online, U.S.	Database of 20,000 new technologies and IP in several fields. Provides online access via subscription. Also provides online expert consultancies on patent licensing, venture capital, etc., via email.	\<www.teonline.com\>

British Technology Group, U.K.	180 employees company with offices in London, Philadelphia, Tokio—over half being scientists, engineers, patent attorneys, lawyers, and accountants. Provides wide range of services in technology transfer business. Goal is to create partnerships between technology users and sources of technology.	\<www.btgplc.com\>
Venture Capital On Line, U.S.	Links venture capital companies and technology start-ups and vice versa. Also offers services that streamline the deals.	Red Herring On Line News, "New Start-Up Plays Matchmaker", January 21, 1999
Steinbeis Foundation, Germany	Extensive network of German regional intermediaries and institutions that link companies asking for technology development services and product/engineering design to German universit es, technical schools, and government research labs.	\<www.steinebis.com\>
CORDIS, European Union	Official online service of the EU. Provides information on research and technology outputs of EU funded R&D programmes. Also provides bulletin board for demand and supply of technologies for licensing, co-development, co-marketing, and other agreements. Some few thousands technology deals listed.	\<www.cordis.lu\>

microprocessors, provide a useful comparison. MicroUnity attempted to integrate downstream by setting up its own fabrication plant. The considerable costs of semiconductor fabrication facilities led Micro-Unity to close its plants before production was started. This hurt its ability to raise financing. The focus on manufacturing and the lack of additional funding from the financial market prevented the company from investing in the development of other technologies.

In contrast, Broadcom stayed with a strategy of licensing its technology to established manufacturers and has found strong support from the financial market. By staying with its natural specialization in design, Broadcom is gradually developing other technologies. MicroUnity's failure is considered to be related in part to unrealized expectations about the growth of the broadband communications chip market. Possibly, MicroUnity's strategy might have succeeded if the market had taken off in the late 1990s, as the company expected. Its story is a clear warning for companies that do not have the required capital resources and organizational capabilities to move downstream. In addition, unlike Broadcom, the considerable investments MicroUnity made in manufacturing prevented it from expanding its portfolio of technologies that could be licensed to others (See *Red Herring Magazine* 1997.)[19]

Like the biotech industry discussed in the previous section, a significant fraction of the specialized technology suppliers in the semiconductor industry are likely to exit the market through mergers and acquisitions. Some business experts are also concerned about the quality of some of these firms' technologies. Further, one drawback of many of these companies' licensing strategy is that they may depend too much on the vagaries of the relationships with few key clients. Even a leading company like Rambus is said to have had some difficulties because Intel did not push the alliance with the vigor and speed that Rambus had hoped for, as Intel was largely distracted by events in its main PC business. Announcements of delays in the introduction of the Intel chip based on Rambus technology led to a fall in Rambus's stock price, after a significant rise in previous years. Moreover, Rambus still gets only 25 percent of its revenue from technology licenses, with the rest being accounted for by contract work.

But as the discussion of biotech highlighted, one should not confuse the fortunes of the individual firms with those of the industry as a whole. A natural feature of a market characterized by a high degree of "exploration" is that many companies are likely to fail. Even the life of some of the companies with leading technologies may not be longer than that of their technology. What is important, however, is that this pattern, whereby downstream semiconductor manufacturers or the design companies themselves look for specialists to supply "plug-and-play" circuits and subcomponents to be embedded in their products, is becoming increasingly common in the industry. This reinforces our theory that division of labor is gradually taking place. This structure may outlive the individual firms that currently compose it. Thus, while any consolidation and reduction in the number of ASICs and design companies would not come as a surprise, this is likely to act as a selection mechanism for firms operating in the upstream industry, rather than foretelling the impending demise of the entire sector.

Finally, one cannot fail to recognize the association between the new industry structure in the United States and the resurgence of the U.S. semiconductor industry in the world market during the 1990s. It is well known that during the previous decade, the U.S. industry faced intense competition from Japan, which came to dominate the world market of DRAMs and memories. The Japanese dominance in this market became so pronounced that by the mid–1980s, the share of the Japanese industry in the world semiconductor output rose above that of the United States. The U.S. response in the 1990s was to move into design-rich segments. This strategy produced a significant increase in their competitiveness vis-à-vis the Japanese and other foreign producers. Since the mid–1990s, the U.S. world semiconductor production share has risen well above that of Japan. The U.S. dominates the microcomponent segment with a world production share of nearly 75 percent, compared to Japan's share of less than 25 percent (see Langlois and Steinmueller 1998; Macher, Mowery, and Hodges 1999).

While many factors can account for the resurgence of the U.S. competitiveness in this sector, the new industry structure undoubtedly played an important role. The U.S. division of innovative labor in semiconductors introduced two main advantages. First, it gave rise to industry-wide economies in the innovation process, similar to those for the software industry discussed earlier. These economies, documented by Langlois and Robertson (1992) for the PC and stereo system sectors, arise from the presence of many independent component and subsystem providers which creates opportunity for industry-wide experimentation, magnifying the innovation potential of an industry. Put differently, this industry structure is particularly apt for conducting extensive explorations of new trajectories vis-à-vis the exploitation of existing ones. As suggested by Levinthal and March (1993), this enhances the learning processes and the rate of product innovation. Second, the increasing costs of semiconductor R&D and manufacturing implied that proper arrangements for risk-sharing among the many participants in the industry had to be devised, which turned out to be another natural consequence of the extensive networking in U.S. semiconductors during the 1990s.

3.6 Conclusions

This chapter discussed some developments in four high-tech industries wherein transactions in technology in various forms are taking place. We began by discussing the chemical engineering sector. This is probably one of the first examples of an extensive division of innovative labor in industry, whereby specialist producers of engineering and technological knowledge served a large number of downstream firms.

The story of the SEFs provides several interesting lessons. First, it shows how the advantages of specialist technology producers lie in the industry-wide economies of specialization gained by focusing on technology. Second, it is suggestive of one important factor encouraging specialization, namely the development of standard bodies of knowledge. Without chemical engineering as a well-defined body of knowledge and discipline, SEFs would have had to become involved in the production of specific chemicals in order to accumulate the expertise to design processes and plants for the those chemicals. The existence of SEFs also encouraged chemical firms to license their technologies, as we shall discuss more fully in chapter 7.

Software is a quintessential example of a market for knowledge services and technology. Though some types of software are akin to products, there are several cases in which software has proved to be a powerful instrument for codifying knowledge and technologies, thereby making technologies more easily transferable across independent organizations. The development of standard architectures and the increasing need for reuse are fostering the development of software components for sale. This is encouraging the rise of specialized producers, including individuals, which develop these components. Finally, there are many software companies that are focusing on licensing their technology rather than moving downstream into the business wherein their technologies are used.

Although the natures of the pharmaceutical and biotechnology sectors are different from those of software and electronics, some of its patterns regarding technology trade appear to be consistent with those of these other industries. The clear vertical division of innovative labor in this sector (e.g., biotechnology firms supplying technology to pharmaceutical firms downstream) is being enriched by more complex and networklike patterns. New biotechnology firms are entering market niches, and many are combining information technology and biotechnology. Moreover, several new biotech companies of the 1990s have focused on computerized drug research tools, which combine expertise in biochemistry and biotechnology with expertise in software, semiconductors, and computer sciences.

The focus on these tools illustrates another critical feature of the division of innovative labor. Instead of leveraging only the superior productivity of research, which their small and flexible organizational structures tend to provide, biotechnology firms can benefit from a much larger market size when they focus on developing tools or capabilities that cut across drugs or therapeutic categories (or varieties of agricultural chemicals, for that matter). In this way, specialized firms focusing on tools are able to tap a larger market than a pharmaceutical company that develops a new tool.

Finally, the growing market for chip design modules in the semiconductor business has striking similarities with software, biotech, and chemical processing industries discussed earlier. Standard architectures, well-defined bodies of knowledge, as well as the need for partitioning complex technological problems, and the need for reusing knowledge and design, are leading to increasing specialization. Fabless and even chipless companies which chose to license their technologies rather than engaging in downstream operations, are growing rapidly. Moreover, like software and biotech, the new specialization relies heavily on patents and intellectual property rights. While licensing and cross licensing of semiconductor patents by semiconductor manufacturers may be mainly in response to the complex nature of the product, patents are also being used increasingly as a means for defining the property rights on inventions to facilitate the trade of these property rights. The creation and enforcement of intellectual property, while far from sufficient for a division of innovative labor, is clearly a precondition.

II

Limitations and
Determinants

4 Context Dependence, Sticky Information, and the Limits of the Market for Technology

4.1 Introduction

The previous chapters provided quantitative and qualitative evidence, culled from a variety of sources, on the extent of transactions in the markets for technology. A natural question to ask at this stage is what factors limit or inhibit the growth of markets for technology? In this and the following two chapters, we examine what we regard as being the three main limitations to the rise of markets for technology.

The best known of these is the so-called appropriability problem. Property rights are far easier to define and enforce on tangible goods than on intangible goods such as designs, ideas, or technologies. In Arrow's formulation of the problem, once information or an idea is disclosed to a potential buyer, it is possible for that buyer to use the information without paying for it (Arrow 1962a). Anticipating this, a potential seller would be reluctant to disclose the idea, thereby denying potential buyers the opportunity to evaluate the merchandise. Of course, without being able to evaluate the idea, buyers would be unwilling to pay the price asked by the seller. The net result is that such transactions may not take place at all, a canonical example of what economists label "market failure."

Patents define a property right for certain types of knowledge and, in principle, provide a way for sellers to disclose information or knowledge while preventing others from using the information without the patent holder's permission. Since much useful technological knowledge, or know-how, is typically not protected by patents, Arrow's argument is taken to mean that appropriability problems might seriously retard interfirm technology transactions (Teece 1986; Williamson 1991; Balakrishnan and Koza 1993). As we show in chapter 5, the appropriability problem is for the most part overdrawn. Fairly simple and robust contracts can accomplish the efficient transfer of know-how.

Appropriability concerns are not the only factor affecting the efficiency of technology transactions; they are also limited by what we call "cognitive factors," which are rooted in the nature of knowledge and in the way in which humans comprehend and process knowledge.[1] Applying knowledge or technology developed in a specific context for a specific use, to another context and use, is rarely simple or straightforward. Often, the transfer of technology to another context requires extensive adaptations, the costs of which sometimes approach those required to develop the technology in the first place. Obviously, this can substantially reduce the efficiency of the transfer of already-developed technologies, and, in turn, reduce the benefits from a division of innovative labor. Additional constraints on the division of innovative labor include the difficulty of subdividing a given problem-solving task into subtasks. This limits the possibility of assigning selected parts of the problem to agents that do not interact systematically with one another, are physically distant, and belong to different organizations. In short, not only can it be difficult to transfer technologies from the contexts in which they are developed, but it can also be difficult to partition the innovation process into independent, self-contained tasks (Kline and Rosenberg 1986; von Hippel 1990).

As we see here, both the difficulty of subdividing tasks and the problem of using knowledge in new contexts are closely related to the underlying nature of knowledge. Technology transfer requires the technology recipient to undertake many of the activities that are part and parcel of the original innovation process (Cohen and Levinthal 1989; Rosenberg 1990). Therefore, technology transfer itself can be seen as a type of division of innovative labor, where the technology recipient and technology source are responsible for different, possibly overlapping sets of activities that innovation and commercialization involve. Although we focus here on the division of innovative labor, it should be clearly understood that the argument also applies, mutatis mutandis, to the problem of technology transfer and thus to markets for technology in general.

In this chapter, we explore the nature of these cognitive limitations and the factors that determine the severity of their effect. Section 4.2 argues that it is not tacitness alone that determines the cost of knowledge transfer, but also the extent to which knowledge is context-dependent. Whether or not knowledge is codified is not an intrinsic property of knowledge, but instead depends on the nature of the specific knowledge and on economic factors. Therefore, the growth of markets for a specific technology will vary according to the nature of the technology and the objectives and strategies of the firms involved.

Section 4.3 takes a brief detour into the issue of decomposing a problem into autonomous subproblems. Effective decomposability implies that the subproblems are not dependent on one another. This lack of interdependence implies that problem-solving activities can be decentralized with only a minimal cost of information transfer. This directly facilitates a division of innovative labor. In a more indirect sense, decomposability is also associated with a lower cost of technology transfer. The cost of technology transfer depends not only on the cost of transfer per "unit of information," but also on the size and frequency of such transfers. Section 4.4 addresses the parallels between decomposability in the production of tangible goods and decomposability in the production of knowledge. Section 4.5 discusses the link between decomposability and the ability to partition the process of innovation. Section 4.6 argues that advances in fundamental knowledge about natural phenomena, and the tremendous increases in computational resources have greatly enhanced the possibility for effective task partitioning, and therefore, for a division of innovative labor.

4.2 Knowledge as an Economic Resource

One of the starting points of the literature on the economics of innovation is the distinction made by Polanyi (1966) between the so-called tacit and codified dimensions of knowledge. Polanyi argues that a great deal of the knowledge that individuals possess is tacit, in the sense that it is difficult, if not impossible, for them to articulate, and therefore difficult to communicate and transfer to others. Nelson and Winter's (1982) evolutionary theory places this distinction into a meaningful economic framework by extending it from individuals to organizations. Nelson and Winter study how firms and economies grow and the role of technical change as one of the driving forces behind this process. They posit that firms are repositories of a complex set of knowledge bases, competencies, and skills, which are embodied in "organizational routines." The embodiment of knowledge, skills, and competencies into routines stems from the repetition of coordinated activities by the individuals operating inside the organization. Because of the often unintentional way in which routines are conducted, they create organizational knowledge and capabilities that are tacit, and therefore difficult to transfer and to imitate by other organizations. In contrast, knowledge that has been codified can easily be passed along in the form of patents, blueprints, white papers, journal articles, and increasingly, software programs.[2]

Winter (1987) made a significant advance by recognizing that knowledge, and hence corporate knowledge, is a more complex object than the simple dichotomy between codified and tacit suggests. He noted that for many purposes, what matters is the extent to which knowledge can be transferred or imitated. Accordingly, Winter (1987) developed a taxonomy whereby he distinguished among eight pairs of attributes of knowledge: articulable or tacit; teachable or unteachable; articulated or nonarticulated; observable or nonobservable; simple or complicated; system-independent or system-dependent; context-independent or context-dependent; monodisciplinary or transdisciplinary. The first element of each pair denotes forms of knowledge that make it easier to transfer across individuals or organizations, while the second makes transferability more difficult.

Winter is also one of the first authors to recognize that tacitness and codification are not inherent properties of knowledge. The counterpart of tacit knowledge in his taxonomy is not codified knowledge, but knowledge which is "articulable," suggesting that knowledge can indeed be articulated, and therefore made easier to transfer. The nature of knowledge can make it difficult to articulate—for example, when knowledge is complex or cannot be observed in use. In some cases, the cost of making the knowledge explicit can be so high so as to make it impractical to articulate. However, the important point is that the extent to which knowledge is codified, or more generally, the extent to which it is easy to transfer, is an economic decision rather than an inherent property of knowledge.

Winter also discusses the reasons why individuals or organizations may want to invest in making their knowledge explicit. The fear that rivals may competitively use a firm's knowledge encourages the firm to keep it in forms that reduce the risk of "leakage." In these cases, the knowledge will be kept in the intangible, tacit forms that are closer to the second set of attributes of Winter's taxonomy. In some cases, however, a firm could obtain higher economic value from its knowledge by supplying it to other parties who can provide complementary assets. For example, the producer of the knowledge may not have the necessary downstream assets to exploit it commercially. The producer may therefore find it profitable to license the technology or enter into cooperative agreements with other firms. In so doing, it will attempt to make its knowledge explicit for the purpose of reducing the cost of transferring it to others.

Nonaka (1991) makes a similar point (see also Nonaka and Takeuchi 1995), positing that organizational performance depends on how well the organization manages internal knowledge. He sees knowledge creation as a process of knowledge exchange among the individuals within an organization. Nonaka (1991) identifies four modes of knowledge exchange: From tacit to tacit (socialization), from explicit to explicit (combination), from tacit to explicit (articulation), from explicit to tacit (internalization).[3] Socialization, or the exchange of tacit knowledge, requires that individuals act and operate together in physical proximity, exchanging knowledge that cannot be transferred through articles, blueprints, and the like. Combination is the act of joining together pieces of explicit knowledge, for example, the combination of different individuals' knowledge into a manual or workbook. Nonaka argues that socialization and combination are not really actions that create new knowledge, as they simply put together or transfer pieces of existing knowledge. New knowledge is created in the other two cases: articulation and internalization. Articulation is the act of making tacit knowledge explicit, of deeply understanding one's tacit expertise and casting it in standard forms such as explicit routines, blueprints, and embodying it in software programs. Internalization is the act of making these blueprints part of the deep-seated knowledge base and skills of the individuals and the organization, enabling them to use the knowledge naturally and repeatedly within their ordinary activities without making reference to the blueprints.

Unlike Winter, Nonaka looks at knowledge exchange within an organization and its diffusion across the individuals that belong to it, rather than across organizations. However, like Winter, Nonaka emphasizes that the act of making knowledge tacit or explicit is an economic or managerial decision rather than an attribute of the knowledge itself. Of course, different pieces of knowledge may be more or less amenable to the conversion from tacit to explicit or vice versa.

Kogut and Zander (1992) provide another important contribution to our understanding of these issues. They argue that markets for technologies may not exist for reasons other than the classical market failure or appropriability problems. There are cognitive aspects to be taken into account. Specifically, the fact that knowledge or technologies are embedded into organizational routines seriously constrains the choice to transfer them to other agents. In a later paper, Kogut and Zander (1993) offer some rare empirical evidence on this issue. They analyze eighty-one instances of international technology transfer by one hundred Swedish firms, differentiating between transfers to unaffiliated parties and those to wholly owned subsidiaries. Using a questionnaire survey and interviews about the technologies being transferred, they constructed measures of the codifiability, teachability, and complexity of the technology, along with other attributes to use as controls. Their results indicate that technology transferred to unaffiliated parties is more likely to be codifiable and teachable. Conversely, more complex technology lacking these qualities is less likely to be transferred to unaffiliated parties.

In addition, Kogut and Zander (1993) compare their results with those in the literature. For instance, Teece (1977) analyzed twenty-seven projects, and estimated the cost of transferring technologies to other parties ranged from 2 percent to 59 percent of the total. He also showed that transfer costs were lower in the case of more mature technologies and when more firms were using the same technology. Kogut and Zander correctly point out that these variables are proxies for more fundamental attributes of technology. In their own analysis, they use the age of the technology at the time of transfer and the number of firms using the same technology as additional measures of the maturity of technology. Using a logit regression specification, they find that these variables are statistically insignificant, yet codifiability and teachability retain their magnitude and significance. Kogut and Zander (1993) conclude that the firm is a more efficient vehicle for transferring complex, tacit, and difficult to teach technologies. Markets for technologies, in contrast, are more likely to arise when technologies are more codified and therefore easier to transfer across organizational boundaries.

Following Winter (1987) and Nonaka (1991), Arora and Gambardella (1994a) argue that the extent to which knowledge can be made more or less explicit is fundamentally an economic decision. The payoff to codifying knowledge is increased when it must be transferred and applied broadly (see also Dasgupta and David 1994). Similarly, fuller and deeper theoretical understanding of problems reduces the cost of codification. Articulation requires other changes as well. The knowledge must be recast into universal categories rather than idiosyncratic and narrow ones. With more precise instrumentation and increased computational power, articulated knowledge could be exploited more fully, further increasing the payoff to codification. In other words, technological knowledge does not exist in codified form simply because it has matured and become standardized. Rather, the "changing technology of technical change," the term Arora and Gambardella (1994a) use to point to the greater scientific intensity of engineering disciplines and the increased use of formal mathematical and computers models, offers the possibility of casting knowledge in more universal and less context-dependent forms. In turn, using more universal representations for knowledge makes it easier to use knowledge in contexts different from those in which it was generated. Simply put, knowledge can be transferred more effectively across space, organizations, and domains.

For example, as suggested by the semiconductor and biotechnology case studies in the previous chapter, the increased availability and falling costs of computational power has enabled many companies to make increasing use of simulations in product and process design and development. Unlike actual physical tests, simulations require that one first develop a software program that mimics the conditions under which the object is tested in the real world. But to do so, one must first understand the static and dynamic properties under which the process takes place, and translate them into mathematical and software language. By its very nature, this means articulating and codifying these properties—and the underlying knowledge embodied in individuals or their organizations—into general and abstract forms. Similarly, better theoretical understanding of problems means elucidating them, thereby making the underlying knowledge of a phenomenon more explicit. These are powerful forces in making knowledge less context-dependent, and therefore more amenable to interorganizational transfer.

4.3 The Complex Organizational Design of a Division of Innovative Labor

Because of the form in which knowledge is held, even if the unit cost of knowledge transfer is low, total transfer costs might be high if it must be exchanged frequently. That is, a division of innovative labor is also affected by the interdependencies between the various activities or stages involved in the innovation process. Simply put, successful division of innovative labor requires that the innovation process be decomposable.

Herbert Simon's work (e.g., Simon 1962) explains that the decomposition of a complex problem into separate, more elementary subproblems, is an organizational design issue. The extent to which one can design an overall problem-solving activity so as to reduce the interdependence among tasks influences the extent to which one can create coarser or finer partitions. For instance, the precapitalistic artisan, who performed all the activities related to the conceptualization and manufacture of his products, found it difficult, both mentally and functionally, to separate his business into independent operations. In contrast, the Fordist system of manufacturing and Adam Smith's pin factory were each able to attain very fine partitions.

The decomposition of a complex problem into relatively independent tasks is particularly difficult in the development and commercialization of new technologies. This is because the subtasks are intertwined and difficult to disentangle from one another. Often, these tasks draw upon a number of different bodies of knowledge and practice, and a variety of scientific disciplines. Vincenti's (1990) history of the growth of engineering knowledge in the aeronautical industry illustrates this point in the context of engineering design. Engineering design requires the mastery of theoretical knowledge in several disciplines, fundamental and operational design knowledge and concepts, the ability to perform and understand practical experiments, the design and creation of tools, a deep understanding of the function of the device in practice, knowledge and information about the manufacturability of the product at different scales, and information about users' needs and characteristics (see also Freeman 1982; Rosenberg 1982). Given this complexity, the innovation process, from research to engineering design, to manufacturing and commercialization, relies on the work of a number of different groups of experts (teams), each specialized in some area. These activities, however, are difficult to conduct in isolation and imply a great deal of communication between various groups. For instance, the development of flight related quality specifications for airplanes during the 1930s required such close relationships between aeronautical engineers and testing pilots that Vincenti labeled the former "research pilots" and the latter "flight research engineers" (Vincenti 1990, 76).

The automobile industry provides additional examples of the interdependence among several specialists and tasks in engineering design. In the late 1980s, it became clear that the ability to create more effective product designs in shorter times was a key to the growing success of Japanese car manufacturers as compared to their Western rivals (see Womack, Jones, and Roos 1990, and especially Clark and Fujimoto 1991). This ability was traced to the Japanese manufacturers' strategy of integrating the various stages of product development. For example, in Japanese firms, product design was intimately connected with process design, so as to avoid potential conflicts between the overall design of a new car and its components, and the process to manufacture them. Similarly, marketing considerations and information about users were considered early on in the product development process. One key advantage of the Japanese approach was that the early connections among the various functions reduced the need for later, and much more costly, product or process design changes.[4]

These interactions, along with the difficulty of organizing the innovation process around independent tasks, imply that market-based contractual mechanisms for procuring innovation services may entail serious transaction costs. Teece (1988) addressed this issue, arguing that the interdependencies among tasks in the innovation process, and the natural uncertainty associated with development and commercialization of innovations, create at least three sources of transaction costs. First, it is hard to provide detailed specifications of the task requirements at the outset of the innovation process. These specifications can be defined more precisely while undertaking the process, necessitating contracts that are largely incomplete, and which potentially leave either party open to opportunistic behavior by the other.[5] Second, if a company develops tight interactions with one technology supplier, the interplay of relationships may generate sunk costs, which can give rise to switching costs and "lock-in" problems. Finally, releasing precontract information to bidders may require the companies to share valuable proprietary information, and increases the risk that competitors will discover its R&D plans.

Teece (1988) concludes that these reasons explain why the creation, development, and commercialization of new products and processes have traditionally been integrated within a firm. Grossman and Hart (1986) and Hart and Moore (1990) argue that vertical integration, and the authority it confers, helps solve the problems of opportunistic behavior that arise when contracts are incomplete. In the case of innovation, this means that the firm can specify and organize the actions of the various agents involved in the innovation process while the process takes place.[6] Though not part of this framework, integration has other benefits as well. For example, being part of the same organization helps the various specialists to acquire a better understanding of each other's problems and needs, to share common objectives and beliefs, and to adopt a common language (Arrow 1974; Teece 1988). This facilitates collaboration and information exchange, and increases the productivity of the innovation process itself.[7]

Teece (1988) points out that the problem is more severe in the case of more complex technologies, such as systemic technologies that require profound interdependencies among many activities, as compared to "stand-alone" innovations (see also Chesbrough and Teece 1996). He therefore acknowledges that the advantages of integrating the innovation tasks within the same organization can differ across industries and technologies. However, he also provides numerous examples showing how the lack of proper integration of R&D with manufacturing and commercialization led to poor innovation performance. Similarly, Vincenti (1990) highlights the role played by the National Advisory Committee for Aeronautics (NACA) located in Langley Field, Virginia, a U.S. government research center that was responsible for many of the technological developments during the first half of the twentieth century discussed in his book. Apart from basic engineering research and design capabilities, NACA had facilities to undertake full scale wind tunnel tests and other experiments, including actual test flights. Moreover, many NACA projects were undertaken in collaboration with aeronautic producers like Douglas or airlines like United or Pan American.

To summarize, the difficulties in separating the innovation activities into independent tasks explain why markets for technology have not been common thus far. Correspondingly, division of labor in innovation has been less pronounced than in other economic activities. In this respect, one limitation of technology as an economic good is that the transaction costs associated with the complexity and interdependence of the innovation activities can prevent the companies from "decoupling" them from one other, and from other activities of the firm, like manufacturing and commercialization. But this also means that many companies have had to give up the opportunity of exploiting industry- and market-wide economies of scale in technology production and R&D, exploiting only the more limited economies at the level of the firm.

4.4   Modularity

A section of the management literature has argued for an isomorphism between product decomposability and organizational decomposability, arguing in essence that if companies can divide products into separate components or "modules," the organizations responsible for commercializing the product can also be modularized. It is easy, with suitable relabeling, to read into this a theory of division of innovative labor. In other words, Simon's notion of product design, where the design should maximize interaction within components and minimize interactions between components, is argued to apply to optimal organizational design as well.

The idea of modularity has been used to understand the way companies design their products, and the implications for the generation of innovation. Clark (1985) noted that product design is a hierarchical activity, with a "core" design concept around which the various components are conceived and designed. This led to the idea that many new products have a general "architecture" which specifies the way the components have to interact with one another and within themselves. The architecture can be designed and developed independently from the individual components (Henderson and Clark 1990; see also Abernathy and Clark 1985). One implication of this approach is that it is possible to improve components independently from one another, provided of course that the architectural interfaces are not affected. As noted by Henderson and Clark (1990), this adds the possibility of "architectural innovations" that may imply radical changes in the components (e.g., when moving from blade and motor room fans to air conditioning) or not (e.g., from large ceiling-mounted room fans to portable fans).

Modularity in product design has received some attention in recent years due to its perceived advantages for innovation, particularly in view of shorter product life cycles, which reduce time-to-market and the growing value of product customization. Baldwin and Clark (1997) note that while modularity in production has existed for some time, modularity in product design is a relatively new trend.[8] The basic distinction is between products that can be looked at as relatively integrated "appliances" (e.g., the phonographs before the 1930s, which were basically composed of one entire piece—see Langlois and Robertson 1992), and products that are composed of many different and interchangeable parts. The computer industry led this revolution, especially with the introduction of the first modular computer, the IBM System/360 in 1964. Before the IBM System/360, each model of computer was designed with its own specific operating system, processor, peripherals, and application software. In contrast, the System/360 was conceived and designed as a family of machines of different sizes, which were suited for different applications, but shared designs of components and similar operating software or peripherals (see Langlois 1992; Langlois and Robertson 1992).

This had natural implications for innovation. Most notably, provided that one did not change the required interfaces, a great deal of innovation could take place in the components without requiring the redesign of other components or of the entire architecture. Of course, sometimes significant innovation in the components implied that they could no longer be accommodated within the available architecture. For example, as noted by Langlois (1992) and Langlois and Robertson (1992), the forty-column display of the Apple II model and its inability to run CP/M operating software (one of the standards in the early 1980s) and the limited internal memory of the IBM PC's 8088 microprocessor, necessitated the development of more advanced models with new architectures. Yet a great deal of innovation in the components could take place even within the same models.

Although this process was most apparent in the evolution of the computer industry, the approach toward a modular design is evident in other industries as well (e.g., Pine 1993; Langlois and Robertson 1992). This trend also introduced some fundamental changes in industry structure, since modularity makes it possible for distinct firms to independently design and improve components. Again, the history of the PC exemplifies this. Once the Apple II and the IBM PC were conceived as modular systems, several firms entered the market specializing in the design and innovation of various "adds-on" to the hardware and software parts supplied with the machine. Component suppliers have always existed in the industry, but the novelty of the computer industry in the 1980s was that these suppliers did not produce parts according to well-defined specifications of the manufacturer. The modular nature of the product meant that the suppliers had greater autonomy in designing them (as long as the components were compatible with the system interface), and this meant greater opportunities for independent innovation. Other authors have noted the implications for industry structure. Sanchez (1995) and Sanchez and Mahoney (1996), for instance, argued that modularity in product design brings about modular organizations. In particular, they emphasize that the standard interfaces of a modular design provide a sort of "embedded coordination" among independent firms and innovators, which can coordinate their activities independently of a superior managerial authority. For instance, the firm that commissions the innovative design to a specialized supplier no longer needs to specify all the underlying features of the good, provided that the supplier can generate a device that fits the required interface specifications. This reduces the transaction costs, and enhances the opportunities for market-based contractual arrangements. Baldwin and Clark (1997), while recognizing the potential benefits, also note that modular systems that are also open (i.e., where the interfaces are not proprietary standards) make market leaders more vulnerable to competition. While modularity can accelerate overall product innovation, because of the contribution of several specialists, the presence of many specialists can also lead to tougher competition and greater entry (see also Farrell, Monroe, and Saloner 1998; Arora, Bokhari, and Morel, 2000).[9]

4.5 Task-Partitioning and "Sticky" Information

The idea of modularity in the design of artifacts has an obvious analogue in modularity in problem solving itself. Eric von Hippel (1990, 1994, and 1998) has made an important contribution to our understanding of the economics of partitioning problem-solving tasks. Building on Simon's idea (Simon 1962) of decomposable systems, von Hippel notes that greater efficiency can be achieved by dividing the overall problem-solving effort into tasks, showing maximal interaction within them and minimal interactions across them. In doing so, one can reduce one fundamental source of inefficiency, notably that actions in one particular innovation stage or activity may require information or even changes of actions in several other innovation stages or activities. This is a source of inefficiency because of the extensive coordination and information flows that this process requires and the potential disruptions that may be brought about by these interdependencies.

As a heuristic example, there is a straightforward reason why the design of an airplane is partitioned so that one company designs the aircraft body and another designs the engine, instead of the first company designing the first half of the airplane, while the other designing the second half. The latter arrangement would require far more problem solving at the boundary between the two tasks than the former. However, von Hippel (1990) also suggests that the extent to which one can partition the innovation process can vary across industries and technologies. For instance, in the production of printed circuits there is little interdependence between circuit designers and manufacturers, who can accommodate the production of a variety of circuits without any process adjustment. In contrast, in the automobile industry there exists a large amount of overlapping information and joint problem-solving activities between the designers of the sheet-metal parts that make up the surface of an automobile and the designers of the dies used to produce these parts. In this case, it would be difficult to partition this problem into independent tasks.

Von Hippel (1990) also argues that the extent to which the innovation process is integrated within one firm instead of being divided among many specialists depends on the extent to which an innovation activity can be effectively task-partitioned. Thus, an effective partitioning of the tasks that comprise the innovation process can have implications for the division of labor among firms and the role of suppliers. Firms could specialize in different segments of the innovation process and, in addition to reducing information exchange costs, an effective partitioning may also yield economies of specialization.

In subsequent work, von Hippel (1994, 1998) analyzes in greater depth the role of tacit knowledge in task partitioning. He argues that the development of innovations often relies upon information that is in the domain of different agents (e.g., the user and the manufacturer), and that some of this information can be "sticky" in the sense that it can only be transferred at very high costs to other parties. This information arises from tacit knowledge and the routines that are normally associated with the ordinary activities performed by each agent or organization. Thus, for instance, while a producer would draw upon its knowledge about the technical features of the product, the user would rely upon his or her own knowledge about the need to be satisfied and the context in which the good has to be employed. The traditional approach in this type of situation has been to try to move the sticky information. For example, in the development of information systems, the system developers would first undertake a great deal of work at the user site (e.g., a bank or an insurance company) to understand the needs for the system to be produced. Once they acquired this information, the developers returned to their company and designed it. By contrast, von Hippel argues that a more effective approach would be to move the locus of the problem-solving effort. The user and the producer could then draw only upon their own local and idiosyncratic information sets, without having to move between locations.

Hofman and Rockart (1994) and Brady, Tiernay, and Williams (1992) discuss case studies in which they show how information system providers increasingly develop information system "templates" that are built rapidly from initial user specifications. The templates are passed on to the users who try them and single out problems or functions that do not satisfy their requirements. The system is returned to the producer, who performs the required adjustments, and the process is repeated until the product is perfected. Through these successive iterations, the users and the producers no longer move the information, but they move the problem-solving activity. Neither party needs to acquire the sticky information of the other. Each relies on his own information.

This approach is naturally related to task partitioning as one way to achieve effective iterations by dividing the problem into tasks that use only the sticky information of one party and little of the sticky information of the other. In this respect, von Hippel adds a second element to his framework. Under certain conditions it is possible to "unstick" the information. To show this, he presents a detailed example of the development of the application-specific integrated circuits (ASICs). As discussed in the previous chapter, integrated circuits can be of amazing complexity, with millions of transistors or small systems of electronic components ("gates") in a single chip. Along with other features (e.g., size, number, and types of transistors and gates), the way these components are interconnected determines the function of the device. Unlike more standardized products (e.g., the circuits commonly used in a PC), ASICs are integrated circuits designed for specific applications, such as telecommunications switches, cellular phones, and digital cameras. ASICs therefore require special features (e.g., high power, in the case of military applications) and special interconnections among the various electronic components.

The traditional way in which ASICs have been developed is through "full customization." This means the product is designed and developed "from scratch," according to the requirements of the users. This often implies close interaction between the circuit designers, who specify the interconnections and hence the function of the circuit, and are normally located at the user end; and the semiconductor device designers, who know how to design and develop the product, and are normally located at the manufacturer end. These two groups of engineers have rather different competencies, and typically semiconductor engineers know little about circuit design, and conversely, the circuit designers may not be aware of the potential and constraints under which semiconductor device designers operate. In recent years, two trends have contributed to unstick the information located at the supplier end and separate the tasks to be performed by the semiconductor and circuit designers.

The first trend was the development of a new ASIC architecture that reduced the amount of semiconductor engineering information required by a circuit designer to design his own chip. The idea is that the manufacturers develop small, prespecified systems that perform specific functions likely to be employed for different uses. As a consequence, the manufacturer no longer has to consider the overall specialized circuit to be produced for a given user. Such prespecified systems can be combined with each other and the combination allows the circuit designers to simply choose the functions that they need and interconnect them in the desired ways. In so doing, the circuit designer does not need to know how the function was built. He only needs to know how this function interconnects with other functions to obtain the desired performance of the device—that is, he only needs to rely on information located in his own information set.[10]

The second trend has been the development of software tools, located at both the designer and manufacturer end, that coordinate the integration between the two information sets. Software tools available at the designers' end enable them to translate their functional specifications into a description of a network of interconnected logic elements that will perform the desired function, and simulate these functions so as to be able to correct errors or problems. Given these functional specifications, software tools at the manufacturer's end translate them into the physical geometry of the device. Typically successive iterations between the designers and the manufacturers take place before a final design is agreed upon, and the information in the manufacturer's tools is sent to the computerized fabrication equipment.

Thus, the development of devices defined in terms of functions and of software tools offered the opportunity to unstick the manufacturer information, and reduced the need for direct and systematic interactions between the two key players in the ASIC design and development process. In addition, von Hippel shows that the new approach has rapidly diffused in the industry, and it is now becoming the standard way to design and develop these products. His figures indicate that the total market size of ASIC increased from $4.7 billion in 1986 to $13.5 billion in 1994, and to a predicted $23.6 billion in 1999. Moreover, while in 1986 full custom devices represented 52 percent of the total ASIC market, this percentage dropped to 20 percent in 1994 and to an estimated 12 percent in 1999 (von Hippel 1998, 636).

The ASIC example suggests a few final remarks. First, the task partitioning implied by the new approach induced the entry of many new firms focusing on specialized tasks (see also chapter 3), which, in turn, gave rise to an upsurge in market transactions for the exchange of the technologies. Second, it is obvious that the role of these suppliers differs substantially from that of suppliers that produce components according to well-defined specifications of the final manufacturers. In other words, these are independent suppliers, not mere sub-contractors. Third, in an obvious analogy with codification of tacit knowledge, unsticking sticky information depends on the growth of computer and software technologies and the resulting advances in computational capability. Finally, also analogous to codification of tacit knowledge, unsticking sticky information is an investment process. As the ASIC example shows, firms had to devise ways to incorporate the manufacturer's knowledge bases into well-defined tools, or to develop new circuit architectures that would enable them to prepackage electronic functions. Moreover, unsticking the information meant that the manufacturers had to generalize their knowledge bases and products. Their devices were no longer a series of full custom products linked to a number of specific applications, but a set of more standardized, general-purpose elements that could be adjusted to fit several uses.[11]

4.6   Task-Partitioning in Innovation and the Technology of Technical Change

The problem of effectively partitioning the development of a complex product is subtler than modularization. One reason is that even though one can build systems by using autonomously designed modules, these products may still entail a certain degree of what has been called "systemic uncertainty" (Bonaccorsi and Pammolli 1996). Systemic uncertainty means that even if one knows and has perfectly tested the functions performed by the different modules, there is still uncertainty about whether the system as a whole will perform as expected. This is because, while the individual modules can be independently designed and tested for their performance, the functioning of the interfaces among them can only be assessed when the full system is assembled and tested.

In the development of software systems or superchips, the test of the whole system can be done to some degree through simulators. But in the case of large systemic products, like an airplane or a large manufacturing plant, simulations are clearly inadequate. In the first place, airplanes or plants have to operate in a much more complex environment than chips or software, and that environment is more difficult to accurately reconstruct in a simulator. Second, large complex systems are subject to scale-up problems. That is, the properties of the system can change at larger scales because of the increased importance of phenomena that were negligible or did not occur at the pilot or prototype scale. Testing the whole system is the only way to assess the interconnections among the modules.

In one of the first systematic empirical examinations of the link between modularity and division of labor, Brusoni and Prencipe (1998) discuss the cases of innovation in the aero-engine industry and in chemical plants. These are complex systems composed of thousands of highly interdependent components. Moreover, they are developed through the contributions of several firms and with high involvement of the users themselves. Especially over the past decade, the design and development of these two products have led the trend toward design modularity. For instance, in the case of aero-engines, not only have these products been increasingly designed as interconnections of independent modules, but the leading producers have also gradually outsourced a growing share of design activities to their suppliers.

However, the leading producers have not given up their competencies and in-house knowledge in the component technological areas. This is because, with systemic uncertainty, the final integration of these parts requires a deep understanding of the functions of the various modules by someone able to detect errors or the reasons why the system does not work as expected. Brusoni and Prencipe (1998) conclude that in the development of these products the leading producers preserve an important role as technology integrators, and therefore continue to maintain in-house expertise in a broad range of component technologies even though they outsource component design. Moreover, when they do outsource, they tend to provide fairly precise specifications to their suppliers. In short, large complex systems may well exhibit features that limit the extent to which one can create an effective division of innovative labor.

In addition to the narrow technological concern of ensuring that all modules operate together in predictable and expected ways, technology integration has another aspect. Langlois (1999) points out that, in environments marked by Knightian uncertainty—transaction costs include not only the problems of hold-up, bargaining, and imperfect contracts, but also what Langlois calls dynamic transaction costs. For instance, Langlois argues that Henry Ford's consolidation of all production steps in a vertically integrated company was critical to the successful introduction of the Model T in the 1920s. As is well known, the Model T was the result of a successful process innovation. It required, among other things, new types of machinery and equipment. In some cases, existing suppliers were either unable to provide such equipment, or believed, incorrectly, that it was not possible to produce equipment that conformed to the specifications that Ford provided. This prompted Ford to integrate backwards, developing some of the necessary equipment in-house. Langlois argues that had the various stages of production remained under separate ownership, Ford would have had difficulty experimenting with new techniques, machines and parts, all which had to fit with each other. In other words, until the overall architecture of the product, in this case the Model T, was settled, the costs of coordinating the actions of independent parts suppliers and machine makers would have been restrictively high.

A second related limitation to an effective task-partition of the innovation process is due to the distinctive properties of knowledge as an economic commodity. In particular, since buyers of knowledge have to be knowledgeable themselves, a division of innovative labor will require that even firms downstream in the innovation process will have to invest in substantial in-house absorptive capacity (Cohen and Levinthal 1989; Rosenberg 1990). Moreover, in-house capability can also act as an effective outside option in negotiating with technology suppliers (e.g., Gans and Stern 2000).

The need for in-house technical capability, for absorptive capacity or for improving bargaining power, injects a continuous dynamic tension into any division of innovative labor. If the producer of the system has to keep in-house capabilities in the component technologies, he can always switch back to in-house production and design, thereby eliminating the division of labor. Indeed, if maintaining absorptive capacity requires investing in research and development in the relevant field, as aero-engine manufacturers appear to do even in areas where they rely on suppliers, it is likely that such in-house research efforts may scale up to the point where outside technology suppliers may become unnecessary. More to the point, outside technology may be perceived as unnecessary or inferior to in-house technology. Since the in-house R&D departments are likely to be those used to screen and evaluate outside options, self-interest, pride, and blind spots may all create a "not-invented-here" (NIH) syndrome (Allen and Katz 1982).

To be sure, this limitation is another way to reaffirm the same point. The need to keep in-house absorptive capacity means that the interfaces between the tasks are not always well defined, and that a lot of problem-solving takes place at the boundaries between tasks. That is, systemic uncertainty, or other factors implying that one party has to keep an in-depth understanding of the many technologies that compose a complex product, are natural manifestations of the lack of a standardized structure of the architectural interfaces. As noted by Sanchez and Mahoney

(1996), this suggests that there are limited opportunities for "embedded coordination," and one has to resume stronger forms of managerial coordination.

This leads to our final considerations. The recent evolution of technology and knowledge bases, or the "changing technology of technical change," has created greater opportunities for task partitioning (Arora and Gambardella 1994a). As von Hippel also notes, "the primary irreversible factor that we speculate is making user-based design an increasing attractive option is technological advance" (von Hippel 1998, 642). For instance, he notes that while in principle it has always been possible to create and store information about a manufacturer's technology in a booklet or technical guide, the fact that that information can be embedded in a software tool or simulator makes it much easier to use it without continuous guidance and interactions with its producer.[12]

Specifically, the main force behind the changing technology of technical change is the complementarity between increased computational power and greater scientific and technological understanding of problems. Biotechnology is one of the most apparent examples of this complementarity. As discussed in the previous chapter, the industry is witnessing a convergence between information technology and the life sciences. Bioinformatics has given rise to several specialist biotech companies focusing on automated testing tools, combinatorial chemistry techniques to develop the structure of millions of new chemical compounds, and genetic databases and related software and "chips" to analyze them and help identify relevant pathologies and assess new drugs or therapies. These are tools that, like those discussed in the case of software or microelectronics, are useful for unsticking specific bodies of knowledge and information (e.g., knowledge about genetics, and information about gene functions and characteristics), and making them available to other researchers and agents whose comparative advantages lie in other bodies of knowledge or assets (e.g., the large firms).[13]

4.7 Conclusions

Whether technology and innovation are to be integrated within one firm or can be the subject of a division of labor has been the topic of a considerable debate. Stigler (1951) himself argued that division of labor could also embrace the innovation process and industry evolution would lead to the rise of stand-alone R&D labs selling their research outcomes to other parties. Thus far, this prediction had not come true.

Mowery (1983) showed that employment of scientific personnel in independent research organizations dropped between the two wars. More generally, the historical evidence suggests that since the nineteenth century, manufacturing companies have increasingly internalized R&D operations (Chandler 1990). Nelson and Winter (1982) and Teece (1988), along with others, have explained this by emphasizing the tacit and idiosyncratic nature of knowledge and technologies.

Stigler's emphasis on the benefits from division of innovative labor and the later emphasis on transaction costs and other types of barriers are two different starting points for thinking about a complex problem. Indeed, the extent of the division of innovative labor depends both on the efficiency benefits to be realized, but also on the costs involved. In addition to the well-known concerns about appropriability, there are other types of costs. These costs arise because a division of innovative labor entails transferring information across organizations. The costs depend on how frequently the information has to be transferred and the cost per transfer. Roughly speaking, the state in which information is held, the extent to which it is context-dependent and codified, affects the unit cost of transfer. The frequency of transfer depends also on the interdependence between the different actors in the innovation process. In other words, if the innovation process can be effectively decomposed, this reduces the frequency with which the different actors have to exchange information, making it economically feasible to partition the process among them.

Advances in scientific understanding decrease the costs of articulating tacit and context-dependent knowledge and reduce the cost of technology transfer. Further, such knowledge can be embodied in tools, particularly software tools, which make the knowledge available to others cheaply and in a useful form. We believe that advances in science and the tremendous increase in computational capabilities have greatly contributed to extending the division of innovative labor. Such advances have been uneven in time and across industries, consistent with interindustry differences in the division of innovative labor itself. But any division of labor is subject to contradictory dynamic pressures. In particular, the need to maintain absorptive capacity and preserve bargaining power leads large users of technology to make substantial investments in in-house R&D. As well, since the costs of bargaining and contracting with independent firms can be substantial, particularly when there is uncertainty about technological or economic options, firms may maintain in-house R&D as a strategic option. The in-house

R&D investments can, over time, reduce the system-wide benefits of a division of labor in innovation.

In our view, therefore, it is unlikely that a division of labor or a market for technology will exist in all industries or at all times. Though we strongly believe that such markets can have substantial benefits by encouraging more extensive use of existing technologies and an increase in the rate of technological change, the absence of such markets may not always reflect missed opportunities, but instead reflect the important costs that such markets entail.

5   Intellectual Property Rights and the Licensing of Know-How

5.1   Introduction

Context dependence and stickiness of information not only directly increase the cost of transfer of technology but also have an indirect impact on technology transfer across organizational boundaries.[1] This impact is due to the possibility of opportunistic behavior that arise because context dependence increases the likelihood that some technical knowledge is tacit.

The costs of transferring tacit knowledge are particularly salient when the transfer takes place across different organizations for at least two reasons. First, there is a greater cognitive distance between organizations, which raises the cost of transferring tacit and context dependent information. Different units within an organization are more likely to evolve a common shared understanding and a common code for communicating the knowledge than different units in separate organizations. The shared context lowers the relative cost of transferring tacit knowledge inside an organization. Second, the transfer of know-how is difficult to verify by a third party such as a court, due to the tacit nature of know-how. Contracts involving the transfer of tacit knowledge—henceforth know-how—are therefore subject to the risk of opportunism.

Specifically, arm's-length contracts for know-how are marked by double-sided, moral hazard problems. For instance, once the licensor has been paid, she may not send her best engineers or managers over to the licensee to help or provide the technical service, or she may provide the licensee's engineers with only limited exposure to her own operations. Some important trade secrets may not be revealed to the licensee. Given this possibility of moral hazard on the part of the licensor, the licensee would like to make the bulk of the payments after being satisfied that the full technology, including the tacit part, has been transferred.

However, once the licensee has learned the know-how, she cannot be forced to "unlearn" it. Hence, a licensee may refuse to pay the agreed upon amount in full after the know-how is transferred.

There are ways through which the efficiency of contracts for know-how can be enhanced. These include reputation building in the context of repeated contracting, and the use of output-based royalties. However, output-based royalties may not solve the moral hazard problem. Indeed, the amount of output produced by the licensee is often private information and hard to assess by the licensor or a third party. In addition, output-based royalties can handicap a licensee in the product market, especially in oligopolistic markets (Katz and Shapiro 1985), and possibly for this reason, the use of output-based royalties to compensate the licensor for technical assistance is uncommon (Contractor 1981).[2] Reputation building through repeated contracts, while a potential solution, requires a greater degree of integration among the partners. Markets normally imply "anonymous" transactions, and our aim here is to see whether transactions for technology can arise even without established reputation and long-term relationships among the contractors.

In this chapter we propose another solution. Key to our argument is that efficient contracts for the exchange of technology can be written by exploiting the complementarity between know-how and any other technology input that the licensor can use as a "hostage." With complementarity, the use of the know-how is more valuable when used in conjunction with the complementary technology input that can be withdrawn. This allows the licensor to use her ability to withdraw the latter to protect herself against opportunistic behavior by the licensee.

The licensee protects herself by postponing a part of the payment till the know-how has been transferred. If the licensee does not make the second payment, the licensor can withdraw from the contract and withdraw the use of the complementary input. As long as the additional benefit of having the know-how and the complementary input from the licensor is greater than the second period payment, the licensee will make the payment. As long as the second period payment is greater than the cost to the licensor of supplying know-how and the complementary input, the licensor will honor the contract as well. Thus, the problem of opportunism can be mitigated through simple and self-enforcing contracts.

Patents and other types of intellectual property (IP) can function well as the complementary input provided by the licensor. Thus, a prototypical case would be one in which the technology to be transferred is composed of both a patented component and complementary know-how (e.g., experience with using the technology). In such cases, the licensor can withdraw the patent rights from the licensee if dissatisfied about the realization of the contract. With strong, well-defined patents, the licensee cannot derive much value from the know-how alone. Other types of complementary inputs include proprietary machines and equipment, or the engineering and construction services.

The role of intellectual property rights (IPRs) in our discussion is especially interesting in light of the prominence of this issue in many high-tech industries today. Our argument gives a new twist to the role of patents. Their traditional role has been thought to be one of providing ex ante incentives to innovate. But this comes at the cost of restricting the diffusion of the technology. Thus, strong protection of intellectual property can be socially undesirable ex post. However, our analysis suggests that stronger IPRs can enhance the efficiency of technology transfers, and hence encourage the diffusion of technology, including parts of the technology that patents do not protect.

The chapter is organized as follows. Section 5.2 discusses the contracting problems implicit in the sale of know-how. Section 5.3 develops a basic model that formalizes our intuition. This section contains the main implication of the chapter, concerning the relationship between the strength of IPRs, complementarity between know-how and technology inputs, and transfer of know-how. Section 5.4 provides an empirical test of the main proposition of the model using a sample of 144 technology import agreements by Indian firms. Section 5.5 concludes the chapter. The appendix provides some additional details about the data used in section 5.4 and their sources.

5.2 Opportunistic Behavior in the Licensing of Know-How

Technology licensing involves more than just the transfer of blueprints, drawings and specifications. In many cases, the information required for successful utilization includes heuristics, rules of thumb, and other tricks of the trade. These routines and rules of thumb arise as a firm develops its technology base over a long period, often through "trial and error" search processes (Sahal 1981; Nelson and Winter 1982; Pavitt 1987). Thus, a large fraction of knowledge acquired is tacit. The transfer of this know-how is especially important when the firm that is licensing in the technology does not have a great deal of experience with that particular class of technologies. This would typically be the case in international technology transfers (especially North-South transfers), when new and undeveloped technologies are transferred (e.g., biotechnology) and in transfers across industrial sectors.[3]

The question of know-how has been largely neglected by the theoretical literature on licensing, even though there is a great deal of empirical evidence that points to its importance.[4] For instance, over two thirds of a sample of U.K. firms reported that "most" or "all" their licensing agreements had know-how provisions (Taylor and Silberston 1973). In his study of international technology licensing, Contractor (1981) shows that the principal criterion used by licensors for determining payments was the extent of technical services provided to the licensee. The transfer of know-how is costly because it is usually accomplished through the training of personnel, trips by the engineers of the licensor and other services (Teece 1977; Contractor 1981). The quality or the extent of such services may vary according to the efforts made by the licensor. Even though the parties involved can observe the quality and extent of the services, third parties such as courts are unlikely to be able to verify adequately variations in quality. Verification may require monitoring of the process, which is likely to be prohibitively costly.[5]

If third party verification is difficult, both sides may behave opportunistically. Once the know-how is transferred, the buyer may try to avoid paying for it, since it would be difficult to force her to unlearn what she has been taught. On the other side, given the cost of transferring know-how, the licensor may be tempted to skimp on the know-how provided. Faced with the possibility of opportunism, one can always reach the optimum by "selling the firm"—that is, letting the licensor be the residual claimant. This may not be feasible if the licensee also provides complementary inputs that the licensor cannot provide. For instance, the licensor may be a small, research-intensive biotech firm, which is unable to finance or manage expensive clinical trials. There may also be legal problems such as antitrust (domestic licensing) or restrictions on foreign investment (international licensing).[6] Reputation or long term relationships may be other means by which the problem may be ameliorated. However, many licensing contracts do not involve repeated licensing or long-term relationships. Moreover, as noted in the previous section, our objective here is to try to understand how contracts for the exchange of technology can arise even among parties that have not built such a mutual reputation over time.

5.3   The Basic Model

5.3.1   Model Structure

Using a basic Principal-Agent framework we show that simple contracts, where know-how is bundled with codified technology (protected by patents), can successfully achieve the transfer of know-how. The model developed in this section illustrates the role of patents in overcoming the problem raised by the double-sided opportunism.

Suppose that the technology package consists of a patent and know how. We assume that the scope of the patent, which can be thought of as a measure of the strength of the IPR regime, affects the cost of "inventing around" the patent (Gallini 1992). We examine contracts with only lump sum payments. This assumption keeps things simple while also being close to the facts. Royalty rates tend to vary very little across licensing contracts for any given industries. By contrast, there are large variations in the lump sum payments, which are said to reflect differences in the amount of know-how being transferred (Bidault 1989; Taylor and Silberston 1973, 20; Contractor 1981).

We assume that the lump sum payments are made in two stages: The licensee makes part of the payment after the contract is agreed upon but before any know-how is transferred. The rest of the payment is made when the licensor has provided the know-how. The licensee can withhold the second period payment, and thus can guard herself against the possibility of the licensor undersupplying know-how. The licensor can withdraw the patent (i.e., deny the licensee any right to use the patent) if the licensee fails to make the second payment. Here the assumption that know-how is complementary to the patented component of technology is crucial. The mutual "hostage taking" allows a self-enforcing contract in know-how to work, even though no externally enforceable contract exists. This intuition is formalized below.

5.3.2   Definitions and Notation

To understand the logic of the argument, it is easier to begin with the case where the amount of know-how that has to be transferred is fixed. In this case, the only choice that a licensor has is either to transfer the know-how or not. Let x represent the index for the transfer of know-how, and y be the index for the transfer of the complementary input. Thus, $x = 1$ means that the know-how is transferred, and similarly $y = 1$ implies that the patent rights are transferred to the licensee. Let T_2 represent the payment that the licensee makes to the licensor after the know-how is provided, whereas T_1 is the payment made before know-how is transferred.[7]

The (gross) value for the licensee is as follows: V_{xy} if both x and y are provided by the licensor, V_x if only the know-how is provided by the licensor, V_y if y is obtained from a different source than the licensor, and 0 if neither is provided. Finally, let C_x and C_y represent the costs incurred in transferring x and y respectively, and C_{xy} represent the costs if both are transferred by the licensor. Both parties know all magnitudes with certainty.

The complementarity between the patented and tacit components imply that the value is greater if they are obtained together from the licensor, so that $V_{xy} - V_x - V_y > 0$.[8] If we interpret y more broadly as other technology components such as proprietary machines or designs, then there may also be complementarities in supply, for instance, economies of scope in the supply of the two inputs, so that $C_{xy} - C_x - C_y < 0$. In what follows we will assume that the complementarities are in the use of knowledge and not in supply conditions, so that the cost of supplying both inputs is simply the sum of the individual costs, that is, $C_{xy} = C_x + C_y$. Also, since y is interpreted as patent rights here, we can set $C_y = 0$ without further loss of generality.

Suppose that the licensee only gets the know-how but not the patent rights. In that case, she could invent around the patent, at some cost represented by P_y. In order to analyze the effects of patent scope, it is helpful to parameterize P_y by expressing it as a fraction of the payoff from possessing the patented component, $k \cdot V_y$, $0 \le k \le 1$.[9] An increase in k represents an increase in patent scope. Given that, licensee's payoff from inventing around (ignoring any payment to the licensor) would be given by $L = V_x + V_y - k \cdot V_y$. In other words, L is the payoff to the licensee from inventing around the patent of the licensor if the contract is terminated and no complementary input is supplied by the licensor. The difference between V_{xy} and L is given by $(V_{xy} - V_x - V_y) + k \cdot V_y$. As can be readily seen, this depends on two dimensions. First, it is greater, the greater is the complementarity between the knowledge in the patent and the know-how. Second, the difference is greater, the greater is the cost of inventing around the patent.

To focus on the role of complementarity, we assume that the licensor has all the bargaining power, and offers to supply the patent rights and know-how in exchange for two lump sum payments by the licensee.

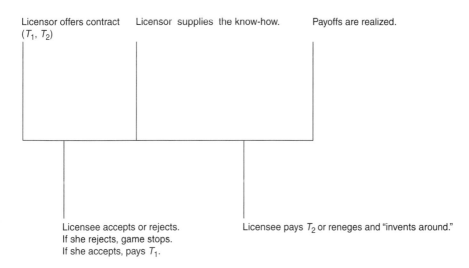

Licensor offers contract   Licensor supplies the know-how.   Payoffs are realized.
(T_1, T_2)

Licensee accepts or rejects.   Licensee pays T_2 or reneges and "invents around."
If she rejects, game stops.
If she accepts, pays T_1.

Figure 5.1
Stages in the technology contracts

This is equivalent to saying that the licensor makes a take-it-or-leave-it offer to the licensee. The contracting is assumed to unfold as follows (see figure 5.1). In the first period, the licensor offers a contract $\{T_1, T_2\}$, where the licensee agrees to pay T_1 immediately and T_2 after the licensor has provided the know-how, in the second period. If the contract is accepted, then the licensor supplies the know-how after the first period payments have been made. Note well that by assumption, third parties such as courts cannot observe if the know-how has been transferred, although the licensee can. Hence, no externally enforceable contract is written on the provision of know-how. Instead, the contract allows either party to terminate it if they are not satisfied with the behavior of the other.[10]

The termination of the contract would imply that the licensee loses the right to use the patent of the licensor. Thus, if the licensee wished to produce, she would have to invent around the licensor's patent. The licensee cannot, however, be forced to unlearn: If the contract is terminated, the licensee would naturally like to make use of what she has learnt through the technological know-how to invent around the patent of the licensor.

We begin with the second stage. After the know-how has been supplied, if the licensee goes through with the contract, her payoff is $V_{xy} - T_2$. If the licensee decides to renege on the contract, her payoff is $V_x + V_y - P_y$. Thus, she will go through with the contract only if $V_{xy} - V_x - V_y \geq T_2$

$-P_y$.[11] In addition, notice that a promise by the licensor to supply know-how is credible only if $C_x \leq T_2$—that is., the second period payment covers the cost of supplying the know-how.[12] Thus $x = 1$ only if $V_{xy} - V_x - V_y \geq C_x - k \cdot V_y$. This condition can be rewritten as

$$(V_{xy} - V_x - V_y) + k \cdot V_y \geq C_x \Leftrightarrow V_{xy} - L \geq C_x. \tag{1}$$

Inequality (1) illustrates the key conditions for know-how transfer to take place. It says that the know-how must be valuable, complementary to the patent, and that it must be difficult to invent around the patent, so that the net payoff from inventing around is small.

We also have to ensure that the licensor could not do better by simply transferring patent rights without any know-how. If only y is transferred, the maximum payment that the licensee would be willing to make is V_y. The licensor's payoff when only y is transferred is therefore V_y. Formally, we have the following inequality

$$T_1 + T_2 - C_x \geq \cdot V_y. \tag{2}$$

Finally, we have to guarantee that the licensee will agree to sign the contract, that is, that the overall participation constraint (also called the individual rationality constraint) for the licensee is satisfied. This happens if the value the licensee derives is greater than the total payments she makes, so that

$$V_{xy} - T_1 - T_2 \geq 0. \tag{3}$$

Together, inequalities (2) and (3) imply that

$$V_{xy} - \cdot V_y \geq C_x. \tag{4}$$

Inequalities (1) and (4) constitute the necessary and sufficient conditions for know-how transfer to take place. If such condition are satisfied the optimal licensing contract stipulates $T_1 = L$ and $T_2 = V_{xy} - L$. If know-how were contractible, we would simply require that there be positive gains from trade, namely that, $V_{xy} - V_y \geq C_x$. Before proceeding with the discussion of some generalizations, we summarize the main results of this simple model with the following proposition:

PROPOSITION 1   Simple lump sum based contracts can accomplish the efficient transfer of know-how. This is more likely to happen when there exists complementarity between know-how and technology input and when the patent scope is broad.

5.3.3   Generalizations of the Basic Model

The intuition formalized above proves to be surprisingly robust to a variety of extensions and generalizations.

No Reneging in Equilibrium
One can show that as long as transferring know-how increases the joint surplus enjoyed by the licensee and the licensor, it is in the licensor's interest to ensure design contracts where the licensee makes the second period payment. Formally, one can show that there is no reneging by the licensee in any equilibrium of the game show in figure 5.1. Although Arora (1995) contains a formal proof, the intuition is straightforward—if the contract is such that the licensee would renege in the second period, then the licensor will not transfer know-how in the first period. This is equivalent to transferring only the patent rights, a condition that is ruled out by inequality (2).

Choosing How Much Know-How to Transfer
It the amount of know-how transferred varies, one can show that the licensor's decision problem can be rewritten so that she maximizes the joint surplus, subject to a constraint which is simply a modified version of inequality (1).

$$\underset{x}{\text{Max}}\ V\,(x) - C\,(x)$$
$$\text{s.t. } V\,(x) - L\,(x) - C\,(x) \geq 0 \tag{5}$$

In (5), $V\,(x)$ is the payoff to the licensee if, in addition to the patent, it also gets x amount of know-how, $C\,(x)$ is the cost to the licensor of transferring that know-how, and $L\,(x)$ is the payoff to the licensee if it gets the know-how but not the patent. In other words, the interpretations are similar, albeit modified to take into account that the licensor can now choose how much know-how to transfer.

If the constraint (5) does not bind, this implies that not only will know-how be transferred, but the amount of know-how transferred will be what would have taken place if there were no contracting difficulties due to tacitness. Moreover, the greater the complementarity between know-how and the patent and the broader the patent scope, the less likely it is that the constraint will bind. Furthermore, in this case, one can show that the two lump sum payments are as follows: $T_2 = V\,(x) - L\,(x)$ and $T_1 = L\,(x)$. It also follows that both payments are greater, the greater is the amount of know-how transferred, under the plausible assumption that $V_x(x) > L_x(x)$, for instance, the marginal value of know-how is higher when it is used together with the patented part of the technology.

If the constraint binds, then the amount of know-how, x, is defined by $V(x) - L(x) = C(x)$. In this case, it is easy to see that x is greater the greater the patent scope is.

Bargaining and Renegotiation
We have assumed that the licensor has all the bargaining power. Furthermore, the contracting process was simplified in that after the know-how was transferred, the parties could not renegotiate the contract. These assumption are important though not critical for the transfer of know-how to be accomplished. In particular, if the licensee can "hold-up" the licensor after the know-how has been transferred then this will reduce the amount of know-how being transferred, particularly if the licensee has a substantial amount of bargaining power.

Asymmetric Information
One can also extend the model to situations where the licensor is uncertain about how valuable the know-how is to the licensee. The remarkable result, proved in Arora (1995) is that even in such situations, the simple contract works. Indeed, the first period payments play a critical role, because the licensee can use higher up-front payments as a signal that it values know-how.

5.3.4   Discussion and Implications

Though very simple, this model has strong implications. The model explains why patents and know-how contracts are bundled together, even though the majority of the licensees claim that they are mainly interested in know-how.[13] It explains why technology contracts often have payments made over time, and the crucial role that these payments play in such contracts. It also predicts that the amount of know-how transferred will vary directly with lump sum payments, as reported by Contractor (1981) who found that the technology transfer costs were positively correlated with the disclosure payments and other lump sum payments for engineering services.

From the perspective of division of innovative labor, this model explains why technology licensing may be an inefficient means of extracting rents from innovation.[14] Arrow (1962b, 355) notes:

Patent royalties are generally so low that the profits from exploiting one's own invention are not appreciably greater than those derived from the use of others' knowledge. It really calls for some explanation why the firm that has developed the knowledge cannot demand a greater share of the resulting profits.

In terms of the model, as the difference between V (x) and L (x) becomes small (either due to narrow patent scope or weak complementarities between the patent and know-how), the amount of know-how transferred falls, and so does the net return to the licensor. In the context of innovation policy, the model suggests that a broader patent scope would be beneficial to the extent that the chief sources of innovation are small research intensive firms who rely upon licensing to appropriate the rents from innovation.

The model also implies that if patent protection is sufficiently strong, then the joint surplus maximizing amount of tacit know-how is contracted for and provided.[15] In a policy context, the controversy over intellectual property rights in forums such as the GATT has received a great deal of attention. Chin and Grossman (1990) have pointed to the potential benefits of stronger patent protection to the South (in addition to the North) arising from a higher rate of innovation in the North. Our results above imply that stronger patent protection would benefit the South by increasing the flow of know-how, even without any incremental inducement to innovation in the North.

5.4.   Testing The Model: Do Patents Enable the Transfer of Know-How?

5.4.1   Data Sources and Description

In testing the model, the first question is what an appropriate test of the model is. The point can be made simply. The model predicts that if the licensee values know-how more than it costs the licensor to transfer know-how, then the licensor can accomplish the transfer by bundling the know-how with a patent or other complementary technological inputs. Finding data on the value and the cost of know-how transfer is extremely difficult. It is easier, although still difficult, to find information on licensing contracts, and particularly whether or not technical services were provided, and whether the know-how to be transferred is bundled with complementary inputs.

We use a sample of 144 technology import agreements by Indian firms during 1950–1975.[16] For these agreements, the database reported infor-

Table 5.1
Variables and Descriptive Statistics

Variable	Description	Mean	S.D.	Min.	Max
YEAR	Beginning year of the agreement minus 1969	5.83	8.17	−20	15
LINK	1 if prior links between licensor and licensee; 0 otherwise	0.22	0.41	0	1
LARGE	1 if licensee is an MRTP company; 0 otherwise	0.35	0.48	0	1
PREVIOUS	1 if licensee had previously imported technology; 0 otherwise	0.17	0.37	0	1
EQUIP	1 if supply of machinery and equipment are included in the agreement; 0 otherwise	0.33	0.47	0	1
PATENT	1 if patent rights are included in the agreement; 0 otherwise	0.47	0.50	0	1
PLANT	1 if the agreement includes the commissioning of the plant by the licensor; 0 otherwise	0.32	0.47	0	1
TRAIN	1 if the agreement includes training of personnel; 0 otherwise	0.19	0.40	0	1
QC	1 if the agreement includes quality control services; 0 otherwise	0.41	0.50	0	1
RD	1 if the licensor helped set up an R&D unit; 0 otherwise	0.76	0.43	0	1
NON-ELECT. MACHINERY	1 if agreement is in non-electrical machinery; 0 otherwise	0.31	0.46	0	1
ELECTRICAL MACHINERY	1 if agreement is in electrical machinery; 0 otherwise	0.25	0.43	0	1
TRANSPORT EQUIPMENT	1 if agreement is in transportation equipment; 0 otherwise	0.10	0.29	0	1
CHEMICALS	1 if agreement is in chemicals; 0 otherwise	0.12	0.32	0	1

Note: Number of observations is 144, except for YEAR, where $N = 141$.

mation on various types of technical services associated with the contracts, which we use as indicators of whether know-how is transferred or not. The data are discussed in greater detail in the appendix. Table 5.1 lists the data used in the empirical analysis and presents descriptive statistics.

The technology contracts in our sample provided information about three technical services that we used as indicators for the provision of know-how: TRAIN, QC, and RD are three dummy variables which take the value one if the agreement includes respectively training of person-

Table 5.2
Relationships Among the Three Technical Services
(a) RD & QC

	QC = 0	QC = 1	
RD = 0	81	35	116
RD = 1	4	24	28
	85	59	144

(b) RD and TRAIN

	TRAIN = 0	TRAIN = 1	
RD = 0	34	82	116
RD = 1	1	27	38
	35	109	144

(c) QC and TRAIN

	TRAIN = 0	TRAIN = 1	
QC = 0	32	53	85
QC = 1	3	56	59
	35	109	144

Note: The last column lists the row totals; column totals are listed in the last row.

nel, quality control services, assistance by the licensor in setting up an R&D unit, and zero otherwise.

Training of personnel (TRAIN) is the most broadly defined of the services and is included in about 75 percent of the cases.[17] Quality control services (QC) are included in about 40 percent of the sample agreements. Assistance in setting up an R&D unit (RD) is included in about 20% of the sample agreements. Tables 5.2a–c also shows that there is fairly well defined hierarchy in these services in that almost all contracts that included R&D also included quality control services, and almost all contracts including quality control services also involved training. This suggests that training of personnel is defined quite broadly. The other two services should not suffer to the same degree from the problem of variability in extent and quality.

In addition to the three technical services, our contracts enabled us to identify three complementary "inputs"—patent rights (PATENT), commissioning of plant (PLANT), and equipment (EQUIP). These variables take the value of 1 if patent rights, plant commissioning to the licensor, or supply of equipment are involved in the agreement, and 0 otherwise. As already discussed, the extent to which patents can be used to protect know-how depends upon the degree to which the know-how being provided is complementary to the technology covered by the patent, and upon the strength of patent protection. A patent that is easily circumvented, or one whose infringement is difficult to prosecute is not likely to be much of a bargaining tool. In India, certain important categories of patents, such as product patents in chemicals and pharmaceuticals, are not permitted. This would tend to reduce the effectiveness of patents as a device to protect tacit knowledge in the chemical industry, a fact that is reflected in the results below. However, it is important to distinguish between limited patent rights and poorly enforced rights. The Indian situation is characterized by the former rather than the latter. Therefore, where patent rights are protected, they can be used to protect know-how that is complementary. Since patents protect recent technology, it is reasonable to expect that the complementarity with patents will be the strongest for R&D related know-how, and the weakest for routine training and maintenance.

As far as the possibility of bundling equipment with know-how is concerned, all else held constant, machinery and equipment that is proprietary to the licensor will be complementary to the know-how being supplied by the licensor. In these cases, the licensor can restrict the supply of the equipment if the licensee does not abide by the contract. The evidence on the extent to which licensors provide proprietary equipment is, however, mixed. Balcet (1985) notes that Italian firms supplying technologies to Indian companies often required that the local partner imported components and equipment exclusively from the technology exporter. On the other hand, Bell and Scott-Kemmis (1988: 53–57) find that in their sample of British suppliers, when sales of machinery, equipment, or instrumentation were associated with the technological collaboration agreement, the supplier firm usually procured the equipment on behalf of the licensee from other firms. The mixed evidence suggests that the ability to use equipment to protect know-how would be limited. However, it is likely that know-how about matters such as operating procedures and maintenance of the machine will be complementary to the machine. Know-how about product design, or process control is less likely to be complementary to the machine. The foregoing considerations suggest that know-how about quality control and labor training should have stronger complementarity with equipment than R & D.

Plant commissioning is likely to be bundled with know-how, and it can provide some hold-up opportunity against the licensee, primarily because the licensor is likely to be a low cost supplier of such services. In the data, plant commissioning is highly correlated with performance guarantees, as well as with the provision of machinery and equipment. This suggests that plant commissioning is similar to a turnkey arrangement. The licensor would therefore find it less costly to provide technical services if the licensor were also responsible for plant commissioning.[18] Under some conditions, there may even be direct complementarity, because know-how supplied by the licensor may not be as useful if the plant were being set up by someone else.

In addition to the three complementary inputs, there are other ways in which contracts for know-how could be made to work. As noted earlier, reputation building in the context of repeat contracting may be one such way. The data set contains measures of prior contacts between the two parties. LINK is a dichotomous variable which is equal to 1 if the two parties had prior linkages, and 0 otherwise. For instance, in some cases, the licensee had previously acted as a sales agent for the licensor. Less frequently, the licensee had acted as a supplier. We also used other controls. PREVIOUS is a binary variable indicating whether the licensee had previously purchased technology (for the same project) or not. In the sample period, large private sector firms in India have been subject to special regulations under the Monopolies and Restrictive Trade Practices (MRTP) Act.[19] A value of 1 (and 0 otherwise) for the variable LARGE indicates that the firm in question is a large private firm.

5.4.2 Characteristics and Limitations of the Data

The agreements in our sample range over a number of industrial sectors, primarily electrical machinery (25%), nonelectrical machinery (30%), transport equipment (10%), and chemicals (12%). This distribution corresponds well with the overall distribution of technology licensing contracts in India (Cooper 1988, 10). Also, the agreements range over a period of a little more than three decades, although the vast bulk of them are concentrated in a shorter period. The reason why this time spread may not be a serious problem is that the analysis is conducted conditional on the firm having decided to import technology, and having succeeded in entering into a technology import agreement. Since there are significant transaction costs of negotiating with the technology supplier and with the government, the major impact of the changing economic environment is likely to be on the number of technology agreements. While there is a distinct possibility that there may be changes in the value placed upon know-how, it is unlikely that there has been any systematic change in the relationship between the different elements of the technology package.[20]

A more serious issue is the absence of direct information on the licensor. In terms of our model in the previous section, this creates a serious problem because it implies that one lacks direct measures of the cost of supplying the complementary input or the technical service in question. For instance, one does not observe if the licensor was unwilling to supply a particular service. While some characteristics of the licensee are covered, the coverage is limited. Thus data limitations rule out any structural estimation and any direct tests.

Despite its limitations, this is a unique and valuable data set. It contains detailed information on the composition of technology agreements, enabling us to analyze with greater precision issues that have hitherto received only qualitative analysis. The usefulness of this data set can best be appreciated in relation to the existing literature on technology imports in developing countries, which consists almost exclusively of regression studies using crude measures such as regressions of the expenditures on imports of technology on various firm characteristics.[21]

5.4.3 Empirical Analysis

A direct examination of the theory is not possible if independent measures of the degree of tacitness of know-how content of a technical service are absent, or if the degree of complementarity between an input and technical service and licensor characteristics are not known. The second best option is to analyze the extent to which technical services and other inputs are bundled together. This implies that we have only indirect evidence to present in support. Nonetheless, as we argue below, the evidence is strongly suggestive.

Since there are three technical services and three complementary inputs, and a sample size of 144, it seemed reasonable to test the hypothesis that the conditional probability of a complementary input being present—conditional on a (related) technical service being present—is higher than the unconditional probability.[22] Such an analysis has the virtue of placing the least amount of a priori structure. However, contingency tables become quite cumbersome when one controls for factors such as industry effects, especially because of the rather small cell counts for particular cells. Therefore we also use probit estimates as a second best way to test for the association between the provision of technical service and the presence of complementary inputs.

Table 5.2 suggested a near hierarchical relationship among the three services. So we begin by pooling all three technical services, as well as the three inputs, to test whether the technical services and inputs are distributed independently. Table 5.3a reports the expected and actual frequencies, and overwhelmingly rejects the null hypothesis of independence.[23] Moreover, the difference between the expected and actual frequencies is negative for the diagonal and positive for the off-diagonal elements. This supports the notion that technical services are bundled with inputs in technology packages.

Tables 5.3b–d report the probability of the provision of different complementary inputs, for each of the three technical services. As the tables show, the conditional probability of each of the complementary inputs is higher when any technical service is provided, than when the service is not provided. The results indicate that equipment sales are strongly related only to TRAIN. Patents are associated with RD, and more weakly, with QC; plant commissioning is related to the provision of all three services, although the association with TRAIN is weak.

5.4.4   Interactions, Industry Effects, and Other Heterogeneity

To see whether some of the observed relationships merely reflect higher order interactions, we tested for association amongst the three complementary inputs themselves. As table 5.4 shows, PATENT is not associated with either PLANT or EQUIP, but the latter two are positively associated with each other. This suggests that complementarities or economies of scope in supply of inputs alone are not likely to be the cause of the observed association between inputs and technical services. Further support is provided by conditioning on the inclusion of a technical service. Table 5.5 shows that conditional on RD being provided, there is a strong positive relationship between the provision of PATENT and PLANT, even though on average (unconditional) there is no association. In general, there is a stronger positive association between any two inputs when a technical service is provided, and the effect is most marked for RD.

This result suggests that both patent rights, as well as turnkey arrangement are associated with the transfer of sophisticated technological know-how, and that usually both need to be present in order to facilitate the transfer of such know-how. In other words, for technically

Table 5.3

Association Between Technical Services and Complementary Inputs

(a) Technical Services and Complementary Inputs, Total Number

	Input = 0	Input = 1	Input = 2	Input = 3	
Tech = 0	16 (9.7)	12 (10.2)	3 (10.0)	1 (2.0)	32
Tech = 1	17 (15.6)	18 (16.3)	16 (15.9)	0 (3.2)	51
Tech = 2	9 (11.6)	15 (12.1)	11 (11.9)	3 (2.3)	38
Tech = 3	2 (7.0)	1 (7.3)	15 (7.2)	5 (1.4)	23
	44	46	45	9	144

Notes: Row = total number of technical services (RD + QC + TRAIN) in the package. Column = Total number of complementary inputs (PAT + EQUIP + PLANT) in the package. The expected frequency under the null hypothesis of independence is given in parentheses. Value of chi-squared statistic and associated probability under the null hypothesis are 41.05 and 0.001, respectively.

(b) PATENT and Technical Services

	RD = 0	RD = 1	QC = 0	QC = 1	TRAIN = 0	TRAIN =1
PATENT = 0	67	8	50	25	22	53
(75)	(60.4)	(14.6)	(44.3)	(30.7)	(18.2)	(56.8)
PATENT = 1	49	20	35	34	13	56
(69)	(55.6)	(13.4)	(40.7)	(28.3)	(16.8)	(52.2)
Column Totals	116	28	85	59	35	109

Notes: $N = 144$. The row totals are given in the parentheses in the first column. The expected frequency under the null hypothesis of independence is given in parentheses. The value of the chi-square statistic and the associated probability under the null hypothesis are as follows:

RD – 7.699, 0.006
QC – 3.776, 0.052
TRAIN – 2.151, 0.143

sophisticated know-how, individual inputs may not be very useful by themselves; a larger package of inputs may be needed. Moreover, the advantages of bundling several inputs together appear not to be related to economies of scope, but instead to the presence of technical services. This issue is further explored in the regression analysis.

Another possible explanation for the results relates to heterogeneity across licensing agreements. To test for possible industry effects, we analyzed the distribution of inputs and technical services in the five major industry groups represented in the data. This analysis, using contingency tables showed, and table 5.6a confirms, that the provision of in-

(c) PLANT and Technical Services

	RD = 0	RD = 1	QC = 0	QC = 1	TRAIN = 0	TRAIN = 1
PLANT = 0	93	5	71	27	30	68
(98)	(78.9)	(19.1)	(57.8)	(40.2)	(23.8)	(74.2)
PLANT = 1	23	23	14	32	5	41
(46)	(37.1)	(8.9)	(27.2)	(18.8)	(11.2)	(34.8)
Column Totals	116	28	85	59	35	109

Notes: See notes to table 5.3b. The value of the chi-square statistic and the associated probability under the null hypothesis of independence are as follows:
RD – 40.28, 0.000
QC – 22.84, 0.000
TRAIN – 6.63, 0.010

(d) EQUIP and Technical Services

	RD = 0	RD = 1	QC = 0	QC = 1	TRAIN = 0	TRAIN = 1
EQUIP = 0	79	17	57	39	30	66
(96)	(77.3)	(18.7)	(56.7)	(39.3)	(23.3)	(72.6)
EQUIP = 1	37	11	28	20	5	43
(48)	(38.7)	(9.3)	(28.3)	(19.7)	(11.7)	(36.4)
Column Totals	116	28	85	59	35	109

Notes: See notes to table 5.3b. The value of the chi-square statistic and the associated probability under the null hypothesis of independence are as follows:
RD – 0.554, 0.457
QC – 0.014, 0.905
TRAIN – 7.549, 0.006

puts differed across sectors.[24] The occurrence of plant commissioning was relatively higher in chemicals, while that of patents was relatively lower. Of the other sectors, only electrical machinery had a relatively higher occurrence of patents. Plant commissioning was less likely for all types of machinery, while equipment sales were more likely. However, table 5.6b also shows that there are no major differences across sectors in terms of the provision of technical services. With the exception of electrical machinery, where the provision of R&D is relatively lower, the hypothesis of independence cannot be rejected. But even this exception has mixed implications at best because electrical machinery has lower probability of R&D despite the higher (than average) probability of patents, although it does have a lower probability of plant commissioning. Although not reported here in the interest of brevity, we also

Table 5.4
Relationship Among Complementary Inputs
(a) Association between PLANT and PATENT

	PLANT = 0 (98)		PLANT = 1 (46)	
PATENT = 0 (75)	52	*(51.04)*	23	*(23.96)*
PATENT = 1 (69)	46	*(46.96)*	23	*(22.04)*

Notes: The value of the chi-square statistic and the associated probability under the null hypothesis of independence are 0.12 and 0.73, respectively. $N = 144$. The row and column totals are given in the parentheses. The expected cell frequency is given in each cell in italics.

(b) Association between PATENT and EQUIP

	EQUIP = 0 (96)		EQUIP = 1 (48)	
PATENT = 0 (75)	53	*(50)*	22	*(25)*
PATENT = 1 (69)	43	*(46)*	26	*(23)*

Notes: The value of the chi-square statistic and the associated probability under the null hypothesis of independence are 1.13 and 0.29, respectively. See notes to table 5.4a.

(c) Association between PLANT and EQUIP

	EQUIP = 0 (96)		EQUIP = 1 (48)	
PLANT = 0 (98)	73	*(65.33)*	25	*(32.67)*
PLANT = 1 (46)	23	*(30.67)*	23	*(15.33)*

Notes: The value of the chi-square statistic and the associated probability under the null hypothesis of independence are 8.45 and 0.004, respectively. See notes to table 5.4a.

analyzed the relationship between the complementary inputs and the technical services for each of the major industry groups separately. As in table 5.3, PATENT is associated with RD, and in many cases, with QC as well, but rarely with TRAIN. Only TRAIN is associated with EQUIP. All three technical services are associated with PLANT, although the association is weak in the case of TRAIN. Hence it is unlikely that the results of table 5.3 are due to industry effects.

One problem that contingency tables often posed was the small cell counts for particular cells. To get around this we performed multivariate probit regressions. Note that these regressions should not be given a causal interpretation both because it is incorrect, and because in this case, theory does not ascribe causality. They are best interpreted as a parameterized estimate of the strength of the individual relationships,

Table 5.5
Probabilities of Complementary Inputs, Conditional on Presence of Technical Services

	PATENT = 1 | PLANT = 1	PATENT = 1 | EQUIP = 1	PLANT = 1 | EQUIP = 1
RD = 0	21.74	51.35	35.14
RD = 1	78.26	63.64	90.91
QC = 0	28.57	57.14	25.00
QC = 1	59.38	50.00	80.00
TRAIN = 0	40.00	60.00	20.00
TRAIN = 1	51.22	53.49	53.66
	PLANT = 1 | PATENT = 1	EQUIP = 1 | PATENT = 1	EQUIP = 1 | PLANT = 1
RD = 0	10.20	38.78	56.52
RD = 1	90.00	35.00	43.48
QC = 0	11.43	45.71	50.00
QC = 1	55.88	29.41	50.00
TRAIN = 0	15.38	23.08	20.00
TRAIN = 1	37.50	53.49	53.66

Notes: The table reports the probabilities, expressed as percentage, of the first input being included, conditional on the second input being included. For instance, the first column gives the probability that PATENT = 1, conditional on PLANT = 1.

controlling for the presence of other inputs and characteristics of the licensee. The regressions were tried with four specifications. The first has only the complementary inputs as right-hand-side variables. Next, the right-hand-side variables are comprised of industry dummies, and licensee and relationship specific variables. In the third specification, we included the three complementary inputs to the variables in the previous specification. In the fourth specification, we added interaction terms between the three inputs. Note that the specification involving only the complementary inputs correspond to the contingency tables 5.3b–d, with additional linearity restrictions.

Tables 5.7a–c show the results of the regression estimation to be consistent with those reported in tables 5.3b–d. Also, the coefficients of the variables common across specifications are relatively stable. In particular, the coefficients of LINK, LARGE, and PREVIOUS are stable, albeit with some change in their statistical significance. The specification that includes the interaction terms generally yields insignificant coefficients, presumably due to the greater collinearity in the regressors. Consistent with table 5.5,

Table 5.6
Inter-Industry Differences in Technology Packages
(a) Probability of Chi-Square Statistic for Strength of Association between Industry Sector and Complementary Inputs

	PAT	EQUIP	PLANT
NONELECT. MACHINERY	97.6	52.2	71.4
ELECT. MACHINERY	0.27**	10.2	02.3**
TRANSPORT	87.0	32.0	13.6
CHEMICALS	03.2**	71.5	00.0**

Notes: Probability of the chi-square statistic, under the null hypothesis of independence using Pearson's chi-square test. For instance, the first cell gives the probability of obtaining a chi-square statistic as high or higher than that obtained, under the assumption that PATENT is independent of NONELECT. MACHINERY. **signifies that the null hypothesis can be rejected at the 5 percent level.

(b) Probability of Chi-Square Statistic for Strength of Association between Industry Sector and Technical Services

	RD	QC	TRAIN
NONELECT. MACHINERY	80.0	27.4	58.2
ELEC. MACHINERY	01.5**	14.2	21.7
TRANSPORT	60.8	88.0	08.9
CHEMICALS	65.0	58.7	60.1

Notes: See notes to table 5.6a.

only the interaction term between PATENT and PLANT is significant, and that too in the R&D equation alone. Turning to other coefficients one observes that the coefficient of LARGE is positive and significant in the more parsimonious specifications of the R&D and QC equations, implying that large firms are more likely to purchase know-how. The coefficient of LINK is usually insignificant, and is negative in the QC equation.[25]

In general, the results of the regressions conform to our a priori expectations of the extent of complementarity between the various types of know-how and the different inputs. EQUIP is significant only in the TRAIN equation. The observed result is consistent with the observation made by Bell and Scott-Kemmis (1988, 53–57) that in many instances, the licensors merely procure the equipment from others on behalf of their Indian licensee. PATENT is positive and significant in both RD and QC, but not in TRAIN. PLANT is positive in all three, although the coeffi-

Table 5.7
Probit Estimates: Dependent Variables R&D, Quality Control, and Training

(a) Probit Estimates, Dependent Variable: RD

CONSTANT	-2.00**	-1.38	-1.79	-1.76
	(0.29)	(1.34)	(1.83)	(1.43)
LINK	0.66	0.53	0.59	
		(0.34)**	(0.40)	(0.42)
LARGE		0.46	0.28	0.21
		(0.28)*	(0.36)	(0.36)
PREVIOUS		0.57	0.56	0.71
		(0.36)	(0.43)	(0.46)
EQUIP	-0.27		-0.29	0.32
	(0.31)		(0.38)	(0.79)
PATENT	0.78**		0.81	0.08
	(0.29)		(0.33)**	(0.53)
PLANT	1.75**		1.96	0.83
	(0.30)		(0.41)**	(0.65)
PAT*PLANT				1.87
				(0.79)**
EQUIP*PLANT				0.02
				(0.81)
PAT*EQUIP				-0.73
				(0.79)
Log-Likelihood	-47.58	-59.02	-39.08	-36.19

Notes: Standard errors are given in the parentheses. ** and * signify that the coefficient is significant at the 5 percent and 10 percent level of significance respectively in a two-tailed test. The coefficients for the time and sector dummies are not reported here. The number of observations is 141.

cient is insignificant in the TRAIN equation. Moreover, the coefficient of PATENT is smaller than that of PLANT in all three equations, which may reflect the somewhat relaxed intellectual property regime in India during this period.[26]

The equations reported in table 5.7 were estimated independently of one another. Mindful of the quasi-hierarchical relationship among the technical services, we also estimated an ordered probit equation where the dependent variable was the number of services provided. As table 5.8 shows, the results are consistent with those in tables 5.3a and 5.7. Total number of services and the total number of inputs are strongly associated (compare table 5.3a), as are the individual inputs (compare tables 5.7a–c).

(b) Probit Estimates, Dependent Variable: QC

CONSTANT	−0.74**	−1.99	−2.20	−2.06
	(0.18)	(1.12)**	(1.28)**	(1.24)**
LINK		−0.26	−0.46	−0.50
		(0.40)	(0.31)	(0.31)
LARGE		0.60	0.45	0.41
		(0.24)**	(0.26)*	(0.26)
PREVIOUS		0.34	0.27	0.31
		(0.31)	(0.33)	(0.33)
EQUIP	−0.34		−0.11	−0.11
	(0.25)		(0.29)	(0.53)
PATENT	0.47**		0.43	0.47
	(0.23)		(0.24)*	(0.32)
PLANT	1.22**		1.14	0.62
	(0.25)		(0.29)**	(0.45)
PAT*PLANT			0.49	
			(0.56)	
EQUIP*PLANT				0.63
				(0.58)
PAT*EQUIP				−0.46
				(0.58)
Number of param. estimated	4	9	12	15
Log-Likelihood	−83.00	−88.51	−77.37	−76.02

Notes: See notes for table 5.7a.

Although we have tried to control for unobserved heterogeneity in the analysis, it is obvious that potential sources of heterogeneity remain. Thus, the results reported here are consistent with a situation where weaker intellectual property rights may have dissuaded certain potential licensors from the market, or induced licensors to offer only older technologies. In the latter case, patents may proxy for the vintage of the technology, and the association with technical services merely reflect the greater need for such services in transfers involving new technology. However, previous studies suggest that it is unlikely that many Indian firms were able and willing to use the most recent technologies (Scott-Kemmis and Bell 1988).

5.5   Summary and Conclusions

In the imperfect market for technology, problems of moral hazard, asymmetric information, and opportunistic behavior often arise. These

(c) Probit Estimates, Dependent Variable: TRAIN

CONSTANT	0.25	0.86	–0.07	0.25
	(0.17)	(1.18)	(1.30)	(0.47)
LINK		0.50	0.38	0.51
		(0.35)	(0.37)	(0.37)
LARGE		0.44	0.40	0.38
		(0.28)	(0.29)	(0.29)
PREVIOUS		(0.77)	0.95	0.91
		(0.44)*	(0.49)*	(0.47)*
EQUIP	0.62**		0.88	1.01
	(0.29)		(0.35)**	(0.58)*
PATENT	0.26		0.14	0.20
	(0.24)		(0.28)	(0.34)
PLANT	0.60**		0.55	0.52
	(0.29)		(0.35)	(0.99)
PAT*PLANT				0.07
				(0.67)
EQUIP*PLANT				–0.04
				(0.71)
PAT*EQUIP				–0.41
				(0.66)
Number of param. estimated	4	8	12	15
Log-Likelihood	–72.68	–72.38	–65.73	–65.54

Note: See notes for table 5.7a.

problems are likely to be acute in the transfer of tacit knowledge or know-how. In this chapter we developed a simple model that shows how know-how can be transferred through arm's length contracts, provided it is bundled with complementary inputs. The empirical analysis shows that the provision of technical services is accompanied by the provision of complementary inputs. This result persists even after controlling for industry characteristics and the size of the licensee, as well as for prior linkages between the two parties. Moreover, in view of India's weak patent regime, the strong association of patent rights with the provision of technical services is somewhat unexpected. If, however, as argued in this chapter, this result is indicative of the fact that even relatively circumscribed patents are being used to protect tacit knowledge, then the finding is of great significance. The significance lies in the fact that a benefit, hitherto unappreciated, of stronger intellectual property rights would be a more efficient flow of tacit knowledge from the tech-

Table 5.8
Ordered Probit Estimates, Dependent Variable: Total Number of Technical Services

CONSTANT	0.54	0.30	0.24	0.06
	(0.42)	(0.45)	(0.44)	(0.38)
LINK	0.22	0.05	0.075	0.075
	(0.24)	(0.24)	(0.38)	(0.24)
LARGE	0.52	0.44	0.40	0.52
	(0.20)**	(0.21)**	(0.22)*	(0.21)**
PREVIOUS	0.50	0.51	0.52	0.63
	(0.29)*	(0.32)	(0.33)	(0.34)*
EQUIP	0.10	0.48		
		(0.26)	(0.51)	
PATENT		0.53	0.34	
		(0.21)**	(0.28)	
PLANT		1.33	0.74	
		(0.25)**	(0.36)**	
PAT*PLANT			1.12	
			(0.45)**	
EQUIP*PLANT		0.01		
		(0.53)		
PAT*EQUIP			−0.51	
			(0.53)	
INPUTNUMB				0.60
				(0.11)**
Log-Likelihood	−184.73	−162.87	−159.77	−168.56

Notes: The coefficients for the time and sector dummies, and for the threshold parameters in the ordered probit, are not reported here. INPUTNUMB = PAT+EQUIP+PLANT (the total number of inputs included in contract). See also notes to table 5.7a.

nology sources to unaffiliated technology users. Thus better IPR laws in countries which rely upon licensing (as opposed to direct foreign investment) as a source of technology transfer would enhance the inflow of know-how and make the technology transfer more efficient.

Furthermore, an important benefit of broader patents would be to encourage innovation by research intensive firms, such as small biotechnology firms or semiconductor design companies, which lack the capabilities for commercializing innovations. For such firms, the expected revenues from licensing the innovation would be an important part of the payoff, and a policy that enhances the efficiency of the market for know-how would increase their incentives to invest in new knowledge.

We do not mean to suggest that there are no disadvantages of broader patents. As we see in chapter 10, for instance, if contracting is very costly, broader patents may inhibit the development of technologies that have a strong cumulative nature (Merges and Nelson 1990). In international technology transfer, stronger patent protection may increase the share of the rents of the North vis-à-vis the South. Stronger patent protection may also increase the market power of licensees in the markets of the South. Our point is simply that a major benefit of broader patents would be that complementary know-how, critical to the utilization of technologies, could be bought and sold more efficiently. In other words, tacitness of technology is not an insurmountable barrier to a market for technology.

Appendix: The Data Set

The dataset used in this chapter is derived from a survey carried out by The National Council of Applied Economic Research, New Delhi (NCAER). The NCAER mailed questionnaire surveys (followed by an interview) to Indian firms that had licensed technology from abroad during 1962–1982, of which 211 responded. However, sufficiently complete data are available only for some 144 agreements. Further details about the survey are given in Alam (1988).

The unit of analysis is a technology agreement. The responding firms listed the components of the technology package that were included in the contract. The identities of the firms, and indeed, any information other than that provided as answers to the questionnaire, are not available.

The Monopolies and Restrictive Trade Practices Act (MRTP), was aimed at large privately owned (i.e. non-public sector) firms. In particular, it only applied to those that satisfied, in 1985, one or more of the following three criterion: (1) assets larger than Rs 1,000 million; (2) under the joint management/ownership of one or more firms with assets collectively larger than Rs 1000 million; (3) market share of 25 percent or more and assets larger than Rs 10 million. In each instance, the limits have been raised over time. For further details of the provisions, the reader is referred to the Monopolies and Restrictive Trade Practices Act of the Government of India 1970. An MRTP firm needed special clearance to invest in many sectors and even expansion of existing capacity was subject to special approval from the appropriate state agencies. The recent policies of economic liberalization in India have considerably softened the bite of MRTP regulations.

6

Markets for Technology and the Size of the Market: Adam Smith and the Division of Innovative Labor Revisited

6.1 Introduction

Much of the discussion so far has focused on the factors that affect the cost and efficiency of technology transactions.[1] However, one of the key features of markets is the possibility of multiple contracting—for instance, a seller can supply more than one buyer. This possibility is particularly important in the case of technologies because, once developed, they can be deployed at only a fraction of the cost of the initial investment. This leads directly to Adam Smith's well-known observation that "the division of labor is limited by the extent of the market" (Stigler 1951). Thus, even if one could successfully solve the contractual problems, a full-fledged division of labor in the production and utilization of knowledge and technologies would depend on the size of the market for their applications.

To understand this limitation, one has to better define what is meant by size of the market. Suppose that a certain body of knowledge or a certain technology is specific to a given application by a particular firm. The context-specific nature of the knowledge and technology would then imply that it is difficult to reuse that technology for other applications. In these cases, the R&D cost can only be spread on the volume of production of the good associated with that application. But this implies that the potential supplier would not have any economic advantage in the R&D activity compared to the firm that produces and sells the good, because the market size of the technology would not be much larger than that of the good to which it is applied. Moreover, the comparative advantages of the supplier would not increase, if the size of the market (for that good, and hence for that application) increased. In other words, if a specialized supplier is restricted to a single buyer, there is no advantage to specialization that can offset the inevitable costs, transaction and others, involved.

Specialization advantages arise only if a supplier that incurs the fixed costs can serve a number of different producers at a nominal additional cost. This requires that the technology or the knowledge base of the supplier not be totally idiosyncratic to specific contexts or environments. In other words, while the technology may have to be adapted to various applications or users, at least parts of the technology and knowledge bases can be reused at zero or very low incremental costs. Under these conditions, specialized suppliers would have an advantage over any individual user because although the user could also reuse the knowledge, she would do so much less frequently than would a specialized supplier serving a number of users.

In short, what we suggest here is that markets for technology and specialized technology suppliers are more likely to arise in the case of general-purpose technologies (Bresnahan and Trajtenberg 1995; Helpman 1998; Rosenberg 1976), or when the technology relies on "general and abstract knowledge bases" (Arora and Gambardella 1994a). General-purpose technologies, or GPTs, are technologies that encompass several applications. Since the fixed cost of developing a GPT can be spread over many potential applications, the efficiency of specialized GPT suppliers increases as the number of applications to which the GPT is applied increases. Thus, specialization advantages arise with increases in the size of the market, insofar as the increase is due to an increase in the number of potential users of the GPT rather than an increase in the size of the individual user or application.[2]

In what follows we will use GPT to denote the technology developed by specialized technology suppliers, who will collectively be referred to as the GPT sector. The technology developed in-house by users will often be referred to as "local" technology. The logic of the argument is little changed if the users are individual firms or entire sectors. Accordingly, we will use the term application sector or user interchangeably.[3]

We assume that each user can develop in-house technology that is specific to its needs, whereas the GPT, once developed can be used in all possible applications. However, the GPT is more "standardized" and less suited to any specific application than the local technology, produced in-house and customized for that particular application. This lack of customization will either reduce the value of the final output or increase the cost of delivering a particular level of functionality or both. This can be represented as an additional unit cost of production of the final good that is incurred by the downstream firms when using the GPT, and that it is not incurred by them when they use the local technology, developed in-house. We label this additional unit cost d to denote the "distance" created by the GPT from the customized, local technology.

We first discuss a simple model that compares two alternative industry structures, one in which various application sectors (or firms) develop their own idiosyncratic technologies, and another industry structure in which an upstream sector produces a GPT that is used by the downstream industries. We then ask, Which of the two industry structures minimize industry costs? We show that as the size of the applications increases, the industry structure with individual users developing local technology is more likely to be the one that minimizes industry costs. By contrast, as the number of potential applications increases, users' buying from the GPT sector is more likely to minimize industry costs.

Thus, the basic argument is simple: All else held constant, markets for technology are more likely to arise when the breadth of potential applications is larger and there are many distinct potential uses of a given technology. An increase in the size of each application—greater depth—is more likely to induce users to develop their own technology. An extension of this basic model shows that as the number of applications increases, the upstream GPT industry invests in reducing d, further enhancing the efficiency and the extent of the division of innovative labor.

The chapter is organized as follows. The next section presents a simple model which formalizes the relationship between the division of innovative labor and breadth and depth of the market. Section 6.3 uses the key insights of the model to analyze several historical and contemporary GPT industries. While section 6.4 extends the basic model allowing the GPT sector to invest in increasing the generality of the technology it supplies, section 6.5 provide further evidence that supports the predictions made in this chapter. Section 6.6 summarizes and concludes the preceeding discussion.

6.2   GPTs and Industry Structure

6.2.1   GPTs in Old and New Industries

GPTs are not a recent phenomenon. In the first and second industrial revolution, many "general specialties," as Stigler (1951) labeled them, exploited scale economies in production. Stigler's examples of general specialties include railroads and shipping, the London banking center, specialized production of intermediate materials (such as steel and chemicals), and capital goods (such as machine tools, electric motors, and lights). Similarly, Rosenberg (1976) analyzes how the capital good industry in the nineteenth century formed the basis of a profound "technological convergence." This convergence led to significant economies in the production of general purpose machine tools, embodying fundamental principles of shaping, bending and cutting metal, that could be applied to a host of industries such as firearms, bicycles, sewing machines and automobiles.

The creation of new general specialties continues unabated. Specialized science and engineering-based "high tech" industries lead this trend. The electronics industry, for instance, has seen a sustained increase in specialization as hardware, software, and networking have become separate engineering subdisciplines. These are general specialties, in the sense that the fruits of their inventions are sold to a variety of distinct types of users. Similarly, we saw in chapter 3, that many biotechnology firms are focused on the development of general-purpose drug research tools.

Thus, both today and in the past, industrial development is marked by the creation of whole new bodies of specialized knowledge and by whole new industries selling to many others.[4] These general specialties are an important source of economy-wide scale economies and economic growth (Bresnahan and Trajtenberg 1995; Helpman and Trajtenberg 1998; Helpman 1998; Romer 1986, 1990).[5]

6.2.2   Cost-Minimizing Industry Structure: Division of Labor vs. Vertical Integration

In a seminal article, Bresnahan and Trajtenberg (1995) provide the micro-foundations of how GPTs contribute to industry and economic growth.[6] Their model of industry structure is based on an upstream GPT industry that produces an input that is distributed to several downstream sectors. However, Bresnahan and Trajtenberg do not discuss the conditions under which a GPT sector would arise. Put differently, under what conditions is it cost efficient for different users to rely on a common source of technology as opposed to developing it in-house? To address this question, we present a simple model that compares two types of industry structures. The first one features an upstream sector specialized in the production of a GPT which can be supplied to various downstream users. In the second industry structure there is no GPT sector, and each downstream user develops its own "local" knowledge or technology. This technology is idiosyncratic to the application sector that develops it and cannot be employed in other sectors.[7] The local technology is likely to be context-specific and tacit, possibly developed through trial-and-error processes, and difficult to apply outside of the context in which they were developed. The GPT instead can be used by all user sectors. However, the GPT is less suited for each of the applications than the local technology.

To examine these issues, assume that there are N application sectors or users, each producing the final output Q, where for simplicity Q, is assumed to be the same for all sectors. Suppose that the cost borne by an application sector to develop its local technology is equal to K.[8] Hence, if each of the application sectors develops a local technology, the total industry cost of developing technology is $N \cdot K$. In addition, to produce Q each application sector has to incur a unit production cost which we normalize to zero. Instead, when the application sectors employ the GPT, they incur an additional production cost equal to $d \cdot Q$.[9] The parameter $d > 0$ measures the mismatch between the GPT and the use of local technologies. Finally, the cost of developing the GPT is K, which in this case is also the total industry cost to produce the technology.

The total cost in the GPT regime is equal to $K + d \cdot N \cdot Q$, whereas, when local technologies are used, total industry costs are equal to $N \cdot K$. It is easy to see that the cost advantage of the GPT structure, $K \cdot (N - 1) - N \cdot d \cdot Q$ decreases with Q. Furthermore, if we consider the point at which the two structures have equal costs (i.e., $K \cdot (N - 1) = N \cdot d \cdot Q$), an increase in N will increase the cost advantage of the GPT structure. To see this, note that the first derivative of the cost advantage term with respect to N is $K - d \cdot Q > K - d \cdot Q \cdot N / (N - 1) = 0$. These arguments lead to our key propositions:

PROPOSITION 1. As the size of the market of each application Q increases, the cost minimizing industry structure can move from GPT to vertical integration, but not vice versa.

PROPOSITION 2. As the number of distinct application sectors of an economy N increases, the cost minimizing industry structure can move from vertical integration to GPT, but not vice versa.

Thus, in economies or industries with many different users of a basic technology, one is more likely to observe a division of innovative labor. This will hinge upon the creation of generalized technologies and knowledge bases, which can be applied to a wide spectrum of downstream uses. By contrast, when the size of the market increases not because of new users, but because of the growth of the existing users, the cost minimizing industry structure is likely to be the one in which the downstream sectors develop their own local and specific technologies.

In other words, when it comes to market size, what matters for the division of innovative labor is breadth rather than depth. This consideration can also help distinguish between division of innovative labor and outsourcing. Although from a certain perspective, both involve the purchase of an input, there is one important difference in the reason for their existence. A division of innovative labor is based on economies of specialization. Typically, these arise because a given knowledge or competency, once developed, can be applied repeatedly and for different users, at a much lower cost than the cost of creating the knowledge in the first instance. Simply put, there are economies of scope across different users. Outsourcing, such as in the familiar automobile industry model where a large firm is served by a number of suppliers, each supplying a very large fraction of its output to a single buyer, is more likely to be driven by other factors like the desire to preserve flexibility in hiring. In uncertain environments, outsourcing may help shift adjustment costs to suppliers, who may have lower adjustment costs because of their smaller size and less rigid organization.[10]

When it comes to technology, the distinction between outsourcing and a division of innovative labor is especially important. R&D outsourcing is possible, but unless the R&D supplier is leveraging a knowledge base or competence that is applicable and useful for a number of users, R&D outsourcing is unlikely to be a sustainable proposition given the transaction costs advantage of doing the R&D in-house. One important exception is when there are some organizational reasons that disadvantage in-house R&D. For instance, some organizations may be too rigid or bureaucratic to attract and motivated talented researchers. Similarly, researchers can be given better incentives (Landau 1998; Arora and Merges 2000), and information flows may be more efficient in smaller organizations (Arrow 1974). As a result, a firm may prefer to outsource even without substantial economies of scope across users. Even so, if outsourcing is going to persist for a long period, it may be better for one firm to acquire the other while keeping the organizations distinct. This appears to have been the case with Genentech and Hoffman LaRoche. Initially, Hoffman La Roche and Genentech were involved in a number of joint R&D and licensing agreements, with Genentech supplying technology. During the 1990s Hoffman La Roche first acquired a minority stake in Genentech, which was then converted later on to outright acquisition. Genentech remained organizationally and geographically distinct from Hoffman La Roche, functioning as a captive R&D supplier. More recently, Genentech has been spun-out again as an independent firm.

6.3 A Historical Look at the Gains from a Division of Innovative Labor

Our objective in discussing the historical evolution of GPTs is twofold. First, to show that our assumptions about K and d are grounded in reality. Further, the historical evidence suggests, as each GPT was created, observers noted the problems in applying the GPT across sectors. This led to attempts to lower d, to make the general specialty more adaptable and widely useful—in a word, to make the general specialty more general. The importance of this kind of change and the way it drew on formal science and engineering, is an important part of our discussion, and particularly of our extension of the basic model in the next section.

The rise of the railroad industry in the nineteenth century, as also noted by Stigler (1951), is probably one of the first major examples of industry-wide increasing returns. Long-run increasing returns to scale in this industry had two distinct facets. First, the physical capital of a railroad was efficiently shared across many classes of shipments. Second, the (very considerable) invention costs of improvements in steam power, in steel rails, in the telegraph, and in management structures to control large transport systems could be similarly spread out. The cost for any user of building dedicated transportation lines linking a particular shipper's most frequently used routes could be considerable. Individual shippers, even very large ones, were unable to generate enough transportation demand to justify these set-up costs.

The corresponding ds were not zero. Shippers of different kinds cared differently about speed, reliability, smoothness, and costs. A railroad optimized to deliver fresh fruit or passengers differed from a coal or grain carrier. By relying on specialized suppliers, the users were giving up the opportunity to ship their freight at their most desired times, or along the optimal routes between departure and destination, or under any other very special condition. This happened for the obvious reason that the layout of the railroad system, its scheduled routes, and timing had to be optimized according to the utilization of the network as a whole rather than to fit the needs of individual users. Nonetheless, the combination of operational and invention scale economics swamped these modest benefits of diversity and the general specialty of railroading emerged. In the nineteenth century, railroads witnessed substantial organizational and technological improvements that increased their appeal to a broad class of users (Chandler 1990, 53–56). The U.S. railroad companies pioneered the techniques of modern management. They adopted a "scientific" approach to the scheduling of movements of trains, freight, and passengers, to the optimization of routes and connections between hundreds of locations and destinations, and to the maintenance of railroads and related equipment. This very exact scheduling, which was critical to enhancing the efficiency of transportation, was created by subdividing a vast and very complex set of operations into a hierarchy of smaller and simpler tasks, which were supervised, monitored, and coordinated by different layers of managers. The effect of this advance was to progressively lower the d costs associated with railroads as a transport system.

Fundamental change in the conditions of localization for transport awaited the invention of the automobile and the truck.[11] This technology shifted the boundary between the general and the localized. "Road" continued to be general (and is now provided by the government), whereas rolling stock (automobile and truck) and management became specific to the using sectors. Now a user would own his own vehicles and, subject to a congestion externality schedule his own shipments or travel. Even though motor vehicles are subject to vastly lower scale economies than trains, they have increased flexibility, breaking the rigidity of standardization. A lower K permitted considerable escape from generalist production and from the d costs imposed on users.

A different example comes from the twentieth-century chemical processing industry. As noted in chapter 3, at the beginning of the century, chemical firms used to design and engineer their own manufacturing processes. There was little sharing of process knowledge across makers of different products. The emergence of the chemical engineering discipline changed that radically. Chemical engineering unified diverse chemical processes by conceiving of them as a sequence of "unit operations" like distillation, evaporation, drying, filtration, absorption, and extraction. These operations were applied under different conditions on different types of materials in different uses, but the general analytical principles underlying the unit operations were common. Chemical engineering, with strong roots in science, was able to advance understanding of these general analytical principles and of their mode of application to different materials. Thus, the invention of a general specialty involved a division between the general (process knowledge) and the specific (the application of that process knowledge to particular products). Moreover this created enormous opportunities for specialization of the invention function itself. Thus, since World War II, the specialized engineering firms (or SEFs) supplied process design and engineering services for a number of products such as fertilizers, plastics, and textile fibers.

A single SEF, Universal Oil Products (UOP) has been responsible for a number of important inventions. Indeed, UOP has acted as the R&D department of many small and independent oil refiners and chemical firms. Even today it sells a number of licenses in many oil refining and chemical processing technologies, throughout several countries. Two of UOP's technologies are quintessential examples of general purpose inventions—the first continuous cracking process for producing gasoline, the Dubbs process, developed in the 1910s; and the Udex process for separating aromatic chemical compounds from mixed hydrocarbons, developed in the 1950s.

The value of the Dubbs process was twofold. It worked continuously, without stopping production, and it produced gasoline from either high-quality feedstock or from low-quality "black oil." This was a significant "general-purpose" improvement because hitherto, different kinds and grades of the raw material required specific process technologies. Thus, as noted by a recent history of UOP: "With the Dubbs process, UOP could live up to the 'universal' in its name by cleanly cracking *any* oil, regardless of coke-formation quantities" (Remsberg and Higdon 1994, 50–51, italics in original). Moreover, rather than vertically integrate forward into refining, UOP chose to license its technology to the myriad of local refiners, helping them specialize it to their particular feedstock. This strategy made sense because of the structure of the oil refinery industry in that era, with a larger number of small refiners. Indeed "(P)ractically every little town in the country with access to oil had a small refinery" (Remsberg and Higdon 1994, 50).

During the 1950s, UOP developed the Udex process to separate aromatic compounds (benzene, toluene, and xylene) from mixed hydrocarbon streams. These aromatic compounds are themselves general-purpose inputs used in the making of many distinct chemical prospects. The Udex process was extremely flexible. As noted by Spitz (1988, 191): "Generally, UOP has been able to assemble a combination of processing 'blocks' that would allow a producer to make any desired combination and relative quantity of benzene, toluene and xylene isomers from every conceivable feedstock." These examples show that UOP's expertise was specialized in the sense that it was deep in particular processes, but general in the sense that it cut across many products and petrochemical inputs.

Parallel to the SEFs, university chemical engineering departments played a crucial role in making fundamental process improvements. They helped develop the science of large-scale chemical processes. This basic understanding of phenomena that straddled chemistry and engineering, such as catalyst design, was applicable across a variety of processes. Thus, university chemical engineering departments actually reduced the cost of designing modern, large-scale continuous flow processes for any number of products—that is, they lowered d. To put it quite bluntly, without the development of the science of chemical engineering, it is unlikeiy that there would have been SEFs. It is certainly true that SEFs would have been far less important and far less pervasive in the chemical processing industry.

A related example is the invention of the microprocessor in 1971. Before then, integrated circuits were largely "dedicated" products, in the sense that their operations were defined by the physical wiring and interconnections designed and built by the manufacturer on the chip. Consequently circuits had to be produced by the manufacturers with specific applications in mind. By contrast, the microprocessor, or "programmable chip" as it was aptly named, could be programmed. As Braun and MacDonald (1978) note, it implied "software wiring" as opposed to "hardware wiring." It could then read and process more variable instructions and perform a far larger number of operations. Most importantly, it could be produced without specific applications in mind. The users, who could program the chip according to their needs, could define its functions.[12]

It is then not surprising that the device rapidly found extensive applications. Apart from its core use in microcomputers, it became a pivotal component in telecommunications, aerospace and office equipment, in the control of industrial processes, in the automobile industry, among many others. Its utilization extended the range of applications of integrated circuits. In a sense, this widespread application was the natural consequence of the fact that, whether deliberately or not, the microprocessor was conceived, from its very invention, as a general-purpose object. The impact was to lower d. Ultimately, the microprocessor also changed part of the integrated circuit business into one characterized by a very high K. A general microprocessor is a very complex device, and we now see a small number of firms making long production runs of a few microprocessor designs.

The uses of integrated circuits have varied along the dimension of performance-cost trade-off as well. Hardwiring, despite all the wasteful duplications of design costs it involves (multiple K), offers superior performance in many applications. This is why an "application-specific integrated circuit," or ASIC, industry flourished in parallel to the "general" microprocessor. As discussed in chapters 3 and 4, the division of inventive labor is quite different here. Manufacture of ASICs is performed by general specialists. But unlike Intel or Motorola, these are specialists in the manufacturing process only. They do not design the products they make. Applications sectors design ASICs and solicit manufacturing cost bids from these general specialists. A fundamental organizational innovation has arisen to lower the d-costs in this industry. A language has emerged for describing ASIC designs. It is a computer language, spoken by two very different kinds of computers. The first are computer-aided-design (CAD) workstations used in the application sectors. The second are manufacturing-control computers used in the GPT sector. By this mechanism, even ASICs can have "software wiring."[13] The application sector firms design a logical chip and the general specialist firms make it. Thus, both the substantial scale economies in the plant (high K), and the substantial benefits of localization have been achieved by this d-lowering organizational invention.

In sum, these modern general specialties in the science and engineering based industries, have reduced the tension between localization and generalization by the invention of "lower-d" ways to organize the inventive activity itself. The advantage arises in the use of uniform and systematized knowledge to make the invention by the application sectors easier. As we formalize in the section 6.4, one consequence of this process has also been to draw more application sectors into the ambit of a given GPT.

6.4   Extensions and Generalizations

6.4.1   Differences in User Size and d-Reducing Investments by the GPT Sector

The model discussed in section 6.2 highlights the crucial difference between breadth and depth of the market in terms of the opportunities generated for the creation of an upstream sector of specialized technology suppliers. A number of the restrictive assumptions there can be generalized, as formally demonstrated in Bresnahan and Gambardella (1998). In particular, one can have an arbitrary distribution for the size of the downstream application sectors or users, Q.[14] Further, one can allow users to either produce the technology in-house or buy it from the upstream technology suppliers. Finally, one could also think of situations where the GPT sector can invest in increasing the generality of the technology it supplies, thereby reducing d.

If users differ in terms of size, one can show that there will be a critical size threshold such that users larger than the threshold will rely on in-house technology, while users smaller than the threshold will instead purchase the GPT from upstream suppliers. The intuition behind this result is simple. While the benefits of using the GPT—namely, access to technology at a fraction of the cost of its development—are independent of the volume of output, the costs of using the GPT vary directly (increase) with the level of output. Thus, there is a threshold size beyond which the costs of using the GPT outweigh the benefits and then the users will rely on in-house or "local" technology.

The threshold depends on a number of factors, such as the fixed cost of developing the technology—the higher is K, the greater the threshold required for the use of local technology. The threshold also depends on d. The larger the value of d, the smaller is the threshold. It is reasonable to suppose that technology suppliers, in this case the GPT sector, can reduce d, albeit at some costs. As the examples in our previous section suggest, these costs can really be thought of as investments in generalized knowledge, inventions and technologies, that, by lowering the "economic" distance between all application sectors and the GPT, reduce the penalty from using the GPT instead of a local technology.[15]

If GTP suppliers can invest to lower d then both d and the size threshold are interdependent, because clearly the larger the volume of output that embodies the GPT, the greater the incentive of the GPT sector to invest in reducing d. In other words, the decision to rely on GPT rather than on in-house or local technology, and investments in reducing d are mutually complementary. Formally, this is to say that the strategies of the users in terms of the adoption of GPT, and the strategies of the GPT sector in terms of investments in reducing d are strategic complements. There is by now a substantial literature in economics on the special properties where the strategies adopted by different players are strategic complements (see Bulow, Geneakoplos, and Klemperer 1985; Milgrom and Roberts 1990). Using the results from this literature, Bresnahan and Gambardella (1998) show quite directly that as the number of potential users increases, there is greater investments in reducing d (so that the upstream sector supplies more general technology), and the size threshold for producing local or in-house technology increases. Simply put, an increase in the size (breadth) of the market through an increase in the number of potential users N expands the GPT sector. On the other hand, a proportional increase in the size (depth) of all potential users, Q, implies a smaller GPT sector in the sense that investments in reducing d are lower, as is the size threshold for the production of in-house technology. This is summarized by the following propositions.

PROPOSITION 3.   An increase in the number of users (N) implies a larger GPT sector, in the sense that: (1) d is smaller, and (2) a larger fraction of users buys the GPT.

PROPOSITION 4.   A proportional increase in the size of all firms in the economy (Q) implies a smaller GPT sector, in the sense that (1) d is higher, and (2) a smaller fraction of firms buys the GPT.

Proposition 3 says that increases in the size (breadth) of the market encourage the rise and expansion of a generalist-specialist sector and, correspondingly, of generalized knowledge bases and technologies. One way to interpret Proposition 3 is that a more extensive market means a larger number of distinct uses of a general-purpose technology. With more distinct uses, as Proposition 1 shows, a GPT sector would lower costs. Here we also see that the GPT industries have greater incentives to reduce d. Thus, the innovation process in a diverse market economy involves the creation of GPT industries and systematic attempts to make their technologies more general.

6.4.2   Advances in Science and Complementary d-Reducing Efforts by the User Sectors

In addition to the size of the market, this model also illustrates other factors that encourage the rise of a division of innovative labor. In particular, the state of scientific and engineering knowledge conditions the opportunities for reducing d. Advances in science mean greater ability to comprehend a wider set of previously unrelated phenomena within common explanatory frameworks, and this facilitates efforts to reduce the distance among them (Arora and Gambardella 1994a). Scientific advances have often created technological linkages among formerly distinct industries. For example, greater understanding of solid state physics during the 1950s led to the development of the transistor, thereby inducing a convergence in the technical bases of industries such as telecommunications, office equipment, and consumer products. Similarly, advances in the theory of organic chemistry enabled the German chemical industry during the nineteenth century to link molecular structures to the properties of many different substances. Organic chemistry then became the common basis of sectors such as dyestuffs, pharmaceuticals and explosives. In a very similar way, after World War II, theoretical advances in polymer chemistry provided the common framework to design the molecular structures of new plastics, fibers, or rubberlike products (see Hounshell and Smith 1988; Chandler 1990).

The size and quality of professional scientific bodies also affects the cost of creating general technologies. It has been suggested, for instance, that the United States had provided a more "scientific" education for software programmers than Japan, and this has accounted for some of the difficulties that the Japanese software industry has faced in producing more basic software templates as opposed to specific and often highly customized applications (Cusumano 1991; Nakahara 1993). Similarly, Landau (1998) argued that the systematic training provided by the U.S. universities, MIT in particular, in chemical engineering since the end of World War II, has been critical for the diffusion of highly skilled professionals in the field. The training of U.S. chemical engineers involved a solid grasp of the scientific foundations of chemical process design. In turn, this created a body of professional expertise that could be employed to design and engineer many different types of chemical plants or refineries.

Advances in science lower the cost of reducing d. If we denote θ to be the factors that lower the costs of reducing d, the model shows that an increase in θ implies a fall in d, which results in a higher size threshold. In other words, a rise in θ will increase the fraction of application sectors that buy from the GPT sector. This expansion of market for the GPT will lead the GPT sector to further invest in reducing d, which will further increase the size threshold. The net impact can be summarized in the following proposition:

PROPOSITION 5.   Advances in science (higher θ), or any other factor that lowers the marginal cost of reducing d, implies a larger GPT sector, in the sense that (1) d is smaller, and (2) a larger set of firms buys the GPT.

Proposition 5 also relates to our earlier examination of the cognitive limitations to a division of innovative labor and to the discussion developed in Arora and Gambardella (1994a). There it was suggested that science is a powerful instrument to codify knowledge in ways that enable industries to link seemingly "distant" products and technologies. This led to a division of innovative labor because the fixed cost of producing a given piece of knowledge could be spread over a larger market.

Finally, a natural extension of this framework is one where the individual application sectors can also invest in reducing their own d. As long as these investments are complementary to the d reducing investments made by the GPT sector, all the results above would hold a fortiori.[16] In many high-tech industries users often make such complementary investments. For instance, as discussed in chapter 4, in developing new information systems many software companies develop general "templates." Once developed, the customization of the templates occurs through a "rapid prototyping" process, in which the general system is passed on to users who start using it and suggest ways to make it closer to their actual needs.[17] Here, d is lowered because of efforts made by both parties. Our analysis suggests that users will be more willing to make complementary investments to customize "generic" technology to their own needs (instead of developing technology custom built to their needs) in markets where there are many uses in the economy (N) or high scientific skills (θ), or the uses are of proportionally smaller scale (Q).

6.5 Applying the General Framework

6.5.1 Breadth Versus Depth in the U.S. and Japanese Machine Tool and Software Industries

Our results about the relationships between GPTs and the size of markets state that the division of innovative labor is associated with markets that feature a greater number of distinct uses of a basic technology. These larger markets expand the boundaries of the GPT by widening its breadth of applications and by encouraging investments that reduce the cost of using the GPT vis-à-vis more specific solutions. In this section, we look at two industries that permit the examination of this point from two different perspectives.

The first example is the software industry in the United States and Japan especially up to the mid–1990s. From the founding of the computer industry through the mid–1970s, large mainframes were the only significant commercial computers. Users were large organizations, such as large firms or the U.S. military that could afford large mainframes and utilize them extensively. Software was customized. Consultants, systems integrators, or the employees of a particular user would handcraft software applications for it. A "packaged" software industry, selling "standard" tools for many users, arose only in the 1970s and was associated with the development of minicomputers and later on of the PC. The much cheaper PCs and minicomputers meant that many more types of users were using computers, often in ways very different from how mainframes were used. Many of these users were small (in the sense of small Q) and hence they could not afford to purchase or develop customized software. But there were millions of them, definitely large N.

To be sure, there was a good deal of technical advance in computers and in software, which may well have shifted out the supply curve of independent software vendors. But a cross-country comparison suggests that technical advance cannot be solely responsible for the rise of standard packaged software. For many reasons, the diffusion of minicomputers and PCs in Japan has been slower than in the United States (Cusumano 1991; Nakahara 1993). As table 6.1 shows, in the late 1980s the comparative value of large hardware systems in Japan vis-à-vis the United States was much higher than in the case of smaller systems and PCs. The numbers are striking. While the sales of large systems in Japan were approximately as high as in the United States (8.7 vs. 9.1 billion dollars), the U.S. PC market was worth 19.6 billion dollars as opposed to 4.2 billion dollars in Japan. There the computer still appeared to be the province of large users, who could afford and manage the large systems, and its diffusion among the vast population of smaller users had been slow. Table 6.1 also shows that the U.S. market of packaged software dwarfed the corresponding Japanese market: 13.1 vs. 1.4 billion dollars. By contrast, the figures about custom software are of comparable size (9.6 vs. 10.1 billion dollars).

One can be skeptical of this evidence given the names of the countries in it. After all, market organization is generally more important in the United States, relationship organization for commerce is generally more important in Japan. Another example shows that our inference is not country-specific. The history of the computer numerical control (CNC) machines during the 1980s is similar to that of software, but the positions of the United States and Japan are reversed. CNCs are machine tools whose automated tasks are controlled by a computer. The latter can be easily re-programmed to enable the machine to perform a variety

Table 6.1
Japan-U.S. Hardware and Software Comparison (1987), in 1987 billion U.S. dollars

	Japan	U.S.
Hardware Shipments	21.0	45.6
Large Systems	8.7	9.1
Medium Systems	3.1	8.7
Small Systems	5.0	8.2
Personal Computers	4.2	19.6
Software-Vendor Revenues	13.0	24.8
Total packages*	1.4	13.1
Custom software & system integration	10.1	9.6
Facilities management & maintenance	1.4	2.1
Total market	34.1	70.4

Source: Cusamano 1991, 49. * indicates that they include systems/utilities, application tools, and application packages.

of tasks. CNCs, which first emerged in the early 1980s, advanced the earlier technology of numerical controls (NCs) in which the automatic movements were controlled by computer punch tapes.

The United States pioneered this industry, and CNCs were actually invented in the United States. But while the United States had been the world leader in machine tools since the 1970s, Japanese producers expanded dramatically in the world market during the 1980s and increased considerably their exports into the United States. Japanese producers entered with smaller, microprocessor-based CNCs, whereas the U.S. producers had remained with large mainframe and minicomputer-based CNC machines.

The early NC machines were developed by the U.S. Air Force in the 1950s. Since then their diffusion in the United States occurred largely in two sectors, aerospace and automobile, and within the latter predominately among the "big three"—GM, Ford, and Chrysler. In the 1970s, about one-third of the total U.S. market of NCs was in the aerospace sector and the share of the automobile market was a little smaller (Finegold 1994, Vol.1: 37). With the introduction of CNCs, the US machine tool producers kept focusing on "large, sophisticated users in the automobile and aerospace industries with the available resources and complex requirements to enable adoption of large, expensive, difficult-to-use mainframe- and minicomputer-based CNC machines" (Finegold 1994, 116; March 1989). This also meant that these machines were largely designed for the special purposes and requirements of these users and that the competencies of many machine tool makers were to a good extent sector-specific (Finegold 1994; March 1989).

By contrast, Japanese CNC makers immediately focused on smaller microprocessor-based CNCs for many more types of users. Fujitsu Automatic Numerical Control (FANUC) rapidly became the world leader and the firm that set the world standards. What FANUC and other Japanese producers did was to develop machines with fairly standardized, "commodity"-type characteristics. This enabled them to reach the many smaller firms, in a variety of industries, that were unable to afford large and expensive customized systems. Even by the end of the 1980s, the number of adoptions of NC or CNC machines by Japanese small and medium sized firms was about 40 percent higher than of small and medium U.S. firms (Finegold 1994, 112).

Moreover, because their market was composed of many different buyers, with distinct features and needs, Japanese producers made significant investments in "modularizing" their production and design operations. This was a real revolution in the organization of their work and in the design of their products, which enabled them to take advantage of economies of scale while still maintaining the ability to customize products to meet customer demands. For instance, they made considerable effort to identify parts of machines for different uses that could be standardized without much loss of specificity of the application (Finegold 1994, 13). By mixing and matching standardized components, they could then package machines that were suited for different uses—the classic d-lowering strategy for a GPT.

6.5.2 General-Purpose Tools in Biotechnology

Another example of the relationships between GPTs and industry structure comes from the biotechnology industry. Chapter 3 noted that a leading trend in the biotech industry during the 1990s had been the development of general-purpose research tools. Many so called platform biotech firms focused on the tools market, which is becoming increasingly important both in absolute terms and relative to the other typical market of the biotech companies, notably that of specific products or compounds. As discussed in chapter 3, these tools are mostly technologies for conducting more efficient laboratory tests, screenings of compounds, tests of the action of a fairly large number of molecules and substances, computerized drug design and research. These tools typically exploit scientific advances in combinatorial chemistry, genetics and information technology. Moreover, the trend is clearly toward higher generality of purpose of these tools. Thus, for instance, the strategies of companies involved in the production of "gene-chips," like Affymetrix or Nanogen, hinge upon the development of technologies that can be rearranged to test for different drugs or pathologies. Similarly, companies like Caliper Technology, or the other companies developing the so-called "labs-on-a-chip," advertise the superiority of their products by claiming that their tools can assess a very wide number of semiconductor design modules (see section 3.4 and table 3.7).

While this establishes the importance of the GPT aspects of the new biotech systems, it naturally leads toward a discussion of how and why these companies have emerged, and why they seem to rely so heavily on the "generic" features of their products. To understand this, it is useful to compare the new platform biotech companies with the product-specific biotech concerns, which were more typical of the 1980s. By the late 1980s, the growing number of biotech and pharmaceutical firms developing new drugs represented a large and growing market for R&D tools and services. Moreover, while some pharmaceutical (or chemical) companies, as well as some of their product markets, are large, pharmaceutical markets are highly differentiated, with a plethora of products and therapeutic categories. This suggests that there are important opportunities for technologies that cut across these sub-markets. Consistent with this, as noted in chapter 3, the platform biotech companies normally offer nonexclusive licenses.

In fact, the large size of some pharmaceutical products and companies can explain the difficulties that product-specific biotech companies may have faced, as well as the reasons why—as also noted by Cockburn et al. (1999)—the "platform" biotech business has developed more rapidly in the 1990s compared to the "product" biotech business. The strategy of product biotech companies is to sell products, or license specific compounds (typically proteins) and the associated knowledge to the pharmaceutical firms. But product-specific research is often closely tied to specific substances and their functions, with limited economies of scope. While there are other possible advantages, such as shifting risk, in licensing compounds from biotech companies, such contracts entail a number of inefficiencies, as discussed in earlier chapters. By contrast, specialized suppliers of platform technologies enjoy economies of scope and thus have an advantage over pharmaceutical firms.[18]

Thus, the large number of potential applications has been an important determinant of the growth of GPT biotech tools in recent years. It may also explain why platform biotech firms try to develop tools that are increasingly more general (lower d). This enables them to gain market shares by enhancing the set of potential buyers of their systems. The growth of the GPT biotech platforms is also related to changes in the "state-of-knowledge" parameter θ. We noted in chapter 3 that the Human Genome Project has given an impetus to many research fields in this area. Considerable advances in instrumentation, as well as in the understanding of the nature and function of genes and proteins, have taken place. These are technologies and scientific advances that are inherently associated with the opportunities of developing biotech platforms. As a result, the d-lowering efforts of the 1990s and the rise of these GPTs, may have been further enhanced by changes in θ.

One could ask why we have observed the rise of companies specialized in the upstream research functions of the pharmaceutical business only since the 1970s, and not earlier in the history of this industry. After all, unlike research in the electronics or mechanical sectors, where feedback from the various stages of the research, production, and commercialization process are important (Kline and Rosenberg 1986), pharmaceutical research has always been characterized by well defined and somewhat independent steps—for instance, laboratory research leading to new compounds, clinical tests, FDA approval, and marketing. While feedback from the clinical tests have occasionally helped focus or enhance opportunities back in the laboratory, most typically the compounds that fail in the clinical tests are rejected outright and other often entirely new substances are tried (Gambardella 1995).

The absence of strong interdependencies among the different stages of the innovation process in pharmaceuticals suggests that the integration of these activities within the same company or organization may not be as crucial as in other industries. To put it in the language of our chapter 4, a natural degree of task partitioning exists among the various facets of pharmaceutical innovation. Thus, one might well have observed upstream activities undertaken by some specialists that offered their compounds to the larger firms. Indeed, in the early history of the pharmaceutical industry, independent scientists or researchers, often within universities or research institutions, were sometimes responsible for new compounds that were developed and marketed by the large firms. After World War II, however, the vast majority of new drugs have been developed largely within the laboratories of the large pharmaceutical firms that also conducted the clinical tests and marketed the products (Schwartzman 1976).

There are many reasons for this pattern, which persisted until the 1980s. One is the absence of a substantial comparative advantage for specialist research companies vis-à-vis the leading pharmaceutical firms in the traditional drug discovery and development paradigm, prior to the advent of biotechnology, and the advances in molecular biology, and genetics. In turn, this is related to the fact that there were few opportunities to share knowledge across research projects for new drug products. Until quite recently, drugs were discovered through trial and error, by running large numbers of substances and compounds through a number of screens to detect various types of biological activity. Not only is this expensive, requiring substantial investment in equipment and research facilities, but it also has limited opportunities for knowledge spillovers across therapeutic areas. Although a firm specializing in research may still have enjoyed a modest advantage, it is likely that this advantage would be outweighed by transaction costs involved in licensing potential drugs to companies that would develop, manufacture and commercialize the drug. With only limited advantages to specialization, forces favoring integration proved to be hard to offset.[19]

6.5.3   Externalities and the Role of History and Chance

In their seminal article, Bresnahan and Trajtenberg (1995) pointed out the externalities inherent in the process of division of labor. In any division of labor involving specialized firms that serve a number of users, there are both horizontal and vertical externalities. The vertical externalities arise because the more efficient the suppliers, the greater the value of the investments that users make in using the supplied input. Conversely, the greater the investments that users make in using the supplied input, the greater the demand for the input and hence, the greater the payoff to firms that supply the input. The horizontal externalities arise because, in any division of labor, each upstream supplier will supply more than one downstream user. Thus, any improvements in cost or quality of the supplier will benefit the users. In turn, when a given user makes an investment that enhances the value of applying the input supplied by the upstream supplier, this will induce the supplier to also make complementary investments that improve cost or quality. The benefits of improvements will spill over to other users.

One implication of these externalities is that market outcomes may not be efficient and collective action, such as user-producer research consortia, can improve over the market outcome. Another is that the actual process through which a division of labor can emerge is likely to be strongly conditioned by history and chance. Indeed, Arora, Bokhari, and Morel (2000) find both to be true. They analyze a model of industry evolution where the final output consists of two "components." Firms differ in their ability to produce the two components. Firms enter and exit in each period. At the time of entry, each firm decides, based on current period prices, whether to specialize or to enter as an integrated firm. Since a firm is unlikely to be equally good at producing both components, there are advantages to specialization. On the other hand, there are transaction costs involved in putting the two components together. Also, the payoff to a specialized firm is greater, the greater the number and productivity of specialized firms producing the complementary input.

Thus, Arora, Bokhari, and Morel (2000) are dealing with a more general structure compared with Bresnahan and Trajtenberg (1995), with many users and suppliers, and where the division between users and suppliers is not exogenously imposed, but arises from the dynamics of the model. Their results show that early events in the history of an industry can have an important effect on the extent of division of labor. Thus, an industry that becomes heavily vertically integrated early in its history is more likely to remain that way for a considerable period, even when the cost-minimizing structure involves division of labor. Conversely, once a division of labor begins to unfold, the industry structure may evolve away from integration, even if the latter is the cost-minimizing structure. If one now expands the model to include horizontal externalities, in the sense that a greater division of labor reduces transaction costs or otherwise lowers costs, we find that industry structure may permanently deviate from its long-run-cost-minimizing structure.

To clarify the logic of this argument, one could think of a market where downstream firms are vertically integrated. This implies that there is a small market for independent upstream suppliers because the firms in the industry will produce the upstream input internally. As a result, if there is any entry by another firm in this market, it can do so only by vertically integrating itself, since there is no upstream industry supplying the technology or the upstream input more generally. And this would be the case even if the alternative equilibrium, where the downstream firms are vertically disintegrated, is more efficient.[20] Moreover, the more costly strategy of having to be vertically integrated can limit the possibilities of new entry.

For example, Europe has a very limited division of labor in software and biotech because, unlike the United States, the presence of highly vertically integrated manufacturers in Europe has limited the size of the market for independent suppliers. In turn, this reinforced the trend of the established companies to vertically integrate. Only exogenous changes can modify this situation. The entry of U.S. SEFs in Europe after World War II, or of U.S. software or biotech companies that venture outside the United States, is one of such factor. As we see in chapter 8, this international transmission mechanisms can be a powerful tool for spreading the benefits of division of labor, even when historical conditions prevent the shift toward a more disintegrated industry structure.

6.6 Conclusions

This chapter discusses the endogenous emergence of a division of innovative labor and the creation of GPTs or general-purpose technologies. Division of innovative labor is limited by the extent of the market. However, the size of the market as it is commonly understood, namely the volume of demand of a given good, is not what matters. Rather, what matters is the breadth of the market—the number of different types of uses for the input provided by the specialized suppliers.

In fact, a larger volume of a given application tends to encourage the creation of local technologies that are produced by the users themselves and that are customized for their purposes. By contrast, the existence of distinct and heterogeneous users leads to the development of technologies that are more "generic." Though not as well suited to any given application compared to a custom developed technology, by being widely applicable, such generic technologies have lower unit costs. Moreover, a large number of potential users can induce investments by the GPT suppliers in making the GPT more general and hence more effective for each users. In turn, this encourages investments by the users themselves to improve the functionality of the general technologies for their needs. Not only is the resulting division of innovative labor more efficient, it is also more extensive in the sense that more users employ the GPT rather than use their own custom developed technology. Advances in scientific and technological bases can have similar effects.

Understanding the different ways in which the depth and breadth of the market interact with the process of specialization also has important normative implications. Reserving a more detailed discussion for chapters 9 and 10, we briefly summarize implications for business and public policy. Firm strategies on whether to develop in-house competence or to outsource from the outside have typically been evaluated largely from a transaction cost perspective. By adopting a systemic or industry-wide approach, this chapter offers a different view. In a nutshell, when possible, specialized upstream firms should supply those technologies that are generic and applicable to a large variety of uses and users. Therefore, unless a firm has a large scale of operation in a particular area, developing an in-house version of the technology is not sensible. One exception is where the firm plans to spin off that technology as a stand-alone unit, thereby creating in effect a specialized supplier of the GPT. For a firm planning to specialize in supplying technology, a key question is whether its technological competencies are applicable broadly. If not, the firm's plans should include ways of integrating forward into the application area. Alternatively, the firm may plan, as many such firms do, to be acquired by a major user of the technology. However, if the technology is broad based or generic, specializing in technology and maintaining independence will have the highest payoffs.

From a policy perspective the discussion in this chapter suggests that in order to encourage an efficient and extended market for technology one has to rely on the creation of multiple opportunities for the application of given basic technologies. For instance, the "closed" domestic markets of many European countries often feature only few large producers, especially in basic industries (e.g., the so-called national champions). Closed markets can prevent the creation and efficient utilization of GPTs. Therefore, an insufficiently appreciated benefit from the opening of the European market will be the gains from industrywide economies based on various forms of division of labor.

This also points to the relationship between industry growth, competitiveness and the size of the domestic markets. Specifically, it has often been argued that one advantage of the United States lies in the opportunities that a large domestic market creates for economies of scale at the level of the firm. While this has an element of truth, we argue that a much more significant advantage of the large U.S. market stems from the diversity and the number of the firms that operate in it. This has given rise to considerable economies at the level of entire industries. We discussed in some of our earlier chapters the extent of the exploration and experimentation that has been observed in the U.S. personal computer or semiconductor business, and the beneficial impacts on innovation. Similar effects have been observed for the creation of GPTs and a division of innovative labor. For instance, the large number of users of drug research tools in the United States has certainly contributed to the rise of the biotech toolmakers in this rather than in other advanced countrics. Likewise, the large and diversified U.S. industry, compared to other countries, has largely been responsible for the development of important GPTs in sectors such as software, semiconductors and the like, or in chemical processing even earlier in the twentieth century. One could even argue that the U.S. competitiveness in the world today is comparatively higher in sectors that have exploited the size of the domestic market to gain industry-wide economies (e.g., software, biotechnology, semiconductors) than in sectors that exploited it to enjoy economies of scale at the level of individual firms (e.g., automobiles).

III

Functioning and
Economic Implications

7   Licensing the Market for Technology

7.1 Introduction

As discussed earlier, profiting from intellectual property through arm's-length contracts, such as licensing, faces a number of impediments. Such impediments notwithstanding, chapter 3 provided extensive evidence of the increasing use of licensing in technology based industries such as chemicals, software, electrical and nonelectrical machinery, biotechnology and computers. It is not too surprising that small firms or research labs license despite the inefficiencies of arm's-length contracts. Lacking the downstream manufacturing and marketing capabilities, they may have no other way to appropriate the rents from innovation.

More surprising is that large established producers are active in the market for technology as well. Firms such as Union Carbide, Procter & Gamble, DuPont, Boeing, Hoechst, IBM, Texas Instruments, AT&T, and Phillips Petroleum are now explicitly considering licensing revenues as a part of the overall return from investing in technology. These firms are well established, have large market shares in the product markets, and are capable of exploiting the technology on their own.

Licensing by firms like IBM defies conventional wisdom, which holds that an innovator can best profit from innovations by commercializing the innovations itself (Teece 1988). In this view, licensing is undesirable, not only because contracts are inefficient, but also because licensing increases competition and, hence, dissipates rents. Until recently, many research-intensive firms have reflected this traditional wisdom by treating their technology like "family jewels."

Traditional explanations for licensing build on the idea that firms license if they are less efficient at exploiting the invention than potential licensees, or they license to establish their technology as a de facto standard. Although these explanations have some validity, they cannot fully explain the kind of licensing behavior we are witnessing. In this chapter we propose a different explanation which complements the traditional ones. Specifically, we argue that the interaction between a market for technology, where firms sell their technology through licensing, and a product market, where firms sell their output, helps explain licensing. We show that competition in the product market creates a strategic incentive to license. Further, the competition from other technology holders heightens this incentive, even though licensing reduces the joint profits of all technology holders. We use this theoretical apparatus to explore how licensing decisions are affected by factors such as the nature of demand, transaction costs, and patent protection.

The next section provides evidence of substantial licensing activity by large established producers in a number of technology-based industries. In section 7.3 we show that our key departure from the literature on licensing is the relaxing of the assumption of a monopolist innovator. In turn, this affects the magnitude of the two main forces driving licensing decisions by technology holders: the *revenue effect* and the *rent dissipation effect*. Section 7.4 provides a simple example, which highlights main results of our theory and the underlying intuition. We formalize it in section 7.5, where we develop a model to study how licensing strategies are affected by the nature of demand, transaction costs and the bargaining power of the licensor. Some evidence is provided to support our theory. Section 7.6 examines the licensing behavior of small firms and research labs. Its implications are confronted with data on licensing in the chemical industry. Section 7.7 shows that, with multiple licensors, increasing the efficiency of licensing contracts can diminish profitability and hence the incentives for R&D. Section 7.8 pulls together our main findings.

7.2   Licensing by Established Producers

There are some well-known examples of large companies consciously adopting a strategy of licensing for generating revenues. The chemical industry is a particularly rich source of such examples. For instance, Union Carbide is reported to have earned $300 million from its polyolefin licensing in 1992 (Grindley and Nickerson 1996). Similarly, Phillips Petroleum is thought to cover about a third of its chemicals R&D from licensing expenses. More recently, both DuPont and Dow Chemicals, two chemical firms with a long tradition of exploiting technology

Table 7.1
Licensing Activity by a Sample of Large Chemical Producers during 1980–1990

		A	B	C	D
AS	Air Separation	596	55%	59%	32%
FC	Fertilizers	1000	73%	16%	12%
FP	Food Products	308	25%	12%	3%
GH	Gas Handling	1014	28%	15%	4%
IC	Inorganic Chemicals	1249	45%	33%	15%
IG	Industrial Gases	613	63%	39%	25%
MM	Metals	532	26%	8%	2%
OC	Organic Chemicals	1084	38%	49%	19%
OR	Organic Refining	2246	56%	26%	15%
PC	Petrochemicals	2155	70%	41%	29%
PH	Pharmaceuticals	747	16%	48%	8%
PL	Plastics	1474	56%	69%	38%
PP	Pulp and Paper	396	23%	0%	0%
TF	Textile and Fibers	438	66%	36%	24%
	All subsectors	14897	50%	37%	18%

Source: Our calculations from Chemintell 1991.
Column A = Total number of plants constructed or under construction worldwide during 1980–1990; column B = Share of plants for which information about the licensor was disclosed; column C = Share of plants licensed by a sample of 153 large chemical corporations (all North American, European and Japanese chemical corporations with more than 1 billion U.S. dollar sales in 1988) of all plants with disclosed licensor; column D = Share of plants licensed by our sample of 153 large chemical corporations of all plants reported in the database.

in-house have started to license their technology very actively. Indeed, in 1994 DuPont created a division with the specific task of overseeing all technology transfer activities. Beginning in 1999, this is expected to be a $100 million per year business. Dow Chemicals has also long had a reputation for "never licensing breakthrough technology, and there was an emotional bias against licensing" (Ed Gambrell, V.P., Dow Chemicals). In 1995, it formed a licensing group with the purpose to "create more value" from its technology. Before the group was formed, Dow Chemicals had licensing revenues of roughly $25 million per year. It now expects to earn a $125 million per year by 2000 (Rivette and Kline 1999).

Table 7.1 shows that, during the 1980s, a significant share of chemical process technology sold to unaffiliated firms came from large established producers. The table reports, for selected chemical subsectors, the total number of plants constructed or under construction worldwide during

1980–1990 (column A), the share of plants for which the information about the licensor was disclosed (column B), and the share of plants licensed by a sample of 153 large chemical corporations (column C).[1] Note that these 153 firms, which have large downstream manufacturing and marketing capabilities, account for more than a third of the entire market for technology. In product groups like Organic Chemicals, Air Separation, and Plastics, the firms of our sample license close to or more than 50 percent of all plants for which the identity of the licensor is known.

This trend is not confined to the chemical industry. In semiconductors, IBM has initiated a more active approach to licensing in 1988. Patent and technology licensing agreements earned $345 million for IBM in 1993, increasing to $640 million in 1994. In 1998 IBM patent licensing revenues reached $1 billion, or nearly $750,000 per patent, accounting for over 10 percent of IBM's net profits. To create such profits, it is estimated that IBM would have to sell $20 billion in goods and services. Texas Instruments had led industry moves to take a more active stance on licensing. Texas Instruments initiated its current licensing strategy in 1985, when it successfully asserted its patents in court for a range of inventions pertaining to integrated circuits and manufacturing methods. The company is reported to have earned cumulative royalties of over $1.8 billion between 1986 to 1993, a figure comparable to its cumulative net income during this period (Grindley and Teece 1997). Other firms licensing semiconductor technology include AT&T and SGS-Thompson.

Table 7.2 shows the extent of licensing by leading licensors in a number of selected sectors (SIC at the two-digit level). The table, which has been constructed using information drawn from the SDC data base discussed in chapter 2, reports the most active licensors in some selected sectors along with the number of licensing deals they have signed both as buyers and sellers of technology. Table 7.2 shows that licensing by established producers is not confined to chemicals and semiconductors. Most, though not all, of the firms shown in table 7.2 are large firms with large market share in the product market and enough manufacturing and marketing capability to exploit the technology on their own.[2]

Notice three further aspects of the licensing activity. First, although in semiconductors and electronics there is a substantial amount of cross-licensing, there is substantial affirmative licensing as well, in the sense that patents are not merely being exchanged for other patents. Further, most of the large firms are also active in licensing technology from others. Finally, from the limited description of the licensing agreement in our data set, it appears that only a small fraction of all the licensing contracts are exclusive, especially for technologies licensed by established firms. Exclusivity is most often found when the licensing is combined with an R&D contract, so that the licensing is for technology that is yet to be developed.

7.3   Why Large Firms License Their Technology

7.3.1   A Brief Survey of the Literature

Economics and management literature provides several reasons why even a large successful company might want to license technology to others. An obvious one is the inability of the innovator to exploit its technology to full effect. Typically, this occurs when the technology has application in markets in which the innovator does not typically operate. Licensing is an easy alternative to the expensive move into a different business context.

International licensing is a canonical example. International licensing occurs when companies realize that they cannot serve some foreign markets with their investments, or that it would be extremely expensive or risky to do so. There are obvious added costs of doing business in another country, including communications and transport costs, higher costs of stationing personnel abroad, barriers due to language, customs, and being outside the local business and government network (Hymer 1976). If significant contracting problems described in chapters 4 and 5 are absent, the firm can reap the returns from its technology through a simple licensing contract (Dunning 1981), which implies a low level of exposure to country-specific risk (Hill, Hwang, and Kim 1990; Contractor 1990). In addition the firm has no need to learn how to deal with the local context: it is the licensee that brings in this knowledge (Hofstede 1991).

Similarly, the technology the innovator has developed might not apply to its own lines of business. For instance, Boeing has developed several technologies whose applications are beyond its traditional products. Having patented these applications, Boeing offers them for sale. Some technologies may not fit into a company's overall strategy. Their application may be in product markets that are too small or undesirable, or a company may have ethical objections to their use.

Licensing may also be used to sustain monopoly prices. Specifically, even if collusion in the product market is prohibited, a firm can license

Table 7.2
Leading Licensors, by Sector, Selected Sectors, 1985–1997

Company	Licenses Given	Licenses Taken	Cross-Licenses	Sector
IBM	34	48	69	Business Services
Apple Computer	25	18	15	SIC 73
Sun Microsystems	24	16	16	
Novell	17	17	22	
Hewlett-Packard	13	24	28	
AT&T	11	22	21	
Oracle	10	9	35	
Digital Equipment	8	20	21	
Fujitsu	6	11	34	
Qualcomm	15	0	1	Communication
AT&T	4	3	5	SIC 48
Motorola	3	1	2	
Pacific Telesis group	3	0	1	
Cable &Wireless	2	0	1	
Kokusai Denshin Denwa	2	0	2	
Bell South	1	0	1	
IBM	0	2	5	
Sprint	0	1	3	
General Motors	4	2	3	Instruments and
Honeywell	4	0	4	Related Products
Baxter International	3	4	1	SIC 38
Eli Lilly	3	4	3	
Daimler-Benz	2	0	4	
Hewlett-Packard	2	1	5	
Philips Electronics	2	2	1	
Eastern Kodak	1	3	1	
Siemens	1	3	4	
Johnson & Johnson	0	7	2	
Motorola	23	15	33	Electronic & Other
Intel	19	8	20	Electric Equipment
IBM	18	9	38	SIC 36
Texas Instruments	18	14	39	
AT&T	11	11	36	
Philips Electronics	7	8	35	
Siemens	7	7	26	
Toshiba	5	23	30	
Samsung	4	39	15	
NEC	0	21	27	

Apple Computer	7	6	6	Industrial Machinery
Hewlett-Packard	7	4	15	and Equipment
Digital Equipment	6	0	6	SIC 35
AT&T	5	5	7	
Fujitsu	5	8	10	
IBM	5	10	22	
Hitachi	2	8	9	
NEC	2	9	8	
Matsushita	0	12	2	
Toshiba	0	8	12	
Roche	29	32	21	Chemicals And
American Home Products	21	19	7	Allied Products
Monsanto	14	14	16	SIC 28
Dow Chemical	13	20	11	
Rhone-Poulenc	10	15	11	
Hoechst	7	34	14	
Merck	7	16	10	
Eli Lilly	5	25	12	
Johnson & Johnson	3	22	8	

Source: Our calculations from SDC database on Joint Ventures and Alliances.

its technology to rivals using contracts which set royalties such that the resultant competition yields equilibrium profits identical to what a cartel would have yielded (Fershtman and Kamien 1992). Even if the contract does not directly implement the monopoly price, it might still facilitate tacit collusion (see, for instance, Lin 1996; Eswaran 1993). Further, licensing can be used strategically to control competition and limit entry. For instance, an incumbent firm may license its production technology to reduce the incentive of a potential entrant to develop its own, possibly better, technology (Gallini 1984). Alternatively, the incumbent firm might license a weak rival to crowd the market and deter entry by a stronger competitor (Rockett 1990).

Licensing can be also used as a strategy to enhance demand by creating a second source of supply (Shepard 1987), or by committing the firm to innovate (Corts 1999). Licensing is therefore a way for the innovating firm to make performance or price commitments that otherwise would not be credible. This is particularly important when buyers must make a substantial specific investment to use the new technology.

Licensing could also be motivated by the attempt to create and control de facto standards.[3] Control of these standards can yield large rents.

Licensing is a powerful means to rapidly extend the adoption of a given technology in order to create a critical mass of adopters and suppliers of complementary inputs for the technology. Diffusion of their technology through an active licensing policy partly explains the success of firms like Nintendo and Matsushita in establishing their standards in the video game and VCR markets respectively.

Perhaps the most common occasion for licensing in industries where technology is cumulative and systemic is that firms have to enter into cross-licensing agreements to get access to components patented by other firms (see also discussion in chapter 3). In a sense, these licensing arrangements could be thought of as a primitive type of technology transaction where technology rights are bartered rather than sold. An immediate and important implication is that only firms that own technology can participate in this market. These types of cross-licensing arrangements have typically been seen in electronics and semiconductors, where a number of different firms have controlled important components of the technology (Hall and Ham 1999; Grindley and Teece 1997). With the increase in patenting of gene fragments and research tools in biotechnology, cross-licensing arrangements may increase in the life sciences and chemical sector as well. Although traditionally cross-licensing arrangements have been royalty free, in the last ten or fifteen years, firms with stronger and larger patent portfolios have been demanding and receiving royalty payments. According to industry observers, these payments can amount to tens or even hundreds of millions of dollars (Cohen, Nelson, and Walsh 2000).

7.3.2   Revenue Effect versus Rent Dissipation Effect

In this chapter we propose a different explanation that complements the ones surveyed earlier. Specifically, we argue that the existence of a market for technology changes the incentive of established producers to license their technology. A market for technology implies the presence of several firms owning substitutable technologies. Accordingly, we focus here on the case in which there are at least two independent technology holders in the market. By contrast, the economic literature on licensing has typically focused on the optimal licensing behavior of the monopolist innovator once it has developed and patented a new technology or production process. (In addition to the papers cited above, see also Gallini and Wright 1990; Katz and Shapiro 1985, 1986; Kamien and Tauman 1986.)

The introduction of multiple technology holders might appear to be a minor theoretical extension; instead, it turns out to be very important for understanding licensing behavior.[4] Specifically, licensing imposes a negative pecuniary externality upon other incumbents in the product market, which is ignored by the licensor. As a result, if there are two or more incumbent firms that have proprietary technologies that are substitutes for each other, both firms may find it privately profitable to license, although their joint profits would be higher in the absence of any licensing. This argument will be fleshed out in the example we provide in the next section.

The model we present in section 7.5 is driven by two effects that licensing has on the profits of the licensor. The first, the *revenue effect*, corresponds to the rents earned by the licensor in the form of licensing payments. The second one, the *rent dissipation effect*, is given by the erosion of profits due to another firm (the licensee) competing in the product market. With only one producer the rent dissipation effect typically dominates the revenue effect. The incumbent would earn monopoly profits if it does not license. If it licenses, it can earn at most the sum of duopolistic profits. Since industry profits are typically maximized by a monopoly, the incumbent firm has no incentive to license. By contrast, with two incumbent producers, the losses due to increased competition are shared with the other incumbent in the product market so that the licensor does not fully internalize the rent dissipation effect. This implies that the revenue effect can be larger than the rent dissipation effect. In turn, this means that the incumbent firms compete to supply not only their products, but also their technologies.[5]

The revenue effect depends on transaction costs and the relative bargaining power of the licensor and licensee. Our results confirm that lower transaction costs and greater bargaining power of the licensor lead to more licensing. We will show that the degree of product differentiation across technologies also influences the magnitude of the two effects. If the goods are differentiated the licensee will be a stronger competitor of the technology holder in the product market than of the other producers. This enhances the rent dissipation effect, and reduces the profitability of the licensing strategy. Thus, licensing will be more widespread the lower the degree of product differentiation. Moreover, one would expect that the rent dissipation effect depends on the production and commercial capabilities of the licensor: Large, well-established producers have less to gain from licensing and more to lose from competition. Our results confirm that, all else held equal, research labs or firms with smaller downstream output license more. Interestingly enough, the model also produces a less obvious result. The presence of independent labs may induce a producer-innovator to license more as well.

The latter result is particularly interesting within the framework of this book, because independent technology firms (like the SEFs in chemicals), in addition to supplying technology themselves, can also induce producers in the final markets to become technology suppliers.

7.4   An Example: Licensing in the Market for Lyocell Technology

Lyocell is the first man-made fiber to be created in more than thirty years and some industry experts believe it could prove to be the biggest technological breakthrough since the invention of synthetic fibers one hundred years ago (*Financial Times*, Jan. 8, 1998). Courtaulds, a British textile and chemical firm, developed Lyocell. Shortly thereafter, Lenzing, an Austrian firm, independently developed a similar fiber. Later, an engineering design firm, Zimmer, also claimed to have a rival technology for producing a fiber with similar properties. In what follows, we use this case to develop a simplified example that highlights the main insights of the model. It is important to note that any figures for revenues and profits are not the actual numbers but purely for illustration.

Suppose only Courtaulds has developed and patented the Lyocell process. Assume also that Courtaulds has the ability to commercialize the technology by itself, earning monopoly profit of $150 million. If Courtaulds were to license the Lyocell process to DuPont, it would have to compete with DuPont in the Lyocell market. In turn, competition will reduce total industry profits to $120 million, providing DuPont and Courtaulds each with $60 million in profit. DuPont will not pay more than $60 million for the Lyocell process, implying that Courtaulds could earn no more than $120 million by licensing. Thus, licensing would not be privately profitable.

If Lenzing also develops a competing technology, there will be two producers of Lyocell. To keep with our example, suppose that, absent any licensing, Courtaulds and Lenzing compete with each other and earn net profits of $60 million each. Consider again the decision by Courtaulds to license its Lyocell process to DuPont. If a licensing contract is signed, there will be three producers of Lyocell. Increased competition will reduce total industry profits to $105 million, with $35 million for each producer. If Courtaulds negotiates with DuPont a fee of

80 percent of DuPont's profits from selling Lyocell and incurs transaction costs of $2 million. Licensing is now privately profitable for Courtaulds; the $25 million decrease in its own profits is compensated by $26 million of net revenues from licensing.

One can draw some quick conclusions from this stylized example. First and most important, simply because Courtaulds faces another competitor in the market for Lyocell, it could find privately profitable to license its technology to DuPont, whereas as a monopolist it would not. Second, transaction costs are important. If transaction costs were $4 million, Courtaulds would not license. Third, appropriability of the revenues generated by the Lyocell process is crucial. If Courtaulds could only get 70 percent of DuPont's profit, Courtaulds would not license.

The foregoing analysis has to be modified if the Lenzing process generates a product which is an imperfect substitute for Lyocell. If Courtaulds licenses its technology to DuPont, both Courtaulds and DuPont will produce the same product, which however differs from Lenzing's product. In other words, DuPont and Courtaulds are closer competitors than each is to Lenzing. In this case, DuPont and Courtaulds earn $32.5 million each, and Lenzing earns $40 million from selling the product. Given an 80% share of DuPont's profits and transaction costs of $2 million, after licensing Courtaulds would earn total net profits of $56.5 million. This implies that licensing would not be privately profitable for Courtaulds. This points to another important implication of the theory we develop: Competition in the market for technology generates stronger incentives to license when the final product is homogenous.

Finally, return to the case of a homogenous product market in which Courtaulds finds it privately profitable to license, and suppose that Lenzing can license as well, for instance to BASF, a German chemical company. If Lenzing does not license its Lyocell process, it earns $35 million. If it does, there will be four firms in the product market. Assume that industry profits fall to $90 million and each firm earns $22.5 million. If Lenzing can extract 80 percent of BASF profits through a licensing fee and it incurs a $2 million transaction costs, its total profits after licensing become $38.5 million. This implies that Lenzing finds licensing to be privately profitable. But both Courtaulds and Lenzing earn only $38.5 million if they license, while they would have earned $60 million if they did not license. This is a classical Prisoner's Dilemma problem, as shown in figure 7.1. In the figure, we used the following notation: π (N) are the profits of each producer when there are N producers in the product

Lenzing

		Licensing	Not licensing
Courtaulds	Licensing	π (4) + $\sigma\pi$ (4) –F π (4) + $\sigma\pi$ (4) –F	π (3) + $\sigma\pi$ (3) –F π (3)
	Not licensing	π (3) π (3) + $\sigma\pi$ (3) –F	π (2) π (2)

Figure 7.1
The Prisoner's Dilemma in licensing

market. For example, π *(2)* = *$60m*, π *(3)* = *$35m*, π *(4)* = *$22.5m; F* = $2m stands for the transaction costs; and π = 80 percent is the share of licensee's profits accruing to the licensor. It is easy to see that one Nash equilibrium of this simple game is that both firms license, even though each would earn higher profits if both could credibly commit to a non-licensing strategy.[6] We return to this finding in section 7.7.

7.5 A Model of Competition in the Market for Technology

To provide a more rigorous understanding of the factors affecting patent holders' licensing behavior in the market for technology, we develop a simple model that captures both the intuition and the implications of the story illustrated above. We deliberately keep our framework close to the example. As an extension, we allow incumbents in the market for technology to decide how many licenses they sell to potential entrants. We then study how licensing strategies are affected by factors such as the nature of demand, transaction costs, bargaining power of the licensor, and characteristics of the patent holders.

Assume that two firms have independently developed and patented proprietary technologies for the production of a good.[7] Apart from the two patent holders, we assume that there exist many potential entrants who cannot innovate, but can produce if they receive the rights to use the technology from one of the incumbents. We also assume that entry is costless.[8] Incumbents can therefore both produce themselves (by using their installed production facilities) and license their technology to potential entrants. A licensee produces the same variety of the good as the original licensor. Qualitative results would not change if one assumes the existence of a fringe of firms that can get access to the technology without obtaining a license from one of the technology holders (i.e., through imitation).

Let $k_i - 1$ be the number of licenses sold out by firm i and $k_j - 1$ be the number of licenses sold out by firm j with $i \neq j$; $i, j = 1,2$. This characterization says that each of the two incumbents can enter into non-exclusive licensing contracts, thereby giving rise to k_i and k_j competitors using that respective technology. Differently from our previous example, the strategy set of each patent holder is now enlarged: not only can it decide whether to license or not, but it can also choose how many licenses to sell. For analytical tractability we shall consider k_i and k_j to be continuous variables.

Technology transfer from the licensor to the licensee involves a fixed cost, $F \geq 0$, which captures the transaction costs of licensing. These are the deadweight losses arising from the costs of writing contracts, the costs of gathering information about the technology, the costs of bargaining over the mode and the amount of the licensing payments, the costs of enforcing the agreement. Last but not least, F also stands for the cost of transferring know-how, which has been found to be an important component of the costs of technology transfer (Teece 1977). As discussed in chapter 5, several scholars have argued that the transaction costs of technology licensing are negatively correlated to the strength of patent protection (Arrow 1962b; Merges 1998). Insofar as licensing behavior depends on F, our formulation allows us to analyze how licensing strategies are affected by changes in the patent protection regime.

We also assume that $\sigma \in [0, 1]$ is the share accruing to the licensor of the total profits earned by its licensee through the use of the technology. We assume that $\sigma\Pi$ is a fixed fee collected upfront, and we do not allow for per-unit output royalties.[9] Thus, while F captures the inefficiencies in arms-length contracting, σ accounts for the inability of the licensor to capture all the rents. Both F and σ depend on the actual form of the licensing contract and the strength of patent protection. To keep our analysis manageable, we treat both as parameters. We shall interpret σ as the bargaining power of the innovator in the licensing negotiation. Notice that given our assumption of a large number of potential licensees, σ would be set equal to 1 if it were endogenous to the model. We prefer to keep it as a free parameter to better match the empirical finding that on average licensors capture only a share of the total rents generated in a licensing contract (Caves et al. 1983). There are several other reasons for the licensor being unable to extract the full rents generated by its technology, including asymmetric information (Arora 1995).

Our theoretical framework is a two-stage game. In the first stage, each patent holder decides how many licenses to sell to potential entrants ("competition in the market for technology"). Thus the two incumbents choose respectively $k_i - 1$ and $k_j - 1$. In the second stage, all firms that obtained the technology ($k_i + k_j$) supply the product (competition in the product market). Notice that these two stages correspond to the distinction between markets for goods and markets for technology introduced by the Antitrust Guidelines for the Licensing of Intellectual Property (U.S. Department of Justice 1995) and discussed in chapter 1.

Competition in the Product Market

Assume that competition in the product market generates for each producer profits π^i (k_i, k_j, μ) (gross of any licensing payment) if it gets technology $i \neq j$; $i, j = 1,2$. Here, a key parameter is μ, which stands for the degree of differentiation across the products produced with the two technologies. We assume that $\mu \in [0,1]$, with products being homogeneous for $\mu = 1$ and completely differentiated (independent) for $\mu = 0$. Higher values of μ are associated with more homogenous products. A natural assumption here is that profits increase with the degree of product differentiation, which in our notation implies that π^i is decreasing in μ.[10] Furthermore, since competition erodes profits, we also assume that the producer's profits are decreasing with the number of licenses sold, that is, π^i is decreasing in k_i (and of course in k_j if $\mu > 0$).

Competition in the Market for Technology

Given the outcome of the last stage of the game one can express each patent holder's profits as a function of the number of firms in the product market, k_i and k_j, and of the exogenous parameters, μ, Π and F. That is

$$V^i(k_i, k_j, \mu, \sigma, F) = [1 + \sigma(k_i - 1)] \, \pi^i(k_i, k_j, \mu) - (k_i - 1)F. \tag{1}$$

The first term on the right hand side is the sum of the profits from the patent holder's own production and the licensing payments from $k_i - 1$ licensees. The second term represents the sum of all transaction costs that the licensor has to pay for each of the $k_i - 1$ licensing contracts.

Each technology holder i chooses k_i to maximize its profits given by (1).[11] The first order condition for an interior maximum is therefore[12]

$$V^i_k = \sigma\pi^i + [1 + \sigma(k_i - 1)]\pi^i_k - F \leq 0 \qquad \text{for } k_i - 1 \geq 0. \tag{2}$$

The first order condition (2) shows the two effects discussed in section 7.3.[13] The first one, $\sigma\pi^i$, is positive and it corresponds to the *revenue effect*.

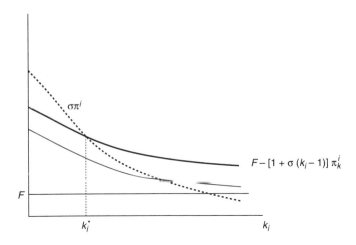

Figure 7.2
Marginal revenue and marginal cost of licensing

This is the increase in profits from additional licensing revenues due to an additional licensee. The second one, $[1 + \sigma(k_i - 1)]\pi_k^i$, is negative and it represents the *rent dissipation effect* from adding one more competitor in the product market. The magnitudes of these two effects and F determine whether the firms license in equilibrium, and if so, how many licenses are sold. This is illustrated by figure 7.2. The dashed line represents the *revenue effect*, or in other words the marginal revenue of licensing. The thick line represents the sum of the *rent dissipation effect* and the transaction costs F, which constitutes the marginal cost of licensing. Holding k_j constant, the optimal number of licenses k_i^* is obtained equating the marginal revenue and the marginal cost of licensing.

In a licensing equilibrium, each firm optimally chooses the number of licenses given the number of licenses sold out by its rival. Figure 7.3 depicts the reaction functions of each patent holder. Each firm's reaction function gives the firm's best response for any given licensing strategy adopted by the rival. We draw the reaction functions as upward sloping.[14] This highlights our argument that competition in the product market increases the incentive to license. The point at which reaction curves cross identifies the equilibrium of the licensing game. Since patent holders are ex-ante symmetric, we focus on the symmetric licensing equilibrium, which we denote k^*.

We present our main results in the form of propositions. We sketch the proofs for all propositions in a technical appendix to this chapter.

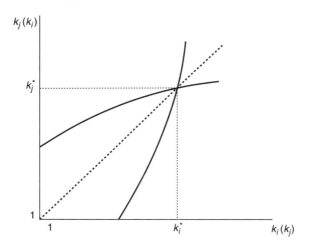

Figure 7.3
Licensing reaction functions

PROPOSITION 1.   Increases in the licensor's bargaining power, σ, and decreases in transaction costs, F, induce firms to license more; that is, k^* is increasing in σ and decreasing in F.

It is straightforward to see why higher transaction costs make licensing less profitable. Both the revenue effect and the rent dissipation effect remain unchanged, but higher transaction costs increase the marginal cost of licensing. Hence, an increase in transaction costs implies a downward shift of patent holder's reaction function. Instead, an increase in the licensor's bargaining power increases both the revenue effect and the rent dissipation effect (see figure 7.4). However, the impact on the revenue effect is greater than that on the rent dissipation effect. Thus an increase in the licensor's bargaining power shifts upward its reaction curve and raises the equilibrium number of licenses.

Proposition 1 implies that any factor that increases the bargaining power of licensors, or decreases the transaction costs involved in licensing will increase licensing. From a policy perspective, the interpretation of changes in F is more interesting.[15] Arora (1995) and Merges (1998) have argued that stronger patent protection reduces the transaction costs of technology licensing (see also the discussion provided in chapter 5). Anand and Khanna (2000) provides empirical support for this proposition. Based on a sample of 1612 licensing agreements over the period 1990–1993, they find that sectors where patents are strong are also those with higher incidence of licensing activity and substantial licensing of prospective technologies. Sectors with weak patent protec-

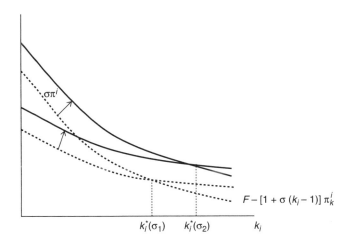

Figure 7.4
Increase in licensor's bargaining power $\sigma_2 > \sigma_1$

tion tend to have higher incidence of transfers to related parties, more cross-licensing, and other such bundled arrangements for transferring technology.

We now state and prove one of the most robust results of this chapter, which can also be most easily tested empirically—namely, that the extent of licensing decreases with the degree of product differentiation. The intuition is quite straightforward. When the good is highly differentiated, each technology holder has a well-defined market niche. Any entrant licensed by the technology holder will be a closer competitor to the technology holder itself than to other technology holders. Instead, when the good is homogeneous, the negative effect due to increased competition is spread across all incumbents, while only the licensor shares in the profits of the new entrants. Greater product homogeneity implies a smaller revenue effect. While it also reduces the rent dissipation effect (see figure 7.5). It turns out that the second force prevails under standard specifications for competition and demand functions, and that the licensors' reaction curves shift upward when μ increases. This implies that k^* increases with μ.

PROPOSITION 2.   Firms license more the more homogenous is the good; that is, k^* is increasing in μ.

Patterns of technology licensing in the chemical industry provide evidence that supports Proposition 2. Using our Chemintell database, table 7.3 reports for some selected chemical subsectors both a measure of

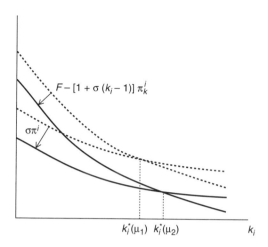

Figure 7.5
More homogenous products, $\mu_2 > \mu_1$

Table 7.3
Licensing and Product Differentiation in Selected Chemical Subsectors, 1980–1990

		Index of Product Differentiation	Average Number of Licenses
AS	Air Separation	9.27	10.2
FC	Fertilizers	13.19	7.96
FP	Food Products	44.59	1.55
GH	Gas Handling	21.55	4.08
IC	Inorganic Chemicals	25.35	3.13
IG	Industrial Gases	18.81	4.8
MM	Metals	25.77	2
OC	Organic Chemicals	47.40	1.23
OR	Organic Refining	21.12	9.09
PC	Petrochemicals	19.88	6.52
PH	Pharmaceuticals	49.97	0.78
PL	Plastics	22.19	3.70
PP	Pulp and Paper	2.66	3.63
TF	Textile and Fibers	11.35	3.91

Source: Our calculations from Chemintell 1991.

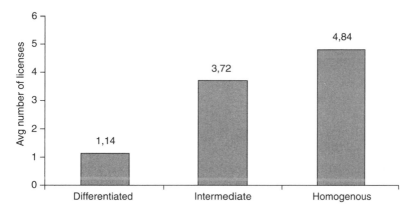

Figure 7.6
Product differentiation and licensing

product differentiation within the product group and the average number of licenses per patent-holder.[16] Note that extensive licensing marks homogeneous product groups like air separation, pulp and paper, and petrochemicals, while we observe only limited licensing by patent holders in differentiated product groups like pharmaceuticals and organic chemicals. Figure 7.6 supports this finding. We classified all twenty-three chemical subsectors reported in the Chemintell database into three broad categories according to their degree of product differentiation: homogenous, intermediate and differentiated. Figure 7.6 shows the average number of licenses per patent-holder decreases with the degree of product differentiation.[17]

7.6   Small Firms and Research Labs

To understand the role of firms with limited manufacturing and marketing capabilities, we shall use again the example developed in section 7.4, where Courtaulds and Lenzing had competing versions of the process technology for Lyocell. Assume that competition in the product market is such that with two, three, and four producers, each makes respectively $60, $35, and $22.5 million profits from selling Lyocell. If the licensing payment is equal to 80 percent of the licensee's profits and transaction costs are of the order of $4 million, neither Courtaulds nor Lenzing have incentive to license. Now, suppose that the second patent holder is not Lenzing, but Zimmer, the German engineering design firm. Zimmer has no downstream production facilities. The only way for

Zimmer to profit from the Lyocell process is through licensing. Suppose that Zimmer licenses its technology to DuPont. We want to see if Zimmer has any interest in licensing its technology to a second licensee, say BASF, thereby diffusing the technology more widely than Lenzing would do. Zimmer's profits from licensing only to DuPont are $44 million (80% of $60 million minus $4 million). Zimmer's profits from licensing to DuPont and BASF are $48 million (80% of $70 million minus $8 million). Hence, other things being equal, Zimmer would license more than Lenzing.

In fact, this is not the end of the story. We must also check whether Courtaulds has any incentive to license, given that Zimmer has licensed DuPont and BASF. If Courtaulds does not license, it will earn $35 million. If it does license, its profits rise to $36.5 million. Hence, not only does Zimmer licenses more than Lenzing, but it also encourages Courtaulds to adopt a more aggressive licensing strategy.

The remainder of the section uses our theoretical framework to analyze how the presence of firms lacking production capability (i.e., small firms and research labs) affects large corporations' licensing strategies. Suppose that patent holders either have manufacturing and marketing capabilities, or they do not. In the latter case, their profit function only depends on the (net) revenues from licensing, that is,

$$(k_i, k_j, \sigma, N, F) = \sigma(R_i - 1)\pi^i(k_i, k_j, \mu) - k_i - 1)F, \qquad (3)$$

where $k_i - 1 \geq 0$ is the number of licenses. As one might expect, small firms and research labs tend to license more than big corporations. With no rents from production, the rent dissipation effect does not matter, and licensing is a more appealing strategy. This is stated below:

PROPOSITION 3.   Firms with no manufacturing capability license more.

Once again, the chemical industry provides a natural test-bed for analyzing this implication of our theory. As widely discussed in earlier chapters, specialized chemical process engineering firms, the SEFs, focus on engineering and process design services for chemical plants and typically lack the downstream manufacturing capability to produce the final products. Licensing is the only way to profit from their intellectual property. Indeed, the Chemintell database shows that around a third of all chemical plants for which the licensor is identified are licensed by SEFs. This share rises to about 50 percent for product groups like Fertilizers, Gas Handling, Organic Refining, and Textile and Fibers.

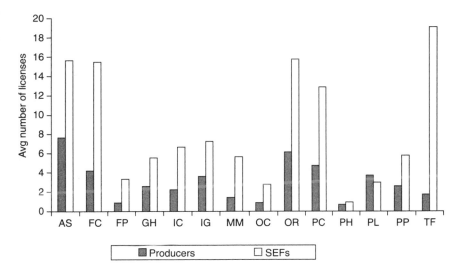

Figure 7.7
Propensity to license by SEFs and chemical corporations

Figure 7.7 provides some support to Proposition 3. It shows, for some selected chemical subsectors, the average number of licenses (total number of licenses divided by number of firms) sold by chemical producers and SEFs, respectively. With the exception of Plastics (PL), the average number of licenses per SEF is larger than the average number of licenses per chemical producers, with the difference being substantial for most subsectors.[18]

Perhaps less obvious is how the presence of research labs (small firms) influences the licensing behavior of firms with installed production facilities (large firms). This is highlighted in the following proposition:

PROPOSITION 4.   The presence of firms lacking downstream manufacturing capability induces large established producers to licensing more.

To understand this result we use our reaction function analysis (see figure 7.8). Upward-sloping reaction functions are critical for this result. We start with the symmetric case where both patent holders are large established producers. The equilibrium is given by point E_1, where the reaction curves cross. Now substitute firm j with a research lab. Proposition 3 implies that a research lab licenses more for any given number of licenses sold by the rival. Hence, its reaction curve shifts upward. The

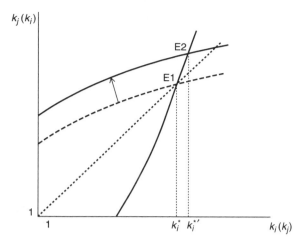

Figure 7.8
The inducement effect

new equilibrium is E2. Notice that since the reaction functions are upward sloping the producer responds with a higher number of licenses as well. As a result, not only we have more licensing because the research lab is more inclined to sell its technology, but we have more licensing because the established producer becomes a more aggressive licensor too.

This result points to an *inducement effect:* The presence of a research lab stimulates the licensing activity of the large corporation at a level that it would not have reached otherwise. Again we use the chemical industry to offer some consistent if not conclusive, evidence. Figure 7.9 classifies the twenty-three chemical subsectors reported in Chemintell (1991) in three broad categories according to the importance of SEFs as licensors. The figure shows that in all subsectors in which SEFs have more than 42 percent of market share during the 1980s, the average number of licenses by chemical producers is 2.8, whereas in the subsectors in which SEFs have less than 18 percent of the market, it is as little as 1.3.[19] Thus, apart from being suppliers in the market for technology themselves, independent technology firms have the additional effect of inducing the producers in the final markets to become technology suppliers as well.

7.7   Incentives for Investing in R&D

So far, we have been arguing that competition in the product market creates a strategic incentive to license. By licensing, firms induce entry and

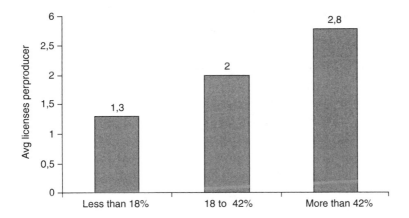

Figure 7.9
SEFs' market share and licensing by chemical producers

further strengthen competition in the product market. As well understood in the literature on innovation, an increase in the rate of diffusion also implies a smaller incentive to develop the innovation in the first place. This is also what occurs in our model where a larger k^* means lower perfirm profits.

PROPOSITION 5.   With ex-ante symmetric licensors, the possibility of licensing reduces the profits per innovator. That is, profit under licensing decreases with k^*, if industry profits decrease with competition.

The intuition for this result was already provided in our example in section 7.4. If firms are ex ante symmetric and they do not license, it is reasonable to assume that they share the market equally. In the equilibrium with positive symmetric licensing, each patent holder's technology (used by the licensor and its network of licensees) still covers half of the market. However, competition among licensees (and licensors) is now stronger, and it is likely to reduce industry profits. A Prisoner Dilemma situation then emerges. Each incumbent earns higher profits under a symmetric nonlicensing strategy, and it also earns higher profits by licensing if the rival does not.

Proposition 5 also suggests that technology holders might have incentives to collude in order to reduce or stop licensing and hence increase profits. An example of such a practice is provided by the history of the chemical sector. Before World War II cartels were widespread. The major technology leaders, which were typically European firms, adopted a strict control over their licensing policies in order to keep market shares, deter entry, and sustain prices above competitive levels (Arora 1997). Such collusion in the market for technology is explicitly addressed in the Antitrust Guidelines for the Licensing of Intellectual Property (U.S. Dept. of Justice 1995, example 2).

The fear of dissipating profits through aggressive licensing might have induced Courtaulds and Lenzing to initially fight fiercely for the patent on the Lyocell process—each firm accusing the other of violating its intellectual property—and later to agree on sharing the property rights on the Lyocell process. Both the legal disputes and the agreement might cover attempts to avoid competition in licensing. Unfortunately for them, Zimmer has also announced that it has discovered its own Lyocell process which does not infringe any of the existing patents.

Finally, proposition 5 underscores the ambiguous effects on the profits of technology holders of factors that increase the efficiency of licensing transactions or enhance the licensor's share. On the one hand, a larger σ (or a smaller F) increases the licensor's profits; on the other hand, it stimulates (by proposition 1) the licensing activity of the rival technology holder, and, hence, it reduces profits. In particular, it is readily apparent that at $k^* = 1$, an increase in the efficiency of the licensing contracts would actually hurt the technology holders.[20] This is stated formally in the following result:

PROPOSITION 6.   At parameter values such that $k^* = 1$, an increase in σ or a decrease in F reduces profits of each technology holder.

Thus, insofar as stronger patent protection encourages licensing (through higher σ or lower F), it may produce the unexpected result that it may even lower industry R&D or reduce the number of firms investing in R&D.

7.8   Conclusion

There is increasing evidence that firms in some sectors are trying to profit from their intellectual property not just by embodying it in their own output but also by licensing it to others, including to potential competitors. This behavior is difficult to understand in the context of models with only monopolist technology holders, who face no competition in the product market. By relaxing the widespread assumption of a monopolist patent holder, this chapter shows that competition drastically changes the incentives for an incumbent to license its technology to potential entrants.

In particular, when there are multiple technology holders, not only do they compete in the product market, but they also compete in the market for technology. Thus, this chapter provides a framework for analyzing the nature and properties of markets for technology.

Within this framework, we showed that increases in the efficiency of licensing contracts and reductions in transaction costs increase the propensity to license. Although licensing profits increase, stronger product market competition may even reduce the overall profits of the innovating firms. This implies that stronger patents may be a mixed blessing for firms in technology intensive industries. Although stronger patents raise barriers against imitation by rivals, they may nonetheless ultimately result in increased product market competition by facilitating licensing. In many respects, this can be seen as a somewhat paradoxical result in light of the traditional view about the role of patent rights, whereby stronger protection is normally seen as a necessary "evil." It reduces competition in order to allow for the necessary incentives to innovate. But to the extent that increased patent protection induces licenses, it may well be associated with an increase in downstream competition. And this arises from the fact that stronger intellectual property rights induce the formation of more extensive markets for technology.

Since licensing partially substitutes for production, small firms and firms lacking adequate downstream commercialization (production and marketing) capabilities are naturally more aggressive licensors. Moreover their presence induces their larger rivals to license more aggressively as well. Therefore, managers in technology-based firms must guard against a common tendency to treat in-house technology like the "family jewels," particularly when smaller, technology-focused firms also develop substitute technologies. Instead, they must be prepared to become effective technology licensors and compete in the market for technology.

The challenges that markets for technology pose for managers are strongest in sectors with relatively homogenous products. Unless the established incumbents also have strong brand identities or other ways of differentiating themselves from others, even proprietary process technologies will not be effective entry barriers if the transaction costs of licensing are low enough. Our model thus provides another important insight—increasing product differentiation not only softens price competition in the product market, it also reduces the propensity to license in the technology market.

Appendix: Proofs

Proof of Proposition 1. The key of the proof is that in a symmetric stable licensing equilibrium the direction of change of k depends only on the sign of the cross partial of the payoff function. One can easily compute $V_{kF} = -1 < 0$ and $V_{k\sigma} = \pi + (k^* - 1)\pi_k > \sigma[\pi + (k^* - 1)\pi_k] > \sigma\pi + [1 + \sigma(k^* - 1)]\pi_k > 0$, thus giving us the required results. ∎

Proof of Proposition 2. By differentiating $V_k \equiv V_k^i |_{k_i = k_j = k^*}$ with respect to μ, one obtains $V_k\mu + \sigma\pi\mu + [1 + \sigma(k^* - 1)\pi_k\mu$, where the former term is negative, while the latter is positive. Thus, the result depends on the characteristics of the profit function. One can show that $V_{k\mu} > 0$ under quantity competition, and linear demand, and under price competition, and multinomial logit demand. (See Arora and Fosfuri 1999.) ∎

Proof of Proposition 3. The first order condition for a research lab is $V_k^i = \sigma\pi^i + \sigma(k^* - 1)\pi_k^i - F = 0$. Evaluating this condition at the k_i optimal for a firm that can operate in the product market, one can see that $V_k^i > 0$, giving us the required result. ∎

Proof of Proposition 4. For this result it suffices to prove that $V_{k_i k_j}^i > 0$. Notice that $V_{k_i k_j}^i = \sigma\pi_{k_j}^i + [1 + \sigma(k_i - 1)]\pi_{k_i k_j}^i$, where the former term is negative, while the latter is positive. Thus, the result depends on the characteristics of the profit function. In Arora and Fosfuri (1999) we derive conditions for $V_{k_i k_j}^i > 0$ to hold. ∎

Proof of Proposition 5. At a symmetric licensing equilibrium, each licensor's profits are: $V(k^*) = [1 + \sigma(k^* - 1)]\pi(k^*, k^*, \mu) - (k^* - 1)F$. Notice that $V(k^*) < k^*\pi(k^*, k^*, \mu)$. Finally, $2\pi(1,1,\mu) > 2k^*\pi(k^*, k^*, \mu)$, since industry profits are decreasing with competition. Notice that $\pi(1,1,\mu)$ are the patent holder's profits in the nonlicensing equilibrium. ∎

8

Global Technology Suppliers and the International Division of Innovative Labor

8.1 Introduction

The benefits of specialization and division of labor are articles of faith for economists. However, the literature has typically focused on benefits that arise within a market. In this chapter, we argue that an important and understudied part of the story lies in the benefits that a division of labor in one market can generate for other markets. We have already explored one aspect of this issue in chapter 6, where we noted that general-purpose technologies, or GPTs, and the industry specialized in their production, can be the vehicles for transmitting the beneficial effects arising in one industry to other industries. The transmission of these effects is inherent in the general-purpose nature of the technology, and it crucially depends on the intermediation of the GPT sector. As we have noted in chapter 6, productivity improvements in one industry generate incentives for the GPT sector to improve its technology. Because this technology is shared by many industries, these industries also benefit from the improved quality of the GPT as well. Indeed, this pattern of technology diffusion and transmission of growth impulses is one of the basic features of a division of innovative labor. Instead, when industries are vertically integrated in the production of technology, there are fewer spillovers across them, with reduced investment and reduced economic growth.

This chapter argues that the potential to transmit these benefits arises not only across industries but also across countries. If the growth of the market in a certain country gives rise to the formation of specialized technology suppliers in that country, then, once the technology is developed, these technology suppliers can sell it to producers in other countries at a lower cost than the initial cost of developing the technology. In this way, followers benefit from investments in technology by leaders.

To examine this issue we study investments in chemical plants in less developed countries (LDCs) during the 1980s. This provides an ideal testbed. Beginning in the 1930s and continuing into the 1960s, the modern chemical industry in the developed countries ("First World") grew rapidly. (See section 8.4 for definitions.) This stimulated the growth of firms that specialized in the design and engineering of the chemical processes, the SEFs. In the 1970s, and especially in the 1980s, as a modern chemical industry emerged in the developing countries, it benefited from the presence of the SEFs that acted as an upstream sector of technology suppliers in the First World. Simply put, the growth of the chemical industry in the First World created an upstream sector, which later spurred the growth of the chemical industry in the developing countries.

To structure our analysis, we first develop a simple theory of international transmission of growth impulses. Our theoretical framework assumes that a larger number of technology suppliers increases the net surplus that the buyers receive from investing in a chemical plant. This is a natural assumption since buyers should benefit from being able to choose from a larger pool of suppliers, and is consistent with a large set of economic explanations that variously emphasize search costs, reduced bargaining power of sellers, and a better "match." The main result of our theory is that if the existing SEFs in the First World are also potential suppliers of chemical firms in developing countries, then a larger number of First World SEFs in a given market for chemical process technology implies greater investment in that market in the developing countries.

We use our theoretical framework to derive two additional results. First, we predict that the larger the number of First World SEFs, the greater the number of plants in developing countries whose engineering services are "bought" from SEFs, and the smaller the number of plants whose engineering services are "made" in-house by the chemical firms. Second, the impact of an increase in the supply of SEFs is greater for less technically advanced companies. This suggests that SEFs are more beneficial for local Third World companies than for the multinational enterprises that invest in these markets. This key result (and empirical finding) implies that technology suppliers, and a division of innovative labor, primarily benefit technically less advanced companies and countries. We test the implications of our theory using data on chemical plant investments in 139 leading chemical technologies and thirty-eight developing countries. These are drawn from the comprehensive Chemintell (1991) data set of more than 20,000 chemical plants announced and constructed during the 1980s.

The chapter is organized as follows. Section 8.2 below provides the conceptual underpinnings of our approach and links it to the literature on economic growth and international trade. Section 8.3 presents our theoretical framework. Section 8.4 discusses the empirical specifications and presents our empirical results. Section 8.5 summarizes our findings and concludes the chapter. The appendix describes our data.

8.2   Division of Labor, Markets for Technology, and International Technology Spillovers

Our analysis in this chapter is related to several strands in the literature on economic growth and international trade. Our emphasis on the lower cost of using technologies compared with the cost of developing them is similar in spirit to the literature on endogenous growth (e.g., Romer 1990, 1996). Following Griliches (1979) and Jaffe (1986), there is a well established line of research on technology spillovers. Coe and Helpman (1995), Eaton and Kortum (1996), and Keller (1998) have provided evidence of the existence of international technological spillovers.[1] We noted in chapter 2 that an important void in this literature is that we lack a firm understanding of the mechanisms that give rise to these spillovers. An important exception is the work of Zucker, Darby, and Armstrong (1998), who find that market mechanisms and other established linkages involving individual scientists may account for what appear to be knowledge spillovers from universities to local firms in California biotechnology.

In this chapter we suggest another mechanism through which spillovers may take place—the intermediation of an upstream sector which sells technology inputs through a full-fledged market for technology. Note that in our analysis both real and pecuniary spillovers may be involved. SEFs may lower technology transfer costs for developing countries, and competition among them may lower the price as well, a purely pecuniary effect.[2] Rich as our data are, we cannot empirically distinguish between the two mechanisms. Thus, although our theoretical explanation focuses on the pecuniary externality, real externalities may be present as well.

It is natural to ask whether our story is not simply a story about international trade. It is, but with one difference. While the standard Heckscher-Ohlin trade model locates comparative advantage in natural resources or factor endowments, we locate it in the fact that chemical engineering services are based on cumulative learning and experience, and that the (fixed) costs of acquiring this expertise are already sunk when the developing country markets arise. Put differently, the First World has a comparative advantage in engineering services simply because First World engineering firms were founded more than fifty (and in some cases, more than 100) years ago in response to the growth of the oil and chemical sectors in their own countries.

By stressing the historical sequence in the rise of new markets, our perspective also differs somewhat from Rivera-Batiz and Romer (1991), who argue that international economic integration increases growth because, with integration, the fixed cost of producing "ideas" can be spread over a larger market. In our story, integration is beneficial to the follower countries even though the number of SEFs in the First World does not increase when the First World and developing country markets are integrated. Our primary reason for assuming that SEFs do not develop in response to growth in developing countries is that it is more faithful to history. As a historical fact, most SEFs arose to serve the First World market, and their investments were not motivated by the hope of serving developing country markets that did not yet exist.

Finally, our analysis in this chapter is related to the literature on the product life cycle (Vernon 1979), whereby as technologies or products mature, they are transferred from the First World to developing countries. This literature has focused on one mechanism through which this transfer occurs—multinational enterprises (MNEs) operating in final product markets. This has often been justified by the assumption that while downstream products are tradable, upstream inputs are not (Nadiri 1993; Rodriguez-Clare 1996). In fact, in the chemical industry as in many other high-tech industries, a key upstream input—intangible knowledge and expertise—is easier to move across locations, while the final products (chemicals such as ammonia and ethylene) are costly to transport. MNEs are undoubtedly an important vehicle for technology transfer. However, when technologies are based on systematic body of knowledge like chemical engineering, MNEs are not the only, or even the most important, way of transferring technology. Instead, as in the chemical industry, specialized technology suppliers competing amongst themselves can be the predominant means of technology transfer.

8.3   Theoretical Framework and Empirical Implications

Figure 8.1 summarizes the two effects that drive our theory.[3] First, the growth of the First World market for a given chemical process encour-

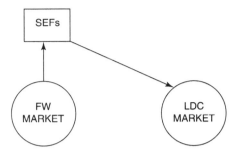

Figure 8.1
The transmission of growth impulses

ages the rise of engineering firms specialized in the design of chemical plants for that process. This result is completely intuitive. It only requires that entry as an SEF have a fixed cost (corresponding to the cost of acquiring technical expertise), and that the price-cost margins (profits per unit of output) that SEFs earn, decline with the number of SEFs in that sector.[4]

The second effect is the impact SEFs in the First World have on the size of the developing country market. To understand this effect, suppose that First World SEFs did not exist. Then, apart from relying on multinationals, either developing country firms would have to provide the services themselves or rely on any domestic SEFs that may exist. In either case, developing country firms would face very high costs. Having fewer SEFs to choose from increases search costs, lowers the bargaining power of the buyer, and reduces the likelihood of getting a more advanced or appropriate technology. As a result, the expected surplus of setting up a plant would be lower, and this implies lower investment in chemical plants. Given the high transportation costs for many chemical products, this would imply slower growth of chemicals.

Instead, assume that the First World market for chemical process technology has already emerged and a division of innovative labor achieved. In other words, assume there are k SEFs that have entered the market for engineering services in the First World. If SEFs can cheaply supply their technology to producers in developing countries, with technology-specific costs already sunk, then the number of SEFs which can potentially serve the developing country market is equal to k as well. Note that k is independent of the developing country market size.[5] In addition if the expected surplus of setting up a plant is increasing with the number of available SEFs, we can show the following:

PROPOSITION 1.   The total investment in a given developing country market is greater, the greater is the number of (potential) technology suppliers, k.

Now consider the investment decision of a downstream chemical firm. It has three possible alternatives. It can either not invest (and hence earn zero profits), or it can "buy" engineering services from SEFs, or it can "make" (engineer) the plant by itself. Proposition 1 simply states that the sum of "buys" and "makes" increases with the number of SEFs.

However, the availability of a larger number of technology suppliers also affects the relative profitability of developing the technology in-house vis-à-vis buying the technology. The availability of SEFs lowers the cost of buying the technology from external sources but leaves unchanged the costs and benefits of developing the technology in-house. So, the larger the number of technology suppliers the more profitable the strategy of buying becomes relative to the strategy of making. This leads to the following proposition.

PROPOSITION 2.   The expected number of "buys" increases with the number of SEFs, k, whereas the expected number of "makes" decreases with k.

Finally, we analyze how the benefits from an industry of specialized technology suppliers depend on the technological capability of the investing firm. For simplicity, consider only two sets of firms: firms with a high level of technological capability and firms with a low level. Firms that are technically competent have a greater possibility to engineer the plant on their own, whereas firms with little technological capability must necessarily rely upon specialized technology suppliers if they want to invest. These are the firms that benefit the most from the existence of a market for technology. Insofar as MNEs have greater technological capabilities than developing country chemical firms, SEFs are more valuable for developing country firms than for MNEs. This is summarized by the following proposition:

PROPOSITION 3.   Investments by domestic LDC firms respond more to the number of SEFs than investments by MNEs.

Our theory relies strongly on the assumption that the critical input, technology, is easily "tradable" across countries. It is therefore important to understand why this input is tradable. To illustrate this point we borrow an example from the history of another industry. In his study of the U.S. machine tool sector in the nineteenth century, Rosenberg (1976) noted that the various downstream industries using machine tools for their operations did not emerge at the same time. For instance, firearm manufacturing emerged earlier than sewing machines, typewriters, or bicycles. The growth of the firearm industry then spurred the growth of a machine tool sector specialized in the production of machines to cut metals into precise shapes. As Rosenberg points out, when the bicycle and other mechanical industries arose a few decades later, they had to perform metal cutting operations that were very similar to those of the firearm industry (e.g., boring, drilling, milling, planing, grinding, polishing, etc; see Rosenberg 1976, 16), and these were performed using very similar machines.

Thus, the bicycle industry could rely upon the suppliers of metal cutting machines that were already serving the larger firearm industry, which were more numerous than the suppliers that the bicycle industry could have supported by itself. The key factor here was that what was learned in the firearm industry to produce the metal cutting machines did not have to be learned again in bicycles. Hence, the machine tool producers could move across sectors even though bicycles are very different from firearms. The "commonality" in the learning process across the industries, or what Rosenberg called "technological convergence," was critical for the transmission of growth through the intermediation of an upstream sector.

If we look at this issue across countries rather than across sectors, we have a similar argument. Even though an ammonia plant in the United States is a different object from an ammonia plant in India, what remains unchanged are the basic principles of how an ammonia plant should be designed and engineered. Clearly, applying what one has learned in one place in another is not always easy, and technology transfer is certainly not costless (Teece 1977). Such costs are likely to depend on the very nature of the knowledge embodied in the technology (see chapter 4), with tacit and less articulated knowledge being more difficult to transfer, but also on the "absorptive capacity" of the recipient firm (Cohen and Levinthal 1989). However, the important point is that the transfer cost must be substantially smaller than the cost of developing the technology in the first place. It is in this sense, that the fixed cost of developing or inventing the technology is paid by the industries or countries that emerge earlier (firearms or U.S. fertilizer producers), while the industries or countries that come later (bicycles or Indian fertilizer producers) pay only the marginal cost. Technological convergence is the factor that makes possible the transmission of growth mediated by division of labor.

8.4   Empirical Analysis

8.4.1   Sample and Variables

To test our theory we used data on thirty-eight developing countries and 139 chemical process technologies. This gave us 5,282 "markets," where the unit of observation is a process-country pair. Plant-level data on the 139 chemical processes were obtained from the Chemintell (1991) data base, which covers all new chemical plants (over 20,000 in all) announced all over the world during the period 1981–1990. The database and the construction of the variables used in the empirical analysis are described in more detail in the appendix. We included all thirty-eight developing countries for which we could obtain complete data from two main sources: United Nations Statistical Yearbooks, and Barro-Lee (1994). These countries account for about 80 percent of all the chemical plants located in developing countries in the database. In what follows we define "First World" to be the Western European countries, the United States of America, Canada, Japan, Australia, and New Zealand. All the other countries, except the so called Eastern Bloc countries are included in "developing countries."

We constructed the following variables. $SIZE_{ij}$ is the total investment in millions of U.S. dollars in our 139 processes i and 38 countries j. This is obtained by multiplying the number of plants in ij by the average investment cost of a plant in process i in all developing countries.[6] Similarly, we constructed BUY_{ij} and $MAKE_{ij}$, which are the total dollar investments in plants whose engineering services are bought from an unaffiliated contractor, and the total investment in plants whose engineering services are made in-house (or by an affiliated SEF). DOM_{ij} and MNE_{ij} are the total dollar investments by developing country and multinational firms respectively.[7]

$SIZE\_FW_i$ is the total value of investment in process i in the First World. This is obtained by multiplying the total number of plants in process i in the First World by $COST\_FW_i$, the average investment cost of a plant in process i in the First World. SEF_FW_i is the number of firms (SEFs) that provide engineering services in process i in the first world.

We constructed two other process-specific variables, $NOVEL_i$ and $PROCPAT_i$. They are two measures of the nature of the technology. $PROCPAT_i$ is the total number of U.S. patents granted for the chemical process i in the period 1976–1997. It covers only the patents relating to the process itself rather than to the use of the output produced by the process. $PROCPAT_i$ is a good measure of the complexity of the process technology, and of the potential for multiple inputs, pathways, and final product qualities.[8] $NOVEL_i$ is the growth rate between the two periods 1986–1995 and 1976–1985 of all the U.S. patents whose title contained the exact name of the process i. Unlike $PROCPAT_i$, $NOVEL_i$ does not distinguish between process and product patents. Thus, for instance, this variable also includes the development of new uses of the product. $NOVEL_i$ is then likely to be a measure of the rate of technological change. We use these two variables to control for the maturity and complexity of the technology. Our objective here is to rule out the possibility that the estimated coefficient of SEF_FW_i reflects the effect that developing countries are more likely to invest in older and more mature processes. In turn, these two variables may also help to control for differences in the technology transfer costs.

Finally, the database classifies plants into twenty-one chemical subsectors, we grouped in nine sector dummies (listed in the appendix). Our country-specific variables include measures like GDP, population, energy consumption, openness, and human capital, and are listed in table 8.1 along with their source. Table 8.2 presents descriptive statistics for the variables used in our analysis.

8.4.2 $SIZE_{ij}$, BUY_{ij}, and $MAKE_{ij}$: Specification and Empirical Results

We begin by estimating three equations linking $SIZE_{ij}$, BUY_{ij}, and $MAKE_{ij}$ to the number of First World SEFs. We employed a logarithmic specification of the form

$$\log(X_{ij}) = const + aY_j + bZ_i + e_{ij}, \tag{1}$$

where X_{ij} is $SIZE_{ij}$, BUY_{ij}, or $MAKE_{ji}$, Y_j is a vector of country-specific characteristics, Z_i is a vector of process specific characteristics, and e_{ij} is an error term. We note that the results are robust to alternative specifications such as linear or exponential. A logarithmic specification allows the marginal effect of SEFs on investments to diminish with the number of SEFs. Bresnahan and Reiss (1991) have also shown that four to five suppliers in a market may be enough to make the market competitive (the average number of SEFs in our sample is 12). This favors a functional form that accounts for the diminishing returns of an extra supplier.[9]

As country-specific characteristics we used measures of the economic size of the country (log (GDP_j), log (POP_j), log ($ENERGY_j$), log ($AREA_j$)), and measures of human capital ($HKAP_j$), openness to imports of intermediate goods ($OPEN_j$), geographic area dummies. We also used dummy variables for the presence in the country of oil or gas reserves,

Table 8.1
List of Country Characteristics

GDP_j	Real GDP of country in 1985 in billions of U.S. dollars. Obtained from per capita GDP of country (Barro-Lee) times population.
POP_j	Population of country in 1985 in millions. (Barro-Lee)
$ENERGY_j$	Total energy consumption of country (1985–1987 average) in thousand metric tons of coal equivalent (UN Statistical Yearbook).
$AREA_j$	Size of land in thousands square Km (Barro-Lee). In regressions we also used $AREA_j$ interacted with sector dummies for inorganic chemicals, agricultural chemicals, minerals & metallurgy $(ICHEM_i + AGRI_i + MM_i)$
$HKAP_j$	Human Capital. Average schooling years of population over 25 in the country (Barro-Lee). Equal to zero if data is missing in Barro-Lee (missing data for China, Egypt, Morocco, Nigeria, Saudi Arabia).
$DHKAP_j$	Dummy equal to 1 for countries for which $HKAP_j$ is missing in Barro-Lee.
$OPEN_j$	Own-import weighted tariff rates of the country on intermediate inputs and capital goods. (Barro-Lee) This is Barro-Lee's variable $OWTI$. Equal to zero if data is missing in Barro-Lee (missing data for Burma, Hungary, Poland, South Africa).
$DOPEN_j$	Dummy equal to 1 for countries for which $OPEN_j$ is missing in Barro-Lee.
$DOIL_{ij}$	Dummy for countries with oil reserves interacted with dummy for processes in the oil refining sector. Countries with oil reserves: Algeria, Argentina, Brazil, China, Colombia, Ecuador, Egypt, India, Indonesia, Iran, Iraq, Kuwait, Malaysia, Mexico, Nigeria, Saudi Arabia, Syria, Venezuela. (Main countries with oil reserves listed in World Atlas, 1990.)
$DGAS_{ij}$	Dummy for countries with natural gas reserves interacted with dummy for processes in the gas processing sector. Countries with natural gas reserves: Algeria, Argentina, Indonesia, Mexico, Venezuela. (Main countries with natural gas reserves listed in World Atlas, 1990.)
Geographical Area Dummies	Africa, Eastern Europe, Middle East, Central and South America, Far East.

Table 8.2
Descriptive Statistics

Variable	No. of Obs.	Mean	Std Dev	Min	Max
$SIZE_{ij}$*	5282	78.1	431.4	0	17751.7
BUY_{ij}*	5282	75.3	422.9	0	17751.7
$MAKE_{ij}$*	5282	2.8	33.9	0	1321.1
DOM_{ij}*	5282	62.8	364.6	0	13313.7
MNE_{ij}*	5282	15.2	129.7	0	4437.9
$SIZE\_FW_i$*	139	2761.4	6277.5	2.0	45555.6
$COST\_FW_i$*	139	76.5	145.5	0.8	1190
SEF_FW_i*	139	11.94	11.77	0	60
$NOVEL_i$	139	0.17	0.65	−0.78	3.600
$PROCPAT_i$**	136	61.19	60.65	1	345
GDP_j	38	171.28	323.40	19.63	1918.79
POP_j	38	84.90	204.40	1.70	1059.50
$ENERGY_j$	38	61.26	126.70	1.48	765.18
$AREA_j$	38	1311.4	2039.4	1.0	9537.0
$OPEN_i$***	34	0.237	0.23	0.00	1.32
$HKAP_j$***	33	4.85	2.18	0.91	10.75

*In millions of U.S. dollars.
**Missing values for specialty chemicals, resins, and refinery.
***Missing values. See table 8.1.

and interacted them with the sector dummies for oil refining plants and gas plants ($DOIL_{ij}$ and $DGAS_{ij}$). We interacted log ($AREA_j$) with a dummy for the three sectors: inorganic chemicals, agricultural chemicals, and minerals and metallurgy ($ICHEM_i + AGRI_i + MM_i$). This is because larger countries are more likely to possess natural resources that are the basis for the production of inorganic chemicals and minerals. Similarly, it is more likely that bigger countries have large areas for extensive agricultural production. Apart from log (SEF_FW_i), we used the following process-specific characteristics as controls: sector dummies, log ($SIZE\_FW_i$), log ($COST\_FW_i$), log ($PROCPAT_i$), and $NOVEL_i$.[10]

Table 8.3 presents the results of our OLS estimations of equation (1). The estimated elasticities, with respect to SEF_FW_i, of $SIZE_{ij}$ and BUY_{ij} are large and statistically significant (0.46 and 0.52 respectively). By contrast, the elasticity of $MAKE_{ij}$ is very small, and insignificantly different from zero. The marginal effects of SEF_FW_i, computed across all observations in our sample, are 3.01 million U.S. dollars for $SIZE_{ij}$, 3.28 million U.S. dollars for BUY_{ij}, and a mere 4,690 U.S. dollars for $MAKE_{ij}$. Therefore, the marginal effect of SEFs is greater for the buys than for the

Table 8.3
Determinants of Total Investment, "Buys" and "Makes": OLS Estimates
$\log (X_{ij}) = \text{const} + aY_j + bZ_i = e_{ij}$

	$SIZE_{ij}$	BUY_{ij}	$MAKE_{ij}$
Constant	−9.95	−10.95	−4.21
	(1.44)	(1.62)	(0.55)
$DOIL_{ij}$	0.51	0.51	0.14
	(0.14)	(0.16)	(0.05)
$DGAS_{ij}$	−0.34	−0.37	−0.01
	(0.21)	(0.24)	(0.08)
$DHKAP_j$	−0.12	−0.11	−0.09
	(0.12)	(0.14)	−0.05
$(1 - DHKAP_j) \times HKAP_j$	−0.04	−0.05	0.01
	(0.02)	(0.03)	(0.01)
$\text{Log}(GDP_j)$	0.44	0.42	0.26
	(0.16)	(0.18)	(0.06)
$\text{Log}(POP_j)$	−0.29	−0.31	−0.07
	(0.11)	(0.12)	(0.04)
$\text{Log}(ENERGY_j)$	0.39	0.47	−0.05
	(0.07)	(0.08)	(0.03)
$\text{Log}(AREA_j)$	0.07	0.08	−0.02
	(0.03)	(0.04)	(0.01)
$(ICHEM_i + AGRI_i + MM_i) \times \text{Log}(AREA_j)$	0.13	0.15	0.01
	(0.03)	(0.04	(0.01)
$DOPEN_j$	−0.18	−0.22	0.11
	(0.15)	(0.17)	(0.06)
$(1 - DOPEN_j) \times OPEN_j$	0.62	0.72	0.07
	(0.18)	(0.20)	(0.07)
$\text{Log}(SIZE\_FW_i)$	0.38	0.41	0.07
	(0.05)	(0.06)	(0.02)
$\text{Log}(COST\_FW_i)$	−0.31	−0.35	−0.07
	(0.06)	(0.06)	(0.02)
$NOVEL_i$	−0.16	−0.17	−0.03
	(0.05)	(0.05)	(0.02)
$DPROCPAT_i$	−0.35	−0.49	−0.01
	(0.20)	(0.23)	(0.08)
$(1 - DPROCPAT_i) \times \text{Log}(PROCPAT_i)$	−0.13	−0.15	0.00
	(0.03)	(0.03)	(0.01)
$\text{Log}(SEF\_FW_i)$	0.46	0.52	0.02
	(0.05)	(0.06)	(0.02)
Adj. R^2	0.25	0.24	0.04
No. of observations	5282	5282	5282

Note: Standard errors in parentheses. All regressions include sector dummies and dummies for geographical areas of country.

chemical plant investments as a whole, and the effect on the makes is almost zero. This supports propositions 1 and 2.

The important result of table 8.3 is that the effects of SEF_FW_i on $SIZE_{ij}$ and BUY_{ij} are sizable and statistically significant despite the extensive controls for the size of the chemical process and country markets. Note also that our measures of market size (e.g., GDP_j, $ENERGY_j$, $AREA_j$, $SIZE\_FW_i$) are generally significant in all three equations. Finally, in all three equations, the cost of a "typical" plant ($COST\_FW_i$), and our measures of technological change and complexity ($NOVEL_i$ and $PROCPAT_i$) have the expected sign. As predicted by the product lifecycle theory, costly and complex processes are associated with lower investments by developing countries.

Since our dependent variables, $SIZE_{ij}$, BUY_{ij} and $MAKE_{ij}$, are non-negative, we also estimated Tobit specifications (not reported here). The signs of the explanatory variables in the Tobit specifications were similar to the ones in the OLS specifications. We have also explored a possible economic interpretation of the many "zero" observations, namely that there exists a threshold level below which setting up a chemical plant is not economically profitable. To capture this additional subtlety we used a generalized Tobit model (see Amemiya 1985) that allows such a threshold to vary across observations. Results (not reported here) suggest that first world SEFs increase the probability of investment in LDCs and, given the threshold, increase investment as well. For further details, see Arora, Fosfuri, and Gambardella (2001).

8.4.3   Measurement Error and Unobserved Heterogeneity

Our empirical procedure in section 8.4.2 raises two important issues. First, our measure of potential suppliers ignores the possibility that an SEF operating in a certain market could be a potential supplier for a related process. This assumption is plausible but if it is invalid, it implies that SEF_FW_i is measured with error.[11] In turn, this would mean that our estimates are likely to be biased toward zero, and the true effect is likely to be larger than the estimated effect. As a check of robustness, we estimated a specification (not reported here) where we used SEFs operating in an entire sector (e.g., synthetic fibers) in the First World as being potential suppliers for all processes (e.g., polyester and nylon) belonging to that sector. The estimated impacts of the number of first world SEFs were qualitatively similar to those reported in table 8.3. Therefore our measure of the supply of SEFs is not likely to be key to our empirical results.

A more important problem is that we are likely to measure the potential size of the market with error. If this error is correlated with the number of First World SEFs our estimates will be biased. For instance, if unobserved increases in the size of the developing country process markets induce more SEFs to operate in those process markets in the First World, the correlation between investment and the number of SEFs represents the common effect of a larger market, not a causal effect. This is a typical case of endogeneity bias. However, there is both qualitative and quantitative evidence that our estimates are not seriously biased.

If the coefficient of SEF_FW_i were driven largely by unobserved market size effects, one would expect a statistically significant impact in the $MAKE_{ij}$ equation. Instead, the estimated coefficient is almost zero, while measures such as the size of the first world market and GDP are large and statistically significant. Evidence from the industry's history provides further support. Most of the SEFs, and virtually all the major SEFs in the United States, Europe or Japan, were founded before or immediately following World War II, and most chemical process technologies were developed twenty to forty years ago when the developing country chemical markets were still quite small or nonexistent—and by that time SEFs had already accumulated considerable expertise in these fields (Arora and Gambardella 1998). Moreover, First World SEFs maintain strong linkages with their country of origin, and from our database we confirmed that it is rare for SEFs to supply engineering services to developing countries in a process unless they also do so in their home markets.[12]

Nonetheless, it is still possible that the growth of developing country markets led to further accumulation of expertise by SEFs, or that developing country demand prevented some SEFs from exiting the industry. If so, unobserved variations in developing country demand for chemical plants are correlated with our measure of SEFs. The standard approach in this case is to find instruments for First World SEFs. There are two possibilities: exploit differences among countries according to the extent to which they are open to the inflow of foreign technologies or use differences across processes in the nature of technology. Since the market for chemical processes is a truly global market with SEFs supplying even the more protected countries, there is insufficient cross-country variation in the effective supply of SEFs for this to be a useful way to identify the impact of SEFs.[13]

Instead, we exploited the differences across processes in the nature of the technology, which is an important source of variations in the number of SEFs. Specifically, some processes are based on standard and codified technologies, which encourage specialization and increases the number of SEFs. Using process-specific instruments we have run a GMM estimation of the $SIZE_{ij}$ equation, which we do not report here for brevity of exposition. The GMM estimate of the elasticity with respect to SEF_FW_i is 0.44, very close to our original OLS estimate of 0.46, and shows that the potential endogeneity bias of SEF_FW_i is quite modest. For further details, see Arora, Fosfuri, and Gambardella (2001).

8.4.4 Assessing the "Marginal" Effect of SEFs

To get a sense of the magnitude of the impact of an upstream sector of technology suppliers on the total investment of the downstream market, we compute the effect of one additional SEF in a typical process market on the expected total dollar value of investment in the developing countries in that process market (we used estimated elasticities from our GMM estimation). Average investment in a process-country market is $78.1 million, whereas the average number of First World SEFs in a process market is 11.94. So, an additional SEF would increase investment by (0.44 × 78·1/11 94) million, or about $3 million per year per country. As figure 8.2 shows, this increase is greater for larger countries like China and India, and smaller for smaller countries, like Algeria and Kuwait. For the thirty-eight developing countries as a whole, the increase in investment in a typical process would then be $114 million, or a little less than one extra plant over the ten-year period (the average investment cost of a plant in developing countries is about $120 million). The impact of an additional SEF is small, as expected, given that most markets already have more than five or six SEFs.

Recall, however, that this is the average effect over the sample: It varies by the size and nature of the process. For instance, figure 8.3 shows that the effect diminishes with size. Processes with a large number of Third–World plants are likely to be less affected than processes with fewer plants. There are two forces at work here. On the one hand, a given percentage increase in investment implies a larger dollar increase if the base-level investment is high (as it is in this case). On the other hand, an additional SEF in the market is more important when the number of SEFs is small than when the number of SEFs is large. Our results suggest that the "diminishing returns to the number of SEFs" effect dominates when there is a large number of plants. Thus, the results indicate that division of labor is important, but that in many sectors it has proceeded far enough that further entry of specialized suppliers would only have a smaller impact.

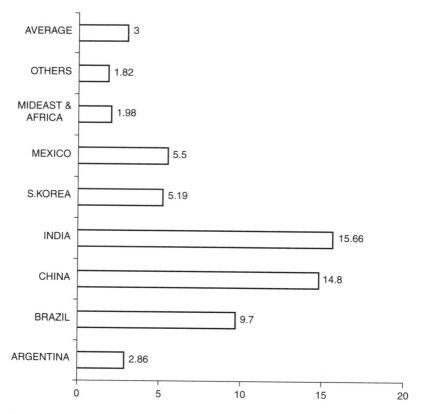

Figure 8.2
Estimated impact of an additional SEF—additional investment per process, by country, in millions of U.S. dollars, 1981–1990

Finally, our estimates also show that the impact of an additional SEF is likely to be greater in more mature processes. This is borne out by figure 8.4. This figure shows that processes, where the technological frontier is moving rapidly, are likely to be affected less than more mature processes.

8.4.5 The Differential Effect of SEFs on LDC and Multinational Firms

If our story is correct, proposition 3 implies that SEFs ought to benefit developing country firms much more than First World MNEs, which are likely to have substantial in-house technological capabilities. We estimated two equations for the total dollar investment by domestic firms and multinationals using the same specification and variables employed earlier. Table 8.4 presents the results of these estimations using

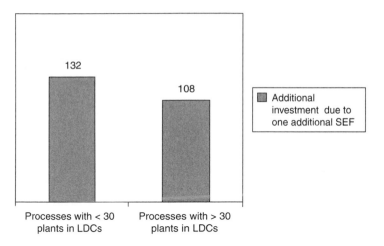

Figure 8.3
Estimated impact of additional SEFs on investment in developing countries—by size of process market, in millions of U.S. dollars, 1981–1990

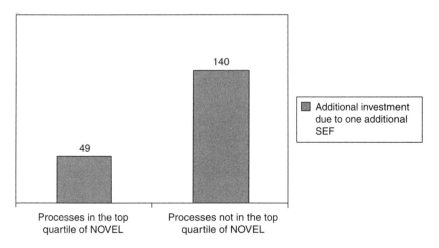

Figure 8.4
Estimated impact of SEFs on investment—by type of process, in millions of U.S. dollars, 1981–1990

Table 8.4
Investments by MNEs and LDC Firms in LDCs—DOM_{ij}, MNE_{ij}: OLS Estimates
$\log(X_{ij}) = const + aY_j + bZ_i + e_{ij}$

	DOM_{ij}	MNE_{ij}
Constant	-7.81	-7.40
	(1.54)	(1.04)
$DOIL_{ij}$	0.6	-0.06
	(0.15)	(0.10)
$DGAS_{ij}$	0.16	0.35
	(0.23)	(0.15)
$DHKAP_j$	0.02	-0.25
	(0.13)	(0.09)
$(1 - DHKAP_j) \times HKAP_j$	-0.01	-0.05
	(0.03)	(0.02)
$\text{Log}(GDP_j)$	0.17	0.52
	(0.17)	(0.12)
$\text{Log}(POP_j)$	-0.18	-0.32
	(0.12)	(0.08)
$\text{Log}(ENERGY_j)$	0.48	0.02
	(0.08)	(0.05)
$\text{Log}(AREA_j)$	0.10	0.00
	(0.03)	(0.02)
$(ICHEM_i + AGRI_i + MM_i) \times \text{Log}(AREA_j)$	0.14	0.03
	(0.04)	(0.02)
$DOPEN_j$	-0.51	0.40
	(0.16)	(0.11)
$(1 - DOPEN_j) \times OPEN_j$	0.85	0.28
	(0.19)	(0.13)
$\text{Log}(SIZE\_FW_i)$	0.38	0.23
	(0.06)	(0.04)
$\text{Log}(COST\_FW_i)$	-0.31	-0.22
	(0.06)	(0.04)
$NOVEL_i$	-0.17	-0.09
	(0.05)	(0.03)
$DPROCPAT_i$	-0.48	-0.02
	(0.22)	(0.15)
$(1 - DPROCPAT_i) \times \text{Log}(PROCPAT_i)$	-0.15	-0.02
	(0.03)	(0.02)
$\text{Log}(SEF\_FW_i)$	0.44	0.06
	(0.05)	(0.04)
Adj. R^2	0.23	0.07
No. of observations	5282	5282

Note: Standard errors in parenthesis. All regressions include sector dummies and dummies for geographical areas of country.

least squares (OLS).[14] The key result in table 8.4 is that the estimate of the impact of First World SEFs is sizable and significant in the domestic firm equation, whereas it is small and nonsignificant in the MNE equation. This is an interesting result for it suggests that SEFs are likely to have encouraged entry of developing country firms into new chemical markets by transferring to them the chemical technologies. This result is consistent with other findings; the presence of SEFs lowers entry barriers and makes markets more competitive (Lieberman 1987). The finding that SEFs do not have a similar impact on MNEs suggests that First World SEFs are a source of increased competition for the very same First World companies that gave rise to these SEFs in earlier periods. We return to this issue in chapter 9.

8.5   Conclusions

Markets for technology are a precondition for the existence of specialized technology suppliers operating in vertical markets. Specialized suppliers can act as a mechanism for knowledge transfer that resembles technological spillovers across firms, a subject that has attracted a great deal of attention from economists (Griliches 1979; Jaffe 1986; Coe and Helpman 1995). However, a part of what are called spillovers may in fact be market-mediated transfers of knowledge.

The thesis we developed in this chapter is that the intermediation of an upstream sector of technology suppliers can be a powerful mechanism through which spillovers can take place. As noted, for instance, by Bresnahan and Trajtenberg (1995), in a division of innovative labor R&D or other investments by downstream companies could induce greater investments in complementary R&D by technology suppliers, which would enhance the performance of other downstream firms.

The economics of the mechanism we propose in this chapter is very simple. As Romer (1990) has emphasized, the development of technological capability is a fixed cost activity, while the productive application of the technological capability is a (low) marginal cost activity. In our story, firms in the upstream sector invest in learning to design the production process. If the upstream sector is competitive, these costs are ultimately paid by the downstream sector. The expertise and the technologies that they supply are process- and not location-specific and, thus, can be made available to downstream firms in other countries. Competition between the suppliers implies that the benefits of the acquired expertise will be made available to users in other countries, or in other sectors of the economy, at prices close to marginal cost because the development costs have already been sunk.

In short, what our results imply is not that the observed rates of investment in chemical plants in developing countries are being fueled solely by specialist process technology suppliers from the First World and could not be achieved without them. Rather, we interpret our results as suggesting that the investment is taking place earlier and more rapidly than if developing countries had to rely solely upon chemical producers in the First World to transfer the technology, or even worse, if they had to "reinvent the wheel"—that is, develop process technologies and the broader engineering expertise required to design and construct chemical plants domestically.

The organization of industry in the First World "matters" not just for the growth of the first world but also for the growth of other nations. Moreover, our results suggest that not all firms or countries benefit equally from spillovers. In other words, the existence of specialized technology suppliers implies that there are benefits to being a "latecomer" to the process of economic development. This also has natural implications for corporate management and policies, which we discuss more fully in chapters 9 and 10.

In a somewhat different context, one might have conceptualized the phenomenon discussed in this chapter as international technology transfer. Undoubtedly, SEFs are important sources of chemical technology, but many large chemical firms also transfer technology overseas. However, as discussed in chapter 7, chemical producers have to trade off gains from selling technology against losses in actual or potential revenues from selling the downstream product. On the other hand, SEFs provide technology with few strings attached, and will sell their technology and expertise to all. In so doing, they have truly helped create a market for technology, from which many developing countries have benefited.

Appendix: Description of the Data

Plant Data

Our main source of plant-level data is Chemical Age Project File (Chemintell 1991), a database compiled by Pergamon Press, London, and now held by Reed Elsevier Publisher, London. From this data source we obtained information on 20,581 plants announced or constructed the world over, in the broadly defined chemical sector during 1981–1990. The database is organized by plants. It reports the name of the company that ordered the plant, the name of the engineering company for that plant (or "staff" for in-house engineering), the location of the plant (city and country), the name of the chemical process or of the product being produced, the date in which the investment was first reported in the specialized trade press, along with other information. For about 40 percent of the plants, Chemintell also reports the total cost of investment in the plant in millions of U.S. dollars. Finally, the data base reports the status of the plant along with the date in which the information was last updated. In most of the cases the information was updated in 1988–1989, which suggests that we can reasonably assume that this was the status of the plant at the end of our sample period. There are 14,893 plants in the database that are either "completed" or "under construction." The others are "planned," "under study," "abandoned," "canceled," "delayed," or "other."

We focused on the plants that were either completed or under construction. Thus, $SIZE_{ij}$, BUY_{ij}, $MAKE_{ij}$, DOM_{ij}, MNE_{ij}, and $SIZE\_FW_i$ were obtained by using only the 14,893 plants that are completed or constructed. In counting SEF_FW_i, we used information from all the 20,581 plants in the database. This is because even plants that were planned, under study, abandoned, or other, provided useful information about whether a given SEF was a potential supplier for that technology. For similar reason, we used all the available information about plant costs to compute $COST\_FW_i$ and the average plant investment cost in LDCs, which was used to compute the dollar values of the variables mentioned above. The vast majority of the firms counted in SEF_FW_i are independent SEFs, or engineering subsidiaries of larger industrial groups (especially for European and Japanese companies). These normally act as independent companies and can also be considered as full-fledged SEFs. There are a few chemical firms that provide engineering services to other (nonaffiliated) chemical companies, which were included in SEF_FW.

Chemical Processes

Chemintell plants cover 2,081 different chemical processes. We focused on the 139 largest processes with twenty or more plants in the database. Gathering information for all processes for our measures of technological novelty and complexity, is very difficult, and often, prohibitively so.

In fact, our sample is a comprehensive set of all the important and widely diffused chemical technologies in the world. It covers 10,145 plants that are completed or in construction, for instance, almost 70 percent of all the 14,893 plants completed or in construction in the database. In addition, in an earlier working paper we reported qualitatively similar empirical results using a larger sample of processes, albeit without the extensive controls that we use here (Arora, Fosfuri, and Gambardella 1996). Similar analyses using a cross-section of all the 2,081 processes and aggregate variables for the LDCs did not change the results.

Sectors

Chemintell classifies its plants in the following twenty-one sectors (in parenthesis the number of plants completed or under construction): Agricultural Chemicals (116), Air Separation (596), Coal Refining (32), Desalination (40), Engineering Materials (110), Environmental Technologies (75), Fertilizers (1,000), Food Products (308), Gas Handling (1,014), Inorganic Chemicals (1,249), Industrial Gases (613), Minerals and Metallurgy (532), Miscellaneous (505), Organic Chemicals (1,114), Oil Refining (2,246), Petrochemicals (2,155), Pharmaceuticals (745), Plastics and Rubber (1,474), Pulp and Paper (396), Synthetic Fuels (135), Textiles and Fibers (438). The sector dummies that we actually used in all our regressions were obtained, however, after aggregating these twenty-one sectors in nine classes of relatively homogeneous sectors. The nine aggregate sectors are: OIL REFINING, PETROCHEMICALS, MINERALS & METALLURGY, PLASTICS & RUBBER, INORGANIC CHEMICALS, AGRICULTURE (Agricultural Chemicals and Fertilizers), GAS (Gas Handling, Air Separation, and Industrial Gases), ORGANIC CHEMICALS (Organic Chemicals, Explosives, Textile and Fibers, Food Products, and Pharmaceuticals), and MISCELLANEOUS (the rest).

Nationality of Companies and Subsidiaries

We used Predicast's (1991) and other company thesauruses to group all the companies that were subsidiaries of other companies in the data base under the names of their mothers companies, and assign nationalities to companies. We treated the SEFs that were subsidiaries of larger chemical groups as independent firms. However, when an SEFs provided services for its parent company, this was counted as a "make." We do not find any SEFs from LDCs operating in the First World.

Limitation of the Database

Chemintell is a commercial database, and is constructed from various sources such as questionnaires and reports in the trade press. Its vast coverage suggests that biases are unlikely. For about 17 percent of the plants in our sample the name of the engineering company is not given. Conversations with data providers in the industry suggested that these blanks could arise for a number of reasons. Companies may still be looking for suitable engineers, or they do not want to disclose the name, or the information is simply missing. However, we cross-checked using another database (Hydrocarbon Processing Unit or HPI, compiled by Gulf Publishing, Texas). The check was inconclusive because a number of the identified plants in the other database were also missing the relevant information. However, since most of the identified plants that did report the name of an engineering company in the other database were "buys," our check ruled out the possibility that the blanks are predominately "makes."

We performed all our empirical analyses under different assumptions about the blanks—that is, all the blanks are buys, all the blanks are makes, the blanks are 50 percent buys and 50 percent makes, the blanks are distributed between buys and makes in the same proportion as in the case in which the name of the engineering company (or "staff") is observed. The results presented here are those where we assume that all the blanks are buys. It turns out that all other assumptions about the blanks had even more favorable results for our theory.

Construction of PROCPAT$_i$

We selected all relevant patents using a keyword search with the process as the keyword. From these, we selected and read the full abstracts of patents that exactly fit our criterion. The patent classes (and subclasses) into which these patents were classified were examined to ensure that the invention was in fact a process invention. These subclasses of the U.S. patent classification system were used along with the process name as the basis for Boolean queries of the U.S. patent database to generate the final set of patents, one set for each process. The titles (and some abstracts selected at random) of the patents in the final sample for each process were examined to ensure that the final sample did not contain irrelevant patents.

Countries

In all our analyses, and for all the variables that we constructed, we defined First World to be all the OECD countries except Mexico, the Czech Republic, Hungary, Poland, South Korea, and Turkey. These countries joined the OECD only very recently and for our purposes, it was more appropriate to include them in the LDC category. Therefore our first world countries are all the Western European countries, the United States of America and Canada, Japan, Australia, and New Zealand. The thirty-eight countries in our sample are: Algeria, Argentina, Bangladesh, Brazil, Burma, Chile, China, Colombia, Ecuador, Egypt, Hong Kong, Hungary, India, Indonesia, Iran, Iraq, Kuwait, Malaysia, Mexico, Morocco, Nigeria, Pakistan, Peru, Philippines, Poland, Saudi Arabia, Singapore, South Africa, South Korea, Sri Lanka, Sudan, Syria, Taiwan, Thailand, Tunisia, Turkey, Venezuela, and Yugoslavia.

IV

Implications for
Public Policy and
Corporate Strategy

9   Implications for Corporate Strategies

9.1. Introduction

Markets for technology have natural implications for the technology strategies of companies and influence their overall corporate strategy. Of course, neither technology management nor licensing practices are new phenomena. However, as we have earlier argued, the incidence and importance of technology licensing and technology related transactions have greatly increased in recent years, and it is therefore important to understand the implications for corporate strategy.[1]

As discussed in chapter 2, companies, and particularly large companies, are recognizing that not all technologies they develop are used commercially. As a result, many firms have chosen to devote their attention to discovering new opportunities for profiting from their technologies and increasing returns from R&D. At the same time, recent studies have documented an increase in licensing revenues earned by U.S. firms (Degnan 1998), as well as an upsurge in patenting activities (Kortum and Lerner 1999). More generally, the recognition of the value of their technological portfolios has prompted many firms to take serious steps toward more effective management of their know-how, technologies, and intellectual capital (Grindley and Teece 1997; Teece 1998; Granstrand 1999; Rivette and Kline 1999).

Markets for technology affect the role of companies both as technology users (they can "buy" technologies) and as technology suppliers (they can "sell" technologies). At the very least, markets for technology expand the strategy space: a firm can choose to license external technology instead of developing it in-house. Similarly, a firm can choose to license its technology to others instead of, or in addition to, investing in the downstream assets needed to manufacture and commercialize the end-product. Thus, for example, an entrepreneurial start-up may choose to narrow its focus to the development of new technology rather than its implementation, relying on licensing to appropriate returns from innovation. Given that manufacturing and commercialization require substantial resources, which smaller firms may be unable to mobilize, markets for technology may be critical for the very existence of high-tech start-ups. For technology users, the monitoring of externally available technologies becomes a strategic imperative, although external research and internal development are not mutually exclusive options. Moreover, markets for technology can undermine the privileged access to technology that incumbent firms in an industry may enjoy. Both competitors and entrants may acquire similar technology from alternative sources of supply in the market. At an industry level, markets for technology lower the barriers of entry into the industry, increase competition, and compress product lifecycles—all changes that require appropriate strategic responses.

Growth of markets for technology also has profound implications for the theory of the firm. Drawing on the resource-based theory of the firm, we argue that markets for technology can imply a fundamental reconsideration of the appropriate boundaries of the firm. We document our arguments by drawing on cases and examples of specific companies to show that some of the leading corporations of the world are actively engaging in licensing their technologies. In some instances, this is a significant change from the traditional view that technologies must be retained in-house. Indeed some companies are creating internal divisions specifically focused on managing the sale of their technologies and intellectual property.

The ramifications of a market for technology extend beyond large R&D conducting firms to smaller, technology-based firms and high-tech start-ups as well. In particular, we argue that markets for technology offer these companies the opportunity to specialize in technology development without having to invest in the more costly downstream assets. From a normative perspective, our argument points to the risks that such companies may face when they try to integrate downstream instead of remaining focused on upstream technological developments.

Teece's seminal paper pointed out that if a firm cannot appropriate rents from innovation through licensing ("weak appropriability"), in order to profit from the technology, the firm should acquire assets that are co-specialized with the innovation (Teece 1986). Pisano (1990) argues that new product development is more likely to be internalized in those areas where the (external) R&D market is less efficient. Iansiti

(1997) claims that in a world of increasing technological options, firms' competitive advantages are rooted in the ability to monitor and quickly seize external opportunities.

A somewhat different tradition, influenced perhaps by Schumpeter's vision of even innovation becoming routine inside large firms, has emphasized the payoff from coordinated and large-scale investments. Commercial success, Chandler stresses, depends on complementing investments in R&D with parallel investments in manufacturing and marketing (Chandler 1990). This view, which is closely linked to the resource-based theory of the firm, depicts firm growth as a process of exploiting slack resources within the company (Penrose 1959; Nelson and Winter 1982; Shane 1996). These accounts implicitly assume that such slack resources are best employed by the firm itself. In this chapter, we depart from the widespread premise in the technology management literature that innovations are best exploited in-house, and, instead, we examine the implications that a well functioning market has for technology and corporate strategy.[2]

We begin in section 9.2 by analyzing the consequences of "missing" markets for intangible assets, and how the behavior of companies can be affected once markets for such assets arise. Section 9.3 focuses on large, established firms. We discuss how some of the established technology leaders are modifying their strategies for appropriating rents from innovation by incorporating technology licensing as an important option. Section 9.4 examines the distinct challenges faced by smaller firms, especially technology-based start-ups. Section 9.5 deals with the external acquisition of technology—that is, the effects of markets for technology on the strategies of companies as technology buyers. Section 9.6 discusses the implications of markets for technology on entry and competition. Section 9.7 summarizes our main conclusions.

9.2   Markets for Technology and Corporate Strategies

9.2.1   The Effects of "Missing" Markets for Corporate Assets

To understand the corporate strategy implications of markets for technology, it is useful to begin with a more general discussion of markets for assets that distinguish a firm from its competitors.[3] These assets include technology, production expertise and facilities, strong brand-name reputation, human assets, supplier networks, and established marketing channels. The resource-based theory of the firm suggests that to be a source of sustained above-average performance, resources must meet three criteria: they must be valuable, rare, and imperfectly mobile (Barney 1991; Peteraf 1993; Markides and Williamson 1996). In other words, a competitive advantage must be underpinned by resources for which well-functioning markets do not or cannot exist. The firm builds a sustainable competitive advantage by having assets that its competitors cannot access. Barney (1986) notes that the possession of such assets must be rooted in imperfections in the factor market, that is, the market where the factors used to create such assets are traded. These imperfections ultimately arise from differences in the expectations that firms hold about the future value of the assets (Barney 1991). Cool and Dierickx (1989) point out that not all the assets required to sustain competitive advantage can be bought and sold and instead must be accumulated internally. Similarly, much of the thinking on technology strategy has approached the problem by implicitly or explicitly assuming that technological assets cannot be directly bought and sold, and the services of such assets cannot be "rented." This chapter therefore builds on the resource-based view of the firm by analyzing what happens when some assets that were not tradable become tradable.

What are the consequences of such a missing market for technology? The immediate consequence is that the innovator must exploit the technology in-house.[4] That is, in order to extract the value from the technology, it (or rather, its services) must be embodied in goods and services, which are then sold. Such goods and services must have lower costs or command higher prices to deliver returns that are greater than the competitive rate of returns—firms earn "quasi-rents."

Consider a case where a firm has developed a new cost-reducing technology for producing semiconductors. In order to extract value from the technology, the firm must use it to produce the semiconductors. Not only does this require the firm to have access to complementary assets (such as expensive semiconductor fabrication facilities, marketing channels, and so on), but the returns would also depend on the volume of output that the firm can produce and sell. If the complementary assets are themselves not traded in a competitive market, or if firms differ in their access to them, then firms that have superior access to these complementary assets will be able to derive greater value from the technology.[5] Similarly, firms that can exploit the technology on a larger scale will be able to derive greater value (Cohen and Klepper 1996; Klepper 1996).

Following this logic, larger firms or firms with superior access to complementary assets will have a greater incentive to invest in the technology in the first instance. Taking this one step further, firms investing in technology would be well advised to also invest in those complementary assets that cannot be easily and efficiently acquired from the market. In other words, as Teece (1986) put it, firms must invest in creating cospecialized assets to maximize their returns from developing new technology. In sum, absent a market for technology, a firm must often acquire other assets in order to extract profits from the technology. Insofar as these other assets are themselves expensive and illiquid, large well-capitalized, integrated firms that possess such assets have greater incentives to invest in developing new technologies (Nelson 1959). Conversely, smaller firms face major hurdles in developing and commercializing technology.

The situation is quite different when the asset can be sold or rented. Complementary assets need not be owned or even directly accessed by the technology developer. The relative importance of complementary assets within the boundaries of individual firms diminishes compared to the existence of the same assets at the level of industries or markets. Ultimately, a market for the asset provides the innovator—a firm that has developed new technology—with more options. Instead of embodying a newly developed technology in goods and services, a firm may choose to sell or license that technology to others. Other firms may license technology instead of developing it in-house.

This does not mean that firms would only acquire technologies from external sources. A company that aims to be an industry leader will strike a balance between external acquisition and in-house development of technologies. For companies with lower in-house technological capabilities, however, the existence of external technology sources could be critical in enhancing their ability to produce and sell more innovative goods (Iansiti and West 1997). Similarly, a market for technology assets does not mean that innovating firms will become pure licensing companies, although several smaller firms have been successful as specialized technology suppliers. Rather, as we shall discuss below, the appropriate strategy in the presence of markets for technology depends on the efficiency of markets for other types of assets, including finance. Moreover, when examining the manner in which a market for technology conditions strategies, there is one other industry-level force that must be considered. Markets, particularly efficient markets, are great levelers. A market for technology lowers entry barriers and increases competition in the product market, which often implies the rethinking of existing strategies. In turn, when a well-functioning market for an asset exists, such an asset cannot be a source of sustainable competitive advantage, and firms must look somewhere else for opportunities to gain an edge over competitors.

9.2.2 Markets for Technology and Strategies for Appropriating Rents

Teece (1986) identifies several critical dimensions for the appropriability of the returns of a firm's intellectual property: nature of technology, strength of property rights regime, complementary assets, ease of replication, and ease of imitation. Appropriation through licensing works best when there exists a substantial gap between the costs of replication and imitation. If the technology is easy to replicate and transfer but difficult to imitate, the innovator can capture a large part of the rents simply by licensing. Hence, when the underlying knowledge base is sufficiently codified and not context specific, and intellectual property rights (IPRs) are well defined and protected, licensing can work well (Williamson 1991; Kogut and Zander 1993).

As discussed earlier a large market for chemical processes and engineering services exists. The development of chemical engineering played an important role in developing more general and abstract ways of conceptualizing chemical processes. As well, patents typically work more efficiently in chemicals than in other industries (see Levin et al. 1987; Cohen, Nelson, and Walsh 1997). In addition, many processes, especially in petrochemicals, are designed around a specific variety of catalyst that can be kept proprietary because of the difficulty of imitation from simple structural analysis alone. The licensor can therefore use the catalyst as a credible hostage; failure by the licensee to respect the initial agreement can trigger a cutoff in the supply of the catalyst.

However, Teece (1988) argued that the appropriation of the returns from innovation through licensing is the exception and not the rule. In other words, the best way of appropriating the rents from technology is by directly embodying it into goods and products. In a more recent paper, Teece (1998) recognizes that the formation of markets for technology might change this view. He notes that the separation of intellectual property from products generates a new environment for knowledge management where the focus is on how to capture value from knowledge assets. At the same time, he warns that "becoming a pure licensing company not directly involved in the production market and increasingly remote from the manufacture and design of the product itself can be a risky strategy" (Grindley and Teece 1997, 80). Since risk is sometimes worth the additional reward, the innovator now has the option to balance her ability to extract value from the asset by embodying it in products and services, against the transaction costs involved in trading the technology. In this respect, licensing is an option not mutually exclusive with self production. Hence, with a market for technology, a firm needs to recognize what its core competencies are, as well as which sources of competencies are tradable, and which are nontradable. Having done so, it can then decide whether a given discovery or technological competency is to be exploited in-house or through licensing. In many instances, firms might possess some "non-core" technologies (in some cases, of substantial value) that can be profitably licensed.

The decision whether or not to exploit the technology in-house depends on several factors. First and foremost it depends on the distribution of complementary assets. If the firm has superior access to the complementary assets as compared to its rivals, in-house exploitation is clearly an attractive strategy. Conversely, if the firm lacks the complementary assets, it may consider selling or licensing the technology. An important special case arises when the technology in question is generic in terms of its application—a general-purpose technology or GPT. In this case, only an extraordinarily large and well-diversified firm will be able to exploit the technology satisfactorily in-house. Otherwise, it is far more likely that the relevant complementary assets will be more broadly distributed, so that licensing the technology would yield higher returns.

The foregoing example highlights the importance of the transaction costs involved in the markets for different types of assets. If the transaction costs of acquiring complementary assets such as production and marketing capabilities are lower than the transaction costs involved in selling or licensing the technology, an innovator lacking the complementary capabilities may nonetheless choose to exploit its technology in-house. There are many factors that affect transaction costs for technology exchange. Foremost among them are well-defined and enforced property rights. Property rights are easier to define and enforce, and transaction costs for technology licensing contracts are lower, when the knowledge is articulable (Winter 1987), and can be represented in terms of general and abstract categories (Arora and Gambardella 1994a). Such representations reduce the context dependence of the technology, freeing it up to be used more generally and reducing the cognitive barriers to technology transfer (see also Von Hippel 1990 and 1994; chapter 4).

Difficulty in valuation can significantly increase transaction costs. Accurate valuation is particularly important in cases where the firm lacks downstream assets to commercialize the technology. Current accounting practices and norms, derived as they are from times where measuring tangible and material assets was their crucial task, have to be modified in order for technology markets to flourish. This is a complex issue that is well beyond the scope of this chapter (see Deng, Lev, and Narin 1999; Lev and Zarowin 1999).

What is less well understood is the role that technology markets themselves can play in improving the accounting for intangible technological assets. A market for technology improves the accuracy of any valuation attempt. It does so in the most obvious way: by providing an objective measure of the value, if the asset itself has been traded in the past, or if similar assets have been traded. Needless to say, technology is highly differentiated, and its "price" is likely to reflect factors that are idiosyncratic to the buyer and the seller. Thus, any monetary measure is likely to be imperfect. That said, such problems are not unique to the measurement of the value of technology. A flourishing market for paintings by the Old Masters (e.g., Rembrandt, da Vinci, etc.), for instance, shows that product differentiation and idiosyncratic sources of value do not preclude the existence of a reasonably well functioning market.

Moreover, when investing in R&D, firms are implicitly making such measurements, as do investors when they value the firms in capital markets. Markets for technology allow for the possibility of valuing the contribution of technology separately from that of other assets the firm may possess. In turn, such valuation may enable firms to specialize in developing technology without necessarily having to acquire downstream capabilities.

In addition to transaction costs, the decision regarding in-house exploitation also depends on the extent of competition in the different markets in the "value chain" of innovation. For instance, the innovator may face much greater competition in the product market than in the market for technology. In this case, the returns from in-house exploitation are likely to be small, limited by the ability of the innovator to increase its sales and gain market share, typically a slow process. The innovator may face much less competition in the technology market, and may be able to extract much higher returns there. For example, these exact considerations led Qualcomm to exit from producing handsets embodying its CDMA (Code Division Multiple Access) technology and focus on technology licensing. In the early 1990s, Qualcomm introduced a wireless telephone technology, based on CDMA technology, which was markedly superior to the existing technology. It embodied this technology into cellular phones (handsets) and grew rapidly, with a turn-over of $4 billion, and a net income of more than $200 million in 1999. However, recently Qualcomm decided to drastically refashion its business. Citing falling margins in the CDMA handset operations, it divested itself of manufacturing and focused on generating and licensing its CDMA technology. As Irwin Jacobs, Qualcomm's chairman and CEO, put it, "We'll let others deal with wrapping plastic around chips" (*Business Week* 1999). On an annualized basis, Qualcomm earned nearly $400 million in licensing and royalty revenues in 1999, which was slightly more than what it spent on R&D in the same year.

9.3 Licensing and Related Technology Strategies by Large Firms

9.3.1 Revenue Effect vs. Rent Dissipation Effect

The recognition of the potential of the licensing market has been prompted by several related factors. First, globalization is increasing the demand for technologies. Globalization allows the exploitation of technology on a large scale in a relatively short time through licensing. Second, the improved organization and functioning of the market for technology increases opportunities for licensing. Finally, R&D costs are increasing. These factors have prompted many established companies to manage their technology and intellectual property portfolios more effectively. On the demand side, increased competitive pressures, falling tariffs and regulatory barriers to entry have created a large pool of potential technology buyers, firms that see their core competence not in creating technology but rather in exploiting it.

As discussed in chapter 7, the decision by a large established company as to whether or not to license is the result of two main forces pushing in opposite directions: the revenue effect and the profit dissipation effect. Licensing forces a trade-off. Licensing revenues (the revenue effect) have to be balanced against the lower profits that the increased competition (the rent dissipation effect) from the licensee implies. Although the licensor has many different strategies to limit the extent of this latter effect (for instance, the contract might impose quantity restrictions or exclusive territories, or unit royalties might be fixed such as to control the licensee's output), an entrant is nevertheless a potential threat to the licensor's. This implies that firms with a large market share in the product market (and by implication, possessing the required complementary assets) are better off exploiting the technology in-house. On the other hand, if its market share is small, the firm may be able to increase profits by licensing in addition to in-house exploitation. Similarly, licensing is more attractive when the licensee operates in a different market and is unlikely to be a strong competitor.

These arguments, which summarize the results of our model in chapter 7, are exemplified by the different ways in which BP Chemicals has approached the acetic acid and polyethylene businesses. In acetic acid, BP has strong proprietary technology and a substantial market share. It licenses very selectively, typically only granting a license to get access to markets it would otherwise be unable to enter. In polyethylene, by contrast, BP's market share is small. Although it has good proprietary technology in polyethylene as well, there are a dozen other sources of technology for producing polyethylene. Thus, BP has licensed its polyethylene technology aggressively, competing with Union Carbide, the market leader in licensing polyethylene technology. Even here, BP initially tried not to license in Western Europe, where it had a substantial share of polyethylene capacity. However, other licensors continued to supply technology to firms that wished to produce polyethylene in Western Europe, with the result that BP found it was losing potential licensing revenues without any benefits in the form of restraining entry.

BP is not alone in choosing to appropriate rents by licensing its technology. As we shall see in the next section, a number of other firms, including Dow Chemicals, DuPont, and Monsanto, which have traditionally neither licensed their technology nor acquired technologies from the outside, have embraced technology licensing as an integral part of their technology management strategy.

The trade-off between the revenue from licensing and the rent dissipation that licensing entails can create conflict between business units and the licensing department, which is often part of the R&D or IP management group. The form and severity of these conflicts depend on how licensing is organized in a firm. Usually, the intellectual property group, typically part of the R&D department, is responsible for technology licensing. In many firms, the intellectual property group or the R&D labs that generated the technology retain licensing revenues. Business units tend to oppose licensing because it will create competitors. In other firms, these licensing revenues are shared with the business unit, partly mitigating the problem. Sharing licensing revenues is also more likely where R&D is supported by business units.

However, revenue sharing is not enough. Management incentives also matter. If business managers have strong incentives to increase market share, they will oppose licensing even if the revenue effect outweighs the rent dissipation effect. Licensing revenues, even in successful licensors, are rarely comparable to the revenues from sales of products, but the cost of generating a dollar of licensing revenues is significantly lower than that cost of generating a dollar of product sales. However, managers who are rewarded for sales growth or market share will tend to overlook this, and resist licensing.

An interview with the Vice President of R&D at Firm P, a U.S. petrochemical producer, provided an interesting example of this conflict.[*] Firm P has several important innovations in plastics polymers, which it produces in substantial quantities. Although this firm has licensed its technology on occasion, for the most part it has treated its technology as its crown jewels, preferring to profit from its innovations by embodying them in its own output. With increasing competition in most of the major plastics markets, profit margins have shrunk. Firm P had an opportunity to license its proprietary technology to a producer in a large Asian country. However, the business unit producing the plastic opposed the decision, arguing that licensing to a competitor would create competition for a plant that Firm P was planning to construct in the Persian Gulf region. Even though the business unit would get the bulk of the licensing revenues, its managers were more concerned with ensuring that their plants operated at high capacity, leading them to oppose the licensing deal.

Although such concerns are understandable, they appear to be misplaced. Not only were other firms supplying the plastic in that country, there were many suppliers of the technology as well. Although, as discussed in chapter 7, the plastic produced with other technologies was not identical to that produced by Firm P's technology, the difference was not very significant for many uses. The experience in related products certainly suggests that the opposition to licensing was not in the firm's interest. However, since business managers were typically rewarded in large measure based on market share, sales growth, and capacity utilization, their opposition to licensing is understandable. As this example shows, firms that wish to exploit licensing opportunities have to ensure that the tradeoff between licensing revenues and rent dissipation is well managed. This requires educating business managers about the net value added from sale of products versus that from licensing. Further, it requires that managers have incentives consistent with those of the firm as a whole. In some cases, firms may choose to spin off the entire technology licensing business as a stand-alone unit within the firm or as an independent firm.

A spin-off is especially likely if potential licensees have concerns about licensing technology from a potential competitor. Licensees may be concerned about revealing information about their strategy, investment plans, or proprietary information about production technology. Such information often accompanies technology licensing. Similarly, business managers of a potential licensor may be concerned about leakage of proprietary information to licensees that are competitors, or that may become competitors in the future. A stand-alone licensing operation can ease many of these concerns. Arora and Merges (2000) show that spin-offs can bring other efficiency benefits, when technical services are important for successful licensing.

9.3.2 Changing Licensing Strategies

This changing approach to licensing is exemplified by the recent behavior of several leading large companies, which have paid increasing attention to this new way of profiting from their technological portfolios. Clearly, there are many reasons why firms license (see discussion in section 7.3.1). Firms may license to create demand, to deter entry by stronger rivals, or to dissuade rivals from launching their own R&D projects in the area. Most important, in certain sectors like electronics and software, firms may license their technology to create de facto market standards, which they can control and exploit. However, the examples that follow illustrate the growing importance of markets for technology in encouraging firms to seek additional returns from their R&D efforts by selling technologies disembodied from products. Specifically, they suggest that large firms are actually refocusing their overall business strategy to account for the increasing importance of such markets.[7] Table 9.1 lists the links for the company websites listing technologies and patents available for license.

DuPont is a good example of a large established firm that has substantially changed its attitude toward technology licensing. In 1994, the company created the Corporate Technology Transfer Group, a division with the specific task of overseeing all technology transfer activities. Reversing its tradition of treating in-house technology as the crown jewels, DuPont has begun to exploit technology through an aggressive licensing program. Starting in 1999, this is expected to be a $100 million per year business:

For a long time, the belief about intellectual property at DuPont was that patents were for defensive purposes only. Patents and related know-how should not be sold, and licensing was a drain on internal resources. . . . Our businesses are gradually becoming more comfortable with the idea that all intellectual property . . . is licensable for the right price in the right situation. Rather than let it sit on the shelf, we can take advantage of these underutilized assets and turn them into enormous value for the company. . . . Appropriate licensing of our intellectual property can be seen as just one more opportunity to keep DuPont competitive and to generate value for our shareholders from the assets we own. (Jack Krol, DuPont President and CEO 1997 Corporate Technology Transfer Meeting)

Indeed, many of DuPont's underutilized technologies, or those that do not fit within the company's overall business strategy, are now for sale. In 1998, there were 18,000 active patents at DuPont, but only 6,000 were used to run the enterprise. On its web page, DuPont advertises the technologies available for licensing in several areas including fibers, composites, chemical science and catalysis, analysis, environmental technologies, electronics, and life sciences. In addition, in 1999 DuPont and other founding members (3M, AlliedSignal, Boeing, Dow Chemical, Ford, Honeywell, Polaroid, Procter & Gamble, Rockwell) financially backed the creation of yet2.com, an online market designed to allow members to buy, sell, license, exchange, and research technologies.

Not only has DuPont changed its attitude toward selling technologies, but it has also reversed its historical reliance on using internal resources alone for the development of its technologies. Indeed, by strategically pooling its resources with those of universities, government laboratories, and other companies, DuPont hopes to lower costs, speed developments, and gain access to new ideas.

IBM has a long tradition of licensing and cross-licensing its technology, as a means of both accessing external technology and earning revenues. This tradition dates back to 1956, when an agreement with U.S. antitrust authorities required IBM to grant nonexclusive, nontransferable, worldwide licenses for any or all of its patents to any applicant, in exchange for reasonable royalties—provided the applicant also offered to cross-license its patents to IBM on similar terms (see Grindley and Teece 1997). Although the consent decree is no longer in force, IBM has pursued an active approach to licensing over the past decade. IBM patent-licensing revenues went from $30 million in 1990 to $1 billion in 1998, amounting to $750,000 per patent, accounting for over

10 percent of IBM's net profits. To generate equivalent profits, it is estimated that IBM would have to sell $20 billion in goods and services.

Recently, two large technology agreements have attracted attention and pointed to the revenue-generating potential of IBM's huge in-house stock of technologies. The first deal was with Dell, a $16 billion seven-year contract allowing Dell access to a broad range of microelectronics, networking, and computer display technologies. The second, a $3 billion five-year contract with EMC, covered storage systems.

IBM is also actively advertising the availability for licensing of its portfolio of storage technology and patents. Technologies are available for licensing in areas including magnetic disk storage, magnetic tape storage, optical storage, storage libraries, and storage subsystems. This constitutes a complete range of innovative storage technology for the personal/handheld, mobile, desktop, workstation, and server environments.

Boeing's core business includes the development and production of commercial and tactical aircraft, missiles, and space systems for the U.S. Government. However, some technologies and processes that Boeing develops do not mesh with its traditional products. Some of these technologies are now available for licensing. The set of patents and technologies available is quite large and includes algorithms, laser technology, factory hand tools, measurement systems, video display, and fiber-optic sensors.

Philips holds a significant number of patents on various optical recording systems. Many of these technologies are now offered for sale through licensing. Licensing seems to be motivated by the need to recoup the research, development, and other effort invested by Philips in optical recording technologies as well as in the present and future research. Currently, Philips is offering patent licenses for optical media in five mainstream areas: CD, DVD, SACD (Super Audio Compact Disc), MPEG and AC-3 (related to the Dolby technology).

Texas Instruments instituted its current licensing strategy in 1985. Since then, revenues from royalties and licensing fees have increased steadily, reaching $600 million in 1995. In some years, these revenues have exceeded income from normal operations. Over the last decade or so, Texas Instruments is estimated to have earned over $1.5 billion in licensing and royalty fees. Grindley and Teece (1997) point out that Texas Instruments's licensing strategy benefited from the stronger U.S. treatment of intellectual property after 1982. Indeed, it benefited from what has been referred in the semiconductor industry as the "Texas Instru-

Table 9.1
Selected Web Pages Advertising the Licensing of Intellectual Property

Company	WWW Address	Available for Licensing
Boeing	<http://www.boeing.com/assocproducts/mdip/home.htm>	Algorithms, laser technology and manufacturing, coatings, material processing, composite technologies, materials, factory hand tools, measurement system, fasteners, placement systems, video display, fiber optic sensors and demodulation systems.
IBM	<http://www.ibm.com/ibm/licensing>	Processes used in integrated circuit, hard disk storage technology, device designs, source code.
DuPont	<http://www.dupont.com/corp/science/technologies.html>	Fibers related, composites, chemical science and catalysis, analytical, environmental, electronics, biological
Union Carbide	<http://www.unioncarbide.com/business/busprgde.html>	Ethylene oxide/ethylene glycol, industrial performance chemicals, polyolefin resins and compounds, solvents, intermediates and monomers, coating materials, specialty polymers and products.
Philips	<http://www.licensing.philips.com>	CD, DVD, SACD, MPEG, AC3
Procter & Gamble	<http://www.pgtechnologytransfer.com>	It is P&G's own online market for technology.
Several Founding Members	<http://www.yet2.com>	All types of technology. It is an online market for technology.

ments" effect. Beginning around 1985, Texas Instruments successfully asserted its patents in court for a range of inventions pertaining to integrated circuits and manufacturing methods. This enabled the firm to earn higher royalty payments from other firms in the industry. Texas Instruments also has strategically used its large patent portfolio to establish cooperative R&D agreements and joint ventures, and to negotiate higher royalties in cross-licensing agreements with other players in the industry.

Monsanto spun off its chemical operations in 1997 to form an independent company, which initiated a comprehensive review of its technologies and scouted for potential candidates for licensing. Monsanto is now actively licensing its acrylonitrile technology and recently began soliciting licenses for its acrylic fiber know-how. The company is also looking for opportunities to license processes that it has developed but not used in any of its businesses. At the same time, the company is evaluating opportunities for licensing-in technologies to bolster its R&D and process development efforts. As Bruce Greer, Monsanto's Vice President for Growth and Commercial Development, said, "There's no reason you have to reinvent the wheel" (*Chemical Week* 1997).

9.3.3 The Increasing Importance of Intellectual Property Management

The need for firms to manage their intellectual property effectively is underlined by recent work of Granstrand (1999) and Rivette and Kline (1999), showing that patent data can be used for competitive intelligence, to identify potential licensees, and to identify potential research staff as well as to decide where a firm should focus its research efforts. Grindley and Teece (1997) also note that in some firms, the management of intellectual property has moved from the licensing of non-core technologies to become a central element in technology strategy. They recognize that, in industries such as semiconductors and electronics, licensing and cross-licensing have become a means for generating revenues as an alternative to direct production. In turn, this implies that management must take a more active and positive approach to licensing and intellectual property matters in general. Moreover, firms have to be more careful about efficiently managing their intellectual property, in particular by identifying technological areas in which to apply more forcefully for patent protection. Since both applying and maintaining a patent can be costly, firms are likely to be selective in their patenting strategy.

A 1999 report by the European Technology Assessment Network (ETAN) on IPRs points out that a well-defined system of protection for intellectual property can help develop a market for technological knowledge (see Merges 1998; Mazzoleni and Nelson 1998; Anand and Khanna 2000). The report also stresses the importance of an "intellectual property culture" in firms, especially for European firms, which tend to lag behind their United States and Japanese counterparts.[8]

Firms are still experimenting with how best to manage their intellectual assets; no single organization scheme will suit all firms. However, it is clear that the old system of leaving patenting and licensing decisions largely under the control of the general counsel's office is likely to change drastically.

For instance, Xerox is an example of a firm that has mismanaged its intellectual property, having invented but failed to profit from a number of pathbreaking developments such as the PC and the graphical user interface (GUI). In 1997 Xerox held 8,000 patents but earned only $8.5 million in licensing revenues—not even enough to cover the cost of maintaining the patents. To rectify this problem, Xerox set in motion a process of cataloguing and evaluating its patent portfolio. It then pruned the portfolio, giving away (often to universities) patents it did not wish to keep, and monitoring its use of the rest. To guide the use of intellectual property, a Xerox Intellectual Property Office (XIPO) was established as a separate profit center headed by a vice president-level officer who oversees all patent and licensing decisions, and who reports directly to the top management of the firm. Lucent has adopted a similar structure with an intellectual property business unit as a profit center responsible for managing intellectual property on a corporate-wide level (Rivette and Kline 1999).

Dow Chemicals has taken a somewhat different approach. Dow's licensing business was formerly managed by two executives. Individual business units made licensing decisions independently of each other. The recession in the early 1990s and the need to cut costs brought the over $1 billion R&D budget under close scrutiny. In 1994, Dow significantly restructured the management of its intellectual property. Each of the 29,000 patents was valued and assigned to one of 15 major business units. The new structure established intellectual property managers for each business unit who meet regularly to review patent activity on an enterprise-wide basis. Dow Chemicals now earns $125 million in patent licensing, up from $25 million in 1994 (Rivette and Kline 1999).

9.3.4   Corporate Venturing

As Levinthal and March (1993) note, large firms with their established routines and structures, are better suited for exploitation than exploration. In somewhat different language, large firms may be better adapted to making incremental improvements of existing technologies, and in commercializing existing discoveries than for making new discoveries. With some exceptions, large firms may be particularly unsuited for radical or breakthrough innovations. Indeed, when such firms make a significant discovery, they may not recognize or nurture it adequately, especially if the discovery is not perceived as relating to the firm's core operations and markets, or worse, if it is seen as threatening a firm's core business. Increasingly, firms are spinning off these technologies as new ventures. These ventures are initially funded and managed by the parent company.

Corporate venturing has increased in popularity in recent years; some believe that it may overtake venture capital as the leading source of funding for technology-based start-ups. Chesbrough (2000) compares corporate venturing with venture capital. The advantages of corporate venturing include the ability to provide more "patient" capital, and the ability to leverage complementary cospecialized assets. Moreover, corporate venturing allows a firm to learn from its failures. However, a corporate venture has disadvantages compared to independent startups; there may be detrimental delays in decision making. Considerations about fairness and internal equity often imply that only low-powered incentives can be offered to managers in the venture. Many firms see corporate venturing as a way of earning high financial returns as well as accomplishing strategic objectives. Although a full discussion of corporate venturing is beyond the scope of this chapter, it does appear that corporate venturing, a compromise between in-house development and an entrepreneurial startup, has thus far only met with limited success. Corporate venturing appears to work best when there are strong strategic links between the venture and the parent (Chesbrough 2000). Moreover, corporate venturing is too heavily dependent on the availability of slack financial resources. With increasing capital market pressures, such slack resources are less likely to be available than in the past. Thus corporate venturing is unlikely to become a consistent substitute for trading technology.

9.4   Smaller Firms, Different Challenges

In comparison with leading corporations, smaller firms face a different set of trade-offs in choosing between licensing and self-exploitation. For startups, the choice often amounts to a fundamental choice of the business model itself.[9] The choice depends, not only on the efficiency of a market for technology (should one exist), but also on the efficiency of the markets for the complementary assets. In other words, in deciding how to exploit their technology, small firms and start-ups must balance the costs of acquiring capital and building in-house production, distribution, and marketing capability against the rents that would be lost or shared with their partners in a licensing deal.

A commonplace about technology licensing, particularly from the perspective of small firms, is that the technology owner does not receive the full return from the technology (Caves, Crookel, and Killing 1983). Two main reasons account for the failure of innovators to capture more fully the rents from innovation: inefficiency of contracts for technology and differences in bargaining power (Arrow 1962b; Anton and Yao 1994, 1995; see also chapter 5). Gans, Hsu, and Stern (2000) show that start-up innovators tend to profit from their innovations through licensing as opposed to competing directly in the product market with more established firms when the risk of expropriation of ideas is relatively small, and transaction costs of bargaining are low. A related potential problem is that with a royalty-based contract, the innovator's earnings depend on the effort and investment made by its licensees in commercializing the technology. Thus, the firm is unable to control its own fate, increasing the chances of failure. For instance, Rambus (chapter 3) developed a highly successful architectural interface that speeds up data transfer. The company depends critically upon manufacturers of semiconductor devices, notably Intel, for its survival.[10] In many instances, this dependency leads entrepreneurs to adopt a strategy where they try to acquire the complementary capabilities themselves to avoid having to share rents.

The most obvious potential pitfall in such a strategy is that small firms also have limited bargaining power when it comes to acquiring the capital required to build or acquire the complementary assets they need to exploit the technology themselves. Further, to the extent that many of the complementary assets are themselves not readily accessible through a market mechanism, and to the extent that the entrepreneurial startups may not be efficient at building those assets themselves, in-house exploitation is probably a riskier and possibly less efficient strategy.

The markets for complementary assets are developing alongside the market for technology. The clearest example is the tremendous growth in venture capital, and in capital from "angel" investors who provide seed capital. Additionally, the great success that small startups have had in attracting financing through the equity market has reduced the cost of both technology development as well as the cost of acquiring some of the complementary assets.[11]

Merchant fabricators in semiconductors, such as TSCM, are an example of a market for complementary assets. These firms have invested in large semiconductor foundries for application-specific integrated circuits (ASICs) and other types of semiconductor devices for other firms. A start-up firm that has developed new semiconductor technology can outsource production to a foundry and market its devices itself by developing a marketing and distribution organization. Whether it ought to develop a marketing organization or appropriate the rents from its technology through licensing the technology to others depends in part on whether it is likely to be able to develop and manage a marketing operation efficiently. An innovative startup firm, however, may often not be able to do so. For example, in chapter 3 we discussed the different fortunes of Microunity and Broadcom, which developed new semiconductor technologies for communication. The former attempted to integrate downstream in manufacturing and possibly commercialization, thereby facing serious challenges owing to the high capital costs of semiconductor fabrication. In contrast, Broadcom appears to have done better by remaining a specialized concern in technology development while relying on licensing its technology to firms better equipped to keep up with the manufacturing and commercialization.

Another case in point is Cambridge Display Technologies (CDT), which specializes in conjugated polymer technologies. Light-emitting polymers are one of CDT's key applications. When the technology was first developed in the early 1990s, the CDT founders, mainly Cambridge University researchers, tried to develop and commercialize the technology themselves. The company nearly went bankrupt. When professional managers were brought in, they changed the business model. The key function of CDT is to license the technology to established manufacturers. CDT has entered into licensing and codevelopment and manufacturing deals with companies including Dow Chemicals, Philips Electronics, Seiko-Epson, Hoechst, and DuPont. This arrangement recognizes that although CDT has world-leading ability in the light emitting polymers area, it does not have the manufacturing and marketing skills that are also essential to be a world-class display manufacturer. Through licensing-out patents and transferring its technology, CDT enables its partners to apply their complementary skills to developing specific products for their markets.

There are other important considerations that mitigate self-exploitation. Even if a firm can develop and manage complementary assets efficiently, these assets may be much longer-lived than the technology itself. This puts the innovator in the position of having to develop new technologies to "feed" these complementary assets. If the firm fails to develop such new technologies, it will be left with underutilized manufacturing facilities or marketing networks. Unless these assets or their services can be traded on the market, at least part of their value will be lost.

The case of Syntex illustrates the risk involved when an innovative firm chooses to build up firm-specific complementary assets to exploit an innovation in-house. Syntex was founded in 1944 in Mexico City and relocated twenty years later to Palo Alto, California. During the early 1980s, the firm became extremely successful thanks to a non-steroidal anti-inflammatory drug based on the compound Naprosyn, first marketed in 1976. In 1981, Syntex listed on the New York Stock Exchange; in 1987 it reached $1 billion in annual sales. However, when the patents on Naprosyn expired in 1993 and generic products began to flood the market, Syntex became financially distressed. Its stock price plummeted from $54 a share in January 1992 to $18 a share eighteen months later. In late 1993, Roche Holding, the Swiss pharmaceutical firm, acquired Syntex in a deal valued at over $5 billion. Syntex's operations in Palo Alto, after some restructuring, were transformed into a research facility with support and strategic marketing planning staff.

The proximate cause of Syntex's failure was its inability to discover a new blockbuster when the patents on Naprosyn expired. Indeed, Syntex's strong research abilities notwithstanding, pharmaceutical innovations still depend a great deal upon serendipity. Bad luck combined with large fixed costs took Syntex into financial distress, paving the way for the acquisition by Roche.

Leaving aside the question of whether Syntex's research productivity had declined, consider the role of the business model. If Syntex had not built up a substantial downstream manufacturing and marketing capability, it might have been able to ride out the lean periods, because it would not have had to find the revenues to support its downstream operations. Moreover, this business model also implied that Syntex had to invest in extremely costly drug development and clinical trials to find its potential blockbuster drugs. The problem is not that Syntex had to exit the market. Had Syntex failed because its research ceased to be productive, exit would be both privately and socially desirable. Syntex's research capability continued to be valuable as evidenced by Roche's repositioning of Syntex after the acquisition. The problem is that Syntex failed as a pharmaceutical firm, destroying some of the value of the downstream assets in which it had invested. Even if integration did not hurt its research productivity, the failure of research destroyed the value of the Syntex brand name and reduced the value of other firm-specific assets that Syntex had built.[12]

Finally, and perhaps most importantly from a long-run perspective, integration may reduce the innovative potential of the firm, because the acquisition of complementary assets inevitably increases the size of a firm and causes important changes in the corporate culture and in the speed and fluidity of information flows. As Levinthal and March (1993) note, organizations divide attention and resources between two broad groups of activities. They engage in the pursuit of new knowledge, exploration, and in the exploitation of this knowledge. Exploration is similar to the notion of research and development, while exploitation is closer to the downstream activities of production and marketing. A blend of exploration and exploitation is desirable (March 1991; Levinthal and March 1993), but dynamics within organizations may lead exploitation to drive out exploration or vice versa. For instance, experience-driven learning processes, typically the case in manufacturing and marketing, tend to favor exploitation because it provides clearer, earlier, and closer feedback (Levinthal and March 1993). These dynamics are hard to resist in larger organizations, which are often unable to provide high-powered incentives for exploration. Contrasted with the incentives that stock options and the threat of bankruptcy provide for exploration in small start-ups, and the flexibility and rapid flow of information, larger organizations often fail to provide an environment conducive for exploration.[13]

Further, as Stiglitz and Weiss (1981) have demonstrated, limited liability implies that smaller organizations with fewer fixed assets at stake will be willing to bear greater risk. Large organizations can try to encourage exploration by forming and nurturing small subunits isolated from the rest of the organization. As we noted earlier in section 9.3.4, such "corporate ventures" have inherent limitations. The available evidence on their performance, summarized in Chesbrough (2000), is mixed. Levinthal and March (1993) also note that corporate ventures tend to yield modest returns. In sum, there are reasons to believe that as a research-intensive company converts itself to an integrated firm with in-house manufacturing and marketing units, its research productivity is likely to decline.[14]

9.5   External Technology and the "Not-Invented-Here" Syndrome

Markets for technology also affect the firm in its role as a user of technology. The strategic imperative is not only to maximize the revenues from the firm's actual stock of technologies, but also to identify technologies that are available at a reasonable price and that, if acquired, will increase the value of existing assets (Iansiti 1997; Iansiti and West 1997). This does not imply that firms can simply rely on outside technologies and need not invest in R&D itself. Evaluating technologies and being able to use them requires substantial in-house scientific and technological expertise (Arora and Gambardella 1994b; Cohen and Levinthal 1989). As Mowery (1984) has pointed out, a firm is far better equipped to absorb the output of external R&D if it is also performing some amount of R&D internally. A related but different interpretation of this is provided by Gans and Stern (2000), who argue that technology buyers need to invest in R&D to strengthen their bargaining position in licensing negotiations.

Another powerful argument supports the idea that internal and external R&D are complements, not substitutes. Discussing the complex relationship between basic and applied research, Rosenberg (1990) points out that a great deal of R&D is undertaken to solve problems that arise in the course of production. Indeed, the solutions to some of these problems often lead to fundamental scientific insights. Rosenberg's point is that a firm lacking technical capability will often be unable to frame the problems it faces in ways suitable for systematic scientific investigation. Similarly, von Hippel (1990) notes that many innovations arise as leading users attempt to solve problems that crop up as they try to expand the technology frontier. In other words, a firm on the technology frontier, or one that aims to be a technology leader, cannot rely only on outside technology. In many cases, the problems a leader faces are unique. As we showed in chapter 6, independent technology suppliers have little incentive to provide solutions to such problems, at least not until other users face similar problems. However, many firms have taken this view to the extreme, refusing to face the possibility that others may have solutions to their problems. In many cases, solutions may arise from the outside, without the stimulus of the mechanism described by Kline and Rosenberg (1986). After all, the development of new knowledge is marked by serendipity and chance, and solutions developed in one context can be useful in others.

The ability of the firm to evaluate and use outside technology may be conditioned by its existing organizational structure, which limits information flows and how opportunities are framed (see, e.g., Henderson and Clark 1990). Sometimes firms tend to disregard external technology options completely. The "not-invented-here" syndrome (Katz and Allen 1982) often has legitimate roots, as corporations seek to motivate and instill pride in the achievements of their researchers. Rotemberg and Saloner (1994) develop a model in which a not-invented-here corporate culture may serve a valuable role of committing the corporation to develop the technologies invented by the firm's in-house R&D departments, thereby providing the appropriate incentives to the researchers. However, in a world where R&D capabilities are widely diffused, such a commitment device is likely to be costly.

Simply put, markets for technology increase the penalty of nurturing the not-invented-here syndrome. In the first place, the wide diffusion of new technology producers (other firms, smaller technology suppliers, universities, etc.) makes duplications of R&D efforts likely. Even in a specialized field, several research units may be working on similar problems, or one unit may have already solved a problem just encountered by another. By relying only on internally developed solutions, companies can end up reinventing the wheel.[15]

This also points to the importance of systematic monitoring of external technological developments on a worldwide basis. By using and building upon basic or generic technologies developed elsewhere, companies can focus on developing specialized applications that better suit the needs of their local markets (Iansiti and West 1997). Global markets for technology can therefore improve the innovation potential and the competitiveness of companies in technologically and economically less dynamic regions. They can create an effective division of labor between technology producers located in areas more efficient in the production of technology, and local producers that have their comparative advantage in understanding the needs of their customers. Thus, chemical producers in developing countries can rely upon firms in developed countries to provide both technology and know-how, while focusing their efforts on ways to source raw materials and develop the market for the products (see chapter 8).

This is especially true with general-purpose technologies (GPTs) when there exists a market for these technologies. Under such conditions, it pays for each individual firm to acquire the GPT from a specialist supplier, concentrating instead on the customization of the technology, rather than developing the whole technology or innovation from scratch. For instance, firms in developing countries can specialize in adapting the GPT to their markets, relying on and exploiting their nontradable knowledge of local demand, norms, and regulations. A similar argument can be made across industries rather than across countries. It pays firms to use GPTs from industry leaders, and customize them for their own sectors, markets, or clients, rather than develop their own industry-specific technology.

To summarize, there are at least two main implications of markets for technology for companies as users, rather than producers, of technology. First, markets for technology point to the growing importance of strategies based on monitoring external technological developments. As Cohen and Levinthal (1989) have argued, this also means that companies have to develop adequate internal technological capabilities, because greater internal technological skills are typically associated with greater ability to take advantage of outside technological developments. Second, markets for technology can make it more efficient to "customize" products and technologies. Thus, if basic technologies can be made available to a larger number of competitors in an industry, the sources of competitive advantages move downstream. This explains why several companies are increasing the "service-content" of their products. Services bundled with products can be thought of as solutions to problems that customers have, much the way systems integrators like IBM or Anderson Consulting provide solutions to business problems rather than selling computers or software.

9.6 Entry and Competition

At the industry level, markets for technology can potentially give rise to significant industry-wide economies of specialization in the production of technology, especially if they encourage the formation of specialized technology suppliers. Markets for technology may then provide downstream industries with the classical Smithian and Stiglerian advantages of division of labor (see Smith 1776 [1983]; Stigler 1951).

The story of the SEFs (specialized engineering firms) in chemical processing, discussed in earlier chapters, is a natural example. In particular, while SEFs originated as an American phenomenon, during the 1950s and 1960s, U.S. SEFs became a source of technology for the European and Japanese chemical industry. Later on, SEFs from all the advanced countries supplied chemical process technologies to the producers in the less advanced countries. This enabled the European and Japanese chemical industries, and those of other, less developed countries, to rise and grow. Ultimately, this has meant that the SEFs encouraged greater competition and an increase in the number of producers in the downstream chemical product businesses that employed the manufacturing technologies SEFs originally made available. Note that when the SEFs moved to other countries, the fixed costs of developing the SEF technologies were largely sunk, and, as a result, the cost of acquiring technology was lower than it would have been if the local companies had developed it from scratch.[16]

The story of the SEFs points to another implication of markets for technology. The rise of technology suppliers in one country, possibly stimulated by the domestic downstream industry, can increase the competitiveness of foreign rivals of the very same downstream manufacturers in that country. The U.S. SEFs, spurred by the U.S. chemical and oil industries, encouraged the growth of European and Japanese chemical and petrochemical producers in the 1950s and 1960s. These firms vied with the U.S. companies in their own domestic markets, and in the international market later on. Chemical and petrochemical companies from the developing countries now compete in their own markets with the Western manufacturers largely due to Western technologies.[17] Simply put, in the international context, markets for technology can lead to a dramatic shortening of the product life cycles.

The pattern is similar in several high-tech industries today.[18] Biotechnology largely originated in the United States, and today the vast majority of small high-tech intensive biotech concerns are still in the United States. As discussed in chapter 3, the U.S. biotech industry is feeding the U.S. pharmaceutical and agrochemical companies with several new products. However, their services and technology are also available to European and Japanese companies, which have entered into a number of licensing agreements and other alliances with U.S. biotech firms. It may even be that the services available from U.S. biotech firms discouraged the European and Japanese large companies from promoting a biotech industry in their own countries. But the fixed cost of creating the U.S. biotech industry was largely borne in the United States. Similarly, large companies in Europe and Japan, as well as companies from the developing countries, are taking advantage of U.S. technological developments in industries like software or semiconductors, which are largely created by U.S. specialized technology suppliers.

The market for these technologies has meant that the importance of technology as a source of competitive advantages is greatly reduced. The point is not that technology and technological superiority in a certain industry has become unimportant. Indeed, technologically less sophisticated chemical companies (such as those in the developing countries) were likely to be less effective in taking advantage of the SEF technologies, and gaps between technologically advanced and less advanced firms (or countries) did not disappear. Similarly, some leading corporations in pharmaceuticals or electronics today are still technologically superior to many of their competitors. The issue, however, has to be cast in relative rather than absolute terms. Thus, the presence of the SEFs meant that, in chemicals, the gap between a small set of leading technological firms and their competitors, in the other advanced countries first, and in the less developed countries later on, was reduced. The entry by newcomer chemical firms with no significant technological expertise became possible. Likewise, with biotech firms or semiconductor design companies, the opportunities for new entrants in the industries employing those technologies are greater. As a matter of fact, there are cases of firms that have ceased to produce products that they innovated and in which they have had a great deal of experience in production.[19]

One natural response to the increase in competition produced by markets for technology is the necessity for firms to cut costs, possibly by exiting businesses in which they lack a clear advantage. To the extent that technology becomes a relatively less important source of competitive advantages, another response is that firms have to look for other distinctive competitive assets.[20] Indeed, as discussed in section 9.2.1, the resource-based theory of the firm argues that a competitive advantage is sustainable only if it is underpinned by resources and capabilities that are scarce and imperfectly mobile. This is a reason why detailed knowledge of the specificities of demand can become increasingly important. In turn, this implies that companies should focus on knowledge and information about the local geographic markets in which they operate, or about the peculiar and diverse demands of their clients and users. Moreover, they must make significant investments in capturing information about customer needs or the special requirements of their local markets (Porter 1998).

The heterogeneity of demand is a potential source of distinctive capabilities. In the first place, demand heterogeneity implies that companies can extract greater value from their customers by tailoring products or services to the customers' special requirements. At the same time, customers are often unable to articulate their needs. As a result, information can only be acquired through close relationships between consumers and producers. Put simply, the tacit component of the knowledge bases in industry may shift toward information and expertise about what the individual customers want (von Hippel 1998). This information is less tradable, and therefore likely to become a prominent source of competitive advantage. In short, with markets for technology, companies could take advantage of the lower cost of acquiring technologies, and focus on the combination of internal and external technologies to provide distinct solutions to their customers. These efforts must be based on solid understanding of their needs, along with substantial investments in relationships with customers.[21]

The dynamic response rests on the recognition that in a rapidly moving environment, any sort of competitive advantage or distinctive ability of the company is unlikely to persist for a long time. Thus, firms have to learn how to manage themselves in an environment in which the rate of innovation is high, competition is more intense, and time to market new products is shorter. Dynamic competitive advantages require that companies learn how to reorganize themselves rapidly, continuously deploying new competitive advantages and distinctive assets. Specifically, as markets for technology develop, technological superiority is increasingly going to be meaningless if intended as a long-term advantage from controlling a given set of technologies. By contrast, it can become a critical source of distinctive assets if a company is capable of accumulating technological capabilities in a certain domain and develops continuously new technologies in that field. Moreover, markets for technology could further enhance the returns on these capabilities, as companies may become leading suppliers in these markets as well.

9.7   Conclusions

This chapter has analyzed how markets for technology affect and condition the technology strategies of companies, both as technology users and as technology suppliers. In the former case, the first and most obvious implication for large technology-based firms is that markets for technology enlarge the strategy space; firms can choose to license their technology rather than rely solely on internal exploitation. The licensing decision is driven by the interplay of the rent dissipation effect from licensing that comes through increased competition, and the revenue effect from licensing that is due to the pecuniary compensation paid by the licensee for the access to the technology. Accordingly, licensing is more likely to be chosen in a distant market (where it is costly for the licensor to produce), when the market share of the licensor is small (e.g., "orphan" technologies), and when the downstream market is highly competitive (as profit dissipation from an additional producer is small). In addition, markets for technology increase the value of effective internal management and organization of companies' intellectual property.

For small firms and technology-based start-ups, markets for technology increase the effectiveness of strategies based on the specialization of such firms in technology development. They do not need to incur costly and risky investments in downstream assets, and can profit from their research even if they lack the complementary assets, or if the markets for such assets are underdeveloped.

Since markets for technology also involve firms as technology buyers, the growth of such markets increases the importance of external monitoring of technological developments and the penalty of insularity and the not-invented-here syndrome. Markets for technology can also reduce the relative importance of technology as a source of distinctive advantage, because the advantage of possessing some critical knowledge or technology may be limited by the ability of competitors to acquire the technology from other sources. The natural consequence is that companies have to focus on other internal assets that may provide them with distinctive advantages. Detailed knowledge about the idiosyncratic needs and characteristics of specific markets and buyers is an obvious candidate. Thus, markets for technology may actually increase the importance of downstream strategies for differentiation. At an industry level, markets for technology lower entry barriers, increase competition, and compress product life cycles: all changes that require appropriate strategic responses.

10

The Institutional Context: Problems and Policies

10.1 Introduction

Markets neither arise nor function in a vacuum; they require a supporting infrastructure. This need for a "material" infrastructure is evident in the current context of electronic marketplaces and the rising fortunes of firms that provide or supply this infrastructure. But no less important is the institutional and policy infrastructure, which includes not just the formal laws, policies, and legal settings that govern such markets, but also norms, standards, and other "rules of the game," ranging from formal and codified to implicit and informal.[1]

This chapter examines some of the institutional factors and related policy issues associated with the formation and the growth of markets for technology. We first look at the manner in which standards, technical and legal, and various types of intermediating institutions reduce the transaction costs of technology trade. We next discuss two possible unintended outcomes of markets for technology—the fragmentation of intellectual property rights, and the impact of the privatization of knowledge on academic norms and on the diffusion of research findings. We also examine the implications of global markets for technology on national technology policies, especially in smaller or in developing countries.

Many of the institutions required by markets for technology are similar to those required by any new market. For example, there are similarities between the institutional innovations that gave rise to the growth of commerce in Europe during the fifteenth and sixteenth centuries, and those needed for the development of technology markets today. Apart from well-defined property rights, paralleled by the current attention to "intellectual" property rights, the fifteenth and sixteenth centuries also witnessed the creation of legal standards for commerce (e.g., commercial law, double entry bookkeeping), institutions for encouraging risk-taking behavior (e.g., insurance) and for the reduction of transaction costs (e.g., the bill of exchange). In section 10.2, we discuss the transaction cost-reducing role of these types of standards. We will also look at the institutions that intermediate between buyers and sellers. Section 10.3 focuses on the fragmentation of intellectual property and its impact on academic norms, and section 10.4 discusses the globalization of markets for technology. Policy considerations cut across the various sections; policy interventions can facilitate transaction cost-reducing institutions or mitigate some unintended and undesired consequences.

10.2   Standards and Other Transaction Cost-Reducing Institutions

10.2.1   Standards

The absence of standards can significantly increase transaction costs. David and Greenstein (1990, 4) expressly note that "standards reduce the transaction costs of user evaluations." With standard interfaces, intermediate products or components can be more easily incorporated (and tested) into the larger systems in which they have to operate. This increases the advantage of using components from specialized component makers (compared to internal production). At the same time, standards encourage the growth of independent component vendors, who do not need to acquire the entire set of capabilities required to produce an entire system, and can instead focus on the narrower set of activities involved in the production of an individual component.

Of course, perfect separation between the capabilities, particularly the knowledge based capabilities, required to produce components and the capabilities required to produce the systems in which the components are embedded is almost impossible to achieve. Further, the need for system integration implies that the knowledge and expertise of the producers of the larger system or product must extend to the components.[2] Similarly, standards may not always lead to perfect compatibility, particularly in large and complex systems, and particularly when the technology is changing rapidly. But to the extent that standards introduce some degree of compatibility, they reduce the costs of "plugging-in" the components. David and Greenstein briefly note the implications of interface standards for the vertical specialization of the industry: "[A] product that conforms to an interface standard can serve as a subsystem within a larger system built from numerous components and subsystems *that are provided by different suppliers*, each of whom also conform to the same standard" (emphasis added, David and Greenstein 1990, 4). Steinmueller (1992) deals specifically with the implications of standards for the vertical structure of the U.S. semiconductor equipment industry. He distinguishes between two models for developing flexible production technology equipment in the integrated circuit (IC) industry. One model is based on the creation of standards by the Semiconductor Equipment Manufacturer Institute (SEMI) in developing an "open architecture" with standard connections among individual pieces of equipment and components. The second model is based on the implementation of entire subsystems by individual companies with a lower degree of "task-partitioning" (see chapter 4) and standard interfaces only among parts produced by the same firm. Steinmueller argues that the first model would reinforce the prevailing industry structure of the 1980s, with many different equipment suppliers providing the components that are necessary for a complete manufacturing system. By contrast, the second model would push the equipment suppliers to integrate into the design of larger subsystems, possibly undertaking activities that could overlap with those of the IC producers themselves, increasing concentration in the equipment supplier industry.

Steinmueller also discusses the comparative advantages of the two models. The open system approach fuels the growth of many smaller innovative firms. The presence of several firms for each subsystem or component, and the narrow focus pursued by each firm will lead to a higher degree of experimentation and innovation with a faster rate of technical progress in components. The second model, on the other hand, implies better opportunities for the optimization of the existing system. It also avoids the problems associated with divided responsibility and imperfect interfaces that may affect system performance. Analogous implications of open systems can be found in other industries. As discussed in chapter 4, Langlois and Robertson (1992) have illustrated how the development of an open architecture, based on well-defined architectural interfaces and standards, was critical for giving rise to widespread innovation activities and experimentation with PC components by many independent suppliers.

These patterns are not confined to technical standards. Norms and customs—and institutions more generally—can have similar effects. They can facilitate communication and exchange among independent parties. A notable example is the scientific community. While we shall discuss the importance of its norms and customs for the diffusion of knowledge in section 10.4, here we want to highlight a related effect. As David (1991, 1993) and Dasgupta and David (1987, 1994) point out, the need for peer evaluation implies that scientific findings must be disclosed so that they can be replicated. But this has meant that research findings have to be produced in a "standard language" and according to methodologies that will be understood by other scientists. This is clearly a stylized characterization of scientific research, which may not do justice to the inherent differences in methodological approaches, and in the diversity of research programs even within a field of scientific inquiry. It also ignores the fact that a good deal of scientific knowledge is transferred through apprenticeships, with younger scholars working close to their more senior mentors, or through face-to-face communication (e.g., conferences, workshops, meetings, etc.). However, a substantial amount of scientific communication is codified in standard languages, as exemplified by the diffusion of research findings through journal articles.

In the 1980s, silicon-based CMOS technology was established as a dominant design in semiconductor process technology. A standard manufacturing technology encouraged the rise of the fabless semiconductor design companies (see chapter 3). It facilitated the separation between the knowledge bases and the assets that were needed for product design, and those that were required for manufacturing. Since the capital costs of the latter can be quite substantial compared to those of the former, the entry costs of the specialist design firms were reduced accordingly. In addition, standard CMOS interfaces reduced the transaction costs of the exchange of design modules. Design houses could then specialize in designing integrated circuits for the users and rely on merchant foundries for manufacturing (Linden and Somaya 2000).[3]

Technological standards have become common in today's markets for technology. In chapter 3, we discussed the development of a component-management technology, called CORBA, produced by a U.S.-based nonprofit consortium—Component Management Group (CMG)—with 20,000 members (individuals and companies) in the United States, Canada, Italy, Japan, and India. Along with other standard-setting operations and procedures, CORBA provides standard interfaces for software components that can be plugged into systems without interfering with the basic structure of the architecture. Such standard-setting institutions have arisen concurrently with the creation of electronics markets for software components like Flashline (see chapter 3). Web-based markets like Flashline help match buyers and sellers, thereby reducing search and related transaction costs. The success of standards such as CORBA or of online markets like Flashline is as yet unclear. It is noteworthy however that these sorts of initiatives are being undertaken. It points to the complementarity between the growth of specialized firms and the push for standard component interfaces.

The semiconductor industry provides several other examples. During the 1990s, three major standard-setting alliances were formed. The first one, the Virtual Socket Interface Alliance (VSIA), was established in 1996 by thirty-five founding members including Electronic Design Automation (EDA) software firms, fabless semiconductor design companies, and electronics companies. VSIA's goal was to define and establish open compatibility standards ("virtual sockets") in semiconductor design. VSIA both releases the specifications and actively encourages their use by the participating firms. Another alliance, RAPID (Reusable Application-Specific Intellectual Property Developers), aims to improve access to information about design modules. For instance, RAPID developed a standard catalog for featuring commercially available design modules on the Internet. Similarly, the Virtual Component Exchange (VCX) was created in 1998 by the Scottish economic development agency "Scottish Enterprise" and a few major players from VSIA. VCX is addressing business and legal issues related to design module trade by developing standard contracts, monitoring systems, a matchmaking service, and customized arbitration services (see Linden and Somaya 2000). Recently, a similar effort was undertaken in the form of the Digital Greenhouse initiative in Pittsburgh, a public-private partnership whose objectives include promoting agreement on standards in semiconductor design by forming a consortium of semiconductor firms and local universities.

There are several noteworthy aspects of these efforts. First, the coalitions for establishing the standards have not been confined to the setting of purely technological standards. VCX, in particular, is addressing standardization in areas like contracts for design modules. Thus, standards related to the efficient functioning of various aspects of the market for technology, including norms about legal settings, have been central in the formation of such institutions. Second, some of these coalitions are private initiatives. This suggests that direct policy intervention is not strictly necessary for addressing or solving coordination problems involved in standard-setting. However, public agencies like the "Scottish Enterprise" (for VCX) or the Commonwealth of Pennsylvania (for Digital Greenhouse) can help catalyze such initiatives. Thus, indirect policy interventions, possibly through such agencies, may be important in encouraging the industry to coalesce in order to promote standards.

This argument is not new. David and Greenstein (1990) have already noted that standards can be either "unsponsored" (they have no identified originator, but are nonetheless widely accepted), or they can be sponsored by specific interest-holders or groups (e.g., firms), by voluntary standards writing organizations (including industry-wide consortia), or by government agencies with regulatory authority. These different origins of standards have in turn several different and complex economic and policy implications, discussed at some length by David and Greenstein. It may also be worth mentioning the colorful metaphors introduced by David (1987) who noted that: (1) policy interventions for standard-setting are often effective only within narrow spans of time before industry settles on a standard ("Narrow Windows"), (2) the relevant policy decisions have to be made when most of the information about the costs and benefits of the standards is not yet available ("Blind Giants"), and (3) there may be political maneuvering in a race to create a standard because of the resistance of the users or the sponsors of the losing standards ("Angry Orphans"). To the extent that these issues affect the formation of standards, and the latter affect the transaction costs of technology trade, they are also relevant in the rise and the growth of markets for technology.

10.2.2 Financial and Other Intermediating Institutions

As with any other market, intermediating institutions that help reduce the cost of searching for information will improve the functioning of markets for technology. For example, as discussed in chapter 2, patent attorneys, along with other intermediaries of a similar kind, played this role in the nineteenth and early twentieth-century U.S. patent markets described by Lamoreaux and Sokoloff. In addition to providing patent counseling and related services, they also helped balance demand and supply. Today, several independent firms and technology traders on the Internet also play a similar role. (See, e.g., BTG 1998, and table 3.10.) Public institutions can step in where private initiative is lacking. For example, the European Union has created its own Internet-based information-providing service, CORDIS, which collects information about potential technologies for licensing, as well as requests for technological partnerships. Similarly, the German government, along with the Länders and private investors, has created the Steinbeis Foundation—a large network of German firms, research institutions, and academics, whose task is to match technology demands with the supply of technologies.

A critical feature of markets for technology is the role of specialist technology suppliers. However, such specialized firms, many of which are small startups, face many types of barriers. Obtaining finance is a particularly important one. Financial institutions—and particularly institutions that encourage risk-taking—can therefore play a critical role in fostering or hindering the markets for technology. In particular, venture capital, initial public offerings, and "new" financial and equity markets have grown in parallel with the rise of new business opportunities and innovation in high-tech industries. A discussion of the role of financial institutions, venture capital, and similar institutions is beyond the scope of the present discussion. One feature that we want to note, however, is that institutional innovations like venture capital have proven to be extremely flexible. They have adapted in various ways to the actual needs and conditions for supporting new business activities. For example, many analysts have noted that not only do the venture capitalists provide finance, but also managerial support. Most important, they provide startups with connections to a broader networks of people and resources (see Gompers 1999; Gompers and Lerner 1998). This networking capability has been critical for maximizing the exploitation of the external economies that exist in areas like the Silicon Valley.

To a large extent, these institutions are the result of private responses to profit-making opportunities. Hence, the role of policy has been largely that of creating the general "ambience" in terms of broader policy, legal, and institutional context, rather than taking the form of direct intervention. But in many countries, efforts for encouraging risk taking have taken the form of direct policy interventions as well. For example, in many European countries, the governments of individual member states, often with the financial and political support of the European Union, have invested sizable public resources in the creation of Science and Technology Parks, especially in less developed regions. Moreover, both in Europe and elsewhere there is a wealth of public R&D programs that support R&D activities, particularly those of smaller firms. These efforts are undertaken to provide the necessary infrastructures and external economies, along with inflows of capital funds. The obvious intent has been to reduce the risk associated with the launch of the start-up firms, and to support R&D activities and technology-based companies more generally.[4]

A recent report by a group of experts assembled by the European Commission (ETAN 1999) has suggested three main areas for institutional developments that would encourage risk-taking behavior: changes in fiscal policy, the creation of security interests in intellectual property rights, and changes in insolvency laws. As far as the fiscal incentives are concerned, R&D and innovation tax credit can be useful institutional innovations to favor start-up companies and the markets for technology. These objectives, however, have to be taken explicitly into account when designing the schemes. For example, the U.S. Research and Experimentation Tax Credit issued in the early 1980s was amended in 1993 to extend the underlying incentives to smaller firms. Small firms, new startups, or, more generally, firms that could not claim any R&D expenditures in the previous three years on which to compute the incremental R&D tax credit, were assigned a fixed percentage increase of 3 percent for the first five taxable years beginning after 1993.

Another problem with startups is that they may not be able to enjoy the benefits of the R&D credit because they lack taxable income. In order to make an unused R&D credit a valuable asset, the 1993 Amendment established that firms could carry the credit back three years and forward up to fifteen years. In so doing, the credit becomes a hidden asset that can be unlocked in the future when the company becomes profitable or is sold. Venture capitalists and lenders understand the importance of these hidden assets and may grant more favorable terms if they know a credit exists and can be deployed in the near future.

The problem of accounting for the value of technology, and of the technology-based companies more generally, given that such a value is often made up of intangible rather than tangible assets, is well known. The valuation of intangible assets and specifically the valuation of technology are particularly relevant in cases where the firm lacks downstream assets to commercialize the technology. This is a complex issue and well beyond the scope of the present discussion. However, it is important to note that accounting practices and norms can affect the fortunes of technology-based firms, particularly startups, in important ways. Current accounting practices and norms, derived as they are from times when measuring tangible and material assets was the crucial task, will have to be modified in order for technology markets to flourish

This problem is also closely related to U.S. and European attempts to remove legal obstacles to the creation of security interests in intellectual property rights. Once lenders, investors, or the entrepreneurs themselves can meaningfully assess the value of these assets, they can be used in a variety of ways, including as collateral to obtain financing. When such assets can be "securitized" and traded in a market, the growth of firms specializing in developing technology is encouraged.[5]

The third area identified by the ETAN Report (1999) is insolvency laws. As Rosenberg and Birdzell (1986), among others, noted, the introduction of limited liability in the fifteenth and sixteenth centuries was a major institutional innovation for limiting the risk of the entrepreneurs who set up a new business. However, as the report notes, the limited liability can in many practical cases be more apparent than real. On many occasions, the life savings and dwellings of the entrepreneurs have been used as collateral for company debts despite. This could limit, for instance, a business's ability to invest in expensive equipment needed for research experiments, computerized product designs, and the like. The ETAN Report argues for institutional changes that would further reduce liability for failure in technologically risky industries. The report also argues that, in the United States the Federal Bankruptcy Code Chapter 11 is more favorable to the establishment of new companies for marketing technological innovations than are existing laws in most European member countries. This is clearly a quite complicated area for intervention, as one must properly balance the need for encouraging risky businesses against the possibility that companies take excessive risk or that they exert limited care in avoiding losses. But this only increases the importance of carefully crafted policies.

10.3   Intellectual Property Rights in a Non-Coasian World

10.3.1   Fragmentation of Intellectual Property Rights and Related Issues

In previous chapters (particularly in chapter 5), we argued that intellectual property rights encourage the rise of a market for technology.[6] Similarly, Merges (1998) uses the incomplete contracting approach (Grossman and Hart 1986; Hart and Moore 1990) to argue that well-defined enforceable patents reduce transaction costs, and thereby help increase transactions in technology. Merges (1998) also concurs with Arora and Gambardella's (1994a) argument that patents are likely to have a greater value for small firms and independent technology suppliers as compared to large established corporations. Whereas the latter have several means to protect their innovations, including their manufacturing and commercialization assets, the former can only appropriate the rents to their innovation by leveraging the protection that patents provide. At the margin, an increase in the strength of patents and intellectual property rights increases the returns from investments in technology development more substantially for smaller technology specialists and start-ups than for the larger integrated companies.[7] These arguments implicitly or explicitly assume a Coasean world— where transactions can be accomplished easily and at low cost. Though not always realistic, they do point to the role of patents in facilitating transactions in technology.

This role of patents has largely been ignored in formal economic analysis, where the focus has been on the trade-off between the ex ante incentives to innovate and the ex post advantages of innovation diffusion. As a result, major policy questions have been related to the optimum length (and later, length and breadth) of the temporary monopoly to be granted (see, e.g., Gilbert and Shapiro 1990; Klemperer 1990). But in recent years, the nature of technology and the issues at stake have introduced some important new challenges for patent policies and intellectual property rights more generally. In fields such as chemicals, biology, materials, and electronics, the growth in the scientific understanding of relevant phenomena, and the growing power and use of the abstraction that this understanding makes possible, have increased the opportunities to relate knowledge created in a specific context to a much broader array of applications.

This has posed a serious challenge to the notion that each patent is associated with one innovation. Consider the challenge raised by patenting parts of the human genome. While this is a controversial and emotional issue, our focus here is somewhat different. The structure of a gene provides information about the proteins for which it codes. If one also understands the role of the protein in the context of a disease or disorder, then understanding the structure of the gene provides an opportunity to try to prevent or cure the disease. A patent on the gene would therefore allow the patent holder to share the economic rents created by this therapy. However, these rents would have to be shared with the firm that uncovers the role of the protein coded for by the gene as well as with the firm that uses that knowledge to develop a cure, test the cure in clinical trials, and manufacture, market, and distribute it.

This raises the question of how the different contributors should be rewarded. One might expect that the relative bargaining power of the parties involved would determine the rewards. In principle, the situation is not very different from that of a landowner bargaining with a real estate developer who wants to build a shopping mall on the land. In simple terms, one would expect higher transaction costs as the various parties to the negotiation try to get the best deal for themselves. The major difference in this case is that the knowledge of the structure of the gene (and the operation of the protein) is a nonrival good in that it may be applied in other contexts without reducing the economic value derived from its application in the first context. In other words, there is a strong "public goods" character to knowledge.[8] Indeed, applying the knowledge about the structure of the gene to cure one disease does not reduce the value of applying the same knowledge to cure other diseases. In this sense, knowledge is nonrival. The key here is that the knowledge has multiple potential applications, so that users do not compete.

When knowledge is nonrival, protecting that knowledge through patents creates potential inefficiencies. For instance, in the case of ex ante contracting, a number of different potential users may have to get together to invest in creating knowledge. Such contracts are problematic because users will differ in the value they place upon the enterprise, and consequently, are likely to underreport their value. Similar problems are likely with ex post contracting, with different users being charged different prices. Moreover, the closer a patent comes to covering knowledge that amounts to a basic understanding of the physical phenomena involved, the broader the likely sweep of the patent and the greater its reach over time.

This suggests that in cumulative or systemic technologies, a commercializable innovation may require many different pieces of knowledge, some of which may be patented and owned by people with conflicting interests.[9] An agent holding a patent on an important component may hold up the development of the technology (see Scotchmer 1991; Green and Scotchmer 1995, for further discussion). In a similar vein, Merges and Nelson (1990, 1993) argue that broad patents increase the likelihood that an innovator would try to control future innovations based upon her own innovation, thereby slowing down the pace of technological progress.

However, the essential problem is not caused by patents, but by factors such as negotiation costs that prevent agents from entering into contracts for the use of patents. In a Coasian world with no transaction costs, given any initial distribution of property rights over the fragments, agents will bargain to a Pareto optimal solution. More realistically, the required collection of property rights, although socially efficient, might not occur because of transaction costs and hold-up problems. An agent holding a patent on an important fragment ("blocking patent") may use the patent in an attempt to extract as much of the value of the innovation as possible.

Thus, the issue at stake is the impact that strengthening and expanding patent rights—which is what is actually happening today particularly in the United States—would have on transaction costs. Especially problematic is the case when the property rights are defined around very narrow fragments of knowledge and owned by separate entities. In this case, each patent holder has the right to exclude the others from the use of her piece of knowledge. In other words, when several pieces of intellectual property have to be combined, the transaction costs implied could be so high as to prevent otherwise productive combinations.

This problem has been studied in a broader context as the "anticommons" problem (Heller 1998; Heller and Eisenberg 1998). Suppose that the development of a new technology involves the use of N fragments invented and patented by separate firms. In addition, the technology innovator has to pay ex ante a fixed cost, I, which might be thought of as expenditures in R&D. In order to assemble the new technology, either the innovator must buy licenses on the fragments or "invent around" them. The cost of inventing around depends, among other things, on the strength of the intellectual property rights defined around the single fragments.[10] By definition, a blocking patent implies that this cost is extremely large. Let us assume that in the process of collection of the rights, the parties agree to sign a licensing contract which stipulates an up-front fee negotiated through bilateral bargaining.

Two results follow directly from this setup. First, the higher the costs of "inventing-around" the fragments are, the weaker the bargaining power of the innovator is in the licensing negotiations to collect the rights for the use of the different fragments. This is simply because the innovator's outside option—inventing around the patents on the fragments—is less attractive. Second, the larger the number of fragments of intellectual property that must be obtained, the higher the number of contracts to be signed to guarantee the use of the innovation. If transaction costs are increasing with the number of transactions, a larger N is likely to increase the total transaction costs to assemble the fragments.

A more interesting and less straightforward result emerges when one considers opportunistic behavior of firms holding blocking patents on the fragments. Indeed, the further the innovator goes in the collection of the rights for the use of the fragments, the more resources are subject to an irreversible commitment, and, therefore, the weaker his bargaining power in future licensing negotiations for the collection of the remaining fragments. This implies that in subsequent negotiations he will have little chances to recoup all costs sunk until that moment, that is, the fixed investment, I, along with the fees paid for the rights on the fragments already bought. Furthermore, firms might also try to delay selling their blocking claims in order to hold out for higher "quasi-rents." In other words, since the firm that is going to negotiate its "blocking patent" last has the strongest bargaining power in relation to the innovator and can capture the largest amount of rents, all firms have incentives to be the last. This is likely to further delay the assembling of the technology. Obviously, these hold-up problems are exacerbated when the number of blocking patents on separate fragments increases.[11]

So far we have analyzed a scenario in which there is no uncertainty. Innovation, by definition, is characterized by a high level of uncertainty, making prospects even more difficult. First, it can sometimes be difficult to know N a priori. In other words, it is a hard task to determine whose patents bear on a commercial product. Ensuring access to all potentially blocking rights can, therefore, become extremely cumbersome. Second, when the market value of the innovation is uncertain, the owners of blocking patients might agree to sign royalty-based payment for the use of the fragments. In principle, these offer the advantage to the innovator of delaying payment until profits from the innovation start to materialize. To the patent holders, they offer the opportunity to obtain larger payoffs correlated with the sales of the downstream products rather than certain, but smaller, up-front fees. However, the presence of such royalty schemes negotiated on individual basis might imply that the total amount of royalties per unit of output is inefficiently high both from a private and social point of view.[12]

Third, Langlois (1999) raises the problem of dynamic transaction costs. As explained in chapter 4, Langlois argues that Henry Ford's consolidation of all production steps in a vertically integrated company was critical to the successful introduction of the Model T in the 1920. Had the various stages of production remained under separate ownership, Ford would have had difficulty experimenting with new techniques, machines and parts, all which had to fit with each other. When an innovation is based on combining the intellectual property of several independent agents, the costs of persuading them to "rent" or part with their property for a particular application will be high, because each person's payoff will be contingent on all relevant parties coming on board. The net results might be that the parties involved are unable to reach an agreement.

One example of what might occur when several companies hold patents on different components is provided by the early development of the radio (Merges and Nelson 1990). The Marconi Wireless and Telegraph Company, AT&T, General Electric, and Westinghouse all held important patent positions in the early stages of the industry. The ensuing fragmentation of property rights is said to have retarded technological innovation. For instance, the basic patent on the diode was granted to Marconi, while the patent on the triode vacuum tube was assigned to AT&T. Marconi's patent was needed for using AT&T's triode technology. Because neither party would license to the other, no one used the revolutionary triode for some time.

Similar situations arose in the early stages of development of the automobile and aircraft industries and in the chemical process technology industry. Biomedical research may provide another example. Heller and Eisenberg (1998) are especially concerned with the increasing practice in biomedical research of defining property rights around isolated gene fragments. Since many commercial products, such as therapeutic proteins or genetic diagnostic tests, are likely to require the use of multiple fragments, a proliferation of such patents, held by different owners and licensed with stringent "pass-through" provisions, imply large costs for future transactions aimed at bundling the patents together.[13] Software, semiconductors and computers are other examples of industries where the nature of innovation is systemic and cumulative, and where the intellectual property is fragmented. In these industries, the opportunities for holdup are enormous. Indeed, as reported in Grindley and Teece (1997) and Hall and Ham (1999), this has led industry actors to sign cross-licensing agreements covering whole portfolios of patents related to an entire technical field (including both existing and future patents).

Industry participants have echoed these concerns as well. Cecil Quillen, former Senior Vice President and General Counsel of the Eastman Kodak Company, claims that since the early 1980s the legal costs of intellectual property protection has risen dramatically to the point of substantially raising the cost of innovation itself (Cohen, Nelson, and Walsh 2000). Michael Rostoker, former head of LSI Logic, a semiconductor manufacturer, has also suggested that stronger patent protection has enabled firms holding old technology to command licensing fees from a current generation of innovators, even while the original patent holders have long ceased advancing the state of the art. This has led to a stacking of licensing fees that impede the development of new generations of chips (Hadley 1998).

10.3.2 Policy Responses

One possible policy response is to improve the functioning of patent offices, to limit the issue of "bad" patents—patents that are excessively broad, or vague in terms of what is claimed, or that do not adequately specify the use of the patented invention. The patent office evaluates whether patent claims are enabled under the terms of the statute, or if the patent has the statutory novelty in light of the prior art. The better defined a claim is, the less likely there is to be uncertainty about its scope and validity. This translates into lower transaction costs for technology trade and, hence, improved functioning of markets for technology. Moreover, due to the growing importance of patents, the social cost of "bad" patents has increased, along with the number of patents themselves, as Kortum and Lerner (1999) have documented. This argues for more resources to be made available to patent offices for examining patents, and in particular, for searching for prior art.[14]

One may speculate that larger patent offices and stronger incentives to patent might increase patent disputes and litigation, creating deadweight loss. The spurt in litigation activity that we have witnessed in recent years is not a consequence of a greater number of granted patents alone. Indeed, it also points to the likelihood that patent offices, particularly in the United States, are issuing poorly defined patents, with overly broad scope or of dubious "nonobviousness" and novelty over prior art (see Merges 1999a). Litigation itself is not easy to rationalize in the context of standard economic models. If litigation costs reduce total surplus, all economic models of bargaining would suggest that firms have incentives to settle down ex ante the undergoing dispute. There are several reasons why this might not occur. First, litigation costs may be smaller than settlement costs, so that litigation preferred over ex ante settlement both for the firms and for society. Second, firms might have different beliefs about the result of the trial. In turn, such differences are more likely when there are doubts about the validity or scope of the patent in question.[15] In some cases, firms are also known to use litigation, either actual or threatened, to browbeat opponents. This is especially likely when the two parties differ significantly in terms of financial resources, or where time to market may be of the essence.[16]

Often, broad and imprecise patents are issued because patent offices are underfunded, the patent examiners inadequately trained and lacking the necessary capabilities to search for the prior art. In software, for instance, the U.S. Patent Office has issued what are widely seen as overly broad patents, in large measure because the examiners rely heavily upon previous patent applications to discover prior art (Merges 1999b). Since software patents are relatively new (copyrights having been the typical way of protecting software until recently), the result is bad and socially harmful patents that, nonetheless, carry with them the presumption of validity.

By the same token, patent offices should pay more attention to patenting requirements. In the United States, the patentee is required to "reduce to practice" the invention, demonstrate the best-known way the invention is to be used or "enabled," and show the usefulness or "utility" of the invention. Over the last few years, these requirements have not been seriously enforced, at least in certain well-known cases.[17] For instance, patents on gene fragments (ESTs) have been issued without any clear knowledge of what proteins the gene fragment was coded for, and what functions the proteins performed. In principle, these fragments may prove to be useful in a broad spectrum of applications as yet unknown. If granted, the patent holder may be able to demand a large share of the rents from any such applications or even block such applications, without having contributed to their discovery.

These are all possible policy measures to be adopted ex ante. However, if the intellectual property is already fragmented or there are no good instruments (or they are too expensive for society) to avoid the problem of fragmentation at its roots, there is still room for policy interventions to facilitate the functioning of markets for technology. One possibility is to modify the traditional stance of antitrust authorities on patent-pooling agreements. A patent-pooling agreement typically involves two or more companies with similar or overlapping patents. Rather than pursuing interference proceedings or engaging in long and costly litigation to determine issues such as patent validity or infringement, the two companies put their collective efforts to more productive use. For example, they may form a separate entity to which they assign or license their patents. The entity collects royalty for the service or product and pays out a share to each of the patent owners, according to the terms of the agreement. A similar argument applies to cross-licensing agreements whereby firms agree to license each other the use of their respective fragments.[18]

Traditionally, antitrust authorities in the United States have aggressively scrutinized patent pools and cross-licensing agreements, because such agreements were sometimes used for restricting entry, controlling prices and market shares. However, recently the antitrust stance appears to have changed, favoring the emergence of market-based responses to the problem of excessive fragmentation of intellectual property rights. For instance, Grindley and Teece (1997) attribute the extensive use of cross-licensing agreements in electronics and semiconductors (where innovations are typically based on hundreds of different existing patents) to the large transaction costs required to bundle together patent portfolios. Very recently the Department of Justice gave the green light to a group of nine companies and one university to create a pool of the patents essential to the MPEG-2 video standard. Another patent pool involving eleven patent holders has been agreed for the IEEE 1394 bus, a popular solution for transferring audio and video data.[19] In the chemical process industry, technology-sharing agreements have a long history and were established to alleviate the transaction costs involved in market relationships (Arora 1997). The case of the chemical process industry is also interesting for another reason. SEFs have sometimes acted as technology integrators, helping to bypass the hold-up problem of fragmented property rights. Thus, another potential benefit of specialized technology suppliers is that they can act as technology integrators to limit the hold-up problem created by the fragmentation of intellectual property rights.

A final set of policies whose merits remain under debate is the extension of "eminent domain" (i.e., the legal doctrine that allows the government to take over private property for public purpose) to intellectual property. In principle, the threat that the government may step in and buy out a patent holder at a "fair" price can be a powerful deterrent to the sort of opportunism that underlies the fragmentation problem. But governments may not be the best agencies to take over a technology where considerations of the public good might be quite indirect. Determining a fair price for the patent is an important challenge. A recent paper by Kremer (1998) suggests using an auction as mechanism to determine the private value of patents. The government would use this price to buy out the patents and place them in the public domain. To ensure, truthful revelation, some fraction of the winning bidders would be required to buy the patent at the bid price.

Alternatively, the law may simply allow for "efficient breach"—for example, let people "infringe" the patent, and leave the courts to decide about a fair royalty. The latter is similar in spirit to the compulsory licensing provisions and provisions that require the patent to be "worked." Both of these provisions have been utilized in many countries, and require courts to intervene more aggressively than it is probably desirable.

10.4 The Privatization of Knowledge: Crumbling Academic Norms?

As basic scientific knowledge such as the structure of genes becomes eligible for patenting, universities are pulled and pushed into entering the market for technology. David (2000) describes the trend in policy discourse toward a more instrumentalist view of university research, moving from national defense to national industrial competitiveness to, most recently, wealth creation. These trends have contributed to an increasing amount of pressure placed upon universities and university researchers to demonstrate the economic value of their work. Concomitantly, universities have increasingly resorted to patenting and copyrighting their research. The 1980 passage of the Bayh-Dole Act in the United States allowed universities and government laboratories to claim patents on federally funded research, and is widely believed to be responsible for the rise of university patenting (see Mowery et al., 2000).

Other factors have encouraged the trend toward greater privatization of university-based research. A general expansion of patentable subject matter and a more patent-friendly legal environment (with the 1981 establishment of the so-called patent court, the CAFC or the Court of Appeals of the Federal Circuit) meant that the patents universities obtained would be more valuable. The result was an expansion in university patenting, as well as the establishment of university licensing offices and the encouragement of "spin-offs" to commercialize university-based research.

The number of patents issued to the one hundred leading U.S. research universities doubled between 1979 and 1984. The share of university patents in total U.S. patenting increased from 1 percent in 1975 to 3.6 percent in 1995 (Mowery et al. 1999). Since U.S. patents have grown rapidly during this period as well, it implies that university patents have grown faster still. Moreover, whereas overall patents per $1 billion R&D spending (in constant terms) declined from 780 in 1975 to 429 in 1990, university patenting shows an increase from fifty-seven to ninety-six per $1 billion spent over the same period (Mowery et al. 1999). These increases reflect more systematic attempts by universities to assert rights over inventions, including attempts by university licensing offices to elicit the disclosure of such inventions. Mowery and Ziedonis (2000) note that compared to the period between 1975 and 1979, invention disclosures at the University of California (UC) increased sharply between 1980 and 1984, as did the share of disclosures for which patents were applied.

Alongside their increased patenting activity, U.S. universities stepped up efforts to license their patents. Licensing revenues of U.S. universities that are members of the Association of University Technology Managers (AUTM) have increased, in real terms, from $188 million in 1991 to $607 million in 1997. Mowery and Ziedonis (2000) find that the share of UC disclosures that resulted in licenses more than doubled after 1980, while those that resulted in positive licensing revenues increased from 3.9 percent in 1975–1979 to 5 percent in 1980–1984. Over the same period, the share of invention disclosures at Stanford University more than tripled, and those yielding positive revenue doubled, growing from 9.8 percent to almost 18 percent. In short, universities are beginning to resemble, albeit only partially, both sources of technology and incubators for developing independent suppliers of technology.

These trends raise three concerns. First, to some there seems something wrong with the notion of publicly subsidizing research, the results of which will later be monopolized. Put differently, even if one accepts that the temporary patent-based monopoly is a necessary evil to provide incentives for investments in research, then surely research that is publicly funded does not require the lure of patents. Patents seem both unfair and inefficient. This line of reasoning, however, ignores the other role that patents play—namely, in encouraging the efficient transfer of knowledge between inventors and commercializers. It has been argued that absent such patenting, much of the research now being commercialized would lie fallow and unused. Insofar as this is important, one benefit of university patenting is that university researchers can effectively benefit from the invention by licensing the technology and the know-how, instead of attempting to commercialize the innovation themselves. If the latter were to happen, the university would potentially lose the services of researchers and teachers.[20] Patents affect the commercialization of university technology through another route as well. They provide incentives, not for invention, but for development. Indeed, at the heart of the Bayh-Dole Act was the belief that without some measure of exclusivity, companies would not invest in developing university research.

Recent studies of university licensing indicate that such practice relies heavily on exclusive licensing contracts. For instance, Mowery et al. (1999) report that for the period between 1986 and 1990, the fraction of licensed disclosures through exclusive contracts were 58.8 percent, 59.1 percent, and 90.3 percent for Stanford, Columbia, and the University of California, respectively. Mowery et al. criticize the heavy use of exclusive contracting, arguing that nonexclusive licensing would balance the need for exclusivity with the public interest of broad dissemination of knowledge. The heavy use of exclusive licenses should raise concerns, particularly if those licenses cover technology with broad applicability.

The second concern relates to the nature of university research. For instance, might the push to earn revenues from research increase emphasis on applied research at the cost of basic, or fundamental, research?[21] Paradoxically enough, the analysis of patent citations provides one source of empirical evidence. In a seminal contribution, Henderson, Jaffee, and Trajtenberg (1998) found that the rise of university patenting after 1980 was associated with a decline in the "importance" and "generality" of university patents. Since patents relating to more fundamental and broad-ranging discoveries were likely to score higher on the proxies used to measure importance and generality, this evidence seems to support the concern about a movement toward increased short-term and applied research at universities.

However, a more recent study that controls more carefully for the changing composition of universities that patent, Mowery and Ziedonis (2000) reaches a different conclusion. This study analyzed citations to patents held by Stanford and the University of California and found that, relative to a control group of similar patents by industry, there has been no decline in the importance and generality of patents from these universities. Using data on all university patents, they find that the decline of importance and generality is due largely to the increased share of patents sought by universities new to patenting. Thus Mowery and Ziedonis conclude that the evidence does not support a major shift in the content or culture of university research. As before, we lack systematic evidence to come to a definite conclusion on this issue. However, it is certainly possible that there has been a shift toward more applied research and a neglect of more basic and fundamental research, a trend of which universities and governments should be mindful.

The third, and perhaps most important, concern raised by the growing involvement of universities, university faculty, and researchers in patenting and commercializing their discoveries is the impact on academic norms and the consequences for the growth of new knowledge.

Dasgupta and David (1987, 1994) and David (1991, 1993) have high-lighted the features that distinguish the production and dissemination of university research from that carried out in firms and provided an economic framework for understanding these distinguishing features. They argue that the difference is not so much in the methods of inquiry or the nature of the knowledge obtained, but in the nature of the goals accepted as legitimate within the two communities of researchers, the norms regarding disclosure of knowledge, and the systems of rewards. Roughly speaking, university research is undertaken with the intent of disclosure, and the rewards include the approval and respect of a broad (though largely invisible) college of peers. Inevitably, these differences are associated with differences in the types of questions tackled and the methods for representing and communicating the results of the research.[22]

These differences have evolved along with the corresponding institutions in response to some specific features of research as an economic activity. For instance, David (1991, 1993) argues that an inability of European princes and noblemen in the Middle Ages to monitor the quality and effort of the scientists they patronized provided an impetus for open disclosure of research findings. With open disclosure and peer review, the merits of the research findings and hence the quality of the researcher, would be easy to establish. As noted earlier, this also required consensus on the methodology and terminology. The open and rapid dissemination of research findings and the associated norms of academic scientific conduct, particularly peer review, academic freedom, and apprenticeship-type relationships between research students and professors, have become part and parcel of what we think of as university research. These norms are sustained by the public subsidy for university research, allocated principally through a peer review-based mechanism. In essence, the community of researchers decides how funds should be allocated, subject to a few general guidelines and constraints.

Perhaps even more important are the norms of cooperation and collegiality. As Dasgupta and David (1994) point out, the high importance attached to priority creates a tension between complying with the norm of full disclosure and the individual urge to be the first to publish.[23] Since the solution of scientific problems typically requires research into several sub-problems, full disclosure yields a better outcome in the long run for the community as a whole. However, individual researchers have an incentive to "free ride" by learning from others without cooperating in turn. Although cooperative behavior can be sustained in repeated

Prisoner's Dilemma games by threat of exclusion, Dasgupta and David (1994) argue that scientific norms greatly increase the likelihood that networks of cooperative information sharing will arise because of an increased level of trust between competing researchers. These norms are critical for the formation and sustenance of research communities. In turn, these scientific communities act as the agent of society, punishing those that violate cooperation by withholding findings, reviewing the validity of results, training new researchers, and providing some degree of verification of the quality of the researchers themselves (that the community itself allocates funding for scientific research is vital for these other functions, and underpins the ability of the scientific community to enforce its norms).

Privatization of knowledge weakens these norms by reducing the ability of the scientific community to sanction violators and by increasing the rewards to those violators. To return to Dasgupta and David's analogy with the game of Prisoner's Dilemma, privatization of knowledge increases the payoff to withholding cooperation when secrecy followed by patenting of the results will yield large monetary payoffs. There are indirect effects as well. Focusing universities on earning revenues through research leads to a dilution of the role of the larger scientific community in the allocation of funds for scientific research, weakening the power of the community, and, hence, weakening the hold of the norms of disclosure and collegiality.

To be sure, the foregoing description of academia is closer to the Platonic ideal of university research rather than an accurate description of existing reality. The point is that these norms are valuable and useful, and need to be reinforced rather than weakened. Moreover, although resilient, norms are easier to destroy than build; once a sufficiently large fraction of the research community moves away from them, they will be hard to sustain anywhere. Indeed, the growing commercial applicability of biotechnology research has been accompanied by growing anecdotal evidence of the violation of these norms by scientists, including the withholding of important information, delays in disclosure, refusal to cooperate with other researchers, and tales of abuse of graduate and post-doctoral students (Kenney 1986).

However, the available evidence, limited as it is, does not support any significant shift in norms associated with patenting. Mowery et al. (1999) conclude that the bulk of the increased patenting activity appears to have been associated with the increased importance in software and biomedical research that, though more amenable to patenting, are no less basic or fundamental than other university research. Based on their case study of patenting at Columbia University, Mowery et al. also conclude that the impacts on norms are likely to be limited to a few departments most heavily involved in patenting: Electrical Engineering, Computer Science, and the medical school.

A broader question is whether good research can flourish anywhere without such norms. This is a question of institutional design that we raise, but to which we do not know the answer. The academic model of research has been successful in the last 100 to 150 years. Indeed, there is evidence that successful research-oriented firms have tended to adopt the academic mode of organizing at least to some of their research.[24] In other words, the prevailing western university model has been assumed to be an effective way of organizing research, especially basic and fundamental research. With the growing privatization of knowledge, this assumption will be tested in the future.

10.5 "Global" Markets for Technologies and National Policies

Markets for technology, like other markets, are becoming global. In some ways, this is only to be expected, given the reduced "transport" costs and greater appreciation even by otherwise protectionist governments of the benefits of technology. Rapid advances in communications, the Internet being only the most recent, have only hastened the process of globalization.

Markets for technology are far more likely to arise in large, technologically and economically advanced regions, not developing countries. The latter, therefore, need not focus on developing such markets. Instead, they can focus on developing institutions that will enable their firms to participate more effectively in these markets. The example of the Western European chemical industry in the years after World War II is a case in point. Prior to the war, the industry was technologically far ahead of its U.S. counterpart. The disruption due to the war, the rise of the petrochemical industry, and the associated process technologies in the United States, ought to have provided the U.S. chemical industry with a decisive advantage over its European rivals, whose expertise lay in coal-based processes. Yet, in a period of a few years, the German, British, and French chemical industries had largely switched over to petroleum and natural gas as basic inputs. The availability of U.S.-developed refining and chemical engineering expertise made this switch possible. Further, SEFs played an important role in integrating and supplying technology to European customers. In the 1960s, SEFs played a similar role in Japan. Japanese industrial policy, which tended to restrict the access to the Japanese market by foreign firms, was far more receptive to foreign technology imports. Indeed, the policy focus in this context was in creating the ability to absorb and adapt foreign technology (Arora and Gambardella 1998).

The point is simple and well known: Global markets tend to circumscribe the role of policy in affecting market outcomes. For smaller countries like the individual European countries or less-developed countries, the impact of their own policies, if they are not coordinated with those of other countries, is likely to be small. For example, policies of smaller countries to develop standards or other types of supporting institutions are unlikely to induce the development of technology markets on a substantial scale. Similarly, strengthening or weakening intellectual property rights will probably have little effect on the global market for technology, although this may affect the extent to which technology flows into their country.

Policies for encouraging, coordinating, or controlling the markets for technology will be most effective when they are developed by large countries (e.g., the United States), or by sets of countries (e.g., the European Union). Such policies require coordination among countries and super-national interventions in international policy settings. But it is precisely at this super-national level that policy decisions are harder to make because of the many conflicting interests involved, and the lack of strong enforcement mechanisms. And this is why policies developed by a large country like the United States (e.g., in intellectual property rights or the development of standards) can have a strong impact on the world development of markets for technology. Likewise, the European Union can play a significant role, especially if it can harmonize the policies of the individual member states, and avoid the adoption of different rules and standards by individual member states.

For most other countries, the key policy question may be how to take advantage of the growth in technology trade worldwide. This will require encouraging the effective use of existing technologies, rather than the creation of new ones. As well, policies aimed at monitoring international technological developments increase in importance, as do institutions for enhancing the efficiency of contracts and reducing search costs. Thus, countries should increase their emphasis on the ability to identify and select technology, and develop complementary capabilities.

In sectors where markets for technology are developed, and technology can be traded more effectively, countries or regions should specialize according to comparative advantages. This does not imply that countries should cease to invest in research and development. Rather, it implies that they should be more selective in terms of which sectors and types of activities they focus on, at least in the short-to-medium run. It is well known that R&D and patenting is concentrated in the wealthier countries. In particular, the United States and Western Europe have a head start in terms of basic research and developing "generic" technologies like semiconductors and genetics. Their advantage lies not only in being the first movers, but also in the broader industrial base in which they can apply these findings. These advantages are less salient when technologies and products need to be adapted for local uses and needs. If one accepts that companies or industries located "near" users have an advantage when it comes to communicating with their markets and acquiring the relevant information for adapting the technologies, firms in other parts of the world could seize this niche. Thus, even if the production of more basic technologies is concentrated, other regions can access these technologies and exploit their own proximity to users or their comparative advantage in developing complementary technologies, as long as markets for technology work well. [25]

These recommendations are not new and in some quarters, are viewed as a prescription for perpetual technological "backwardness." Some countries may resist such an international division of labor in technology production and adaptation. The reasons for resistence tend to range from national pride to the desire to control strategic technologies. Thus, some form of not-invented-here syndrome (see chapter 9), at the country level, is likely to operate. Whether justified or not, it is important to know that where they exist, markets for technology increase the opportunity cost of such an attitude, very much as we argued in the case of individual firms in the previous chapter. Simply put, if others have already paid the fixed cost of developing technology, and competition among sellers implies that the price of the technology is related to the marginal cost of technology transfer, a strategy of developing the technology in-house and incurring the fixed cost all over again must provide some additional benefits over mere ownership of the technology. There is little point in national policies aimed at reinventing the wheel except where such reinvention is a part of the process of building "absorptive capacity," or as a part of a long-run strategy to develop international technological leadership.

Second, in a dynamic setting, the international division of labor, with implied specialization in technology production and adaptation, means that countries specializing in the latter need not give up the possibility of becoming technology producers, at least in some well-defined areas. For example, by starting with a policy of developing technologies complementary to imported ones, local firms and industries can gradually learn about the basic technology as well, possibly becoming the producers of some key technologies (see also Rosenberg and Steinmueller 1988). The Indian software industry, for instance, started as a low-end supplier of software components to the major software companies especially in the United States. There are signs that this strategy may gradually allow some of these companies to develop more sophisticated capabilities and enable these firms to undertake large and complex projects. A similar argument can be made for the Irish software companies, that have improved their ability to produce new software products in some niches of the market (Arora, Gambardella, and Torrisi 2001). In short, in a dynamic setting, the pattern of specialization is not immutable. With proper technology policies, the advantages of specialization in lower-end technological activities (adaptation) could become the springboard for a move up the value chain. Learning through systematic interactions with the markets or the technology producers of more advanced countries may be critical for this process to occur.

Indeed, some countries, like Russia and Israel and to a lesser extent India, have relatively well developed scientific and engineering infrastructures. However, they lack the market size and the complementary technological and economic infrastructure that could best exploit their scientific and engineering infrastructure. In this respect, they are similar to specialized technology suppliers. A well-developed and globalized market for technology will enable firms from these countries to derive more value from their investments in science and engineering by supplying technology to those able to develop and commercialize it more effectively. Here too, one may encounter opposition from those who would see this as giving away the store. Once again, our objective is not to act as advocates, for the appropriate policy will depend on the specifics of the situation, but to highlight the option that markets for technology would create.

10.6 Conclusions

Markets do not arise simply because the benefits of having them outweigh the costs. They require institutions to support them. Further, markets develop over time with these complementary institutions. This development has to be understood as a historical process, with the pace and form of the development influenced by starting conditions and chance. Further, the rise of a new market affects other markets and other existing social and economic institutions. Their development raises new challenges for policymakers but creates new policy options as well.

In this chapter, we highlight some of the major policy challenges posed by the development of markets for technology. Intellectual property rights are a sine qua non for the development of such markets. But given the nature of knowledge, property rights (such as patents) in knowledge can create problems. In some cases, they can retard the development and commercialization of innovations, as for instance when their use requires combining the intellectual property rights controlled by a number of independent agents. How serious this problem is in practice is uncertain and further research in this area would be valuable.

The privatization of knowledge can also undermine an important institution of modern capitalism, namely the research university, by weakening academic norms of open disclosure and collegiality. Weakening public support for academic research exacerbates the problem by forcing universities to look to generate additional resources by patenting and licensing their research findings. Empirical research on this topic is just beginning to be undertaken, and the available evidence suggests that the situation is not irrevocable. However, by their nature, norms are easier to destroy than to create, and it seems sensible to modify only very slowly a system of organizing basic research that appears to have worked well.

With markets becoming global, the exercise of national policy has to be more circumscribed. Especially for smaller countries like the individual European countries or the less developed countries, markets for technology imply a focus on how best to benefit from the growth of these markets. We suggest that this would mean becoming more open to outside technology and reexamining arguments for investments based on national pride. It would also mean participating in an international division of labor by increasing the emphasis on using technology and building complementary capabilities, possibly at the cost of investing in basic research. In a dynamic setting, the learning potential embedded in a division of labor with more advanced technology producers can create the opportunities for later specialization in some of the more basic technology areas.

11   Conclusions

This book has attempted to answer the following question: Under what conditions will technology itself resemble a tradable asset, and, if it does, what will be the consequences for the generation and use of new technologies, for the diffusion of technology, and for public policy and business strategy? We have also met with some important ancillary questions: In what sectors of the economy are transactions in technology more likely, and how pervasive are they? Under what conditions will specialized technology suppliers arise? What constraints exist upon technology transactions, and to what extent can policy ease these constraints?

In trying to answer these questions, we have confronted a variety of challenges. Markets for technology are not easy to define. Technologies often change hands embodied in capital or final goods. While our focus is on the sales of technologies disembodied from physical goods, embodying or disembodying the technology may be the outcome of deliberate choice. Moreover, it is difficult to make the distinction between knowledge and technology. In this book the subtleties of the distinction have remained in the background.

A similar qualification applies to what we consider to be a novel concept we have developed here, namely the division of innovative labor. In many respects, the distinction between the traditional division of labor and the division of innovative labor is not straightforward. Although there are important reasons to distinguish between the two, there are important commonalities as well: the properties and implications (e.g., for economic growth) of vertical specialization can extend beyond the case of the manufactured goods to specialization in technology and the innovation process.

We noted at the outset that markets for technology can have both horizontal and vertical components. There are the horizontal markets for technology whereby technology holders, typically firms with stakes in the downstream markets, license their technologies to other companies operating in the same markets. There are several reasons why a technology holder might want to license despite the additional competition that this entails. Some are well known, but others, discussed in chapter 7, are less well understood.

The vertical dimension encompasses the division of innovative labor. It yields the classic advantages of specialization, with specialized technology suppliers showing a comparative advantage in creating new ideas and technologies, and established companies having a comparative advantage in developing and scaling up these technologies, as well as in manufacturing and marketing. Some of the leading high-tech sectors—software, semiconductors, and biotechnology—are marked by a division of innovative labor. Even when innovations arise from the outside, as for instance from lead users, specialized technology suppliers have been critical in generalizing and developing the innovation for broad use and in diffusing the innovation, as the specialized engineering firms (the SEFs) have done in the chemical processing industries for many years. We have also attempted to combine two distinct traditions in the literature. Studies of firms and technologies tend to either focus on individual firms or institutions, as with the literature on transaction costs, or take a systemic view, trying to understand the industry structures that result in the lowest cost or the greatest rate of technical progress. We have taken both of these perspectives into account. Specifically, we have attempted to combine the tradition linked with Coase (1937), Williamson (1975), and Teece (1988), which is centered on firms and transaction costs, with the one arising from Smith and Stigler on the division of labor. To paraphrase Karl Marx, although firms make their own destiny, they do not do so in circumstances of their own choosing. The circumstances under which firms develop and implement strategies depend on industry-wide forces created by the combined actions of all industry participants, and shaped by the nature of the knowledge used in the industry and the institutions supporting it.

Chapters 6, 7, and 8 highlight the importance of these industry-level factors. Chapter 6 explores the development of General Purpose Technologies (GPTs) and their implications for the growth and efficiency of markets, noting that these implications depend on the relative size of the breadth of industry demand for a generic input as compared with the depth of demand for specific varieties of the input. Similarly, chapter 7 points out that a firm's licensing behavior depends, in important ways, on the presence and actions of other firms, and can lead to outcomes not consciously intended by any of the firms. Chapter 8 details the manner in which the division of labor in an industry can lower entry barriers for later entrants. The growth of the market in one region can, through a division of labor, create technology specialists that stimulate growth in other regions.

Chapters 4 and 5, and a good part of chapter 10, concentrate on the factors affecting the costs of trading technology, focusing on the individual technology transaction and the associated costs. Chapter 4 highlights cognitive limitations to the "codification" of knowledge that raise the costs of transacting knowledge and technologies. The role of transaction costs is even more apparent in chapter 5, which focuses on the contractual limitations of technology trade, and the way contracts can be written to potentially reduce transaction costs in the market for technology. Similarly, transaction cost-reducing institutions are central to our discussion in chapter 10.

In developing what we hope is a comprehensive approach to understanding markets for technology, we have also developed a better appreciation for the tasks that remain incomplete. As we noted at the outset, formal trade in technology is not the only means of technology transfer. Technology can also be transferred when it is embodied in intermediate inputs, through the acquisition of companies, and through the movement of people. Our framework does not naturally extend to these different channels of technology exchange. More research needs to be done to understand the boundary between these modes of technology exchange and the factors that affect that boundary. These factors include the nature of the institutions involved; the relative strength of intellectual property rights, whether or not the development of technology is cumulative, and the importance of "integration" of the technology with other assets. This last factor may impinge on the the nature and the boundaries of the firm. Moreover, it is important to understand the significance of the arrangement of technology transfers for industry structure, patterns of entry and exit, and incentives of the parties involved.

Our framework is static. We have been pushed to make it so by taking on a relatively unexplored topic, which involves identifying and fleshing out some of the main issues. However, a theory of markets for technology, or more generally of the mechanisms for technology transfer, requires a better understanding of its dynamic issues and consequences. An important distinction that we have not always emphasized is the distinction between technological capability and technology itself, largely because in practice it is not an easy distinction to make. "Technological capability" denotes accumulated knowledge and expertise, much of it tacit. "Technology" can be thought of as the fruit of this accumulated capability. Technology is a flow rather than a stock, more discrete and divisible than the knowledge required to produce it, and more readily articulable than the competencies that gave rise to it. In this book we have focused on technology as a discrete flow, and it is in this sense that we looked at technology as a tradable object. We recognize that in a dynamic setting, acquiring external technology and developing it in-house can have very different implications for the growth of technical capability, and, by extension, for the ability to generate technology in the future.

There is currently a fairly advanced and extensive literature on the dynamic accumulation by firms of competencies.[1] However, we need a better understanding of the interplay between the acquisition of competencies and capabilities, and the acquisition of specific technologies. For instance, how does the former affect the production and the exchange of the latter? What are the implications of the two for policy and corporate strategy? Another area needing further exploration is the effect of uncertainty on these matters. In this book, we have sought to lay the groundwork for our own and others' exploration of these matters, rather than to provide the definitive work on the subject. Some other areas for future work remain that we wish to highlight. An important one is the development of new business models and the possible tension between strategic responses for the individual firm and public policy in this regard. We noted that larger firms might have comparative advantages in downstream innovation activities, while the smaller firms might have comparative advantages upstream. In chapter 9, we suggested that when markets for technology exist, it might be sensible for smaller firms not to integrate in manufacturing and commercialization. This may seem paradoxical, given that the highest rents in an industry are often downstream, while technology markets can be extremely competitive.

Society at large, not just the individual firm, has a stake in the answers to these questions. If the existence of markets for technology moves firms to specialize in the supply of technology, it is natural to question the time horizon for smaller or newly formed companies and startups. There is a large body of literature suggesting that larger firms are long-lived; indeed many leading companies worldwide were founded many decades ago.[2] Longevity is often implicitly seen as a "good thing," not only for the firm itself, but also for society at large. But if companies are set up to develop and sell a particular technology, the idea that they have to live forever (or at least for a long time) is less compelling. Clearly, the few technology developers that would be bold, fortunate, and skilled enough to become full-fledged manufacturing companies may eventually become sufficiently large to exist for a long time. A technology specialist might also continue to develop new technologies, justifying its long life. But it is at least as likely that a firm that was good at developing a single technology is not well suited for developing future technologies. Our approach raises afresh the old question as to what a firm is and what it does. It also underscores the old but often forgotten truth that the fortunes of the individual companies may not coincide with those of the industry or economy as a whole.

To put it in somewhat provocative terms, might it not be more useful to then think of a firm as rising for a specific purpose, such as the development of a particular technology, to then be dissolved and its assets allocated elsewhere, once that purpose is accomplished? This would make these companies more similar to "projects" (possibly built around some intellectual property rights). In many ways, this is the approach followed by industries or geographical areas where venture capitalists or financiers encourage the creation of wealth by underwriting exploratory ideas for new technologies and new businesses. While there is a substantial literature on this topic (e.g., on venture capital, corporate venturing, spin-offs), further research could assess how markets for technology affect the formation of such new businesses, and in particular whether they encourage the growth of firms created for the sole purpose of developing a specific technology.

The need for new and more precise data on technology trade is also clear. Markets for technology have increased in importance from a qualitative and a quantitative standpoint. In writing this book, we have had to rely on statistics that were fragmented and developed largely for other purposes. It is imperative for our purposes that statistics offices begin to collect more systematic data on the extent of technology licensing and other forms of technology exchange, especially about the "price" of the transaction.

Other directions for further research include deeper understanding of the nature of the technology contracts, possibly by developing better models of technology transactions. We also need a better understanding of the nature of the various institutions that support the market for technology. How must the patent system be modified and improved to better accomplish the objectives of providing incentives for new knowledge, and ensuring the effective utilization of this knowledge? Similarly, can one develop new ways to improve the trade-off between the stronger patent protection that markets for technology may require, and the need to protect the system of open science from the threats of the privatization of knowledge? Can we think of institutional innovations in these areas, and develop institutions that can better manage this trade-off?

Markets for technology have developed largely in the West, especially the United States. This raises the question of the extent to which developing countries can benefit from the growth of an international market for technology. There is substantial literature on international licensing in this context. However, markets for technology along with recent technological developments are giving a new twist to these arguments. For example, countries like India, Ireland, and Israel are becoming increasingly important players in the software industry. To what extent these countries will emerge as suppliers of technology is an open question. Recent reports of technology-based firms from these countries occupying important niches, for example, the Israeli firms that provide information security products, suggest that the issue is not entirely fanciful.

For Europe, the natural question is whether its market for technology will expand. Signs point in this direction. For instance, Europe is nurturing initiatives like the online technology bulletin board Cordis, which puts several potential technology buyers and suppliers in contact with one another (see e.g., table 3.10). Moreover, the E.U. is encouraging the development of small high-tech companies, and revising its policy on intellectual property rights to encourage these firms and creation of technologies more generally. Another question is whether the large European companies will create internal licensing divisions and programs to manage their intellectual properties as the U.S. corporations have done. On the normative side, of primary concern is the ability of the European system to reap the benefits of such markets. Today, many large European companies are seeking linkages (including acquisitions) with the U.S. technology-based companies. The implications of this trend are not clear. On one hand, this implies that the European companies are taking advantage of technology developed elsewhere. On the other hand, this trend does not fuel the growth of the domestic system of small high-tech companies and might hurt long-term European growth.

In closing, we want to emphasize that studying the workings and consequences of a market for technology is not to suggest that large corporations will replace in-house R&D by externally licensed technology. The rise of markets for technology during the past decade is not an inexorable trend but historically contingent. Thus, while markets for technology flourished in nineteenth-century America, by the 1930s, the dominant model for privately conducted R&D had become the large corporation with an R&D laboratory, and with only limited trade in technology. In the last two decades of the twentieth century, technology trades have grown markedly. The question is whether in the twenty-first century the two modes will coexist on a more balanced basis, or whether there will be a new phase, with R&D integrated almost exclusively in large corporations once again. The issue is further complicated by the growth of electronics markets and the digital economy, and by the growing international integration of national economies. These forces are transforming firms, the relationships between firms and their employees, and labor market institutions. Undoubtedly, the transformation of some of the basic institutions of the economic system will profoundly shape how markets for technology evolve. As we look ahead, we hope that a little understanding of the past will prove valuable in dealing with the important transformations that the future will bring.

Notes

Chapter 1. Markets for Technology: Why Do We Sell Them, Why We Don't See More of Them, and Why We Should Care

1. Several authors have addressed international technology transfer through the movement of people, although rarely in a systematic way. See, for instance, Bell and Pavitt 1993; Caves 1996; Blomström and Kokko 1998; and Fosfuri, Motta, and Roende 2001. Economic historians have also stressed the movement of people as a key mechanism for the international transfer of technology. See, for instance, Jeremy 1981 for the later industrialization of North America and Landes 1969 and Henderson 1965 for France and Germany.

2. Apart from the management literature mentioned above, horizontal technology licensing has been the main focus of the economic literature (e.g., Gallini 1984; Gallini and Winter 1985; Katz and Shapiro 1985; Shephard 1987; Gallini and Wright 1990). Typically, this literature deals with the strategic incentives of a technology monopolist to license the innovation to his competitors. See also the discussion thereof in chapter 7.

3. Available at *<http://www.european-patent-office.org/patinfopro/index.htm>*. Last viewed 21 December 2000.

Chapter 2. Preliminary Evidence

1. We are indebted to Max Hernandes for helping put this case study together.

2. There are some new technologies that are not based on metallocene catalysts, most notably a solution-phase technology, Sclairtech, developed and offered for license by Nova Chemicals. In addition, Eastman Chemicals has a catalyst system that it offers in conjunction with BP Chemical's gas phase process technology.

3. Recently, Montel, BASF, and Hoechst planned a merger that would unite the technologies offered by Shell, Montedison, BASF, and Hoechst in this field, considerably reducing competition in the market (Chemical Week 1999).

4. Phillips, which won a long patent battle with Montedison in polypropylene, recently prevailed in a patent suit filed by Exxon. As a result, Phillips could emerge as an important source of metallocene technology as well. Phillips has an active licensing program for both chemical and refining technology, and earned over $95 million in licensing revenues in 1999 (Available at *<http://www.phillips66.com/about/technology.html>*, viewed on 10 Jan. 2001.)

5. For example, Union Carbide's contract for the worldwide rights to the gas phase polyethylene process technology to Exxon was rumored to be worth approximately $275 million. Union Carbide is also the part owner of UOP, the leading technology licensor in refining technology.

6. Professor Ziegler was the developer of the Zieger-Natta catalysts, which were the industry standard for polyethylene. Zieger-Natta catalysts are also used in Unipol.

7. The acquisition is under regulatory review to assess whether Univation would become a monopoly supplier of metallocene technology. Interestingly enough, despite its monopoly status, there is no fear that Univation would not license its technology, attesting to the importance of the market for technology in chemicals.

8. See also chapter 9.

9. This is consistent with our discussion in later chapters (particularly chapters 7 and 9)—namely, that licensing tends to increase entry and reduce margins.

10. These are the so-called specialized engineering firms (SEFs), which we discuss in greater detail in chapter 3.

11. This particular database examined by Lamoreaux and Sokoloff can only distinguish whether the patent was assigned to other parties at the time at which it was issued. Of course, the patent rights can be transferred to other parties after or before the patent has been issued. But the Patent Office cannot record these transactions. Lamoreaux and Sokoloff also analyzed another sample that takes into account transfers of patent rights at times other than issue. We refer to their work for details on technology exchange taking place either before or after the patent is issued.

12. Gavin Wright has pointed out that, strictly speaking, this is evidence of a market for patents, rather than a market for technology. Further historical research is needed to establish whether know-how, designs, or prototypes were also transferred along with patent rights (private communication, July 1999).

13. Lamoreaux and Sokoloff do recognize that by the 1920s, when larger companies started internalizing R&D activities by hiring researchers on longer-term contracts, these markets for technology entered into a period of decline.

14. In this paper, Lamoreaux and Sokoloff also discuss cases of several large companies that in the early twentieth century undertook systematic internal evaluations of external technologies (e.g., new patents, information about technologies from technical journals or simply submitted to the companies by individual inventors). This is consistent with the increasing share of company assignments over time, and with the growth of a market for technology.

15. The inability to estimate the value of their patents was especially pronounced in the case of the Japanese companies, which also have a higher share of unutilized patents.

16. We should note that the issue is far from settled. Some recent survey evidence finds that patents are less important as a means of protecting rents from innovation compared to other means such as secrecy, complementary capabilities, and first mover advantage; and that over time their importance has decreased rather than increased (Cohen, Nelson, and Walsh 2000).

17. To the extent that U.S. firms also have equity stakes in overseas licensees they do not control, this figure will result in an underestimation of the market for technology.

18. This included all technology-intensive sectors: Chemicals (SIC 28); Industrial Machinery & Equipment (SIC35); Electronic & Other Electric Equipment (SIC36); Transport Equipment (SIC 37); Instruments & Related Products (SIC38); Electric, Gas, and Sanitary Services (SIC49); Wholesale Trade—Durable Goods (SIC 50); Business Services (SIC73); and Engineering, Management & Related Services (SIC 87).

19. Anand and Khanna (2000) also use the SDC dataset to examine technology deals. They too find that chemicals, electronics, and other high-tech sectors are those where licensing and other technology deals are most common.

20. Degnan (1998) reports that in the 1990s the U.S. royalty payments and licensing fees from foreign unaffiliated entities increased on average by 12 percent per annum, supporting our hypothesis.

21. In case of a two-way flow of technology, such as cross-licensing or R&D collaborations, we divided the value equally among the partners. Whenever SDC did not clearly code the granting or receiving company, we checked for the granting and receiving company (or mutual exchange) by reading through the detailed description of the deal.

22. The median value of $5 million was used for the "Rest" sector.

23. Recall that a low Herfindahl means high diversification, while a Herfindahl closer to 1 indicates low diversification.

Chapter 3. Markets for Technology and the Division of Innovative Labor in High-Tech Industries

1. We have relied upon specialized online sources and trade journals for many of the examples on software, biotechnology, and semiconductors. The full list of articles is reported in the references.

2. On the origins and history of chemical engineering as a discipline, the role of MIT, and its relationships with the oil companies, see Landau and Rosenberg 1992, and Rosenberg 1998.

3. This database (discussed in more detail in the appendix to chapter 8) provides information on about 20,000 plants worldwide in the chemical, petrochemical, and oil sectors. Along with the name of the chemical company owning the plant, the location of the plant, and the date of construction, Chemintell reports both the name of the company that engineered the plant and the name of the licensor of the technology. The name of the engineering company (including whether the plant is engineered in-house by the chemical manufacturer that owns the plant) is given for 55 percent of the plants; the name of the licensor is available for only 43 percent of the plants. The shares in tables 3.1 (and in tables 3.2 and 3.3) are computed over the total number of plants in which the information about the engineer or the source of technology was available.

4. Notice that these shares are computed with respect to all plants for which the information about the engineer was disclosed in Chemintell, including plants engineered in-house. If one is interested in the shares with respect to the market for engineering services, it suffices to divide these figures by 0.874. For instance, the share of U.S. SEFs would rise to 29.7 percent.

5. UOP and Scientific Design are two of the SEFs that have radical innovations to their credit (on Scientific Design, see Landau 1998). A number of other SEFs have contributed to advances in engineering design. For instance, Kellogg made significant contributions to

developing high-pressure processes for ammonia in the 1930s, while Badger is associated with fluidized bed catalytic processes (in collaboration with Sohio).

6. This arrangement enables the licensor to benefit from the superior ability of SEFs to manage technology transfer. It also provides a buffer between the chemical firm and its licensees, limiting accidental leakage of information. From the customer's point of view dealing with a single source for technology, construction, and engineering reduces transaction costs. The SEF can also provide better operational guarantee than if the contract were a pure technology licensing contract (Grindley and Nickerson 1996). In some cases, the SEF may also be able to "bundle" proprietary technology from different sources, reducing transaction costs and mitigating the "anti-commons" problem (see also chapter 10).

7. The evolution of the software industry has been discussed in detail by several studies and we refer the interested reader to those studies. For instance, Mowery (1996) contains essays on various aspects of the international software industry. Among the others, see also Cusumano 1991, Brady, Tiernay, and Williams 1992, and Torrisi 1998.

8. Indeed, tools for addressing problems on the "cutting edge" are more likely to be developed by leading users. Tools suppliers have incentives to wait until a larger set of users face the same problem.

9. For instance, in 1996, Teleres, a joint venture between Dow Jones & Co. and Aegon USA, entered into a strategic alliance with CyberSafe Inc., whereby Teleres licensed and marketed CyberSafe's Cyberbroker software. Teleres made CyberBroker available to the brokerage industry, enabling subscribers to customize the way they view, analyze, and present real estate data. Customers had the ability to combine Teleres data with their own proprietary data.

10. The growth of this business is stimulated partly by the easier access to electronic patent information from the official patent offices (United States, Europe, and elsewhere) and partly by the growing demand for this information. Apart from their use in research, information about patents can be increasingly valuable as many companies have to deal with the growing threat of patent infringement lawsuits and therefore have to be informed about other patents. Moreover, many companies have now realized the importance of effective management of their patent portfolios, in large part because of the increasing opportunities of licensing them (see also chapter 9). As a result, many service companies are currently offering access to patent information via the Web (i.e., Lexis-Nexis, MicroPatent, IBM itself), and some of these offer additional services in this area.

11. The case of foreign licenses is close to the one normally observed in many industries, whereby a producer in one country offers the technology to a foreign partner because it lacks the assets to operate independently in that market.

12. These problems were stressed by a senior executive at a leading developer of engineering design software tools in an interview with one of the authors. This executive, who is the R&D manager for his firm, claimed that he discouraged his engineers from doing patent searches, relying instead on the firm's own portfolio of patents to negotiate access to any relevant patents that may be uncovered later. Needless to say, this executive was skeptical of the benefits provided by software patents.

13. See, for instance, Pisano, Shan, and Teece 1988, Orsenigo 1989, Sharp 1991, Gambardella 1995, Galambos and Sturchio 1998, and Cockburn et al. 1999. See also the comprehensive annual reports on the biotech industry produced by Ernst & Young since 1987, available at <www.ey.com>

14. See also Orsenigo et al. 2001.

15. The objective of the Human Genome Project was to sequence all strands of human DNA (about 3 billion base pairs) to identify the structure of the about 100,000 human genes. Apart from genetics and related research, the Human Genome Project has stimulated the development of new instrumentation technologies that were required to undertake this massive effort.

16. On the origins and developments of the technology, see Braun and MacDonald 1978, and Malerba 1985. Among the more recent studies of the industry are Langlois and Steinmueller 1998 and Macher, Mowery, and Hodges 1999.

17. Linden and Somaya (2000) stress the rise of superchips as a major factor behind the increasing vertical specialization of the semiconductor industry. They argue, as we do, that the soaring complexity of superchips underlines the need for more efficient design reuse, and encourages an extensive specialization in design activities. They also examine the strategic trade-offs between licensing and integration of semiconductor design, and the determinants of vertically integrated versus specialized industry structure.

18. Clearly, integrating modules into a larger system has not always been easy or without costs. Moreover, modular designs using standard components cannot always deliver the performance that custom built designs can. Chapter 6 develops an analytical framework for analyzing this trade-off between performance and cost.

19. Another example, which we analyze in chapter 9, is that of Cambridge Display Technology (CDT), a company operating in the chemical-semiconductor business.

Chapter 4. Context Dependence, Sticky Information, and the Limits of the Market for Technology

1. The concept is similar to the better-known concept of bounded rationality. The latter, however, is closely associated with imperfections in decision making and the inability to specify contractual terms. In our analysis, we wish to highlight the imperfections in how human beings perceive, organize and use knowledge of the world.

2. Nelson and Winter (1982) spurred a great deal of the literature focusing on the firm as a set of competencies and knowledge bases, and on technical change as a "localized," "path-dependent," and experimental process. Among many others, see Dosi 1988, Pavitt, Robson and Townsend 1987, Patel and Pavitt 1997, 1998, Cantwell 1994, 2000, Teece and Pisano 1994, Teece, Pisano, and Shuen 1997, Chandler, Hagström, and Sölvell 1998.

3. Nonaka uses the term "explicit" instead of "codified." For present purposes, any differences are unimportant.

4. Since this realization, Western auto producers have reorganized their internal design and development processes. All the leading firms now practice "concurrent engineering," whereby the design of cars and their components, the manufacturing process, and the acquisition of information from the customers, are carried out in parallel, with intense communications among the engineers and specialists in these fields (e.g., Clark and Fujimoto 1991, 215–228).

5. This is closely related to the appropriability problem described earlier, and even more closely to the analytical theory of the boundaries of the firm contained in Grossman and Hart 1986, Hart and Moore 1990, and Hart 1995.

6. In a similar vein, Arrow (1975) developed a model showing that one of the determinants of vertical integration is asymmetric information about the quality of the supply. On the

role of asymmetric information and incentives in encouraging the integration of R&D within the firm, see Aghion and Tirole 1994. Also see Zeckhauser 1996 on the difficulties of contracting for technological information.

7. The importance of physical and organizational proximity in innovation is epitomized by the following example. In the early 1990s, BMW created its Munich automobile research engineering center, housing about 6,000 engineers. The center is composed of futuristic towers and buildings linked through multiple walkways, which were designed explicitly to minimize the distance among the various departments and facilitate cross-functional relationships (Financial Times 1992).

8. The empirical distinction seems to boil down to a single product created using standard components, as compared to a family of products that share a substantial fraction of standard components.

9. The implications for industry structure are also the main focus of the papers by Langlois 1992 and Langlois and Robertson 1992. Based on case studies of stereo systems and PCs, they show that not only are the opportunities for "collective" innovation an important consequence of design modularity, but also that the resulting industry structure, marked by a division of labor, is socially superior to that based on proprietary systems. For instance, the larger number of firms that can enter and innovate in the various domains allows the economy to support a larger number of trial and error and learning processes than if only one firm pursued these innovations. In other words, economies can be achieved because of the greater opportunities for exploration in such industry structures (see also Levinthal and March 1993).

10. As discussed in chapter 3, an important development in the semiconductor industry in recent years has been the evolution of "systems on a chip" that incorporate a number of functions previously performed by several chips linked with one another in special ways. Unfortunately, these superchips are so complex to design that it has become impossible to design them entirely from scratch. As a result, the manufacturers are developing predesigned modules that are defined in terms of their functions and can be integrated as "packaged" components in a superchip (Linden and Somaya 1999).

11. Chapter 6 develops a formal model showing how the potential breadth of application is a powerful force in inducing firms to unstick their information and to create more general-purpose goods and technologies.

12. Vincenti (1990) argues in a similar fashion when he suggests that an important trend in engineering development is the tendency toward the creation of what he calls "vicarious trials" (Vincenti 1990, 247–248). These are simulated experiments or analytical tests that can substitute "direct trials." Vincenti also notes that vicarious trials include better theoretical understanding of problems that can greatly help the prediction of experimental results.

13. A related feature of these tools is that they are most typically general-purpose technologies, dealing with problems that are common to many firms and researchers. The "gene chips" discussed in the previous chapter are quintessential examples of the general-purpose nature of these devices. Affymetrix's Gene Chip, for example, was customized to assess genetic mutations of the HIV, but the same product architecture can be used to assess several other diseases like cystic fibrosis, diabetes, and coronary artery disease, as well as it can be exploited in other areas like for instance molecular oncology.

Chapter 5. Intellectual Property Rights and the Licensing of Know-How

1. This chapter draws upon Arora 1995 and Arora 1996.

2. Brander and Spencer's (1983) famous article on strategic trade theory is built on the insight that negative output royalties (output subsidies in their context) can induce firms to become more aggressive in the product market and steal their rivals market share.

3. Spitz (1988, 329) provides a very interesting example of the importance of know-how even to technologically competent firms. In the 1950s Spitz headed a team of chemical engineers from Scientific Design, a pioneering chemical process design company. The team was supposed to design and build a plant with the capacity to process 20 million pounds of phthalic anhydride per year. The patents were held by a German company. Even though the team had access to the patents, and a great deal of technical information about the German process had been made public by the Allied forces after World War II, Spitz reports that the team faced a number of problems with the plant, such as leaks from pipes, accumulation of gasses, fires, and explosions. Eventually, a consultant who had worked in a phthalic anhydride plant had to be called in to set matters right. Hounshell and Smith (1988) provide evidence that Scientific Design was not alone in its inability to utilize German technology without the benefit of know-how.

4. The existence of tacit components in the knowledge that is transferred is typically assumed away by the economic literature on licensing. See Bhattacharya, Glazer and Sapington 1990, or Gallini and Wright 1990, Gallini and Winter 1985, and Katz and Shapiro 1986. A notable exception is Macho and Castrillio (1991), who show that output-based royalties can solve the moral hazard problem due to the tacit component of knowledge (provided that output is verifiable), but only at the cost of making the licensee less efficient.

5. Know-how could be observed by the two parties but not by courts. An analogy with the master craftsman–apprentice situation may be useful in understanding this point. An apprentice will be able to observe and appreciate the tacit knowledge that is being imparted to him by the master craftsman. A third party will be unable to verify this unless the latter observed the interaction between the master and the apprentice over a sustained period. Such observation may be prohibitively costly. Formally, what is required is that while third-party enforceable contracts on know-how are not possible, licensees can observe either the amount, or the value of the know-how being transferred to them. Further, the cost of transferring know-how should be common knowledge to both the licensee and the licensor.

6. The economic literature on licensing, see, for instance, Gallini and Winter 1985, Katz and Shapiro 1985, and Rockett 1990 also examines the issues raised by licensing to rivals. In contrast, here we assume that the licensor and the licensee do not compete in the product market.

7. The latter is the analogue of "disclosure" payments, which are made when the licensing contract is signed but before any of the technology is transferred.

8. Complementarities may arise if inputs purchased from sources other than the licensor may have different technical specifications, or be built to different standards or tolerances.

9. Arrow (1962b) notes that imitation without infringement is costly. Merges and Nelson (1990) cite the example of the Selden patents (automobiles) and the Wright patents (aircraft). In both cases, the patents were broad and the authors claim that this raised the costs

for other producers. Levin et al. (1987) provide evidence that suggests that patent protection raises imitation costs as well as royalty income from licensing.

10. This provision is often found in licensing contracts. An alternative interpretation is that since courts will not be able to determine which party was guilty of a breach of the contract, in practice, if either party were to renege on the contract, there is not much the other party can hope to achieve by way of legal redress. In an earlier version of the model, we allowed for liquidation damages to be paid if the contract were terminated, and we obtained the same results.

11. This inequality is typically known as the incentive compatibility constraint (for the licensee).

12. This is the licensor's incentive compatibility constraint.

13. "Many industrialists whom we consulted said quite categorically that the main purpose of licensing is to exchange know-how, with patents a minor consideration added in the small print at the end of the agreement to lend an extra element of precision and security to the contract" (Taylor and Silberston 1973, 114).

14. Typical explanations have pointed to the problem of establishing the value of information without complete disclosure. This model focuses on a related case, where the issue is not the value of information (which is assumed to be known to both parties) but the problem of opportunistic behavior by both the seller and the buyer.

15. Steinmueller (1989) makes the same point. Klemperer (1990) investigates the role of patents in balancing the inducement to innovate with the social cost of monopoly. Scotchmer and Green (1990) examine the closely related issue of novelty requirement and find that a weak novelty requirement would, in general, be preferred. Similarly, Merges and Nelson (1990) argue from an evolutionary perspective that narrower patents are preferred where technological progress is cumulative. Gallini (1992) finds that broad and short-lived patents are superior. Licensing possibilities are not considered in any of these studies.

16. We treat our 144 observations as independent even though a few licenses in the sample feature in more than one agreement.

17. In Kim's (1988) sample of Korean licensing agreements, labor training is included in 64 percent of the cases, while quality control services are included in 56 percent of the cases.

18. This is one of the reasons why integrated transfers (i.e., direct foreign investment) are thought to be superior to arm's-length licensing.

19. This is a complex classification of firms adopted for regulatory purposes. See the appendix for more details.

20. Cooper (1988) has shown that 1968 was a watershed year in terms of changes in official policy. There was a considerable tightening of the restrictions concerning the duration of agreements, royalty payments, and other provisions of technology import contracts. The beginning year of the licensing agreement, YEAR, is used to control for this effect in the regression analyses. We also experimented with a year dummy for 1968, with very little change in the results.

21. See, for instance, Lall 1983, Kumar 1987, Deolalikar and Evenson 1989, Katrak 1985, 1989, and Raut 1989.

22. This is equivalent to the statement that the probability of the technical service being provided, conditional on the complementary input being provided, is higher than the unconditional probability.

23. We also analyzed all combinations obtained by pooling any two technical services and two inputs. The results are not reported here, but in each case, independence was rejected at the 1 percent level.

24. The contingency tables themselves are too numerous to report here. They are available on request.

25. Kim (1988) reports that prior organizational ties are negatively related to the provision of technical services, but the relationship with size is ambiguous.

26. This could also be because contracts involving plant commissioning have features of turnkey contracts, and thereby imply lower costs to the licensor of supplying these services.

Chapter 6. Markets for Technology and the Size of the Market: Adam Smith and the Divisions of Labor Revisited

1. This chapter draws upon Bresnahan and Gambardella 1998.

2. Bresnahan and Gambardella (1998) also argue that this clarifies an important point about Adam Smith's theorem. The literature has sometimes argued that a larger size of the market gives rise to vertical integration rather than specialization and division of labor. (See, for instance Perry 1989 and the discussion thereof in Bresnahan and Gambardella 1998.) But as this chapter reveals, the confusion arises from a "wrong" definition of the size of the market. To the extent that the latter is meant to be in terms of number of applications, rather than "volume" of each individual application, Smith and Stigler's theorem does lead to the right prediction.

3. Indeed, the logic extends through to a case of a large firm with multiple products or divisions that is trying to decide between a centralized R&D lab as opposed to product- or division-level labs.

4. Despite the fact that his famous example of the "pin factory" concerned the division of labor across workers within the firm, Smith clearly envisaged a much broader division across industries or activities based on deep and generalized knowledge bases. He first argued that "improvements in machinery" are sometimes made by "philosophers or men of speculation" "who . . . are often capable of combining together the powers of the most distant and dissimilar objects." Then he noted that "in the progress of society, philosophy or speculation becomes, like every other employment, the principal or sole trade and occupation of a particular class of citizens . . . it is subdivided into a great number of branches. . . , and this subdivision of employment in philosophy, as well as in every other business, improves dexterity, and saves time" (Smith 1776, 21).

5. We will treat "general specialty" and "general-purpose technology" as nearly identical in meaning. To the extent that there is a distinction, a GPT is body of knowledge, or the people who know it are a general specialty.

6. Helpman and Trajtenberg (1998) also discuss some macroeconomic implications of the rise of GPTs. See also Helpman 1998.

7. In general, we shall refer interchangeably to the downstream "industries" or "firms." This is because, given our objectives in this chapter, no difference would arise if one thinks of the GPT as being a technology that can be used by different industries or by different firms in the same sector as long as the sectors or firms are independent from one another, in the sense that they do not compete. If they are allowed to compete, the basic results are unchanged provided that the extent of the competition among the downstream firms or industries is not too strong.

8. For simplicity, we assume that K is independent of the volume of output produced, Q. Bresnahan and Gambardella (1998) show that the same results apply under a weaker assumption, notably that K increases with Q at a decreasing rate, and that the degree of economies of scale is smaller as Q increases. The latter assumption is crucial.

9. One interpretation of having the adjustment cost be proportional to the output of the application sector is that since the upstream technology is not customized to the application, the output of the application sector is deemed less valuable by consumers, with d measuring this loss of value. Thus, although the expression is suggestive of the upstream input being a material input, this need not be so, and the input could be an intangible technology as well.

10. We are indebted to Suma Athreye for helpful discussions on this issue. See also Athreye 1998 for further discussion on the role of market size and related issues in the context of markets for technology.

11. See Bresnahan and Gordon 1997 for a discussion.

12. Braun and MacDonald (1978) suggest that the distinction between the microprocessor and the earlier integrated circuits is between a computer and a calculator. The latter can perform only the functions that are "permanently" defined on its chip, and that can be activated by pressing special keys (e.g., numbers or arithmetic operations). The computer instead can read instructions defined in many possible ways (logic, arithmetic, etc.) and can, therefore, perform more elaborate and distinct operations. They also note some intermediate forms, like the erasable programmable read-only memory.

13. That is, they can have software wiring at design time, if not at use time. ASICs are more suitable for use in a wide variety of special-purpose devices than in, say, computers.

14. As in section 6.2.2, Q represents the depth of the market. We are implicitly assuming that the size of each application sector coincides with the total output produced by the sector, which is exogenously given. In Bresnahan and Gambardella 1998, this assumption is removed and all results hold true provided that larger users are also to produce a larger volume of output.

15. Note that these reductions in d can involve improvements in technology. For instance, an electronic design automation sector can produce libraries and testing software that can easily be configured to be compatible with the processes in use in different foundries, or testing software that will work across a variety of applications. A reduction in d, in other words, indicates a more abstract, portable, and reconfigurable technology, as described in the examples in section 6.3.

16. This is also one of the main results in Bresnahan and Trajtenberg 1995.

17. See, for instance, Hofman and Rockart 1994. See also von Hippel 1994, 1998.

18. On the role of generic versus product-specific competencies of the firms and the implications of division of labor, see also Arora and Gambardella 1997.

19. One such force is rooted in the historical origin of pharmaceutical companies, many of which started out in the nineteenth century as pharmacies that progressively integrated back into manufacturing and, then in the twentieth century, integrated back into research.

20. This is clearly a sort of "prisoner dilemma" situation.

Chapter 7. Licensing the Market for Technology

1. The sample includes all North American, European, and Japanese chemical firms with total turnover larger than $1 billion in 1988.

2. In chapter 9 we provide further examples of large firms that have traditionally neither licensed their technology nor acquired technologies from the outside, and that have recently embraced technology licensing as an integral part of their technology management strategy.

3. Network externalities often make standards very valuable. Network externalities exist where the value of a product or service to a user depends on the number of others who are using that product or service (e.g., the telephone). The more a protocol gains acceptance, the greater the user benefits, and the better chance the standard has of becoming dominant. For a fuller discussion of positive feedback, network effects, and network externalities, see Shapiro and Varian 1998, Katz and Shapiro 1994, Arthur 1994.

4. The importance of strategic effects in vertically linked markets is not new and has been discussed in many other multistage models of oligopoly (see Tirole 1988). Within this strand, our analysis relates closely to the literature on delegation. As Vickers (1985), Bonanno and Vickers (1988), and Hadfield (1991) among others have argued, delegation allows a firm to credibly commit itself to alter a behavior and thereby elicit favorable reactions from rivals (see, e.g., Besanko and Perry 1993; Fershtman and Judd 1987; Schwartz and Thompson 1986; Baye, Crocker, and Ju 1996). We apply the insights from this literature to explain why and how much licensing takes place. Indeed, in our model, licensing is a credible commitment to expand production by transferring the output decision to the licensees.

5. In interviews undertaken by one of the authors with R&D and technology managers in firms such as BP, Exxon, and Phillips, it emerged that the consideration of the revenue and rent dissipation effects plays a crucial role in actual technology licensing strategies. Moreover, one of the most often heard phrases was "we license because otherwise other potential licensors would step in and we would lose licensing revenues without being able to restrict entry."

6. More generally, {licensing, licensing} is an equilibrium of this game when $(1 + \sigma) \pi (3) - F > \pi (2)$ and $(1 + \sigma) \pi (4) - F > \pi (3)$.

7. Although we develop our main arguments in a duopoly framework, the intuition and the results we derive hold for any number of incumbents in the market for technology. Moreover, in Arora and Fosfuri 1999, we generalize this model by allowing firms to make their entry decision in the market for technology. In other words, we treat the number of incumbents as an endogenous parameter. Again, under fairly general conditions, all results hold qualitatively unchanged.

8. This assumption could be removed at the cost of messier algebra. Either positive start-up costs or positive opportunity cost would simply put an upper bound on the number of licenses per patent holder. Our analysis would hold unchanged except for this additional constraint. If the constraint binds, it determines the number of licenses at equilibrium and

the comparative statics would be driven by what happens to the (gross) profits of each licensee in the second stage of the game.

9. Output based royalties are typically a response to asymmetric information or moral hazard, or to induce licensees to reduce output (See, e.g., Katz and Shapiro 1986, Gallini and Wright 1990, Wang 1998). We ignore information problems here. Restricting licensee output is suboptimal for the licensor, because the same outcome can be achieved more efficiently by reducing the number of licensees and saving on transaction costs. Therefore, a lump sum payment contract is the optimal contract in our model (see also Fosfuri 1999). We express this fixed sum as a fraction, σ, of the profits. Even when royalties are calculated as based on output, they are frequently capitalized and paid as a lump sum.

10. In terms of our earlier example, this might imply, for instance, that if Courtaulds and Lenzing are the only two incumbents in the market for Lyocell, their profits are $60 million each if they produce identical products, whereas profits rise to $75 million each if the two types of Lyocell are imperfect substitutes.

11. The subscript k denotes the derivative with respect to k_i.

12. We assume that both the second order condition and the stability condition are satisfied at any interior solution, which therefore defines a Nash equilibrium.

13. A third effect is due to the additional transaction costs for each new licensing contract.

14. One can show that this is always the case with linear demand and quantity competition. Similar result holds under Bertrand competition with multinomial logit demand. See Arora and Fosfuri 1999.

15. Notice that F can also be thought of as relative to the size of the market. Therefore, an increase (decrease) in F can be reinterpreted as a decrease (increase) in market size.

16. Our measure of product differentiation was computed as follows. Chemintell classifies the chemical plants within each subsector in more disaggregated process technology classes. We use the counts at this disaggregated level to compute an equidistribution index at the subsector level. Our index of product differentiation takes the value of 0 if the products are homogenous and the value of 100 if they are totally differentiated. We have also tried alternative measures of product differentiation, such as the entropy index and the Herfindahl index, with substantially similar results.

17. The correlation between our index of product differentiation and the average number of licenses per patent holder, computed across all twenty-three subsectors, is -0.53.

18. This also clearly emerged from interviews that we have had with directors of licensing units of big corporations. For instance, Martin Howard has stressed that the business rationale for licensing depends on whether there are many producers in the market, and on the licensor's market share. For instance, in acetic acid where BP Chemicals has a large market share (around 25%) it has licensed very selectively (typically only licensing to get access to markets it would otherwise be unable to enter). By contrast, in polyethylene, where BP Chemicals has less than 2 percent of the market share, it has licensed very aggressively, competing with Union Carbide, who was the market leader in licensing polyethylene technology.

19. The correlation between the SEFs' market share and the average number of licenses by chemical companies computed across our twenty-three chemical subsectors, is equal to 0.42, with a t-statistics of 2.17.

20. Interesting enough, an increase in the size of market, which would work as a decrease in F, might also hurt the licensors.

Chapter 8. Global Technology Suppliers and the International Division of Innovative Labor

1. Our analysis in this chapter does not examine the effects of spillovers on total factor productivity, as the literature on spillovers typically does, but on the flow of investments, because we do not have measures of the total factor productivity at our disaggregate level.

2. Formally, if First World SEFs rationally anticipated the rise of the LDC market, and could practice dynamically optimal pricing, these pecuniary externalities would disappear. Such pricing strategies would require not merely extraordinary foresight but also extensive coordination between SEFs.

3. The interested reader might find it useful to look at Arora, Fosfuri, and Gambardella (1996, 2001) where we provide two slightly different models that formalize the discussion of this section.

4. This latter condition is a standard result in basically all models of oligopoly competition. See, for instance, Tirole 1988.

5. Strictly speaking, this is true only if the size of the LDC market is small enough so as not to induce any further entry of SEFs. Also, our argument here assumes that First World SEFs are not fully forward-looking. Otherwise they would anticipate that a given LDC market would arise in the future and they would adjust their optimal investment (entry) decision. As noted earlier, neither assumption is necessary for LDCs to benefit from First World SEFs.

6. Actual investment costs are reported for about 40 percent of the plants in our data base (see the appendix) and these were used to calculate the average cost per plant in a given process.

7. We assume that the *BUY* and *MAKE* plants and the *DOM* and *MNE* plants have the same average cost because we lack enough observations with cost figures to separately estimate the average cost for them. However, for the few processes in which we had enough observations to compute separate average costs, they were not statistically different across *MAKE* and *BUY* and across *DOM* and *MNE*.

8. Three of our 139 chemical processes were very broad categories, with very large values for $PROCPAT_i$. For these three processes we used a dummy, $DPROCPAT_i$.

9. Since our dependent variables can take zero values, we redefined $SIZE_{ij}$ as $1 + SIZE_{ij}$, and to keep with the adding up restriction we redefined BUY_{ij} and $MAKE_{ij}$ as $0.5 + BUY_{ij}$ and $0.5 + MAKE_{ij}$. This is just to make the results of the three equations comparable. Using $1 + BUY_{ij}$ and $1 + MAKE_{ij}$ did not produce any significant difference.

10. Two of the processes had $SEF\_FW_i = 0$. For these we set $SEF\_FW_i = 1$, and used log (SEF_FW_i).

11. For instance, our database shows that three different sets of SEFs supply the markets for three different types of polyethylene—high-density, low-density, and linear low-density polyethylene—with very little overlap.

12. We also estimated a lower bound for the elasticity based on the assumption that the unmeasured demand variation had a constant elasticity for different types of investors

(LDC firms versus multinationals). Our estimates, available on request, indicate a lower bound to the elasticity of 0.38 of $SIZE_{ij}$ with respect to SEF_FW_i which is very close to the OLS estimate reported in table 8.3.

13. Even countries like South Korea that have protected downstream markets have been open to imports of technology and engineering services. Aggregate measures of openness, such as the ratio of exports and imports to GDP, or even the more nuanced measure we use here, $OPEN_{jt}$, cannot capture this subtlety. Further, the rise of Western European and Japanese SEFs has made the market for chemical processes a truly global market. Even a country like Libya, which is not directly supplied by American SEFs, is served by a large number of European and Japanese SEFs.

14. We have also run a GMM estimation using process-specific instruments for SEF_FW_i and obtained a very similar estimate for the impact of first world SEFs. See Arora, Fosfuri, and Gambardella 2001 for further details.

Chapter 9. Implications for Corporate Strategy

1. We have chosen to focus primarily on the broad implications for corporate strategy and, consequently, do not address issues such as strategic reasons for licensing, including licensing to create standards, to deter entry, etc. There are also aspects of markets for technology that we do not address here (e.g., the funding of smaller high-tech firms by larger corporations, or corporate spin-offs).

2. Granstrand (1999) also analyzes firms' strategies both as technology users and technology suppliers. Malerba and Orsenigo (2000) discuss strategic options when technology is tradable but argue that the conditions for making technology tradable are unlikely to be realized. See also Pavitt 2000.

3. Clearly, assets that differentiate a firm from its competitors differ from standard commodities, as do the markets for such assets. This is particularly true for intangible assets like technology. The value of such assets is driven primarily by use value rather than cost of production and therefore varies with the prospective buyer. Furthermore, intangible assets by their nature are difficult to define and delineate. This implies that the assets may be "lumpy"—their transfer might be an all-or-nothing deal. When such assets are rented, their use is likely to be more difficult to monitor and meter (Teece 1998). Thus, instead of speaking of the absence of markets for assets, it is perhaps more accurate and realistic to speak about the efficiency of such markets and the costs of transacting in the market. The terminology of missing markets should therefore be understood as an expositional device.

4. This is purposely a polar characterization that assumes that either there are markets or there are not. We acknowledge that this statement ignores a variety of "hybrid" organizational arrangements that might be potentially used in the absence of markets. For instance, Pisano (1990) shows that the use of equity as a hostage in biotechnology research contracts can be a hybrid form to exploit research.

5. The literature clearly distinguishes between generic and specialized complementary assets (Teece 1986). When the complementary assets are specialized there is an additional pressure to integration. When the complementary assets are generic, it is more likely that a market for such assets will work well, providing even access to all firms to the assets. By definition, specialized or cospecialized assets face an illiquid and imperfect market. It is only when the market for complementary assets is perfectly competitive that differences across firms in the access to the complementary assets are completely leveled out.

6. The identity of the firm cannot be revealed for reasons of confidentiality.

7. The examples below have been assembled largely from information from specialized online trade magazines and the web pages of the named companies. Additional evidence on licensing practices by large corporations is presented in chapter 7.

8. The ETAN report also argues that patents are also a valuable source of information. Indeed, although not yet routinely exploited (except in chemicals and pharmaceuticals), patent databases are one of the most comprehensive and accessible sources of scientific and technological information. Advances in new information and communication technologies make it possible to use this rich source of data for designing technology strategies.

9. However, many start-ups adopt a business model whereby they begin by licensing technology and doing contract research for others, then use those earnings to acquire the required complementary assets.

10. Rambus licenses its technology to firms that produce microprocessors, DRAMs, ASICs, or PC controllers and chipsets. Rambus itself does not produce any semiconductor devices. It lacks any special advantage in the manufacture of semiconductor devices, a process that requires large investments in fabrication facilities in addition to a great deal of tacit knowledge. By not producing any semiconductor device, Rambus also steers clear of any potential conflicts of interest and avoids competing with its customers.

11. For instance, Amazon.com, the online bookseller, is now investing large sums in building warehouses and distribution centers. An alternative strategy could have been to ally with a firm with a large distribution network, such as Wal-Mart.

12. The reader might wonder whether Syntex could have tried to "rent" its fixed complementary assets to stave off the crisis. Although marketing agreements, which in effect amount to one partner "renting" its marketing asset to the other partner, are known to take place in the pharmaceutical industry, we can only surmise that Syntex's marketing and production capabilities were not sufficiently attractive to potential renters. Indeed, financial stability, threatened by the failure to replace Naprosyn, would appear to be a sine qua non in a marketing or production partner.

13. Some large organizations, notably Bell Labs in AT&T and the Watson Labs in IBM, have managed to create environments conducive to exploration. This is not enough, however. Many wonderful discoveries at Xerox PARC were ignored, and their exploitation delayed, because of precisely the sorts of problems that Levinthal and March (1993) discuss.

14. By comparison, Kline and Rosernberg (1986) explain in their chain-link model of innovation that these assets may also provide valuable feedback to research about customer preferences and manufacturing trade-offs, thereby making the research process economically more valuable. The chain-link model seems to be a very good one for understanding the great success enjoyed by Japanese firms such as Toyota and Sony. Nonetheless, there is a definite opportunity cost to such a tight coupling between the various parts of the innovation chain, in the form of greater emphasis on exploitation at the cost of exploration.

15. To provide some anecdotal evidence, in 1998 one of us (Alfonso Gambardella) participated in a commission for the evaluation of R&D projects submitted for government support funding in Italy. Most of the projects were submitted by large Italian companies, or by consortia of firms and other institutions. Even though the government program did require a state-of-the-art report for the proposed technology to be enclosed with the application, most projects charged costs for internal R&D activities that involved several early steps before the development of the ultimate technology. Few projects mentioned costs for

acquiring externally developed technologies (e.g., licensing costs) upon which their innovation could build. A casual search from existing patent databases revealed that in a number of cases the applicants could have exploited existing technologies to build their innovation, or at least they could have found specialists who could potentially offer valuable technical consultancy services in the specific domain of their project.

16. This reinforces our earlier point that when markets for technology exist, the penalties for not monitoring the opportunities that are created by them, for not using these markets, or, worst of all, from harboring the "not-invented-here" syndrome, can be substantial.

17. Partly as a consequence, the share of industrialized countries engaged in world chemical production has fallen dramatically from 85.7 percent in 1954 to 62.1 percent in 1994. This is not simply a reflection of economic growth elsewhere. The share of industrialized countries in world exports of chemicals has fallen from over 97 percent in 1955 to less than 67 percent in 1993 (Eichengreen 1998).

18. Merges (1998) provides a number of examples of other types of firms that might be thought of as the "SEFs" of the pharmaceutical and fine chemicals industry. Firms such as Catalytica, ChemDesign, and SepraChem are leveraging research and their expertise in asymmetric synthesis to develop new processes for the production of pharmaceuticals and key pharmaceutical intermediates. These firms both develop proprietary technologies, and either license them to pharmaceutical and specialty chemical companies, or enter into alliances to supply the latter with purer and better inputs. Interesting enough, Merges (1998) also notes that this trend has caused some established producers to spin off units, providing contracted process development and manufacturing services to the pharmaceutical industry.

19. Thus, for instance, ICI, which first commercialized polyethylene and polyester, has virtually exited from these markets (Arora and Gambardella 1998).

20. For example, since the 1950s, chemical companies have tried to differentiate their products by developing a range of different grades of their materials targeted to different markets or users. Similarly, control of the production of basic feedstock, through direct investments in oil producing countries, has been for many years a relatively more important source of competitive advantage than technology for the leading oil and petrochemical manufacturers.

21. Porter (1998) argues that, apart from the customers, companies should make substantial investments in developing tight linkages with the wider set of actors, including suppliers and providers of infrastructure services in the individual regions in which they operate commercially.

Chapter 10. The Institutional Context: Problems and Policy

1. See, for example, Rosenberg and Birdzell 1986; North 1990; Alston, Eggertsson, and North 1996; Aoki, Murdock, and Okino-Fujiwara 1997.

2. See also our discussion of these points in chapter 4.

3. Of course, the CMOS standard was not the only factor encouraging specialization and licensing and cross-licensing agreements. Other factors included the development of software tools for implementing "compiled silicon" VLSI designs, which underscored the advantages of common process models and a common language for device description developed by university and industry research. In addition, it became desirable to incorporate "standard" components such as known microprocessor architectures, protected as

intellectual property rights. Finally, creating more generic products has always motivated the industry, while the need for device specialization continues to drive variety in design (Ed Steinmuller, personal communication, Jan. 5, 2001).

4. There is a growing body of literature attempting to measure the performance of such technology programs and initiatives. The available evidence is mixed. See Lerner 1999 and Wallsten 2000.

5. In this respect, another area for further study is the effective prohibition on lawyers undertaking patent infringement cases on a "contingency" basis.

6. Intellectual property rights consist of largely patent rights, copyrights, design rights, trademark rights, trade secret rights. Our focus in this section is on patents.

7. In some cases, policies designed in the naïve hope of encouraging small inventors have encouraged the abuse of the patent system. In the United States, for instance, there have been well-known cases where patents filed in the 1950s were ultimately issued more than twenty years later. In the meantime, the patentee could legally amend the application so that it covered inventions made well after the filing date. Since patents in the United States are published only upon issue, such patents (sometimes referred to as "submarine" patents because they are not visible for long periods after they are filed) have surprised many established firms. The move toward patent harmonization, which will require publication of all patent applications after a certain period, will be helpful in this respect.

8. The point is not that information can be reproduced at low cost or that information is nonrival in the sense that one person's possession of certain information does not preclude another from possessing the same information. A familiar counterexample is as follows. If only one person knows what is going to happen to the price of a stock, he or she is likely to benefit greatly. But if all (or sufficiently many people) were to have the same information, none would benefit. Thus information can be rival in use, although it is physically nonrival.

9. As David (1993) has noted, knowledge is different from the prototypical public goods such as lighthouses and airport beacons. One important point of differentiation is that the acquisition of knowledge is cumulative and interactive: Knowledge itself is an important input into the production of knowledge.

10. Other factors such as company or governmentally imposed standards for output may also raise the cost of inventing around.

11. A related consequence is that nonmanufacturing firms holding patents on key components are likely to bargain more aggressively for licensing fees. The strategies of firms that have significant market shares in the downstream markets (in which the technology is applicable) are more complex. However, they are likely to cooperate, particularly if there is a stable group of such firms. Interesting enough, the ownership of mutually blocking patents can actually support licensing in this context, since each party will have the ability to block commercial development by the other.

12. Consider two patent holders fixing separately their royalty rates for selling their patents to a unique licensee compared with the case in which the two patents are pooled and a single royalty is set up. This distortion is similar to the one generated by the double marginalization in a chain of monopolies.

13. Pass-through provisions allow the technology holder to receive royalties on future innovations produced by using the licensed technology. These provisions are a matter of considerable debate in the biotechnology industry.

14. In a recent paper, Merges (1999a) shows that the U.S. Patent Office budgets about $3000 for each patent application. Further research is needed to assess whether this is the optimal amount to spend. Any such assessment should take into account the impact of intellectual property rights on the functioning and development of markets for technology. Merges also notes that U.S. patent examiners face perverse incentives. In effect, they are rewarded whether they reject or issue a patent. Since rejections involve greater time and effort for the examiner (such as justifying the rejection and dealing with ensuing appeals), absent adequate incentives to ensure that "bad" patents are not issued, at the margin, examiners are better off issuing rather than rejecting an application. Merges notes that a more serious problem may be inadequate training for junior examiners, and the inability of the U.S. Patent Office to retain senior patent examiners due to inadequate pay.

15. This argument also suggests that litigation activity should shrink substantially if courts would adopt a more coherent and standardized interpretation of the intellectual property legislation, which would contribute to dissolving some of the legal uncertainty about the result of the trial.

16. Lerner (1995) finds that poorly capitalized biotech firms avoided patenting in technology areas populated by better-financed rivals.

17. More recently, the U.S. Patent Office announced that it would undertake a more careful examination of prior art for business method patents involving the Internet, and also that it would apply the utility requirement more stringently for gene sequence patents. Available at <http://www.uspto.gov>, viewed April 2000. At the time of going to press, the U.S. Patent office clarified the guidelines by noting that the utility specified in applications for genes or genetic sequences would have to be "specific, substantial and credible." Available at <http://www.nytimes.com/2001/01/09/health/genetics-health.html>, viewed January 2001.

18. Simpler institutional arrangements are also possible. For copyrights, organizations (such as ESCAP) that hold the copyrights for individual singers and songwriters and collect fixed royalty payments for their use on behalf of the artists have worked well.

19. See "Firewire Licensing to Begin immediately." Available at <http://www.maccentral.com/news/9911/15.firewire.shtml>, viewed Jan. 10, 2001. However, in other circumstances, firms have failed to reach a satisfactory agreement for pooling the patents. This is the case for DVD, where after two years of wrangling over royalties, two groups of firms have failed to agree on how to cross-license the rights or to pool them together, largely because of disputes about how to share the royalty payments. ("Royalty dispute foils one-stop DVD patent licensing plan," EE Times.com, Jan. 10, 2001, available at <www.eetimes.com/story/eezine/OEG1990618S0008>)

20. We should also note that there might be many benefits to universities from researchers who choose to leave the university to start firms. These benefits take many forms, including providing the researchers with better information on promising areas of research, and providing teachers with better information on the types of skills and competencies students need. However, for the most part, university spin-offs are celebrated as evidence of the university's contribution to the national and regional economy, ignoring the potentially much greater contributions of universities in terms of training and other types of technology transfer, such as faculty who consult with industry.

21. In this context, one must note that American universities have historically been responsive to industry needs. Collaborative research relationships between university and industry in a broad range of fields have been a distinctive hallmark of the American university system (Rosenberg and Nelson 1994). Rosenberg (1992), in particular, has convinc-

ingly argued the critical role that American universities have played in supporting innovation, often by helping in the solution of practical and sometimes scientifically mundane problems.

22. Dasgupta and David (1987, 1994) distinguish between what they call the realm of science and the realm of technology, associating the first with open, university-type research and the latter with research in firms. It is tempting, though incorrect, to interpret this as implying that researchers in firms never participate in open research, or that university research is never applied or with immediate practical utility. Rosenberg and Nelson (1994) have argued that in the United States at least, university researchers have also performed a variety of important applied activities, such as developing simple chemical assays, for assessing the purity of materials or development of instruments, such as those developed at the University of Wisconsin for ascertaining the fat content of milk.

23. One reason is that the results of one project feed into the next. Full disclosure of the results of one project would put all researchers on the same footing in terms of being the first to complete the next. By contrast, by only imperfectly disclosing the research finding, a researcher completing a stage ahead of others would get a head start on completing the next stage as well.

24. See Gambardella 1995 for a discussion of this point in the context of the pharmaceutical industry.

25. The experience of Reliance Petroleum is relevant. Reliance Petroleum is part of a large Indian conglomerate, the Reliance Group, that originated in the textile industry and then integrated backward into intermediates (purified terephthalic acid for polyesters), and then moved into the production of basic feedstocks and refining. Reliance engaged Bechtel and several other very large contractors and successfully built the world's largest "grassroots" refinery, accounting for 25 percent of India's refining capacity, and downstream plants, in Gujarat, India. This facility came in six months ahead of schedule and under budget. Clearly, although Reliance has invested in chemical engineering capabilities, more critical to its commercial success is the ability to identify sources of technology and manage them. The Reliance experience, that of entering the oil refinery business with no capacity for designing or constructing such a facility, suggests that much technology can be acquired through the marketplace by firms that have the appropriate, in-house managerial skills (see also Rosenberg 2001).

Chapter 11. Conclusions

1. See, for instance, the studies cited in note 2 of chapter 4.

2. See again the work by Pavitt, Dosi, Cantwell, Teece, and Chandler, among others, cited in note 2 of chapter 4.

References

Abernathy, W. J., and K. B. Clark. 1985. Innovation: Mapping the winds of creative destruction. *Research Policy* 14 (1): 3–22.

Aghion, P., and J. Tirole. 1994. The management of innovation. *Quarterly Journal of Economics* 109: 1185–1209.

Alam, G. 1988. India's technology policy. In *Technology Absorption in Indian Industry*, ed. A. V. Desai, 136–156. New Delhi: Wiley Eastern.

Allen, T. J., and R. Katz. 1982. Investigating the Not-Invented-Here (NIH) syndrome: A look at the performance, tenure, and communications patterns of 50 R&D project groups. *R&D Management* 12 (1): 7–19.

Alston, L., T. Eggertsson, and D. North. 1996. *Empirical studies in institutional change*. Cambridge: Cambridge University Press.

Amemiya, T. 1985. *Advanced Econometrics*. Cambridge, MA: Harvard University Press.

Anand, B. N., and T. Khanna. 2000. The structure of licensing contracts. *Journal of Industrial Economics* 48 (1): 103–135.

Anton, J. J., and D. Yao. 1994. Expropriation and inventions: Appropriable rents in the absence of property rights. *American Economic Review* 84: 190–209.

Anton, J. J., and D. Yao. 1995. Start-ups, spin-offs, and internal projects. *Journal of Law, Economics and Organization* 11: 362–378.

Aoki, M., K. Murdock, and M. Okuno-Fujiwara. 1997. Beyond the East Asian miracle: Introducing the market-enhancing view. In *The Role of Government in East Asian Economic Development*, ed. M. Aoki, H-K. Kim, and M. Okuno-Fujiwara. Oxford: Oxford University Press.

Arora, A. 1995. Licensing tacit knowledge: Intellectual property rights and the market for know-how. *Economics of Innovation and New Technology* 4: 41–59.

Arora, A. 1997. Patent, licensing and market structure in the chemical industry. *Research Policy* 26: 391–403.

Arora, A., and A. Fosfuri. 1999. Licensing the market for technology. CEPR Discussion Paper #2282. London, UK.

Arora, A., and A. Fosfuri. 2000. The market for technology in the chemical industry: Causes and consequences. *Revue D'Économie Industrielle* 92 (Special Issue): 317–334.

Arora, A., and A. Gambardella. 1990. Complementarities and external linkages: The strategies of large corporations in biotechnology. *Journal of Industrial Economics* 38 (4): 361–379.

Arora, A., and A. Gambardella. 1994a. The changing technology of technological change: General and abstract knowledge and the division of innovative labour. *Research Policy* 23: 523–532.

Arora, A., and A. Gambardella. 1994b. Evaluating technological information and utilizing it: Scientific knowledge, technological capability, and external linkages in biotechnology. *Journal of Economic Behavior and Organization* 24: 91–114.

Arora, A., and A. Gambardella. 1997. Domestic markets and international competitiveness: Generic and product specific competencies in the engineering sector. *Strategic Management Journal* 18: 53–74.

Arora, A., and A. Gambardella. 1998. Evolution of industry structure in the chemical industry. In *Chemicals and Long-Term Economic Growth,* ed. A. Arora, R. Landau, and N. Rosenberg. New York: John Wiley & Sons.

Arora, A., and R. Merges. 2000. Intellectual property rights, firm boundaries and R&D inputs. Heinz School Working Paper, Carnegie Mellon University, Pittsburgh, PA.

Arora, A., and N. Rosenberg. 1998. Chemicals: A U.S. success story. In *Chemicals and Long Term Economic Growth,* ed. A. Arora, R. Landau, and N. Rosenberg, 71–102. New York: John Wiley and Sons.

Arora, A., F. Bokhari, and B. Morel. 2000. Returns to specialization, transaction costs, and the dynamics of industrial evolution. Unpublished manuscript, Carnegie Mellon University, Pittsburgh, PA.

Arora, A., A. Fosfuri, and A. Gambardella. 1996. Division of labor and the transmission of growth. CEPR Discussion Paper #474, Stanford University, Stanford, CA.

Arora, A., A. Fosfuri, and A. Gambardella. 2001. Specialized technology suppliers, international spillovers and investment: Evidence from the chemical industry. *Journal of Development Economics* 65 (1): 31–54.

Arora, A., A. Gambardella, and S. Torrisi. 2001. Human capital, international linkages and growth: The Software industry in India and Ireland. Paper presented at the American Economic Association Meeting, New Orleans, LA, Jan. 4–8.

Arrow, K. J. 1962a. Economic welfare and the allocation of resources for invention. In *The Rate and Direction of Inventive Activity: Economic and Social Factors,* ed. R. R. Nelson. Princeton: Princeton University Press.

Arrow, K. J. 1962b. Comments on case studies. In *The Rate and Direction of Inventive Activity: Economic and Social Factors,* ed. R. R. Nelson. Princeton: Princeton University Press.

Arrow, K. J. 1974. *The limits of organization.* New York: W. W. Norton.

Arrow, K. J. 1975. Vertical integration and communication. *Bell Journal of Economics* 6 (1): 173–183.

Arthur, B. 1994. Increasing returns and path dependence in the economy. Ann Arbor: University of Michigan Press.

Athreye, S. 1998. On markets in knowledge. *Journal of Management and Governance* 1 (2): 231–253.

Audretsch, D. B., and M. P. Feldman. 1996. R&D spillovers and the geography of innovation and production. *American Economic Review* 86 (3): 630–640.

Backman, J. 1964. *Competition in the chemical industry.* Washington, D.C.: Manufacturing Chemists' Association.

Balakrishnan, S., and S. Koza. 1993. Information asymmetry, adverse selection and joint ventures. *Journal of Economic Behavior and Organization* 20 (1): 99–118.

Balcet, G. 1985. Transfer of Italian technology to India. *Economic and Political Weekly,* Special Number.

Baldwin, C. Y., and K. B. Clark. 1997. Managing in an age of modularity. *Harvard Business Review* 75 (5): 84–93.

Barney, J. B. 1986. Strategic factor markets: Expectations, luck and business strategy. *Management Science* 32 (10): 1231–1241.

Barney, J. B. 1991. Firms resources and sustained competitive advantage. *Journal of Management* 17: 99–120.

Barro, R., and J. H. Lee. 1994. Data set for a panel of 138 countries. Available at <Ftp://www.nber.org/pub/barro.lee>.

Baye, M. R., M. J. Crocker, and J. Ju. 1996. Divisionalization, franchising, and divesture incentives in oligopoly. *American Economic Review* 86 (1): 223–236.

Bell, M., and D. Scott-Kemmis. 1988. Technology import policy: Have the questions changed? In *Technology Absorption in Indian Industry,* ed. A. U. Desai, 30–70. New Delhi: Wiley Eastern.

Bell, M., and K. Pavitt. 1993. Technological accumulation and industrial growth: Contrasts between developed and developing countries. *Industrial and Corporate Change* 2: 157–209.

Besanko, D., and M. K. Perry. 1993. Equilibrium incentives for exclusive dealing in a differentiated products oligopoly. *RAND Journal of Economics* 24 (4): 646–667.

Bhattacharya, S., J. Glazer, and D. E. M. Sappington. 1990. Sharing knowledge in internally financed R&D contests. *Journal of Industrial Economics* 39 (2): 187–208.

Bidault, F. 1989. *Technology Pricing.* New York: St. Martin's Press.

Blömstrom, M., and A. Kokko. 1998. Multinational corporation and spillovers. *Journal of Economic Survey* 12 (3): 247–278.

Bonaccorsi, A., and F. Pammolli. 1996. The economics of technical development and the nature of design knowledge. *International Journal of Technology Management.* Winter.

Bonanno, G., and J. Vickers. 1988. Vertical separation. *Journal of Industrial Economics* 36: 257–265.

Brady, T., M. Tiernay, and R. Williams. 1992. The commodification of industry application software. *Industrial and Corporate Change* 1 (3): 489–514.

Brander, J., and B. Spencer. 1983. International R&D rivalry and industrial strategy. *Review of Economic Studies* 50 (4): 707–722.

Braun, E., and S. MacDonald. 1978. *Revolution in Miniature.* Cambridge, UK: Cambridge University Press.

Bresnahan, T., and A. Gambardella. 1998. The division of inventive labor and the extent of the market. In *General Purpose Technologies and Economic Growth,* ed. E. Helpman. Cambridge, MA: The MIT Press.

Bresnahan, T., and R. Gordon. 1997. The economics of new goods: An introduction. In *The Economics of New Goods,* ed. T. Bresnahan, and R. Gordon. Chicago: University of Chicago Press.

Bresnahan, T., and P. Reiss. 1991. Entry and competition in concentrated markets. *Journal of Political Economy* 99 (5): 977–1009.

Bresnahan, T., and M. Trajtenberg. 1995. General purpose technologies: "Engines of growth"? *Journal of Econometrics* 65: 83–108.

British Technology Group (BTG). 1998. IPR Market Benchmark Study. Available at <www.btgplc.com>.

Brusoni, S., and A. Prencipe. 1998. Modularity in complex product systems: Managing the knowledge dimension. Unpublished Manuscript. SPRU. Brighton, UK: University of Sussex.

Bulow, J., J. Geneakoplos. and P. Klemperer. 1985. Multimarket oligopoly: Strategic substitutes and complements. *Journal of Political Economy* 93: 488–511.

Business Week. 1999. Qualcomm: From wireless to phoneless. *Business Week,* December 6, 96–98.

Cantwell, J. 1994. Introduction. In *Transnational Corporations and Innovatory Activity,* ed. J. Cantwell. London: Routledge.

Cantwell, J. 2000. Technological lock-in of large firms since the interwar period. *European Review of Economic History* 4: 147–174.

Caves, R. E. 1996. *Multinational Enterprise and Economic Analysis.* Second Edition. Cambridge: Cambridge University Press.

Caves, R., H. Crookell, and J. P. Killing. 1983. The imperfect market for technology licensing. *Oxford Bulletin of Economics and Statistics* 45 (3): 249–267.

Chandler, A. 1990. *Scale and Scope: The Dynamics of Industrial Capitalism.* Cambridge, MA: The Belknap Press of Harvard University Press.

Chandler, A., P. Hagström, and Ö. Sölvell, (eds.). 1998. *The Dynamic Firm: The Role of Technology, Strategy, Organization and Regions.* Oxford: Oxford University Press.

Chemical Week. 1997. Turning process know-how into profits. *Chemical Week,* July 23, 45–47.

Chemical Week. 1999. Process technology: Players improve their hands. *Chemical Week,* Nov. 17–27.

Chemintell, 1991. *Chemical Age Project File* (CAPF). London: Pergamon Financial Data Services.

Chesbrough, H. 2000. Designing corporate ventures in the shadow of private venture capital. *California Management Review* 42 (3): 31–49.

Chesbrough, H. W., and D. J. Teece. 1996. When is virtual virtuous? Organizing for innovation. *Harvard Business Review* 74 (1): 65–72.

Chin, J. C., and G. Grossman. 1990. Intellectual property rights and North-South trade. In *The Political Economy of International Trade*, ed. R. W. Jones and A. Kreuger. Cambridge, MA: Blackwell.

Clark, K. 1985. The Interaction of design hierarchies and market concepts in technological evolution. *Research Policy* 14 (5): 235–251.

Clark, K., and T. Fujimoto. 1991. *Product Development Performance: Strategy, Organization, and Management in the Wolrd Auto Industries*. Cambridge, MA: Harvard Business School Press.

Cockburn, I., R. Henderson, L. Orsenigo, and G. Pisano. 1999. Pharmaceuticals and biotechnology. In *US Industry in 2000: Studies in Competitive Performance*, ed. D. Mowery, Washington, D.C.: National Academy Press.

Coe, D. T., and E. Helpman. 1995. International R&D spillovers. *European Economic Review* 39: 859–887.

Cohen, W., and S. Klepper. 1996. Firm size and the nature of innovation within industries: The case of process and product R&D. *Review of Economics and Statistics* 78 (2): 232–243.

Cohen, W., and D. Levinthal. 1989. Innovation and learning: The two faces of R&D. *Economic Journal* 99: 569–596.

Cohen, W. M., R. R. Nelson, and J. Walsh. 1997. Appropriability conditions and why firms patent and why they do not in the U.S. manufacturing sector. Working Paper, Carnegie Mellon University, Pittsburgh, PA.

Cohen, W., R. Nelson, and J. Walsh. 2000. Protecting their intellectual assets: Appropriability conditions and why U.S. manufacturing firms patent (or not). NBER Working Paper #7552. NBER. Cambridge, MA.

Contractor, F. J. 1981. *International Technology Transfer*. Lexington, MA: D. C. Heath and Company.

Contractor, F. J. 1990. Contractual and cooperative forms of international business: Towards a unified theory of modal choice. *Management International Review* 30: 31–54.

Cool, K., and I. Dierickx. 1989. Asset stock accumulation and sustainability of competitive advantage. *Management Science* 35 (12): 1504–1513.

Cooper, C. 1988. Supply and demand factors in Indian technology imports: A case study. In *Technology absorption in Indian industry*, ed. A. U. Desai, 105–135. New Delhi: Wiley Eastern.

Corts, K. S. 1999. Focused firms and the incentive to innovate. *Journal of Economics and Management Strategy* 9 (3): 338–362.

Cusumano, M. 1991. *Japan's Software Factory: A Challenge to U.S. Management*. Oxford: Oxford University Press.

Dasgupta, P., and P. David. 1987. Information disclosure and the economics of science and technology. In *Arrow and the Ascent of Economic Theory*, ed. G. Feinel. New York: New York University Press.

Dasgupta, P., and P. David. 1994. Towards a new economics of science. *Research Policy* 23: 487–521.

David, P. 1987. Some new standards for the economics of standardization in the information age. In *Economic Policy and Technological Performance*, ed. P. Dasgupta, and P. Stoneman. Cambridge, UK.: Cambridge University Press.

David, P. 1991. Reputation and agency in the historical emergence of the institutions of "open science." CEPR Working Paper N.261, CEPR, Stanford, CA: Stanford University.

David, P. 1993. Knowledge, property, and the system dynamics of technological change. In *Proceedings of the World Bank Annual Conference on Development Economics 1992.* Washington, D.C.: The World Bank.

David, P. 2000. A tragedy of the public knowledge "commons"? Global science, intellectual property and the digital technology boomerang. SIEPR Policy Paper, No. 00-002. Stanford, CA: Stanford University.

David, P., and S. Greenstein. 1990. The economics of compatibility standards: An introduction to recent research. *Economics of Innovation and New Technology* (1): 3–41.

Degnan, S. A. 1998. The licensing payoff from U.S. R&D. *Journal of the Licensing Executives Society International* 33 (4): 1–8.

Deng, Z., B. Lev, and F. Narin. 1999. Science and technology as predictors of stock performance. *Financial Analysts Journal*, May/June, 20–32.

Deolalikar, A. B., and R.. E. Evenson. 1989. Technology production and technology purchase in Indian industry: An econometric analysis. *Review of Economics and Statistics*, November.

Desai, A. V., ed. 1988. *Technology absorption in Indian industry.* New Delhi: Wiley Eastern.

Dosi, G. 1988. Sources, procedures and microeconomic effects of innovation. *Journal of Economic Literature* 26: 1120–1171.

Dunning, J. H. 1981. *International production and the multinational enterprise.* London: Allen and Unwin.

Eaton, J., and S. Kortum. 1996. Trade in ideas: Patenting and productivity in the OECD. *Journal of International Economics* 40:251–278.

Eichengreen, B. 1998. Monetary, fiscal and trade policies in the development of the chemical industry. In *Chemicals and Long-Term Economic Growth*, ed. A. Arora, R. Landau, and N. Rosenberg. New York: John Wiley & Sons.

Ellis, W., and A. Chatterjee. 1998. Shakeout on state street: A seismic federal circuit precedent makes patents a potent financial services weapon. *IP Magazine*, November. Available at <www.ipmag.com/98-nov/ellis.html>.

Ernst & Young. 1997. Annual Biotechnology Report. Available at <www.ey.com>.

Ernst & Young. 1999. Biotech 99: Bridging the gap. Annual Biotechnology Report. Ernst & Young. Available at <www.ey.com>.

Eswaran, M. 1993. Cross-licensing of competing patents as a facilitation device. *Canadian Journal of Economics* 27 (3): 689–708.

European Technology Assessment Network (ETAN). 1999. Strategic dimensions of intellectual property rights in the context of S&T policy. European Commission Report EUR 18914. Luxembourg.

Farrell, J., H. K. Monroe, and G. Saloner. 1998. The vertical organization of industry: Incompatibility versus compatibility. *Journal of Economics and Management Strategy* 7: 143–182.

Fershtman, C., and K. L. Judd. 1987. Equilibrium incentives in oligopoly. *American Economic Review* 77 (5): 927–940.

Fershtman, C., and M. I. Kamien. 1992. Cross licensing of complementary technologies. *International Journal of Industrial Organization* 10: 329–48.

Financial Times. 1992. Vehicle manufacturing technology. *Financial Times Survey*, Section IV, June 5.

Financial Times. 1999. On line specialist goes shopping. *Financial Times*, February 3. Available at <www.ft.com/ftsurveys/q3e26.htm>.

Finegold, D., ed. 1994. *The Decline of the U.S. Machine Tool Industry and Prospects for its Sustainable Recovery*. Santa Monica: Rand Corporation.

Fosfuri, A. 1999. Royalty or fixed fees? A note. Unpublished manuscript. Spain: Universidad Carlos III de Madrid.

Fosfuri, A., M. Motta, and T. Roende. 2001. Foreign direct investment and spillovers through workers' mobility. *Journal of International Economics* 53: 205–222.

Freeman, C. 1968. Chemical process plant: innovation and the world market. *National Institute Economic Review* 74: 931–941.

Freeman, C. 1982. *The Economics of Industrial Innovation*, 2d ed. London: Pinter Publishers.

Galambos, L., and J. Sturchio. 1996. Pharmaceutical firms and the transition to biotechnology: A study in strategic innovation. *Business History Review* 72 (2): 250–279.

Gallini, N. T. 1984. Deterrence through market sharing: A strategic incentive for licensing. *American Economic Review* 74: 931–941.

Gallini, N. T. 1992. Patent policy and costly imitation. *RAND Journal of Economics* 23 (1): 52–63.

Gallini, N. T., and R. A. Winter. 1985. Licensing in the theory of innovation. *RAND Journal of Economics* 16: 237–252.

Gallini, N. T., and B. D. Wright. 1990. Technology transfer under asymmetric information. *RAND Journal of Economics* 21 (1): 147–160.

Gambardella, A. 1995. *Science and Innovation: The U.S. Pharmaceutical Industry in the 1980s*. Cambridge: Cambridge University Press.

Gans, J., and S. Stern. 2000. Incumbency and R&D incentives: Licensing the gale of creative destruction. *Journal of Economics and Management Strategy* 9 (4): 485–511.

Gans, J., D. Hsu, and S. Stern. 2000. When does start-up innovation spur the gale of creative destruction? NBER Working Paper #7851. Cambridge, MA.

Gilbert, R., and C. Shapiro. 1990. Optimal patent length and breadth. *RAND Journal of Economics* 21: 106–112.

Gompers, P. 1999. Resource allocation, incentives and control: The importance of venture capital in financing entrepreneurial firms. In *Entrepreneurship, Small and Medium Sized Enterprises and the Macroeconomy,* ed. Z. Acs, B. Carlsoon, and C. Karlsson. Cambridge, UK: Cambridge University Press.

Gompers, P., and J. Lerner. 1999. *The Venture Capital Cycle.* Cambridge, MA: MIT Press.

Granstrand, O. 1999. *The Economics and Management of Intellectual Property.* UK: Edward Elgar.

Green, J., and S. Scotchmer. 1995. On the division of profits in sequential innovations. *RAND Journal of Economics* 26 (1): 20–33.

Griliches, Z., ed. 1984. *R&D, Patents, and Productivity.* Chicago: University of Chicago Press.

Griliches, Z. 1979. Issues in assessing the contribution of research and development to productivity growth. *Bell Journal of Economics* 10 (1): 92–116.

Grindley, P. C., and J. Nickerson. 1996. Licensing and business strategy in the chemical industry. In *Technology Licensing: Corporate Strategies for Maximizing Value,* ed. R. Parr, and P. Sullivan. New York: John Wiley and Sons.

Grindley, P. C., and D. J. Teece. 1997. Licensing and cross-licensing in semiconductors and electronics. *California Management Review* 39 (2): 8–41.

Grossman, S., and O. Hart. 1986. The costs and benefits of ownership: A theory of vertical and lateral integration. *Journal of Political Economy* 94: 691–719.

Hadfield, G. K. 1991. Credible spatial preemption through franchising. *RAND Journal of Economics* 22 (4): 531–543.

Hadley, W. 1998. Repporteur's report. Paper presented at the Conference on Intellectual Property Rights and Competition Policy, Stanford Law School, Stanford, CA, April.

Hart, O. 1995. *Firms, Contracts, and Financial Structure.* Oxford, UK: Oxford University Press.

Hall, B. H., and R. Ham. 1999. The patent paradox revisited: Determinants of patenting in the U.S. semiconductor industry, 1980–1994. NBER Working Paper #7062. Cambridge, MA.

Hart, O., and J. Moore. 1990. Property rights and the nature of the firm. *Journal of Political Economy* 98: 1119–1158.

Heller, M., and R. Eisenberg. 1998. Can patents deter innovation? The anticommons in biomedical research. *Science* 280: 698–701.

Helpman, E. (ed.) 1998. *General Purpose Technologies and Economic Growth.* Cambridge, MA: The MIT Press.

Helpman, E., and M. Trajtenberg. 1996. Diffusion of general-purpose technologies. NBER Working Paper #5773. Cambridge, MA.

Helpman, E., and M. Trajtenberg. 1998. A time to sow and a time to reap: Growth based on general purpose technologies. In *General Purpose Technology and Economic Growth,* ed. E. Helpman. Cambridge, MA: MIT Press.

Heller, M. 1998. The tragedy of the anticommons: Property in the transition from marx to markets. *Harvard Law Review* 111: 621–688.

Henderson, R., and K. Clark. 1990. Architectural innovation: The reconfiguration of existing product technologies and the failure of established firms. *Administrative Science Quarterly* 35 (1): 9–30.

Henderson, R., A. Jaffe, and M. Trajtenberg. 1998. Universities as a source of commercial technology: A detailed analysis of university patenting, 1965–1988. *Review of Economics and Statistics* 80 (1): 119–127.

Henderson, W. O. 1965. *Britain and Industrial Europe 1750–1870: Studies in British Influence of the Industrial Revolution in Western Europe.* Leicester: Leicester University Press.

Hikino, T., T. Harada, Y. Tokujisa, and J. Yoshida. 1998. The Japanese puzzle. In *Chemicals and Long Term Economic Growth,* ed. A. Arora, R. Landau, and N. Rosenberg. New York: John Wiley & Sons.

Hill, C. W., L. P. Hwang, and W. C. Kim. 1990. An eclectic theory of the choice of international entry mode. *Strategic Management Journal* 11: 117–128.

Hofman, D. J., and J. F. Rockart. 1994. Application templates: Faster, better, and cheaper systems. *Sloan Management Review* 36 (1): 49–57.

Hofstede, G. 1991. *Cultures and Organizations: Software of the Mind.* Berkshire, UK: McGraw-Hill.

Hounshell, D., and J. Smith. 1988. *Science and Corporate Strategy: Du Pont R&D 1902–1980.* Cambridge: Cambridge University Press.

Hymer, S. H. 1976. *The International Operations of National Firms: A Study of Direct Foreign Investment.* Cambridge, MA: MIT Press.

Iansiti, M. 1997. *Technology Integration: Making Critical Choices in a Dynamic World.* Boston, MA: Harvard Business School Press.

Iansiti, M., and J. West. 1997. Technology integration: Turning great research into great products. *Harvard Business Review,* May–June, 69–79.

Jaffe, A. 1986. Technological opportunity and spillovers of R&D: Evidence from firms' patents, profits and market value. *American Economic Review* 76 (5): 984–1001.

Jaffe, A., M. Trajtenberg, and R. Henderson. 1993. Geographical localization of knowledge spillovers as evidenced by patent citations. *Quarterly Journal of Economics* 434: 578–598.

Jeremy, D. J. 1981. *Transatlantic Industrial Revolution: The Diffusion of Textile Technologies between Britain and America, 1790–1830s.* Oxford: Basil Blackwell.

Kamien, M., and Y. Tauman. 1986. Fees versus royalties and the private value of a patent. *Quarterly Journal of Economics* 101: 471–491.

Katrak, H. 1985. Imported technology, enterprise size and R&D in a newly industrialising country: The Indian experience. *Oxford Bulletin of Economics and Statistics* 4 (3): 213–229.

Katrak, H. 1989. Imported technologies and R&D in a newly industrialising country: The experience of Indian enterprises. *Journal of Development Economics,* 31 (1): 123–139.

Katz, M., and C. Shapiro. 1985. On the licensing of innovation. *RAND Journal of Economics* 16 (4): 504–520.

Katz, M., and C. Shapiro. 1986. How to license intangible property. *Quarterly Journal of Economics* 101: 567–589.

Katz, M., and C. Shapiro. 1994. Systems competition and network effects. *Journal of Economic Perspectives* 8 (2).

Katz, R., and T. J. Allen. 1982. Investigating the not-invented-here (NIH) syndrome: A look at the performance, tenure, and communications patterns of 50 R&D project groups. *R&D Management* 12 (1): 7–19.

Keller, W. 1998. Are international R&D spillovers trade-related? Analyzing spillovers among randomly matched trade partners. *European Economic Review* 42 (8): 1469–1481.

Kenney, M. 1986. *Biotechnology: The University-Industrial Complex*. New Haven, CT: Yale University Press.

Kim, Y. 1988. Strategic competition in negotiations of international technology licensing: The informational interaction view. Unpublished Ph.D. diss., UCLA.

Klemperer, P. 1990. How broad should the scope of patent protection be? *RAND Journal of Economics* 21: 113–130.

Klepper, S. 1996. Entry, exit, and innovation over the product life cycle. *American Economic Review* 86 (3): 562–583.

Kline, S., and N. Rosenberg. 1986. An overview of innovation. In *The Positive Sum Strategy*, ed. R. Landau, and N. Rosenberg. Washington, DC: National Academy Press.

Kogut, B., and U. Zander. 1992. Knowledge of the firm, combinative capabilities and the replication of technology. *Organization Science* 3: 383–397.

Kogut, B., and U. Zander. 1993. Knowledge of the firm and evolutionary theory of the multinational corporation. *Journal of International Business Studies* 24: 625–645.

Kortum, S., and J. Lerner. 1999. What is behind the recent surge in patenting. *Research Policy* 28: 1–22.

Kremer, M. 1998. Patent buyouts: A mechanism for encouraging innovation. *Quarterly Journal of Economics* 113: 1137–1167.

Kumar, N. 1987. Technology imports and local research and development in Indian manufacturing. *Developing Economies* 25 (3): 220–233.

Kuznets, S. S. 1969. *Modern Economic Growth: Rate, Structure, and Spread*. New Haven: Yale University Library.

Lamoreaux, N., and K. Sokoloff. 1996. Long term change in the organization of inventive activity. *Proceedings of the National Academy of Science USA* 93: 12686–12692.

Lamoreaux, N., and K. Sokoloff. 1997. Location and technological change in the American glass industry during the late Nineteenth and Early Twentieth Centuries. NBER Working Paper #5938. Cambridge, MA.

Lamoreaux, N., and K. Sokoloff. 1998. Inventors, firms, and the market for technology: U.S. manufacturing in the Late Nineteenth and Early Twentieth Centuries. In *Learning by Firms, Organizations, and Nations*, ed. N. Lamoreaux, D. Raff, and P. Temins.

Landau, R. 1998. The process of innovation. In *Chemicals and Long Term Growth*, ed. A. Arora, R. Landau, and N. Rosenberg. New York: John Wiley & Sons.

Landau, R., and D. Brown. 1965. Making research pay. *AIChE-I. Chem. E. Symposium Series* 7: 35–43. London, UK: London Institute of Chemical Engineers.

Landau, R., and N. Rosenberg. 1992. Successful commercialization in the chemical process industries. In *Technology and the Wealth of Nations*, ed. R. Landau, D. Mowery, and N. Rosenberg. Stanford, CA: Stanford University Press.

Landes, D. S. 1969. *The Unbounded Prometheus: Technological Change and Industrial Development in Western Europe from 1750 to the Present*. Cambridge, UK: Cambridge University Press.

Langlois, R. 1992. External economies and economic progress: The case of the microcomputer industry. *Business History Review* 66 (1): 1–50.

Langlois, R. 1999. Modularity in technology, organization, and society. Paper presented at a Conference on *The Roots and Branches of Organizational Economics*, Stanford University, September 26–27.

Langlois, R., and P. L. Robertson. 1992. Networks and innovation in a modular system: Lessons from the microcomputer and stereo component industries. *Research Policy* 21: 297–313.

Langlois, R., and E. Steinmueller. 1998. The Evolution of competitive advantages in the worldwide semiconductor industry, 1947–1996. In *The Sources of Industrial Leadership*, ed. D. Mowery and R. Nelson. Cambridge, UK: Cambridge University Press.

Lemley, M., and D. O'Brien. 1997. Encouraging software reuse. *Stanford Law Review* 49: 672–703.

Lerner, J. 1999. The government as venture capitalist: The long-run impact of the SBIR program. *Journal of Business* 72: 285–318.

Lev, B., and P. Zarowin. 1999. The boundaries of financial reporting and how to extend them. *Journal of Accounting Research* 37 (2): 353–385.

Levin, R. C., A. K. Klevorick, R. R. Nelson, and S. G. Winter. 1987. Appropriating the returns from industrial R&D. *Brookings Papers on Economic Activity* 14: 551–561.

Levinthal, D. A., and J. G. March. 1993. The myopia of learning. *Strategic Management Journal* 14: 95–112.

Lieberman, M. 1987. Patents, learning by doing, and market structure in the chemical processing industries. *International Journal of Industrial Organization* 5: 257–276.

Lieberman, M. 1989. The learning curve, technological barriers to entry, and competitive survival in the chemical processing industries. *Strategic Management Journal* 10: 72–89.

Lin, P. 1996. Fixed-fee licensing of innovations and collusion. *Journal of Industrial Economics* 44 (4): 443–49.

Linden, G., and D. Somaya. 2000. System-on-a-chip integration in the semiconductor industry: Industry structure and firm strategies, draft. Berkeley: University of California.

Macher, J., D. Mowery, and D. Hodges. 1999. Semiconductors. In *US Industry in 2000: Studies in Competitive Performance*, ed. D. Mowery. Washington, DC: National Academy Press.

Macho, I., and D. Castrillio. 1991. Licensing contracts and asymmetric information. *Annals d' Économie et de Statistique* 24: 189–208.

Malerba, F. 1985. *The Semiconductor Business*. Madison, WI: The University of Wisconsin Press.

Malerba, F., and L. Orsenigo. 2000. Knowledge, innovative activities, and industrial evolution. *Industrial and Corporate Change* 3(2): 289–313.

Mansfield, E., J. Rapoport, A. Romeo, E. Villani, S. Wagner, and F. Husic. 1977. *The Production and Application of New Industrial Technology*. New York: Norton.

March, A. 1989. The U.S. machine tool industry and its foreign competitors. In *Made in America: Regaining the Productive Edge*, ed. M. Dertouzos, R. Lester, and R. Solow. Cambridge, MA: The MIT Press.

March, J. G. 1991. Exploration and exploitation in organizational learning. *Organization Science* 2: 71–87.

Markides, C. C., and P. J. Williamson. 1996. Corporate diversification and organization structure: A resource-based view. *Academy of Management Journal* 39: 340–367.

Marshall, A. 1990. *Principles of Economics: An Introductory Volume*. 8th ed. Handmills: MacMillan.

Mazzoleni, R., and R. R. Nelson. 1998. The benefits and costs of strong patent protection: a contribution to the current debate. *Research Policy* 27 (3): 275–286.

Merges, R. 1998. Property rights, transactions, and the value of intangible assets. Mimeo, Boalt School of Law, University of California, Berkeley, CA.

Merges, R., and R. Nelson. 1990. On the complex economics of patent scope. *Columbia Law Review* 90 (4): 839–916.

Merges, P., and R. R. Nelson. 1993. On limiting or encouraging rivalry in technical progress: The effect of patent scope decisions. Mimeo, Columbia University.

Merges, R. 1999a. As many as six impossible patents before breakfast: Property rights for business concepts and patent system reform. *Berkeley Technology Law Journal* 14: 577–615.

Merges, R. 1999b. Who owns the Charles River Bridge? Intellectual property and competition in the software industry. Working paper, The Berkeley Center for Law and Technology, UC Berkeley, CA.

Milgrom, P., and J. Roberts. 1990. Rationalizability, learning, and equilibrium in games with strategic complementarities. *Econometrica* 58: 1255–1277.

Moore, S. K., and A. Scott. 2000. M&A and litigation mold the market. *Chemical Week* 162 (6) 35–37.

Mowery, D. 1983. The relationship between intrafirm and contractual forms of industrial research in American manufacturing, 1900–1940. *Explorations in Economic History* 20: 351–374.

Mowery, D. 1984. Firm structure, government policy, and the organization of industrial research. *Business History Review* 58: 504–531.

Mowery, D. 1996. *The International Computer Software Industry: A Comparative Study of Industry Evolution and Structure*. Oxford: Oxford University Press.

Mowery, D., ed. 1988. *International Collaborative Ventures in U.S. Manufacturing*. Cambridge, MA: Ballinger Press.

Mowery, D., and A. Ziedonis. 2000. Academic patent quality and quantity before and after the Bayh-Dole Act in the United States. Paper presented at the International Conference on Technology Policy and Innovation, Paris, Maison de la Chimie, Nov. 20–22.

Mowery, D., R. Nelson, B. Sampat, and A. Ziedonis. 1999. The Effects of the Bayh-Dole Act on U.S. University research and technology transfer: An analysis of data from Columbia University, the University of California, and Stanford University. In *Industrializing Knowledge*, ed. L. Branscomb and R. Florida. Cambridge, MA: MIT Press.

Nadiri, M. I. 1993. Innovation and technological spillovers. NBER Working Paper #4423. Cambridge, MA.

Nakahara, T. 1993. The industrial organization and information structure of the software industry: A U.S.-Japan comparison. Working Paper, Center for Economic Policy Research, Stanford University, CA.

Nelson, R. R. 1959. The simple economics of basic scientific research. *Journal of Political Economy* 67 (2): 297–306.

Nelson, R. R. 1990. What is public and what is private about technology?, Working Paper No. 90–9, University of California Center for Research in Management.

Nelson, R. R., and S. Winter. 1982. *An Evolutionary Theory of Economic Change*. Cambridge, MA: The Belknap Press of Harvard University Press.

Nonaka, I. 1991. The knowledge-creating company. *Harvard Business Review* 32 (3): 27–38.

Nonaka, I., and H. Takeuchi. 1995. *The Knowledge Creating Company*. New York: Oxford University Press.

North, D. 1990. *Institutions, Institutional Change and Economic Performance*. Cambridge, U.K.: Cambridge University Press.

OECD. 1998. *Main science and technology indicators*. Paris: Organization for Economic Development and Cooperation.

Orsenigo, L. 1989. *The Emergence of Biotechnology: Institutions and Markets in Industrial Innovation*. London: Francis Pinter.

Orsenigo, L., F. Pammolli, and M. Riccaboni. 2001. Technological change and network dynamics: Lessons from the pharmaceutical industry. *Research Policy*. Forthcoming.

Orsenigo, L., F. Pammolli, M. Riccaboni, A. Bonaccorsi, and G. Turchetti. 1998. The evolution of knowledge and the dynamics of an industry network. *Journal of Management and Governance* 1 (2): 147–175.

Pakes, A. 1986. Patents as options: Some estimates of the value of holding European patent stocks. *Econometrica* 54 (4): 755–784.

Patel, P., and K. Pavitt. 1997. The technological competencies of the world's largest firms: Complex and path-dependent, but not much variety. *Research Policy* 26: 141–156.

Patel, P., and K. Pavitt. 1998. The wide (and increasing) spread of technological competencies in the world's largest firms: A challenge to conventional wisdom. In *The Dynamic Firm: The Role of Technology, Strategy, Organization and Regions*, ed. A. Chandler, P. Hagström, and Ö. Sölvell. Oxford: Oxford University Press.

Pavitt, K. 1987. The objectives of technology policy. *Science and Public Policy* 14: 182–188.

Pavitt, K. 2000. Specialisation and the boundaries of the firm. Unpublished manuscript. SPRU. UK: University of Sussex.

Pavitt, K., M. Robson, and J. Towsend. 1987. The size distribution of innovating firms in the UK: 1945–1983. *Journal of Industrial Economics* 35: 297–316.

Penrose, E. T. 1959. *The Theory of Growth of the Firm*. Oxford: Blackwell.

Perry, M. 1989. Vertical integration: Determinants and effects. In *Handbook of Industrial Organization*, ed. R. Schmalensee and R. Willig. Amsterdam: North-Holland.

Peteraf, M. A. 1993. The cornerstones of competitive advantage: A resource-based view. *Strategic Management Journal* 14 (3): 179–191.

Pine, J. 1993. *Mass Customization: The New Frontier in Business Competition*. Boston, MA: Harvard Business School Press.

Pisano, G., W. Shan, and D. Teece. 1988. Joint ventures and collaboration in the biotechnology industry. In *International Collaborative Ventures in US Manufacturing*, ed. D. Mowery. Cambridge, MA: Ballinger Press.

Pisano, G. P. 1990. The R&D boundaries of the firm: An empirical analysis. *Administrative Science Quarterly* 35: 153–176.

Polanyi, M. 1966. *The Tacit Dimension*. London: Reutledge and Kegan Paul.

Porter, M. 1998. Clusters and the new economics of competition. *Harvard Business Review*, Nov.–Dec., 77–90.

Powell, W., K. Koput, and L. Smith-Doerr. 1996. Interorganizational collaboration and the locus of innovation: Networks of learning in biotechnology. *Administrative Science Quarterly* 41: 116–145.

Predicasts Company Thesaurus. 1991. World Headquarters. Cleveland, OH. Annual Edition.

Raut, L. K. 1988. R&D behaviour of Indian firms. *Indian Economic Review* 23 (2): 207–223.

Red Herring Magazine. 1997. Absolutely fabless: An epic contrast between two competing chip designers. May. Available at <www.redherring.com/mag/issue42/fabless.html>.

Red Herring Magazine. 1998a. Chemical attraction: Long preferring to work independently, biotech companies are now considering the advantages of consolidation. May. Available at <www.redherring.com/mag/issue54/chemical.html>.

Red Herring Magazine. 1998b. Biotech: The next great entrepreneurial wave. May. Available at <www.redherring.com/mag/issue54/overview.html>.

Red Herring Magazine. 1999. ARC cores rides platform divergence trend. June. Available at <www.redherring.com/insider/1999/0604/vc-arccores.html>.

Remsberg, C., and H. Higdon. 1994. *Ideas for rents: The UOP story*. Des Plaines, IL: Universal Oil Corp.

Rivera-Batiz, L., and P. Romer. 1991. Economic integration and endogeneous growth. *Quarterly Journal of Economics* 106: 531–555.

Rivette, K. G., and D. Kline. 1999. *Rembrandt in the Attic: Unlocking the Hidden Value of Patents*. Boston, MA: Harvard Business School Press.

Rockett, K. 1990. Choosing the competition and patent licensing. *RAND Journal of Economics* 21 (1): 161–171.

Rodriguez-Clare, A. 1996. Multinationals, linkages, and economic development. *American Economic Review* 86 (4): 851–873.

Romer, P. 1986. Increasing returns and long-run Growth. *Journal of Political Economy* 94, 1002–1037.

Romer, P. 1990. Endogeneous technological change. *Journal of Political Economy* 98 (5): S71–S102.

Romer, P. 1996. Why, indeed, in America? Theory, history, and the origins of modern economic growth. *American Economic Review* 86 (2): 202–206.

Rosenberg, N. 1963. Technological change in the machine tool industry, 1840–1910. *Journal of Economic History* 23 (4). Reprinted in *Perspectives on Technology*, N. Rosenberg. Cambridge: Cambridge University Press.

Rosenberg, N. 1976. *Perspectives on Technology*. Cambridge: Cambridge University Press.

Rosenberg, N. 1982. *Inside the Black Box*. Cambridge: Cambridge University Press.

Rosenberg, N. 1990. Why do firms do basic research? *Research Policy* 19: 165–174.

Rosenberg, N. 1992. Scientific instrumentation and university research. *Research Policy* 21: 381–390.

Rosenberg, N. 1998. Technological change in chemicals: The role of university-industry relations. In *Chemicals and Long-Term Economic Growth*, ed. A. Arora, R. Landau, and N. Rosenberg. New York: John Wiley & Sons.

Rosenberg, N. 2001. The role of the private sector in facilitating the acquisition of technology in developing countries: A new look at technology transfer. Unpublished Manuscript, Stanford, CA: Stanford University.

Rosenberg, N., and L. Birdzell. 1986. *How the West Grew Rich*. New York: Basic Books.

Rosenberg, N., and R. Nelson. 1994. American university and technical advance in industry. *Research Policy* 23: 323–348.

Rosenberg, N., and E. Steinmueller. 1988. Why are Americans such poor imitators? *American Economic Review* Papers and Proceedings 78 (2): 229–234.

Rotemberg, J. J., and G. Saloner. 1994. Benefits of narrow business strategies. *American Economic Review* 84 (5): 1330–1349.

Sahal, D. 1981. *Patterns of Technological Innovation*. Reading, MA: Addison-Wiley.

Sánchez, R. 1995. Strategic flexibility in production competition. *Strategic Management Journal* 16: 135–155.

Sánchez, R., and J. T. Mahoney. 1996. Modularity, flexibility, and knowledge management in product and organization design. *Strategic Management Journal* 17: 63–76.

Saxenian, A. 1994. *Regional Advantage: Culture and Competition in Silicon Valley and Route 128*. Cambridge, MA: Harvard University Press.

Scotchmer, S. 1991. Standing on the shoulders of giants: Cumulative research and the patent law. *Journal of Economic Perspectives* 5 (1): 29–41.

Scotchmer, S., and J. Green. 1990. Novelty and disclosure in patent law. *RAND Journal of Economics* 21 (1): 131–146.

Scott-Kemmis, D., and M. Bell. 1988. Technological dynamism and technological content of collaboration. In *Technology Absorption in Indian Industry*, ed. A. V. Desai. New Delhi: Wiley Eastern.

Schaaftsma, P. 1998. Patently rewarding? *IP Magazine*. March. Available at <www.ipmag.com/98-mar/schaaf.html>.

Schankerman, M., and A. Pakes. 1986. Estimates of the value of patent rights in European countries during the post-1950 period. *Economic Journal* 96 (384): 1052–1076.

Schwartz, M., and E. Thompson. 1986. Divisionalization and entry deterrence. *Quarterly Journal of Economics* 101: 307–321.

Schwartzman, D. 1976. *Innovation in the Pharmaceutical Industry*. Baltimore, MD: John Hopkins University Press.

Securities Data Companies (SDC). 1998. The SDC Joint Venture/Strategic Alliances Database. Newark, NJ: Securities Data Companies.

Shane, S. A. 1996. Hybrid organizational arrangements and their implications for firm growth and survival: A study of new frachisors. *Academy of Management Journal* 39 (1): 216–234.

Shapiro, C., and H. R. Varian. 1998. *Information Rules: A Strategic Guide to the Network Economy*. Boston, MA: Harvard Business School Press.

Sharp, M. 1991. Pharmaceuticals and biotechnology: Perspectives for the European industry. In *Technology and the Future of Europe*, ed. C. Freeman, M. Sharp, and W. Walker. London: Francis Pinter.

Shepard, A. 1987. Licensing to enhance demand for new technology. *RAND Journal of Economics* 18: 360–368.

Simon, H. 1962. The Architecture of complexity. *Proceedings of the American Philosophical Society* 106 (6): 467–482.

Smith, A. 1776 [1983]. *The Wealth of Nations*. Harmondsworth. UK: Penguin Papers.

Sokoloff, K., and Z. Khan. 1990. The democratization of invention during early industrialization: Evidence from the United States, 1790–1846. *Journal of Economic History* 50: 363–378.

Spitz, P. H. 1988. *Petrochemicals: The Rise of an Industry*. New York: John Wiley & Sons.

Steinmueller, E. 1992. The economics of flexible integrated circuit manufacturing technology. *Review of Industrial Organization* 7: 327–349.

Steinmueller, W. E. 1989. Four observations on the creation and protection of intellectual property rights. Paper presented to the Western Economic Association Meeting, Lake Tahoe, July.

Stigler, G. 1951. The division of labor is limited by the extent of the market. *Journal of Political Economy* 59: 185–193.

Stiglitz, J. E., and A. Weiss. 1981. Credit rationing in markets with imperfect information. *American Economic Review* 71 (3): 393–410.

Swann, P., M. Prevezer, and D. Stout. 1998. *The Dynamics of Industrial Clustering: International Comparisons in Computing and Biotechnology*. Oxford: Oxford University Press.

Taylor, C. A., and Z. A. Silberston. 1973. The economic impact of the patent system: A study of the British experience, University of Cambridge, D.A.E. monograph 23, Cambridge, CUP.

Teece, D., and G. Pisano. 1994. The dynamic capabilities of firms: An introduction. *Industrial and Corporate Change* 3: 537–556.

Teece, D., G. Pisano, and A. Shuen. 1997. Dynamic capabilities and strategic management. *Strategic Management Journal* 18: 509–533.

Teece, D. J. 1977. Technology transfer by multinational firms: The resource cost of transferring technological know-how. *Economic Journal* 87: 242–261.

Teece, D. J. 1986. Profiting from technological innovation. *Research Policy* 15 (6): 285–305.

Teece, D. J. 1988. Technological change and the nature of the firm. In *Technological Change and Economic Theory*, ed. G. Dosi et al. London: Printer Publishers.

Teece, D. J. 1998. Capturing value from knowledge assets: The new economy, markets for know-how, and intangible assets. *California Management Review* 40 (3): 55–79.

Teece, D. J., R. Rumelt, G. Dosi, and S. Winter. 1994. Understanding corporate coherence: Theory and evidence. *Journal of Economic Behavior and Organization* 23: 1–30.

Tirole, J. J. 1988. *The Theory of Industrial Organization*. Cambridge, MA: MIT Press.

Torrisi, S. 1998. *Industrial Organization and Innovation: An International Study of the Software Industry.* Cheltenham: Edward Elgar.

UN Statistical Yearbook. United Nations. New York. Issues 38 and 39.

U.S. Department of Justice. 1995. *Antitrust Guidelines for the Licensing of Intellectual Property.* Washington, DC: U.S. Dept. of Justice and the Federal Trade Commission. April 6.

Vernon, R. 1979. The product cycle hypothesis in a new international environment. *Oxford Bulletin of Economics and Statistics* 41 (4): 255–267.

Vickers, J. 1985. Delegation and the theory of the firm. *Economic Journal* Supplement 95: 138–147.

Vincenti, W. G. 1990. *What Engineers Know and How They Know It.* Baltimore, MD: Johns Hopkins University Press.

Von Hippel, E. 1990. Task partitioning: An innovation process variable. *Research Policy* 19: 407–418.

Von Hippel, E. 1994. 'Sticky Information' and the locus of problem solving: Implications for innovation. *Management Science* 40 (4): 429–439.

Von Hippel, E. 1998. Economics of product development by users: The impact of 'Sticky' local information. *Management Science* 44 (5): 429–439.

Wallsten, S. 2000. The effects of government-industry R&D programs on private R&D: The case of the SBIR program. *RAND Journal of Economics* 21: 82–100.

Wang, X. H. 1998. Fee versus royalty licensing in a Cournot duopoly model. *Economic Letter* 60: 55–62.

Williamson, O. E. 1975. *Markets and Hierarchies: Analysis and Antitrust Implications.* New York: The Free Press.

Williamson, O. E. 1991. Comparative economic organization—The analysis of discrete structural alternatives. *Administrative Science Quarterly* 36 (4): 269–296.

Winter, S. 1987. Knowledge and competence as strategic assets. In *The Competitive Challenge: Strategies for Industrial Innovation and Renewal*, ed. D. J. Teece. New York: Harper and Row.

Womack, J., D. Jones, and D. Roos. 1990. *The Machine That Changed the World*. New York: Macmillan.

Young, A. 1928. Increasing returns and economic progress. *Economic Journal* 38: 527–542.

Zeckhauser, R. 1996. The challenge of contracting for technological information. *Proceedings for the National Academy of Science. USA* 93: 12743–12748.

Zucker, L., and M. Darby. 1996. Costly information in firm transformation, exit, or persistent failure. *American Behavioral Scientist* 39: 959–974.

Zucker, L., M. Darby, and J. Armstrong. 1998. Geographically localized knowledge: Spillovers or markets? *Economic Inquiry* 36: 65–86.

Figures and Tables

Figures
5.1 Stages in the technology contracts   121
7.1 The Prisoner's Dilemma in licensing   182
7.2 Marginal revenue and marginal cost of licensing   185
7.3 Licensing reaction functions   186
7.4 Increase in licensor's bargaining power, $\sigma 2 > \sigma 1$ 187
7.5 More homogenous products, $\mu 2 > \mu 1$ 188
7.6 Product differentiation and licensing   189
7.7 Propensity to license by SEFs and chemical corporations   191
7.8 The inducement effect   192
7.9 SEFs' market share and licensing by chemical producers   193
8.1 The transmission of growth impulses   201
8.2 Estimated impact of an additional SEF—additional
investment per process, by country, in millions of U.S. dollars,
1981–1990   212
8.3 Estimated impact of additional SEFs on investment
in developing countries—by size of process market,
in millions of U.S. dollars, 1981–1990   213
8.4 Estimated impact of SEFs on investment—by type
of process, in millions of U.S. dollars, 1981–1990   213

Tables
1.1 A simple typology of markets for technology   8
2.1 Market for polyethylene technology   18
2.2 Leading deal makers in the market for technology
and type of deals, by industry, 1985–1997   34
2.3 The size and sectoral composition of the market for
technology   38

2.4 Values of inter-industry technology licenses, 1988–1997
(millions of U.S. dollars)   42
3.1 The market for engineering services and licenses in
chemicals, 1980–1990, by sector   49
3.2 Market shares of SEFS: Engineering services, 1980–1990
(shares of total numbers of plants by region)   50
3.3 Market shares of SEFs: Licenses, 1980–1990 (shares of total
numbers of plants by region)   50
3.4 Types of technology transactions in software, some
representative examples   58
3.5 Selected 1998 alliances in biotechnology products
and platforms   68
3.6 Biotech equity financing in the United States, 1997–1999
(millions of U.S. dollars)   70
3.7 Selected DBFs developing research tools   72
3.8 Main licensors, cross-licensors, and licensees
in semiconductors, worldwide, circa 1988–1997   82
3.9 Selected technology intermediaries and their services   84
5.1 Variables and descriptive statistics   126
5.2 Relationships among the three technical services   127
5.3 Association between technical services and
complementary inputs   132
5.4 Relationship among complementary inputs   134
5.5 Probabilities of complementary inputs, conditional
on presence of technical services   135
5.6 Inter-industry differences in technology packages   136
5.7 Probit estimates: Dependent variables R&D, quality control,
and training   137
5.8 Ordered probit estimates, dependent variable: Total
number of technical services   140
6.1 Japan-U.S. hardware and software comparison (1987),
in 1987 billion U.S. dollars   159
7.1 Licensing activity by a sample of large chemical producers
during 1980–1990   173
7.2 Leading licensors, by sector, selected sectors, 1985–1997   176
7.3 Licensing and product differentiation in selected chemical
subsectors, 1980–1990   188
8.1 List of country characteristics   206
8.2 Descriptive statistics   207

8.3 Determinants of total investment, "buys" and "makes": OLS
estimates   208
8.4 Investments by MNEs and LDC firms in LDCs—DOM_{ij},
MNE_{ij}: OLS estimates   214
9.1 Selected Web pages advertising the licensing of
intellectual property   237

Index

Anand, B. N., 186
Antitrust policy
  guidelines for markets in goods, technology, and innovation, 5
  proposed change in patent-pooling agreements, 268–270
Application Specific Integrated Circuits (ASICs), 66–67
  computer-aided-design (CAD), 153
  new ASIC architecture, 107–108
  separate manufacture and design of, 153
  traditional development of, 107
Armstrong, J., 28–29, 43, 199
Arora, A., 46, 53, 98–99, 123, 124, 157, 164, 186, 234
Arrow, K. J., 1, 93, 124–125

Balcet, G., 128
Baldwin, C. Y., 103, 104–105
Barney, J. B., 226
Bayh-Dole Act (1980), 270–271
Bell, M., 128, 136
Biotechnology
  chemistry used in, 70–71
  drug discovery and research tools, 70
  information technology uses in, 70–74
  as research tool, 65
  semiconductor technology applications, 74
Biotechnology industry
  dedicated biotechnology firms (DBFs) in, 63–65, 71–75
  development of (1970–80), 63–65
  equity financing for firms in, 67, 70
  general purpose tools in, 160–163
  growth (1990s), 65–70

industry structure and use of GPTs in, 160–163
  platform and product-specific firms in, 160–162
  platform companies, 160–163
  product-specific, 160–163
  robotic techniques used in, 71
  technological alliances in, 66–70
Bokhari, F., 164
Brady, T., 106
Braun, E., 152
Bresnahan, T., 146, 154, 155, 163, 205, 215
British Technology Group (BTG) report, 8, 29, 43
Brusoni, A., 110

Chandler, A., 2, 225
Chemical engineering
  influence in oil and chemical processing industries, 150–152
  U.S. systematic university training, 152, 156
Chemical industry
  licensing of technology in, 187–189
  licensing to generate revenues, 172–174
  use of licensing in, 52–53
Chemical processes
  diffusion through SEFs, 51–53
  market for technology in, 20–22
Chemical processing industry
  influence of chemical engineering in, 150
  licensing of technology in, 52–53
  role of specialized engineering firms in, 46–53, 151
  suppliers of technology in, 45–46

Chesbrough, H. W., 240
Chin, J. C., 125
Chipless companies. *See* Semiconductor
industry; Specialization
Clark, K., 103, 104–105
Coase, R. H., 282
Cockburn, I., 65, 161
Cohen, W., 247
Competition
among SEFs, 49–51
influences incentives for licensing, 172–
182
in markets for technology in chemicals,
20–22
produced by markets for technology,
182–189, 249
in semiconductor industry, 87
Complementarity
of internal and external R&D, 245
in model of know-how transfer, 119–125
in strategies of users and producers of
GPT, 154–155
use of know-how with, 116–117
Complex systems, large
standards in, 254–255
testing, 109–110
Component Management Group (CMG),
56–57
Computer numerical control (CNC) machines, 158–160
Contractor, F. J., 118, 124
Contracts. *See* Know-how contracts
Convergence, technological transmission
of growth with, 203
Cool, K., 226
Corporate venturing, 240
Cross-licensing agreements
antitrust scrutiny of, 269–270
to obtain patented components, 178
patent pools in, 269
royalty payments in, 178
in semiconductor industry, 79–81

Darby, M., 28–29, 43, 66, 199
Dasgupta, P., 256, 273–274
Data sources
for analysis of global technology suppliers, 198, 204–205, 216–220
Chemintell database, 48, 198, 204
on cost of know-how transfer, 125
database of Securities Data Company, 32

on licensing contracts, 125–130, 140–141
model of know-how transfer, 125–130,
140–141
David, P., 254–256, 258, 270, 273–274
DBFs. *See* Biotechnology industry
Decomposition of complex problem, 99–102
Degnan, S. A., 31
Dierickx, I., 226
Digital Greenhouse initiative, 257
Digital signal processors (DSPs), 76
Division of labor
in chemical processing industry, 45, 48–
49
compared to division of innovative labor, 7, 281–282
in global market for technology, 277–
278
horizontal and vertical externalities in,
163
Division of innovative labor
based on economies of specialization, 148
in biotechnology sector, 64, 89
compared to division of labor, 7, 281–282
constraints on, 94
costs to transfer information in, 113
factors influencing extension of, 113
gains from, 149–153
in high-tech sectors, 282
organizational design of, 99–102
in semiconductor industry, 76–79
technology transfer as type of, 94
U.S. competitive advantage from, 81–
88
in vertical transactions, 6
Downstream sector
integration of manufacture in, 83, 86
in vertical market, 6

Economies of scale
exploited by GPTs, 145–146
in railroad industry, 149–150
using ASIC technology, 152–153
Economies of scope
limited by biotech product-specific research, 161
of specialized suppliers of platform
technologies, 161–162
Economies of specialization
as basis for division of innovative labor,
148
of engineering design sector, 47

with task-partitioning, 106, 255
in technology production, 247
Eisenberg, 266
Electronic design automation (EDA), 54–55
Ernst & Young, 66, 67
European Union (EU)
    Commission report on encouragement
        of risk-taking, 260
    CORDIS online service, 83, 258, 286
    encouragement to high-tech firms, 286
    policy interventions of, 259

Fabless companies. See Firms; Semicon-
    ductor industry; Specialization
Firms. See also Biotechnology industry;
    Chemical processing industry; Semi-
    conductor industry; Specialized engi-
    neering firms (SEFs); Suppliers,
    specialized
    fabless and chip design, 77–78, 81,
        256
    intermediation specialists, 81–83
    licensing of technology by large, 175–
        182
    licensing strategies of, 231–245
    longevity of large, 284–285
    markets for technology can affect for-
        mation of, 285
    resources-based theory of the firm, 224–
        226
    strategic response to markets for tech-
        nology, 223–251
    tacit knowledge of, 95–99
Fosfuri, A., 53
Freeman, C., 48–49

Galambos, L., 64
Gambardella, A., 98–99, 154, 155, 157
Gans, J., 241, 245
General-purpose technologies (GPTs)
    biotechnology tools, 161–162
    cost-minimizing industry structure for,
        146–149
    defined, 144
    economies of scale using, 149–153
    history of, 149
    threshold size in use of, 154–155
Granstrand, O., 238
Greenstein, S., 254–255
Grindley, P. C., 2, 9, 238, 269
Grossman, G., 125

Grossman, S., 101
Growth impulse transmission, 197–198,
    200–201

Hall, B. H., 79, 81
Ham, R., 79, 81
Hart, O., 101
Heller, M., 266
Henderson, R., 103, 272
Heterogeneity of demand, 249–250
Hodges, D., 76–78
Hofman, D. J., 106
Hsu, D., 241

Iansiti, M., 224–225
Industry structures
    extensions of model comparing GPT
        and non-GPT uses, 153–157
    and GPT use in some industries, 157–163
    machine tool industry, 157–160
    model comparing GPT and non-GPT uses,
        146–149
    standards in U.S. semiconductor industry,
        255
    and use of GPTs in biotechnology firms,
        160–163
Information
    diffusion of genetic, 71–74
    information system templates, 106
    institutions that reduce costs of, 258–261
    sharing among biotechnology compa-
        nies, 70–71
    transfer in division of innovative labor,
        113
Information, sticky
    defined, 106
    separating out of, 106–107
    unsticking, 107–109
Innovation. See also Division of innovative
    labor
    EU tax credits for, 260
    with fragmentation of knowledge com-
        ponents, 261–267
    markets for, 5–6
    uncertainty of, 265
Innovation process
    conditions for integration of, 105–112
    decomposability of, 99–102
    modularity in, 102–105
    open architecture to promote, 255
    task-partitioning in, 94, 105–112, 255

Institutions
  financial, 258–261
  intermediating, 258–261
  required by markets for technology,
    253–254
  standards as, 254–258
Integrated circuits
  application-specific, 153
  microprocessor extends range of, 152–
    153
Integration. *See also* Application Specific
    Integrated Circuits (ASICs)
  dynamic transaction costs of, 110–111
  in innovative process, 105–112
  of large complex systems, 109–111
  in production of technology, 197
Intellectual property. *See also* Patents
  chip component designs as, 78
  eminent domain policy related to, 269–
    270
  firms' management of, 238–239
  increase in strength of rights for, 80
  Reusable Application-Specific Intellec-
    tual Property Developers, 257
  in semiconductor market, 79
Intellectual property rights (IPRs)
  controversy in GATT over, 125
  current prominence of, 117
  market-based response to fragmented,
    269
  in model of know-how transfer, 119
  policy of European Union concerning,
    286
Intermediation, technological
  effect of upstream sector, 9, 199, 215
  firms specializing in, 81–88
IPSs. *See* Intellectual property rights
    (IPRs)

Jaffee, A., 272
Joint venture, as horizontal transaction, 6

Khanna, T., 186
Kline, D., 238
Know-how contracts
  enhancing efficiency of, 116
  model of transfer of know-how, 119–137
  moral hazard in arm's-length, 115–116
  out-based royalties in, 116
Knowledge
  attributes of, 96

  embodied in software program, 3–4
  forms of technological, 3–4
  high cost of transfer of, 118
  in intangible form, 96
  licensing of, 117
  organization's internal exchange of, 97
  transferability of, 96–99
Knowledge spillovers. *See* Spillovers, tech-
    nological
Knowledge, tacit (know-how). *See also*
    Know-how contracts
  articulated and codified, 96–99, 105–112
  and codified dimensions of, 95
  cost to transfer, 115
  licensing and transfer of, 117–141
  potential for competitive advantage in,
    250
  sticky information in, 106–109
  in task-partitioning, 106–112
Kogut, B., 11, 97–98
Koput, K., 66
Kremer, M., 269
Kuznets, Simon, 1

Lamoreaux, N., 23–27, 56
Landau, R., 156
Langlois, R., 57, 87, 103–104, 110–111, 255,
    265
Lemley, M., 62–63
Less-developed countries (LDCs)
  emergence of chemical industry in, 12–
    13, 198–216
  role of SEFs in, 12–13, 198–216
Levinthal, D. A., 240, 244, 245, 247
Licensing. *See also* Cross-licensing agree-
    ments; Rent dissipation effect; Rev-
    enue effect
  of chemical processes, 20–22
  and cross-licensing among semiconduc-
    tor firms, 77, 80
  as horizontal transaction, 6
  incentives with market for technology,
    2, 178–180
  by industry sectors, 174–176
  international, 175
  of know-how or tacit knowledge, 117–125
  in market for chemical processes, 20–21
  market for technology licenses, 8–9
  of metallocene technology, 19–21
  of polyethylene technology, 21–22
  reasons for, 175, 177–178

for revenues, 19, 172–175, 228
royalty income from technology, 80–82
SEF practices, 52
in semiconductor industry, 79–81
Licensing strategies
competition influences incentives for,
172–182
of firms to profit from their technology,
234–238
of large firms, 231–240
in model of technology market competition, 182–189
of smaller firms, 242–245
Lieberman, M., 51–52
Linden, G., 55, 77

MacDonald, S., 152
Macher, J., 76–78
Mahoney, J. T., 104, 111–112
March, J. G., 240, 244, 245
Markets for assets
competing firms in, 225–228
transaction costs in, 229
Markets for innovation, 5–6
Markets for technology. *See also* Technology transactions
appropriability problem, 93
in chemical processes, 20–22, 46
comparison of industrialized countries',
31–42
defined, 5
dynamic issues of, 283–284
effect on business formation, 285
function of, 8–10
growth (1990s), 43
horizontal and vertical transactions in,
6–8, 281–282
incentives to license with, 178–180
institutions required by, 253–254
in less-developed countries, 198–216
metallocene technology, 17–20
model of competition in, 184–189
most developed sectors in, 33–41
nineteenth and early twentieth centuries, 23–27
promote incentives to invest in R&D, 8
in semiconductors, 76–88
size and scope of, 29–42
specialization advantages in, 144
technological standards in, 256–258
typology of, 7–8

worldwide, 43, 275–278
Marshall, Alfred, 28
Merges, P., 186, 234, 261, 263
Metallocenes
as catalysts for polymers, 17–18
licensors of technology for, 19
market for technology of, 17–20
Microprocessors, programmable, 152
Modularity
in chip design, 78
in problem solving, 105
in product design, 103–104
in production, 103
systemic uncertainty with, 109–111
Moore, J., 101
Morel, B., 164
Mowery, D., 2, 76–78, 113, 245, 270–272,
274–275

Nelson, R. R., 1, 11, 95, 263
Nonaka, I., 97
Numerical controls (NCs) technology,
159–160. *See also* Computer numerical
control (CNC) machines

O'Brien, D., 62–63
Oil industry
specialized engineering firms in, 151–
152
use of licensing in, 52–53
Orsenigo, L., 66–67
Outsourcing, 148

Pakes, A., 30
Patents
as bargaining chips in cross-licensing, 80
blocking, 264–265
define some property rights, 93
as facilitators of technology transactions, 261–267, 271
issues to U.S. universities, 270–275
in model of know-how transfer, 119–125
in model of technology market competition, 182–189
rights in model of transfer of know-how,
119–137
semiconductor, 79–81
software, 60–63
value of, 30
Patent system
influence on markets for technology, 24

Patent system (cont.)
  new patents in 1840–1911 period in
    United States, 23–27
  proposed changes in patent-pooling
    agreements, 268–270
  recommended improvement of, 267–
    268, 286
Pharmaceutical industry
  biotech suppliers to, 161–162
  interdependence in innovation process
    of, 162
Pisano, G., 224
Polanyi, M., 95
Polymers
  production using metallocenes, 18
  production using Ziegler-Natta cata-
    lysts, 17–18
Polyolefin industry, 18
Polypropylene, 19
Powell, W., 66
Prencipe, A., 110
Privatization
  of knowledge, 274–275, 279
  of university-based research, 270
Property rights. *See also* Intellectual prop-
    erty rights (IPRs)
  on tangible and intangible goods, 93
  transaction costs affected by, 229
  when ownership is fragmented, 261–
    267
Public policy
  funding for U.S. university-based re-
    search, 270–275
  interventions of, 259
  recommended improvement of patent
    system, 267–268
  to reduce transaction costs, 254–261
  related to privatization of knowledge,
    270–275
  related to standards and standard-
    setting, 258
  role in global marketplace, 275–279
  role of standards in, 254–258

Railroad industry
  increasing returns to scale in, 149–150
  modern management techniques of,
    150
Reiss, P., 205
Rent dissipation effect
  defined, 179
  in firm's decision to license, 231

in model of technology market competi-
    tion, 182–189
Research and development (R&D)
  European public policy related to, 259–
    260
  firms' need to invest in, 245
  incentives for investing in, 192–194
  knowledge spillovers in, 27–29
  outsourcing of, 148
  technology buyers need to invest in, 245
  U.S. tax credit policy, 260
Reusable Application-Specific Intellectual
    Property Developers (RAPID), 257
Revenue effect
  defined, 179
  in firm's decision to license, 231
  in model of technology market competi-
    tion, 184–189
Rivera-Batiz, L., 200
Rivette, K. G., 238
Robertson, P. L., 57, 87, 103–4, 255
Rockart, J. F., 106
Romer, P., 200, 215
Rosenberg, Nathan, 9–10, 146, 202–203,
    245
Rostoke, Michael, 266
Rotemberg, J., 246

Saloner, G., 246
Sanchez, R., 104, 111–112
Schankerman, M., 30
Schumpeter, J., 225
Scott-Kemmis, D., 128, 136
Securities Data Company, 32–33, 40
SEFs. *See* Specialized engineering firms
    (SEFs)
Semiconductor industry
  chip design firms, 77–78
  fabless and chipless companies in, 77,
    81, 256
  licensing and cross-licensing in, 77
  licensing to generate revenues, 174
  manufacturing technology of, 76
  markets for technology in, 81
  miniaturization process, 76
  software tools used by, 54–55
Semiconductors
  demand for design-intensive, 78
  production increases, 76
  trade in design modules, 77
  U.S. patents for, 79–81
Semiconductor technology

CMOS technology, 256
gene chip development, 74
laboratory on a chip products, 74–75
Simon, Herbert, 99, 102, 105
Smith, Adam, 6
Smith-Doerr, L., 6
Software
compatible component market, 56–57
cost to produce and reproduce, 53–54
developed by dedicated biotechnology
firms, 70–76
electronic design automation, 54–55
industry structure and use of GPTs in,
157–160
as knowledge tool, 54–56
licensed, 53
market for modules and components of,
56–60
patenting of, 60–63
role in markets for technology, 53–63
technology transactions in, 56–60
Sokoloff, K., 23–27, 56
Somaya, D., 55, 77
Specialization. See also Economies of specialization; Specialized engineering
firms (SEFs); Suppliers, specialized
advantages to, 143–144
in chipless companies, 77
in division of innovative labor, 7
in electronics industry, 146
in fabless design firms, 77, 81, 256
firm choices related to, 164
Specialized engineering firms (SEFs). See
also Chemical engineering
in chemical processing industry, 12–13
comparative advantage in industrialized countries of, 199–200
comparative advantage in process design of, 47–51
comparative advantages of, 47–51
conditions for emergence of, 46–51
as independent licensors, 47
as licensing agents, 52
process technology of, 47–48, 52
as suppliers of chemical process technologies, 247–248
as suppliers to less-developed countries, 200–216
Spillovers, technological
effect of, 9
as externalities, 27–28
international, 199–215

as knowledge transfers, 9–20
upstream sector intermediation effect,
9, 199, 215
Spitz, P. H., 51, 52, 151–152
Standards, technological
CMOS interfaces, 256
CORBA component-management technology, 256–257
standard-setting alliances, 257–258
State Street Bank & Trust Co. v. Signature Financial Group Inc. (1998), 61
Steinmueller, W. E., 255
Stern, S., 241, 245
Stigler, G. J., 6, 112–113, 143, 145–146, 149
Stiglitz, J., 244
Sturchio, J., 64
Suppliers, specialized
barriers experienced by, 259
to chemical processing industry, 150–
151
dedicated biotechnology firms as, 64
as developers of GPT, 144
of general-purpose technologies, 144
to less-developed countries, 200–216
operating in vertical markets, 9
of platform technologies, 161–162
in semiconductor industry, 86
of technology in chemical processing industry, 45–46
technology transfers by, 200
Supreme Court decisions about patenting
of software, 61

Task-partitioning, 105–112, 255
Technology. See also General-purpose technologies (GPTs)
accounting for value of assets of, 29–30,
260–261
appropriating rents from, 228
choice between outsourcing or division
of innovative labor, 148
distinct from technological capability,
284
efficient contracts for exchange of, 116
embodied in physical artifacts, 3–4
firms' in-house exploitation of, 229–232
forms of exchange of, 2
inter-industry flows of, 31–43
licensing to generate revenues, 172–
174
production of, 6–7
R&D outsourcing in, 148

Technology (cont.)
    role of SEFs in diffusion of, 51–53
    royalties on, 31–32, 40
    as tradable object, 284
Technology transactions. *See also* Transac-
        tion costs
    appropriability problems limited by, 93
    cognitive factors limit, 94
    for creation of new technology, 5–6
    inter-industry, 31–42
    markets in, 4
    need for data related to, 285
    patents as facilitators of, 261–262
    services facilitating, 24, 81–88
    in software, 56–60
    for use and diffusion of technology, 5
Technology transfers
    adaptations and cost of, 94
    appropriability problems of, 93–94
    cost of, 95
    in model of technology market competi-
        tion, 182–189
    multinational enterprises as vehicles for,
        200
    software, 60
Teece, D. J., 2, 9, 11, 98, 101–102, 224, 227,
        228, 238, 269, 282
Tiernay, M., 106
Trajtenberg, M., 146, 163, 215, 272
Transaction costs
    factors influencing, 229–230
    in markets for assets, 229
    in model of technology market competi-
        tion, 182–189
    recommended policy to reduce, 254–261

Uncertainty
    in innovation, 265
    systemic, 109–111
U.S. Patent Office
    business process patents granted by, 61
    software patents granted by, 61–63
Universities, U.S.
    apply for patents and copyrights for re-
        search, 270–271
    licensing of patents by, 271–272
    in market for technology, 270
    privatization of university-based re-
        search, 270
Upstream sector
    in biotechnology industry, 67–70
    intermediation effect of, 9, 199, 215

in vertical technology transactions, 6

Venture capital
    compared to corporate venturing, 240
    flexibility of firms offering, 259
    R&D tax credit as asset for, 260
    U.S. firms in other countries, 27
Vernon, R., 200
Vincenti, W. G., 100, 102
Virtual Component Exchange (VCX), 257
Virtual Socket Interface Alliance (VSIA),
        257
Virtual Socket Interface (VSI) technology,
        79
von Hippel, Eric, 11, 105–107, 112, 245

Weiss, A., 244
Williams, R., 106
Williamson, O., 282
Winter, S., 11, 95–96

Young, A., 6

Zander, U., 11, 97–98
Ziedonis, A., 271–272
Zucker, L., 28–29, 43, 66, 199